Principles of Vision

Pierre Bourdieu

Principles of Vision

General Sociology, Volume 4

Lectures at the Collège de France (1984–1985)

Edited by Patrick Champagne and Julien Duval,
with the collaboration of Franck Poupeau
and Marie-Christine Rivière

Translated by Peter Collier

polity

First published in French in *Sociologie générale. Volume 2. Cours au Collège de France* (1983–1986) © Éditions Raisons d'Agir/Éditions du Seuil, 2016

This English edition © Polity Press, 2022

Polity Press
65 Bridge Street
Cambridge CB2 1UR, UK

Polity Press
101 Station Landing
Suite 300
Medford, MA 02155, USA

All rights reserved. Except for the quotation of short passages for the purpose of criticism and review, no part of this publication may be reproduced, stored in a retrieval system or transmitted, in any form or by any means, electronic, mechanical, photocopying, recording or otherwise, without the prior permission of the publisher.

ISBN-13: 978-1-5095-2671-0 hardback

A catalogue record for this book is available from the British Library.

Library of Congress Control Number: 2021948928

Typeset in 10.5 on 12 pt Times New Roman
by Cheshire Typesetting Ltd, Cuddington, Cheshire
Printed and bound in Great Britain by CPI Group (UK) Ltd, Croydon

The publisher has used its best endeavours to ensure that the URLs for external websites referred to in this book are correct and active at the time of going to press. However, the publisher has no responsibility for the websites and can make no guarantee that a site will remain live or that the content is or will remain appropriate.

Every effort has been made to trace all copyright holders, but if any have been overlooked the publisher will be pleased to include any necessary credits in any subsequent reprint or edition.

For further information on Polity, visit our website:
politybooks.com

Contents

Editorial Note	viii
Acknowledgements	x

Lecture of 7 March 1985   1
Inventory – Capital and power over capital – The process of
differentiation – Objectivism and perspectivism

Lecture of 14 March 1985   12
First session (lecture): the elasticity of objective structures –
A programme for the social sciences – Reintroducing the point
of view – Reintroducing objective space – A political sociology
of perception – The theory effect – Social science and justice.
Second session (seminar): the invention of the modern artist (1)
– The programme for future painters – What is at stake in the
struggle – A revolution in the principles of vision –
Academic artists

Lecture of 28 March 1985   41
First session (lecture): going beyond perspectivism and
absolutism – Scientific categories and official categories – The
struggle over perspectives – Practical logics – Political creation –
The theory effect and the master thinkers
Second session (seminar): the invention of the modern artist (2)
– Perhaps the writers should write about nothing? – The master
and the artist – A symbolic revolution – Historical painting –
A *lector*'s painting – The de-realisation effect

vi *Contents*

Lecture of 18 April 1985   73
First session (lecture): the sociological relation to the social
world – A materialist vision of symbolic forms – Perception as
a system of oppositions and discrimination – Investing in the
game of the *libidines* – The passage from action to discourse on
action – The political struggle for the right vision
Second session (seminar): the invention of the modern artist
(3) – Writing the history of a symbolic revolution – The surplus
of educated men and the academic crisis – The education system
and field of cultural production – The morphological effects –
The effects of the morphological crisis on the academic field

Lecture of 25 April 1985   103
First session (lecture): thinking the already thought – The liberty
and autonomy of a field – A question about symbolic power
– The political struggle as struggle for the legitimate vision –
Symbolic capital and gnoseological order – The law as the right
way to speak of the social world – The verdict of the State in the
struggle for identity
Second session (seminar): the invention of the modern artist
(4) – The psychosomatic power of the institution – The symbolic
work of the heretic – Collective conversion – The strategies of
the heresiarch – A revolution affecting the ensemble of the fields
of cultural production

Lecture of 2 May 1985   133
First session (lecture): collective bad faith and struggles for
definition – Justification of a decision to buy and competing
viewpoints – 'Taking apart' and 'putting together' Subjective
manipulations and objective structures – Managing the symbolic
capital of the group – Effects of the corps
Second session (seminar): the invention of the modern artist (5)
– The alliance of painters and writers – The artist's way of life
and the invention of pure love – Artistic transgression today and
a century ago – The mercenary artist and art for art's sake

Lecture of 9 May 1985   166
First session (lecture): certification and social order – The
principle and justice of distributions – Private charity and public
welfare – The three levels of analysis of a distribution – Where
is the State? – Verdicts and the effects of power – The field of
certification

Second session (seminar): the invention of the modern
artist (6) – Academic painting as a theological universe –
Institutionalising perspectivism – The invention of the artist as
character – The painter–writer couple

Lecture of 23 May 1985   196
First session (lecture): Paul Valéry's insights – Amateur and
professional – Bureaucracy as a massive fetish – Categorial
mediation – Validated perception – Science and the science of
the State
Second session (seminar): the invention of the modern artist
(7) – Polycentrism and the invention of institutions – The false
antinomy of art and the market – The collective judgement of
the critics – The three reproaches

Lecture of 30 May 1985   225
Providing a theoretical perspective – The Kantian tradition:
symbolic forms – The primitive forms of classification –
Historical and performative structures – Symbolic systems
as structured structures – The Marxist logic – Integrating
the cognitive and the political – The division of the labour of
symbolic domination – The State and God

Situating the Later Volumes of *General Sociology* in the Work of Pierre Bourdieu   254
Julien Duval

Summary of Lectures of 1984–85   272

Notes   276
Index   314

Editorial Note

This book forms part of the ongoing publication of Pierre Bourdieu's lectures at the Collège de France. A few months after his final lecture in this institute in March 2001 Bourdieu had published under the title of *Science of Science and Reflexivity*[1] a condensed version of the last year of his course (2000–1). After his death, *On the State* was published in 2012, followed by *Manet: A Symbolic Revolution* in 2013, corresponding to the lectures that he gave in 1989–92 and 1998–2000 respectively.[2] The publication of the 'General Sociology' that he gave during the first five years of his teaching at the Collège de France, between April 1982 and June 1986, was then started. A first volume appeared in 2015, collecting the lectures given during the 1981–82 and 1982–83 academic years.[3] The second French volume collects the three following years. This English translation presents the second of those years, 1984–85, with its nine two-hour lectures.

This edition of 'General Sociology' follows the editorial options defined at the moment of publication of the lectures on the State, which aim to reconcile faithfulness with readability.[4] The published text represents a transcription of the lectures as they were given. In the great majority of cases, the transcription used in the present publication relies on recordings. However, for some of the lectures the recordings could not be found and the text published here is based on the literal transcriptions that Bernard Convert made for his personal use. He kindly sent them to us and we are very grateful to him. Finally, in one case (part of the lecture for 7 March 1985, in a forthcoming English volume), lacking any recording or transcription, Bourdieu's argument has been reconstructed using the only material available: Bernard Convert's notes from the lecture.

As in the previous volumes, the passage from the spoken to the written word has required some minor rewriting, which scrupulously respects the approach applied by Bourdieu himself when he revised his own lectures and seminars: making stylistic corrections and emending oral infelicities (repetitions and linguistic tics, etc.). On one or two exceptional occasions only, we have curtailed the development of an argument, when the state of the recordings did not allow us to reproduce it in a satisfactory manner. The words or passages that were ambiguous or inaudible or that reflected a momentary interruption in the recording have been signalled thus [. . .] when it was impossible to recover them, and have been placed between brackets when their accuracy could not be guaranteed.

Acknowledgements

The editors would like to thank Bruno Auerbach, Amélie and Louise Bourdieu, Pascal Durand, Johan Heilbron, Remi Lenoir, Amín Perez, Jocelyne Pichot and Louis Pinto for their collaboration. They particularly wish to thank Bernard Convert and Thibaut Izard for their continual and often essential help.

Lecture of 7 March 1985

Inventory – Capital and power over capital – The process of differentiation – Objectivism and perspectivism

Inventory

I would like to briefly introduce the form that my lectures will take this year. I am moving towards the end of the long marathon that I started out on four years ago. I am nearing the end of the set of lectures that I promised, which is the point when I hope that their coherence will become more apparent and the logic of the whole will emerge. In the first session each week I shall continue the lectures, and in the second sessions, after Easter, I shall present you with a series of analyses of the relations between the literary field and the artistic field, in fact primarily the field of painting and secondarily the field of music in the nineteenth century.[1]

Today I shall draw up a brief inventory of what we have established so far [. . .] and try to open up the third stage of my argument, that is the stage where we set out the relations between the dispositions of the agents and the social spaces within which they operate.

Over the last few years I have explained what I mean by the 'habitus' and above all the theoretical functions that I assign to this concept. I have tried to show how the notion of habitus allows us to avoid a certain number of alternatives that shackle the social sciences, in particular the alternative between subjectivism and a form of mechanist objectivism. I shall not linger over this point. I then tried to expose what I saw as the logic behind the functioning of what I call the 'field'. I formulated a certain number of general propositions concerning fields of force, giving examples taken from the literary field in particular. I tried to

Lecture of 7 March 1985

undertake what you might call a sort of social physics, describing social relations as a balance of power within which the behaviour of agents may be defined. The structures of the spaces that I call 'fields' may be understood as structures of the distribution of powers or different species of capital. Thus to characterise a field such as the literary, academic or political field, you have to use a certain number of indicators to determine how the force that underpins the structure of the field in question is distributed among the different agents or institutions. It seems to me that we can also call this force a 'capital'. Studying this structure enables us to become aware of the constraints that will affect the agents entering into the space being considered.

One problem for empirical research is obviously how to identify the best indicators of a force that is never revealed directly, but only through its symptoms. I would like to bring this point to the attention of any among you who might have a naively substantialist representation of the notion of power. Scientific analysis differs from ordinary experience in that the latter tends to assume that power is a thing that you can locate in a place and which can be manipulated by powerful people. Experience claiming to be based on scientific evidence is not always clearly separated from everyday experience: one famous work of political sociology is entitled *Who Governs?*,[2] a question which supposes that there are people out there who wield power. Inherent in my notion of a field is the idea that the very question of finding out who governs us is naive: what we need to identify is the space within which we can find something like the power to govern, so that we may grasp the distribution of those attributes of power through which the structure of the distribution of powers is made manifest . . .

Having defined the structure of the field, a structure that can be grasped through the structure of the distribution of powers or species of capital, I needed to define the different forms that this power or capital may assume, in order to formulate a fundamental proposal, which is that there are as many species of capital or forms of power as there are spaces within which these species of capital and forms of power can manifest themselves. I tried to describe the species of power or capital which I judged to be fundamental, reminding you all the while that these fundamental species are subdivided into yet more specialised forms of capital or power. I distinguished two major species, economic capital and cultural capital, leaving to one side a form of capital that it occurred to me to establish but which I now have doubts about, social capital. (I shall return to this point: in one of my forthcoming lectures[3] I shall try to show how what I called 'social capital' and isolated as a particular species of capital is perhaps something entirely different. We

Lecture of 7 March 1985

can all make mistakes, and it's a good job, too . . . It seems to me that social capital is something that I shall call an effect of the corps. I shall return to this, I just wanted to point it out here in case anyone was surprised not to find this form of capital in my list.) I thus identified two fundamental species of capital, economic and cultural, and I tried to define their specific properties, as well as the laws of transformation through which one form of capital can be transformed and converted into another. Briefly, I also described the process of codification and formalisation through which the forms of capital or power tend to be constructed juridically.

Capital and power over capital

This is where I had got to [at the end of last year]. One possible path of development of my research would be a theory of what you might call the field of power (rather than the 'dominant class'). I hesitated at length before deciding on what I have now chosen to present you with. One logical development would have been to immediately exploit what I had established on the species of capital in order to try to identify a number of seemingly transhistorical properties in the fields of power and the dominant classes, seen as a set of agents holding positions in the fields of power. Here I make a distinction between 'field of power' and 'dominant class'. It is a distinction that I had never made before, but if anyone involved in empirical research into the question 'Who Governs?' fails to do so, they will make serious mistakes.

You might think that it is sufficient to study the people who hold positions of power in order to study the structure of power. It is true that in empirical research it is usually only possible to study the structure of power through the distribution of power among the powerful. Thus we can only study academic power by studying the properties of academics holding academic power. But this does not mean that the structure of power, that is, the structure of the academic field, can be identified with the whole set of academics, or with those we call 'mandarins'. The distinction that I have just briefly sketched between 'field of power' and 'dominant class' reminds us of the property that I described just now: the structure of a field is not reducible to the space of the distribution of properties among the agents who hold positions within the structure. Consequently, although in studying an academic field I may have to show the distribution of academics within the field, this does not mean that the structure of academic power is equivalent to its manifestation in the distribution of academics according to their power in the academic field. This may seem to be a subtle distinction, but it took me years to come round to it and it does seem useful, both theoretically and empirically, in helping us to better understand what we are doing when we study a social space.

To follow the logic of my argument through, then, I should examine the space within which the species of capital are distributed, that is, the field of power, which is defined precisely by the structure of the way power over the different species of capital is distributed. A rigorous definition of the field of power would be roughly this: it is a space whose structuring principle is the distribution, not of capital (the social space in its entirety would be such a space), but of power over the different species of capital. This difference corresponds to the distinction that economists quite frequently establish between holders of capital such as small shareholders, and holders of capital who wield power over the capital. Things would be the same in the cultural field: for instance, all secondary school teachers are holders of cultural capital, without forasmuch having power over capital, that is, the power granted by a certain type or quantity of capital, or a certain position of power over the agencies that grant power over capital. Thus a major publisher can have power over capital without necessarily having a great cultural capital him- or herself. Likewise, the editor of a cultural weekly, or a journalist presenting a television programme, can have power over cultural capital, which does not necessarily imply the possession of a great amount of personal cultural capital. I offer these examples in order to clarify this distinction, which I believe to be important.

I want to allude here to something that I shall return to later [. . .]. I was talking about a process of historical evolution and I would like to recall it briefly, once again to help us understand the notion of species of capital and the notion of a field. I was saying just now that any field implies its particular form of capital and any particular form of capital relates to a particular field: for instance the academic type of capital is valid within the limits of a certain state of a field, but there are crises of academic capital, just as there are crises of financial capital, when a field within which capital has formed, circulated and generated profit collapses. I also endeavoured to show that the events of May 1968 were partly due to the collapse of the conditions of functioning of a certain type of academic capital, with a certain number of changes in the structures of the academic market, for instance.[4]

Lecture of 7 March 1985 5

The process of differentiation

This link between a field and a species of capital leads me to think that the subdivision of capital, in other words the differentiation between powers and forms of power, corresponds to a process of differentiation at work within the social world. I believe that this is important. All the major sociologists have noted this process of differentiation. The person who has given the best description of it is no doubt Durkheim, who always insisted on the fact that archaic societies (which were his particular interest) were particularly undifferentiated, or rather undivided, that is, they did not differentiate as we do between the orders that we judge to be distinct:[5] art, religion, economics, ritual, and so on were profoundly indistinct, so that practices we might call religious, for instance, had at the same time an economic dimension, or acts of restitution of debt were very often conceived of in terms of sacrifice. It looks as if we have gradually emerged from this kind of initial indifferentiation through the establishment of relatively autonomous universes that have their own laws of operation. This is another way of presenting the notion of field: the social, economic and religious fields, for instance, are the never completely finished products of a process of differentiation, at the end of which each universe acquires its own logic and you might say its own fundamental law.

Thus the economic field becomes a universe within which the logic of economics rules as completely as possible. The fundamental law of a field is what makes a field what it is, it is the 'qua', for instance it is economics qua economics. Fundamental laws are often expressed in terms of tautologies – we say 'business is business'. Which means that there is no place for feelings in business. The fundamental law of the economic field, for example, is the maximisation of profit. An economic field is established when this fundamental law is cleansed of all its accretions, for instance of all the links between economic relations and relations of kinship, between what matters for agents involved in economic exchange and what matters for family relations, when the logic of the market is dissociated from the logic of personal relations. We can say the same thing for the artistic field. What I shall study in the lectures that I shall devote to the nineteenth century is the process whereby the fundamental law of the artistic field called 'art for art's sake' is established. We observe a process analogous to that of economics. Just as people started to say 'business is business', they started to say 'art is art', which means that art is not politics, or ethics, or education. This was a particularly laborious process. Artists died, in a way, to invent this specificity, this fundamental law of art as art. The process of

6 *Lecture of 7 March 1985*

differentiation and the notion of the field are therefore linked. A field is the outcome of a historical process of autonomisation at the end of which a space becomes autonomous (the word 'autonomy' captures the whole argument), that is, independent of external forces, and at the same time behaves in such a way that everything occurring within it obeys a law which is specific to it, the law of 'business is business', or 'art is art', and so on.

Linking the analysis of the process of differentiation that I have just made to my analysis of the different species of capital should lead to a theory of the forms that the field of power may take in different societies. A comparative history of the 'ruling classes', that is, of the fields of power, must of course immediately enquire into the degree of differentiation of the different fields of power. It is probable that the fields of power in very ancient societies or in contemporary but relatively undifferentiated societies will not be of the same kind as the fields that we know: since the different fields are less differentiated, the different powers will be less differentiated and we will find examples of 'Cultural Imperialism', that is, the kind of universe where possession of economic or military capital implies a religious, cultural or aesthetic authority. If we look at the more differentiated forms of the social spaces (I would have said more 'highly evolved', but the term 'evolved' is treacherous), we move closer to the fields of power, and therefore of the dominant classes (as universes of agents holding positions in the field of power), that are much more differentiated, and complex relations between holders of different species of capital will appear. Thus one important aspect of the history of art throughout the nineteenth century turns on the relations between bourgeois and artists, as a confrontation between the holders of economic power and their rivals who are holders of cultural power.

Starting with such an analysis of the species of capital, we might move towards an analysis of the structure of the field of power and the forms of internal struggle within the field of power – as I intend to do in due course. We often think in terms of the class struggle, but I think that we shall not understand much of the historical process if we fail to see that there are struggles within the field of power itself. And I think that people very often confuse the class struggle with struggles within the field of power. These internal struggles, for instance to impose one species of capital as the dominant species, or to upset the hierarchy of power, can only be understood by rooting our study in the specific species of capital and the structure of the field of power [. . .].

Lecture of 7 March 1985   7

Objectivism and perspectivism

I now wish to address an entirely different issue. I started by formulating a theory of the habitus and went on to discuss a theory of the field as field of forces. I shall now move on to enquire into the relations between habitus and field, starting from the idea that the theory of the field as field of forces, as a structure of potential forces within which all agents are contained, is abstract and incomplete because it edits out the fact that the social agents who enter these fields have what I call a habitus, that is, dispositions socially organised to perceive and interpret what is happening in the field, which means that social actions cannot be described as a mechanical effect of the forces of the field. We cannot describe social agents in terms of iron filings swept hither and thither by the gravitational forces of the power relations that structure the field. In fact, for the purposes of my analysis, I might present everything that I have to say this year as a kind of commentary on Pascal's famous dictum: 'By space the universe encompasses and swallows me up like a mere speck; by thought I comprehend the universe.'[6]

In fact I think that social science falls between two stools. It can be a kind of social topology or, to use the language of an eighteenth-century philosopher like Leibniz, an *analysis situs*, that is, the analysis of a structure of positions. In this case the analysis of the field as field of forces is a sort of social physics. This physicalism ignores one property of social agents, which is that they perceive the social world, and represent it to themselves. For the social world cannot be reduced to an *analysis situs*. Agents have views of the world that they inhabit. The object of study needs to include the perception of it as an object by other parts of the object. To view the object correctly we must acknowledge that there are struggles between its constituent parts. Sociology must not follow a physicalist path into dissolving or eliminating this specific characteristic of the social world.

In considering this problem[7] we may recall the parallel relation between sociology and the theory of knowledge (see *Sociology in Question*).[8] As regards our knowledge of the social world, we note the existence of two positions. There is an objectivist, materialist and realist position represented by Marx and Durkheim. This consists in studying the social world in itself, considering it as a thing[9] (which is in fact what I have been doing in my lectures up to now). The social world is thought of as existing independently of the representations made of it both by scholars and by ordinary, lay social agents. Using this approach the scientists put themselves in the place of Leibniz's God: he is the '*geometral* [geometrical focus] of all perspectives'.[10] They ignore

8   *Lecture of 7 March 1985*

particular points of view, which they see as biased representations, labelled ideologies by Marx, who defined them as a universalisation of particular interests,[11] and seen by Durkheim as pre-notions that the scientist must dismiss in order to operate a scientific approach.[12] Science, according to this approach, must immediately dismiss these particular viewpoints in order to construct a social topology (that is, the space of positions specific to the field). This view of things reduces the representations made by social agents to illusions, or a fabrication of justifications (Weber speaks of religion as a theodicy,[13] a justification of positions held, and further, a justification of being what one is). In this view, the agents' individual perspectives are biased and subjective.

If psychoanalysis is less objectionable than the anti-personalist position of the sociologist, it is because it guarantees and respects the unity of perspective, whereas the sociologist situates the viewpoint as a view from one point, and thus dissipates the viewpoint and its claim to objectivity. Sociology thus conceived institutes an epistemological break which consists in passing from the simple viewpoint of the ordinary social agent to the overview of points of view that is the position of the scientist. It implies a break between the scholar and the layman because it supposes an initiation separating the scholar from the layman. It is doubtless for this reason (among others) that sociology fascinates the young. But for sociology to become a science it is absolutely bound to pass through this objectivist phase which makes a break with common sense.

The second position on knowledge of the social world is diametrically opposed to the objectivist position. It is the idealist, perspectivist, phenomenological position that corresponds to that of Nietzsche[14] and, among our contemporaries, interactionists or ethnomethodologists. It amounts to saying that there is no intrinsic social world (existing objectively and independently of the social agents). The social world is only my representation and my will, in Schopenhauer's terms.[15] It is only what I think it is, what I see it as, what I want to make of it. In other words, reality is constructed by the social agents' perceptions.

Within subjectivism we may identify two positions. There is a solipsistic subjectivism which sees the world as my representation, and my discourse as an individual discourse claiming universal status (to which common sense might reply for instance: 'But after all the rich and the poor really do exist, we all know they do!). In the second position, which we might designate as 'marginalist subjectivism', the social world is not my representation. The social world is composed through the integration of the whole set of people's representations and wills. But this social world still only exists through individual representations of it. For instance, respect as we note it in the social world is only the integration of all the acts of respect that we observe in a given social world. Which means that the social world can be changed by a contrary decision, which in this case would be refusing to produce acts of respect.[16]

For marginalist subjectivists the social world is a continuous creation. It is a theatre where social agents act out their identity, strut their stuff, persuade us to believe what flatters them most, and discredit their rivals' shows, as Goffman has analysed it.[17] The idealist philosophy of the social world is inseparable from a rejection of the epistemological break (see Schütz).[18] For a subjectivist there is no inaugural break founding the sociological approach: science is a prolongation of common sense, the sociologist merely makes an account of the accounts rendered,[19] social science recounts what is recounted by the social agents, who are well-informed informers. Ultimately, the sociologist is a phenomenologist who makes the social agents' lived experience of the social world explicit, which procures less satisfaction for the scholar than objectivism does, for there is no break between scholarly knowledge and the layman's knowledge. Objectivism is rather more elitist, with the scholar being a discoverer of hidden truths (Bachelard) and knowing things that ordinary social agents are ignorant of.

(A parenthesis in passing: whereas in philosophy the theory of knowledge *stricto sensu* is located in the pure heavens of the idea – see Kant and Hume et al. – where the social world is concerned, the theory of knowledge always assumes a political dimension. Objectivism is the tendency preferred by the more scholarly and is accompanied by a preference for political centralism, whereas marginalist subjectivism is more a refuge for the less scholarly, and is associated with leftist tendencies. Here we find an echo of the Marx/Bakunin divide.)[20]

The subjectivist approach places the sociologist in a position rather closer to that of the writer or the creative artist than that of the scholar, who is separated from the layman by the epistemological break. That said, the subjectivist sociologist does nonetheless transform the non-thetic into the thetic [that is, he reveals social processes that ordinary social agents suffer unwittingly]. He finds himself in the position of a midwife.[21]

These two positions lead to two very different ways of apprehending the social world. If for example we take the problem of social class, the objectivists will say that the social classes have an objective existence whereas the perspectivists will say that they are a construction, whether scholarly (as in nominalism) or political. Now each of these two positions taken separately is false unless we can find a way of combining

10 *Lecture of 7 March 1985*

them without eclecticism. For these two contradictory positions create a false alternative insofar as these two forms of analysis are both necessary, and are necessarily related. Social topology consists in constructing the network where the social agents are situated and therefore in constructing the points from which their views are taken. It makes sense then to integrate the two viewpoints, to analyse first the positions (in an objectivist approach) and then the views given by these positions (the subjectivist approach). We need to acknowledge the existence of the positions and the standpoints that are grounded in those positions. That said, even if the standpoints adopted are determined by the positions – which are revealed by social topology – it remains that the standpoints are not reducible to the positions, because the standpoints adopted usually aim to transform the objective definition of the positions by changing the (subjective) view that the agents have of these (objective) positions. This provides a preamble to an analysis of the struggles in the social world, notably the political struggles.

The objectivist position is fascinating because it demonstrates – particularly, but not exclusively, with the help of statistics – that the layman sees the social world back to front[22] (as in the case of the educated interviewee who tells the interviewer, without seeing the contradiction, that 'education is innate'). But in sociology it is not sufficient to replace the social world the right way round, we need to explain why we see it the wrong way round.

Sociology must construct the social space – the space of positions where the standpoints adopted are defined – but must not forget that it is individual viewpoints, which are partial and partisan, that go to make this space, to make it what it is and to transform it. Each field has its own characteristic structure of distribution of the trump cards (species of capital) needed to play in the field. Each field invites discussion of the state of the present distribution of its capital, judging whether this distribution is fair or unfair. There is a permanent criticism of this distribution and sometimes of the game itself – which is, however, very rare, this rejection of the game itself being something improbable that would constitute a veritable revolution.

To conclude, by offering a metaphor of the problem posed by the analysis of the social world, we might say that the objectivist position is the position of God the Father, knowing everything and situating itself outside of a world that it knows objectively (notably through statistical analysis which provides evidence of educational wastage, for instance); while the subjectivist position is the position of God the Son, God descended upon earth, the sociologist using his incarnation and immanence to analyse a world in which he is himself engaged (he prac-

Lecture of 7 March 1985

tises self-analysis and prefers a comprehensive approach to statistical enquiry). Would an approach integrating these be the position of the Holy Ghost? We can see that sociology, when it does not know what it is, becomes a theology. And vice versa.

Lecture of 14 March 1985

First session (lecture): the elasticity of objective structures – A programme for the social sciences – Reintroducing the point of view – Reintroducing objective space – A political sociology of perception – The theory effect – Social science and justice
Second session (seminar): the invention of the modern artist (1) – The programme for future painters – What is at stake in the struggle – A revolution in the principles of vision – Academic artists

First session (lecture): the elasticity of objective structures

I shall pick up my argument where I left off. I would simply remind you that the specific problem of sociology comes from the fact that it must establish scientific knowledge of a world that is, in the first place, the object of acts of knowledge (whether recognition or misrecognition, I shall consider later) that are executed by people who belong to this very world, and which, secondly, is at least partly the product of these acts of knowledge (of recognition and misrecognition). To add to the second point a little, I should point out that the propositions which I attempt to advance on the social space as a whole seem to me to be valid for any type of field, and therefore for any particular subspace: the academic field, the intellectual field, the literary or the religious field, for instance. Claiming universal relevance for my propositions obliges me to be specific: it seems to me that one of the most important principles of differentiation lies in the degree to which the acts of knowledge (of recognition or misrecognition) play their part in composing the social world as an objective entity.

Let me explain briefly, by returning to something I said last year.[1] The elasticity of the objective structures of the social fields depends on the degree to which the specific capital or the specific powers characteristic of the universe in question are objectified in socially (and ultimately judicially) guaranteed mechanisms or institutions. The proportion of representations that constitute the composition of the social world or field at issue will be the greater as the objectification of powers there is lesser. The intellectual field, then, is characterised by a weak degree of institutionalisation and objectification in its specific mechanisms and powers. This means that it is one of the fields that leaves the most room for symbolic strategies aiming to transform its structures. It is important to know this in order to understand some of its properties, such as, for instance, the analogy that it presents with pre-capitalist societies where the powers are also weakly objectified . . . We could even go so far as to imagine a social universe without any capital at all. The game would be rather like roulette, where each round is independent of the previous one, whereas in poker, for instance, the gains accumulated in one round can help to guide or determine the strategies used in the next round.

In the fields where the powers or principles of domination are relatively under-objectified in mechanisms (particularly in those that work to reproduce the structure of the field) or in legal guarantees (property laws or academic qualifications, for instance), the scope left for such strategies as bluff, symbolic challenge or subversion aiming to discredit the holders of capital is more effective. These social universes may be virtually a-structural and subject to a kind of permanent revolution, whereby each social agent is able ultimately to impose their own representation without being contradicted by the structures. We might call these universes 'anarchic', although this is not a very good analogy.

This remark on the way that the different fields generally display differential properties according to the degree to which they are structured is important because it helps us remember that the analyses I am putting forward are valid not only for the social field in general (as in the case of what we usually call the class struggle), but also within particular fields. In addition, we find an indication of the peculiar elasticity of the intellectual or artistic fields in the fact that symbolic attacks may have a real effect on their structures. For instance, the 'hit-parade effect' achieved by rendering a hit parade public is a symbolic effect that can help transform structures, precisely in cases where the hierarchies and powers are relatively invisible and unconstructed. I might refer here to the action of a German artistic impresario, so to speak (studied by a researcher whose name escapes me for the moment), who by publishing a kind of hit parade of paintings for the eyes of a few connoisseurs had a very strong impact on the structure of the market

14   *Lecture of 14 March 1985*

for painting,[2] where such judgements are not merely descriptive but actually constitutive of reality. To illustrate what I am saying, imagine that the social universe were totally unstructured, and I needed to simply say: 'Behold the social world: it has three classes . . .', for it to become what I say it is.

I hope to show how true it is that the social world is much more elastic than people think. It always leaves room for this kind of symbolic injunction, it lends itself to being constructed symbolically, but obviously to very different degrees at different historical moments and in different areas of the social space. You must always bear in mind that whereas the fields have invariant properties, there are nonetheless variations in the principles organising their general functions in each specific case. That was a parenthesis, but I think that it is important in showing you what is at stake in my argument.

A programme for the social sciences

If it is true, as I have just argued, firstly, that the social world is characterised by the fact that it is a site of acts of knowledge executed by agents situated within that world, and, secondly, that these acts of knowledge contribute to the composition of this very same world, it follows that social science is faced with a very particular kind of task: understanding, knowing or analysing the social world means taking into account acts of knowledge whose truth we can only know if we know their social determinants. Expressing these things is very awkward and you may think that I am arguing in circles, but these acts of knowledge do not occur in a vacuum (this is what distinguishes my proposal from the subjectivist type of vision that I was analysing last week). They are executed by agents who are themselves located within the space; they are therefore points of view that we can only understand if we know the viewpoints from where they were adopted. To know the social world then is to know both the social world in its objective structure and the viewpoints surveying this space, which owe part of what they are to the positions in this space of those who adopt them.

(I believe that the complications are not of my making, but reflect the fact that it is the social world that is complicated. As I often say, I constantly have the feeling that I am underestimating the complications of reality, and I think, I have to say, that one of the many reasons for the striking backwardness of the social sciences is the fact that, as Descartes said, for practical purposes we need a relatively simple

Lecture of 14 March 1985   15

sort of provisional sociology[3] just to enable us to make our way in the world. Clearly, the sort of procedures that I am trying to elaborate would make life over-complicated, and might even render it unliveable, which is why there have been so many attempts to construct representations of the world that are unconsciously inspired by this need for simplified structures.)

Since the social world is so difficult to perceive, it is very easy to approach it with what I call the 'theory effect', giving the word 'theory' its etymological sense:[4] it is easy to make people believe that they are seeing whatever it is they are told to believe. To give you an example: you would probably be very embarrassed if I asked you to draw the social world on a piece of paper, and you would probably choose some simple form, most likely, no doubt, the pyramid. The problem of the representation of the social world has always been present in every social universe, and, as I said last week, a comparative history of the configurations that historical social universes have given of the social world would be most interesting. The difficulty we have in constructing a simple image of the social world encourages this theory effect: if someone presents an image of the social world which seems coherent, you will easily find it acceptable. In other words, for the time being at least, the theory effect is much easier to apply to the social world than to the physical world. (This justifies the complexities that I am introducing, and ought to help you to accept them, the more so because I do nonetheless think that they are acceptable . . .)

An analysis of viewpoints then is inseparable from an analysis of positions and the *analysis situ*, which means that the analysis of spatial structures and structures of position provides a foundation for the analyses of the visions of the world. More precisely, the analysis of positions is the foundation of the analyses of the habitus as structuring principle of the world. I could have said *analysis visus*, but I say *analysis habitus* because it seems to me that when we want to study these visions of the world, describing the visions themselves is less important than describing the principles which generate these visions, one of the objects of sociology being to grasp not only the space of the positions and the representations that agents have of these positions, but also the structures of perception underlying these agents' visions.

At this level, the problem is finding out how the structures of construction of the social world are themselves constructed. The social world is partly my own construction, but we may suppose that this construction is rooted in objective reality: however elastic it may be, the world resists, it does not let you name or construct it any old how, you cannot match whatever you like with anything that comes to

16 *Lecture of 14 March 1985*

mind, you cannot link employers and workers as easily as you can the whole set of workers with each other. There are therefore limits set by the object [. . .].

There are also limits in the subjects, that is, in the categories of perception used by social agents to construct these visions. These properties of the subject are to be found in the notion of the habitus. They are structures that structure people's perception of the world and it seems to me that we need to look into the genesis of these structuring structures. My hypothesis (which I shall explain further) is that there is a connection between the objective structures of the social world and the structures through which agents construct the social world. This is Durkheim's classic hypothesis that logic, as we know it, has its origins in the structure of groups.[5]

I am therefore defining a sort of programme for social science. Social science cannot be a totally objectivist structuralism, whose ultimate expression would no doubt be found in Althusser's ideas (which do at least have the advantage of being explicit), which reduce social subjects to simple supports of the structure, due to his overtranslation of the word *Träger*, translated as 'bearer', 'bearer of the structure'.[6] Against this vision, which more or less annihilates the social agents in favour of the structure, I think that we must reintroduce the agents, not at all as individual subjects or minds, but as 'producers' of viewpoints.

Reintroducing the point of view

I want to make this definition of the social agent more explicit. The social agent is the producer of a point of view, which means that he is situated, he is placed in a *situs*, and the structure is virtually present in his representations and practices, through the very position that he inhabits. In fact what I have just said is no more than an explanation of the notion of the viewpoint. This marks a very clear separation from what we might call the interactionist vision that I mentioned last week, which attaches great importance to the viewpoints that social subjects adopt towards each other, and ultimately describes the social world as no more than the universe of these perspectives. Thus Anselm Strauss speaks of the 'awareness context':[7] he finds the explanatory principle of social practices in the universe of representations that social agents have of their practices and representations. For Strauss, the determining principle of my action will be the idea that I have of the idea that others will have of what I am doing and of the idea that I have of what I am doing . . . the explanatory principle then becomes more or less

Lecture of 14 March 1985

entirely mental: I am moved in my action by the internalised image of the reception that my action will attract . . .

This is not negligible and it is not wrong, but I think that it is insufficient. Reducing the efficacity (is this the right word?) or the 'influence' (in inverted commas because it is not really right either) of the social, reducing what moves agents to act (the question of what moves agents to act is fundamental to sociology, for it is not at all self-evident, they could choose to do nothing, and just stay put . . .), reducing the source of people's actions to the idea that agents have of the idea that other agents will have of their actions, is no doubt to forget what I have just suggested in saying that the agents are situated. What moves them is not only their representation of others' representations; it is, through the fact that their representation is taken from a specific point, everything that is linked to their location at this point, for instance the interests associated with their position. Thus when you hold a dominant position in a space, you have an overview. I like to quote a very fine phrase that reminds us of the link between certain cognitive structures and the social positions from which they have been constructed: 'General ideas are generals' ideas.'[8]

In the viewpoint, then, there is the point, that is, the whole structure, because in speaking of the field we are speaking of the way in which each point comprehends virtually the whole field and its structure, because by definition a position can only be defined in relation to other positions. For instance, a dominant position is only dominant in relation to a dominated position, as Marx so clearly saw: 'The dominant are dominated by their domination',[9] which very fine formula helps us to understand the relations between the sexes. The objective structure then is not reducible to this perspective on perspectives. To formulate it differently: the truth of the viewpoint is neither in the viewpoint itself nor in its relation to other viewpoints; it is partly in the point from which the view has been taken, that is, in the structure.

What else is implied in the fact of taking the viewpoint as such into consideration? The viewpoint is a structured point of view, it is one of the mediations through which the effect of position operates. This apparently simple statement is in fact very complicated, it contains so much that is implicit. The viewpoint and the view are the product of an agent holding a certain position, but also endowed with a certain structure of dispositions . . . What was implicit in what I was saying just now is the relation between the position and the dispositions, a problem that I have tackled on several occasions and which I shall not rehearse here. In general a correspondence between the positions and dispositions of the inhabitants of a field tends to become established

18   *Lecture of 14 March 1985*

(through extremely complicated mechanisms). I merely remind you of this point which I believe I have developed in the past . . . Briefly, the views are structured by the fact that those who adopt these views are wearing spectacles which are, simply speaking, their cognitive structures, themselves linked partly to the effect of position, which imposes structures of perception on them, and also to the effect of their whole social experience, which may perhaps involve changes of position.

One paradox of the social world then is that the social agents' views of the social world are structured through principles of structuration that are themselves social. I may illustrate this with two examples that I have already analysed. In an early work, 'The Production of Belief',[10] I tried to show that the opposition between Parisian right bank and left bank – as manifested in objective space (for instance in the distribution of theatres and art galleries) which may be grasped in the objective shape of maps and plans and a structure of statistical distributions retranslated into spatial structures – functions largely as a subjective structure and as a category of perception of the world: we perceive plays or theatres, for instance, through categories of perception which have at the very least a correspondence with the objective structures of theatrical productions or the sites of their diffusion; we perceive novels through structures of perception which correspond to the structure of distribution of the publishers, and so on.

These analyses, which I have mentioned only briefly, are also valid in an entirely different context, such as the notorious dualist oppositions which ethnologists discover in most societies: in the case of the Kabyle whom I have studied, the opposition between right and left, etc., has an obvious correspondence in the social structure with the fundamental opposition between masculine and feminine. In other words the division of labour between the sexes, which in this type of society is one of the most powerful, if not the most powerful, principles of division, finds its counterpart in the structures through which it is perceived. This means that the correspondence between the objective structures of the social world and the subjective structures through which the social world is perceived leads to us experience the world as seemingly self-evident.

We can see how the analysis that I have just undertaken can underpin what the phenomenologists and the subjectivists accept as the alpha and the omega of their analyses, that is, a description of the experience of the everyday world as an experience of the self-evident. In Schütz for instance, the phenomenological analysis of the ordinary experience of the social world starts with the acknowledgement of the social world as evident, our lived experience of the social world being an experience of

Lecture of 14 March 1985 19

the world as given and unproblematic. The analysis that I am offering underlies this analysis in a way by saying at the outset that this experience is only valid in cases where there is a correspondence between the objective structures and the incorporated structures. Which is in no way universal: social agents' structures of perception are not always a product of the objective structures to which they are applied. In revolutionary periods, for instance, the objective structures can change while the same structures of perception, which have a certain inertia, continue to be applied. This is the 'Don Quixote' effect: Don Quixote applies to the world structures of perception that are the product of a vanished world. This particular inertia of the structures of perception vis-à-vis the structures that have produced them is what I call the problem of the 'hysteresis' of the habitus.[11]

That said, in pre-capitalist societies, which are not clearly differentiated in terms of fields (nor perhaps of classes), this kind of correspondence between objective structures and incorporated structures is I think much more fundamental; which is no doubt why ethnologists find these universes so attractive. They are universes where the social agents feel at home, so to speak ... At the same time, they are formidably closed universes. These universes where the structures of perception are objectively adjusted to the objective structures produce a kind of permanent self-confirmation of perception. For instance, the structure of the division of labour between the sexes is constantly strengthened and empowered: we cannot see how anything could disprove it, since the obviousness of the division is all the more reinforced when principles of division that are themselves structured by this division are applied to it. When every proverb says that 'men are better than women', that 'women are twisted and men are straight', that 'a woman cannot be straight, she can only be straightened', the women end up conforming to the definition; all they can do is try to make the most of their definition. The strategies of the dominated consist in exploiting the strategies of weakness that the dominant allow them: cunning, deceit, trickery and secrecy.

(The problem that I am discussing is a very general one: we can see it not only in Kabylia but also in our own universes ... I must not close this parenthesis without underlining the consequences for the anthropologist or the sociologist for the way in which they study themselves. Everything that I have just been saying does in fact mean that the structures these scientists describe as existing in an incorporated state in social agents, exist in themselves as well. They should never forget – although unfortunately, as I often say, we often practise sociology in order to be able to forget this – that the incorporated structures which

20 *Lecture of 14 March 1985*

they analyse are inscribed in their own minds too. Consequently, the work of objectification of these incorporated structures is part and parcel of scientific research, and this sort of psychoanalysis of the mind of the researcher is one of the conditions necessary for undertaking successful research. I shall return to this point.)

Viewpoints, then, are structures, lenses, categories of perception and systems of classification, and we can see that sociology must study not only social classes, as we ordinarily call them, in the sense of divisions that may exist objectively in reality (if indeed there is such a thing as 'reality' . . .), but also the principles and structures of classification, as well as taxonomies (of orientation, of colour, of the sexes, etc.), using the hypothesis that the structures glimpsed through their manifestations in our classifications have something to do with the objective structures.

To return for a moment to the allusions I made concerning the problem of the division of labour between the sexes being based on the question of the vision of this division of labour, a famous and very fine text by Simmel[12] says that we must describe the social world in which we live as a gendered universe, insofar as this universe is constantly constructed objectively around the division between men and women. And he notes all the social signs and places that are marked out as masculine and feminine, all the objective hierarchies of the masculine and the feminine. We must realise that we are more or less born into this universe, which is sexually oriented not in a Freudian sense, but in the sense that the universe we are born into is divided along lines of gender (as with clothing, for instance). We incorporate this world, which becomes constitutive of our mental structures and makes us subjects fashioned in such a way that we apply a type of gendered division to a world structured by this division. Whence the fact that the objective structures and the incorporated structures continually reinforce each other. It follows, among other things, that it is extremely difficult to counter these formidably self-reproducing structures precisely because of this effect of circular reinforcement. There would be more to say, but I shall leave it at that.

Reintroducing objective space

A sociology going beyond the alternative of idealism and realism, of objectivism and subjectivism, such as I suggested last time, should then in the first instance, as I have just said, reintroduce the agents, but as situated and structured points of view. Then it must reintroduce the

Lecture of 14 March 1985

objective space, both as foundation of these viewpoints and as their object. You can look at what I said last year on the subject of the hit-parade effect; to understand this effect you need to refer not only to the objective properties of the space of the writers but also to the incorporated properties of the social agents as they perceive this space. I think that in any analysis of a social fact we need to tackle both of these aspects, and add in the question of the relation between the two. Since social space has a relatively stable form and structure, is not totally elastic, is not constantly changing, is not any old thing but follows rules of logical progression, we can start from what happens at a particular moment in time t and have a fairly precise idea of what may happen, and above all of what absolutely cannot happen. There are these laws of logical progression, and social space also has both form and a formative action which informs our perception of the space, helping thereby to ensure its own stability. It is because the world has form that our vision of the world is informed and structured, and, if I generalise the notion of cultural capital to include a whole lot of properties that this notion previously excluded, what I call 'information capital'[13] is to some extent inscribed in our unconscious, for instance in the shape of classificatory schemas or principles of vision that are the often unconscious incorporation of objective divisions in the social world.

We might also refer to the kind of spontaneous statistical calculation that we all practise, which enables us to acquire what Goffman calls 'the sense of one's place',[14] that is, the sense of our 'right place' and situation in the social world: we generally have a fairly good rough idea of our place in the social world. In a particular field, the field of the writers, any writer, whether he wants to or not, whether he realises it or not, knows more or less what his place is. The fact that, like Villiers, the S.A.S. author,[15] he may agree to strike a pose in front of the Arc de Triomphe alongside his Mercedes (an absolutely real example!) is in a way dictated to him by his social status, whereas if you telephone a writer published by Éditions de Minuit[16] (you might try this) he will not accept: he doesn't have a Mercedes, and even if he did, he wouldn't strike a pose, and especially not in front of the Arc de Triomphe! [*laughter*] This implies that there is a kind of sense of propriety in any determined position. This sense of propriety has nothing to do with morality; propriety for someone is what seems proper to their condition, what they tacitly accept without even formulating it, from the fact of inhabiting their position (for instance, in the case of a writer, the fact of publishing here rather than there, or being published by A rather than B, which is more or less the same thing but it would be rather complicated to explain why it is more or less the same . . .).

22   *Lecture of 14 March 1985*

Information capital, the kind of feel for the game that social agents put into practice, is the product of a game that is relatively structured, as opposed to an absolutely anarchic game that would be constantly changing. This is an elementary principle. In his excellent book on Hume, Deleuze says that ultimately the only axiom or anthropological postulate that Hume accepts is the fact that men (he does not call them social agents) are conditioned by experience. One cannot accept less than this. Sociology does claim a little more, because if men are conditioned, it means that if you get them to do the same thing several times over, they learn, and if it is unpleasant they won't do it again whereas if it is rewarded they will start again. This principle of conditioning, which is obviously presupposed by the theory of the habitus, is what ensures that subjects are historical products. To the axiom of conditioning I then add the idea that social agents are structurable, and the idea that their possession of cognitive structures is linked in part (I don't claim to account for the totality of their cognitive structures) to the fact that the social world is structured, that there are in objective reality a social order and oppositions. This information capital, then, is a whole set of kinds of knowledge, know-how and structures of perception; a social agent is equipped not only with these kinds of knowledge and know-how, but also with structures of perception of knowledge.

A political sociology of perception

Having reintroduced firstly the viewpoints and secondly the space, we now need thirdly (I could have added it to the second point, but I prefer to treat it separately to show it up more clearly) to reintroduce the fact that social agents are in competition with each other for the right viewpoint of the space. There is a kind of politics of the perception of the social world, which is in fact a struggle for the legitimate perception of the social world. In other words we cannot do what phenomenologists like Schütz and Garfinkel do when they create a phenomenology of lived experience, lived in a social world in the abstract. How do they see it? An excellent example is one of Schütz's finest texts, 'Making Music Together',[17] which deals with the experience of acting in a concerted, orchestrated manner. The analysis is very fine, but it is obvious that to have the experience of making music together, you need a certain number of quite specific social conditions, which are bracketed out by Schütz, who never even asks the question . . .

(I praise [and I criticise in the same breath]. You know, if I have made some small contribution to sociology, I think that is because I have tried to show due respect to anything that could help us think more deeply about the social world. I have a lot of respect for the people whom I appear to criticise, and some of my arguments are only possible because they have existed. I am saying this out loud, because this is not the style in a country where we are always supposed to look clever enough to have succeeded all by ourselves, so much so that we can seem original if we don't try to seem original . . . I need to say this, because if I don't say it, I won't be able to prevent myself thinking that you are thinking that I am showing off at Schütz's expense, which would make me unhappy and unable to say all this [*laughter*].)

These people have in fact produced some remarkable analyses. It is extraordinary to have had the idea of analysing things that seem self-evident. Their idea is that our ordinary experience of the world, the 'it goes without saying', is something that does not go without saying. They have worked very hard and produced extraordinary results. That said, they have overlooked a great deal. (One of the problems with intellectual work is that very often to see one thing you have to lose sight of another. This is a good thing, because it leaves something for your successors to work on [*laughter*], but it is true that it is very difficult to cover every angle of a topic in a single intellectual enterprise.) What I regret about their work is that they analyse a point of view as if it were universal. I think the phenomenologists make the mistake that I call the mistake of universalising the particular: unconsciously they are universalising their lived experience. In taking their lived experience and ignoring the fact that it is a particular experience (of a professor, of a philosophy teacher, for instance), they bracket out things that the idea of *situs* allows us to reintroduce.

The phenomenologists have claimed to practise a sociology of the perception of the social world, but I believe that practising a rigorous sociology of perception means knowing that this implies a politics of perception or a political sociology of perception. You cannot rightly describe the logic of the social world (as in Schütz's book)[18] if you forget that the construction of the social world is a subject of conflict. The social world and its perception, designation and explanation are subjects of conflict in which there are very special kinds of power relations, where the holders of a cultural capital enabling the explanation of the social world, for instance, have a tremendous advantage.

24   *Lecture of 14 March 1985*

The theory effect

One capital thing that I mentioned at the outset (even if it may have seemed trivial to you . . .) is the theory effect. If I have managed to discover something new, however minor, it is these three words: 'the theory effect'. The theory effect is difficult to detect because it is the personal privilege of anyone claiming to discuss the social world in theoretical terms. It is the effect that I am exercising at this very moment. It amounts to saying, with a greater or lesser degree of social authority, how the social world works and how we should view it . . . Obviously when you are exercising the theory effect, you don't say: 'I am telling you how you should view the social world', but: 'This is how the social world works, there are three classes out there in the real world, and I am merely noting their existence.' This means that we gloss over the fundamental fact that making this statement ('there are three classes') is already a *coup de force* which is only possible for those who conceive that there is something to say about the social world and that it is legitimate to make this kind of statement, which is in itself quite an extraordinary aim . . . (Not to mention the aim of analysing one's own ordinary experience of the social world: which would seem extremely mad to three quarters of the human race – although this does not mean that it is not interesting.) I have launched into this rather lyrical and dramatic tirade because I think that the point might run the risk of seeming banal, whereas it is a very important one.

When we practise a sociology of perception, therefore, we practise a political sociology of perception, reintroducing space as an issue in the struggles that aim to transform our vision of the world. Which is made possible by the second principle that I announced at the outset: the social world is partly the product of acts of knowledge. It is because agents' viewpoints contribute to making their space that the fight to make the space visible, and make people believe in the vision of space that we have to offer, is neither crazy nor absurd. It is objectively founded: it has a good chance of being understood (other people understand very well what it is all about) and a good chance of producing an effect.

Social science and justice

I shall stop here by saying a few words on the notion of prediction. I have perhaps already told you this, but it is relatively important. You know what an enormous part prediction plays in political conflict, with the two grand strategies that consist, one in rethinking the past in the light of the present and the other in saying what the future will bring. These two strategies are typical of political struggles because a prediction that is presented as a prediction is an action on the social world that is presented as an affirmation. In other words it is a form of the theory effect that amounts to saying: 'This is how things are' . . . The (extremely complicated) effect of this theory will be all the more effective, the more the person practising it is something other and more than a simple theoretician. If the theory effect is practised *ex cathedra* in a situation like the present [such as the lecture situation], there is an element of symbolic effect, but if it is practised by someone who has a hold over a group of believers (and therefore a kind of statutory right to be believed), who has what we call an 'authorised' viewpoint, that is, a point of view that ceases to be a point of view, a point of view that is the right point of view (the judicial viewpoint would be the point of view par excellence), it is self-authenticating . . . If I have the authority and I say that tomorrow everyone will demonstrate at the Bastille, there will be people at the Bastille tomorrow (how many, we will have to see . . . [*laughter*]). Whereas if I were to say it here and now, there's not much chance . . . But this is a very serious point.

Prediction as a 'self-fulfilling prophecy', as described by Popper,[19] has a social foundation, it is not a fantasy. The leader of a sect, for instance, spends his time making self-fulfilling prophecies within certain limits and to a certain extent, whose limits and extent we should of course measure. The struggle over the meaning of the social world is then a struggle over legitimate perception, a struggle in which the different social agents – you must remember what I was saying about the two previous points – invest the capital that they have acquired in the previous phases of the struggle. When I said at the beginning that symbolic relations are a particular kind of power relation this is what I was alluding to.

In the summary I gave you last week of my previous lectures, I said that the structure of a field could be grasped from the structure of the distribution, in statistical terms, of the capital or specific power which is effectively at work in the field (the key word is 'distribution'). This is perhaps the articulation between the two points that I have been developing today: the structure of a field is a certain distribution; this field is an object of perception. In other words, social agents will perceive and appreciate this distribution and they will perceive and appreciate it as just or unjust. Here we could discover the Aristotelian meaning and context of the use of the notion of distribution.[20] Social science, which describes distributions by decisively bracketing out any

26 *Lecture of 14 March 1985*

judgement of the value of this distribution (this would be the definition of positivism) – this divine science that says: 'This is how the distribution is, there is no need to question it, it is how it is and moreover it is self-perpetuating, there is nothing to change . . .' – brackets out the fact that there is still an issue of distribution in the space which is structured by that distribution. There is still an issue of the justice or injustice of distribution in the space structured according to the distribution of economic, symbolic or religious power . . . The fact that distribution is an issue in the structure is one of the factors that enable the distribution to be transformed or even revolutionised. This question of justice then is not something that sociology, if it aims to be scientific, should bracket out.

The question of justice is an integral part of social science. Not in the sense of Durkheim's 'Morale théorique et science des moeurs'[21] – whose tired clichés are not the newest aspect of Durkheimian thought, and are the most closely bound to their historical and political context. I am not trying to say that we can use a science of distributions to derive a science of just distribution. I am simply saying that, like it or not, the very structure of a distribution calls into question the legitimacy of the distribution. We might even think that someone's position in the structure of distribution helps to determine the likelihood of their perceiving the distribution as just or unjust. I shall attempt to show you how an analysis in terms of fields can lead us to take a very new approach – surprisingly different from my usual way of thinking – to the traditional problem of justice and injustice which has become fashionable again with a certain number of books published in the United States[22] . . . I shall return to this problem.

Second session (seminar): the invention of the modern artist (1)

I want now to return to a question that I touched on in passing two years ago,[23] the problem of the birth of the modern artist in the nineteenth century, in the context of Impressionism. Let me make it clear straight away that this has nothing to do with the current fashion for Impressionism,[24] since I have been working on this subject for the last three or four years. There is what you might call the substantive interest, as well as the methodological interest, of trying to see more clearly than I have in the past what an analysis in terms of field can bring to the knowledge of an artistic movement. What I want to do is relate the history of the field of painting to the history of the field of literature in the nineteenth century, starting, let us say, with Romanticism.[25]

Lecture of 14 March 1985 27

I believe that a certain number of phenomena cannot be understood for as long as we look at them on the scale of a single field, because a certain number of innovations, in particular those that I intend to analyse, are only comprehensible on the scale of several fields. I have not mentioned the field of music and I shall mention it only in passing, because my work in this area is much less advanced,[26] but also because I find the connections between the fields of painting and literature much more important and significant. Moreover, the studies of music that are pertinent (from my point of view, of course) are far fewer, which means resorting much more to first-hand sources – and consequently the work takes much longer . . .

My project is to try to understand this sort of historical innovation that we fail to notice because it has become an institution, and therefore banal and invisible. It is the 'it goes without saying' effect. Our minds being structured according to structures that were invented in the nineteenth century, we don't see the phenomena that were invented in the nineteenth century, nor, *a fortiori*, the structures through which we see them, which are produced by them.[27] This is an illustration of what I was saying just now. In fact you could call my plan: 'The Invention of the Artist' or 'How did the modern artist invent himself?'[28]

The programme for future painters

To situate the problem, I shall read you a text by Jules Laforgue, whose date I don't know.[29] It has been re-published with a preface that talks about psychoanalysis, etc., but with no mention of the original date (that is typical of French publishing . . .), and I haven't had time to check it out for the moment. It is in the *Mélanges posthumes* which have been re-published by Éditions Slatkine, who re-publish long-lost works with lavish prefaces that take thirty pages to say nothing at all.

This is what Laforgue writes:

PROGRAMME FOR FUTURE PAINTERS. Some of the liveliest most daring painters one has ever known, and also the most sincere, living as they do in the midst of mockery and indifference – that is, almost in poverty, with attention only from a small section of the press – are today demanding that the State have nothing to do with art, that the School of Rome (the Villa Medicis) be sold [*which is still debatable*],[30] that the Institute be closed, that there be no more medals or rewards, and that artists be allowed to live in that anarchy which is life, which means everyone left to

28 *Lecture of 14 March 1985*

his own resources, and not hampered or destroyed by academic training which feeds on the past. No more official beauty; the public, unaided, will learn to see for itself and will be attracted naturally to those painters whom they find modern and vital. No more official salons and medals than there are for writers. Like writers working in solitude and seeking to have their productions displayed in their publishers' windows, painters will work in their own way and seek to have their paintings hung in galleries. Galleries will be their salons.[31]

I don't suppose that you will understand all the implications of this text, which I found only after I had completed my research, and as with the phrases that we often consign to an epigraph, whose interest you see only after you have found everything it was referring to, it raises the question of sources in quite a peculiar fashion . . . people who hunt for influences should think about this . . . it is banal enough, Baudelaire said it a hundred times over for Edgar Poe: 'If I translated Edgar Poe, it was because I had been doing Edgar Poe for years.'[32] Laforgue's text is interesting because it says two things, I think. The first proposition: 'Let us liberate artists from the State, through the specific agencies that express the power of the State within the artistic field.' If we take the scientific field (and I'll leave you to translate): 'Let us liberate the scientific field from the specific agencies through which the State exercises its power . . .'. No need to continue, it is very, very subversive . . . The second proposition: 'Let us do what the writers have done' ('no more official salons and medals than there are for the writers').

This text contains one of the central ideas that I want to communicate: to put it succinctly, whereas the literary field had been free of academic constraint since the eighteenth century, the artistic field in the nineteenth century remained subservient to the canons of the Academy, via the Salon and all the schools that prepared candidates for the École des beaux-arts. There came a time then when the painters were able to find in the situation of the writers a kind of model for their own revolution. At a different historical moment, the rebellion of the painters against their specific tyranny ('specific tyranny' meaning tyranny within their field: temporal power being exercised in an order that rejects temporal power) served as a model for the writers to fulfil their liberation, which was much less advanced than that of the painters, who took them as a model, imagined. This is the general schema . . . In detail, things are more complicated.

A second interesting text is a letter from Courbet (23 June 1870) to Maurice Richard, minister for fine arts, who was offering him the

Legion of Honour. It is a very fine text: 'The State is incompetent in matters of art. When it takes it upon itself to reward, it usurps public taste. Its intervention is quite demoralising . . . and fatal for art, which it wraps in official convention and condemns to the most sterile mediocrity. The wisest thing for the State would be to refrain from this. When it does leave us free, it will have fulfilled all its duty towards us.'[33]

Here I approve and underline. I have a personal bias in this enterprise: I am interested in this history because I see in it the history of a process of autonomisation which has, I would argue, produced our modern intellectuals and researchers, but this history is never finished; it is not linear, there are retreats and reversals, and so it is always worth taking the trouble to try to understand it, but also perhaps to draw strength from this understanding.

I would like now to show how in the first instance the painters took up arms against the Salon, won their autonomy, and with it what we take to be the universal definition of art, whereas it is a historical invention, or is at least a historical moment, which does not mean that an institution like the modern artist, or an ensemble of cognitive structures like modern science, are not universal at the same time as historical. (This raises a problem that I intend to discuss if I have time). It seems to me that one of the problems raised by the analyses I am proposing is the question of the historical conditions within which provisionally universal structures are established. This is a difficult problem. I do no more than refer to it in passing to make you aware that it underlies everything that I am saying.

To start with, we have the academic art that we know as 'art *pompier*'. There is a very fine lecture on '*art pompier*' by Jacques Thuillier published by the Éditions du Collège de France,[34] as well as a book by James Harding, *Artistes pompiers*,[35] more interesting for its illustrations than for its text, which is not altogether bad, but is neither very original nor very well informed. The book does have the merit of providing a well-documented collection of reproductions that are useful for following what I am going to say, since I am not going to play at presenting a slide show . . . What I would first like to show is that it would be better to call *pompier* art 'Academic art', insofar as I believe that a good analysis of the functioning of the structures of the academic universes within which the academic painters are produced and reproduced provides the principles that enable us to understand the more specific properties of this painting. This may sound rather arbitrary. The analysis took me an awfully long time and obviously I did not reach my present conclusions straight away. This is a risk involved in presenting research already completed, as I did in the first session, as

30 *Lecture of 14 March 1985*

opposed to research in progress (which is, moreover, one of the issues in the debate between the *pompiers* and the Impressionists: what is 'finished' and what 'unfinished'?): research presented in as finished a form as possible assumes a dogmatic appearance and exercises an effect of closure and enclosure, which is certainly one of the effects sought . . . These are orderly arts, which present closed worlds as opposed to open worlds. The debate between the sketch and the finished work is one of the great debates within the academic order, and it is no accident if it is both aesthetic and political.

In the nineteenth century, then, painting meant academic painting. The painters were more or less entirely submitted to the authority of the Academy, which had the monopoly of the training of painters and also the monopoly of the consecration of their produce. Consequently it was able, through the very form of the artistic practice that it imposed, to impose an implicit definition of painting, which in its simplest and provisionally most general form amounts to saying that painting is a language, that no painting may say nothing; painting must say something. Implicit definitions are the most powerful because they cannot even be challenged. This is the sense of the opposition that I have established in the past between *doxa* and orthodoxy: the *doxa* is what does not even need to be affirmed, because it is self-evident. An implicit definition then, dare I say, is ideologically impregnable because it does not even have to be affirmed explicitly. It is, as the phenomenologists would say, pre-thetic. It is not promulgated as such, it has no need to be formulated as such and therefore does not elicit an antithesis.

What is interesting in the case that I am studying is the fact that this implicit definition becomes explicit as soon as an antithetical definition appears. In fact history has an analytic function and this is what helps, at least in the present case, to explain the reference that Marx, referring to Hegel, made to the owl of Minerva,[36] which is that consciousness follows after. History acts as an analyst, and the interest of this history of painting at the critical moment when academic painting came to be confronted with the Impressionist challenge (in fact with the challenge by Manet, rather more than the Impressionists) is that history accomplishes a sociological study: it brings what is implicit up into daylight.

What is at stake in the struggle

To help us understand what is at stake in the struggle, there is no better document than the famous text by Zola, published in *My Hatreds*. In this collection of critical articles by Zola, where there are a number of texts devoted to Manet, there is a text devoted to Courbet that I want to read to you. It is a kind of protest against a Proudhon-type definition of art. In the nineteenth century, as I have shown elsewhere, writers like Flaubert found themselves in a situation where they had to fight on two fronts, not only against a social art that wanted art to serve a cause, but also against a bourgeois art that wanted art to serve a conservative function, or at least as amusement for conservatives ... This double opposition is also present in painting, and it is in this context that Zola comes to define a kind of art for art's sake, against on the one hand the Proudhonians and Courbet, partisans of a social art, and on the other hand the Salons and the Academy. This text is important because it says a lot of what I want to say:

> See here! You have writing, you have speech, you can say whatever you want to say, and you go address yourselves to the art of lines and colours in order to teach and to educate. Well! for pity's sake, keep in mind that we are not pure reason. If you are practical, leave to the philosopher the right to give us lessons, and leave the painter the right to give us emotions. I do not believe you can require the painter to teach and in any case I flatly deny that a [painting can affect the morality of the crowd].[37]

This text is very complicated and confused ... But since, after the event, we can see the structure of the field and the issues at stake, it is easy enough to clarify: initially, a polemical discourse is typically led to attack its opponent on grounds that are often imposed by the opponent; and we find in its arguments the presence of the dominant discourse of the moment. In my opinion, Zola is trying to say something that he will say much more clearly when discussing Manet, which is: 'Stop asking painting to say something. Stop treating it as a language.' He speaks of the 'emotions' for the sake of argument, but I think that the important plea is: 'Do not ask us to teach' (the word 'teach' is important). 'Do not ask us to fulfil some academic function' ... He says it against Proudhon, that is, against social art, but he could just as well have said it against the Salon. In a very interesting book on the 1848 Revolution by [name of author inaudible],[38] we see the minister for culture of the moment setting as a subject for competition a portrait of the figure of the Republic: the winners of the competition are the most academic painters, who, being accustomed to executing royal profiles for medallions, are able to swiftly adapt to the Republic, whereas the more advanced painters are out of touch because they reject the very idea of art being a language. We can easily see that what is at stake is

32 *Lecture of 14 March 1985*

the very idea that art has a function, the minimal function of having something to say, of communicating.

We should note in passing that when we talk of 'reading a painting', as people did a few years ago when 'semiology' was in fashion (they 'read' everything, including paintings . . .), we are using the word 'reading' metaphorically, and it is an academic metaphor. (It is no accident that semiology was so successful in the academic world: it enabled an *aggiornamento*[39] – the rehabilitation of the old techniques of reading such as the *explication de texte*. This is a rather cruel parenthesis, but I could substantiate it . . .) The perception of a work of art as a reading involves the implicit thesis that works are made to be read and therefore to be taught and become subjects of debate. What Zola says, and this will constantly be repeated by the painters afterwards, is: 'We do not write, we paint', which amounts to affirming the specific nature of painting. This is very important. Since the dominant art is poetry, which is an art of language, painting has constantly been dominated by this dominant definition (*'ut pictura poesis'*),[40] and it is in relation to this dominant definition that it has been condemned to be a kind of writing, destined to be read. This new affirmation of the autonomy of painting, then, is an affirmation of painting's independence of any function, whether assigned to it by the Academy or by the socialist movement, and also of the dominant model of literature (this supplementary move is all the more amazing, because it is a writer who is speaking) . . .

What I want to show you is how the revolution that led painting to be established as painting, painting as such (remember what I was saying last time: the establishment of a field is the affirmation of an 'as such'), distinct from literature, happens in two phases. Firstly, it breaks free from external function – language must say something, it must argue in favour of progress or else describe ancient civilisations, it must give lessons in morality: according to the Academy's definition. In a second phase it breaks free from a second implicit injunction, according to which art too must say something – it doesn't matter what, but as long as art is required to say something, it remains subject to the dominant definition, which is that of literature.

This revolution occurs in two phases, the writers can be the liberating heroes (this, it seems to me, is the paradox of Zola). The part that they play for the painters is analogous to the part played by intellectuals in some movements of national liberation (I believe that this analogy is well founded): they provide the discourse for people who, for social reasons, are not well equipped to produce discourse on their own production; the writers produce the discourse that confers legitimacy; they

Lecture of 14 March 1985

produce categories of perception. That said, little by little, they effect a second liberation, by importing it into their own terrain. But this is not true of Zola, and this is one of the paradoxes: although he was still very young, Zola was able to write about Manet, who is much more advanced, and develop a theory of painting as a specific kind of writing that would lead him to attack literary writing in its very linguistic function; but Zola did not do what Mallarmé did . . . I'm not sure if I am expressing things in the right order. Zola's text, then, seems to me to encapsulate in advance everything that is at stake in this struggle.

A revolution in the principles of vision

I would like now to show how the Impressionist revolution, which was a revolution against domination by academic structures, took advantage of an objective crisis in the foundations of the academic order. (I think that we can say 'revolution' if we think of it within a relatively autonomous field – there are specific revolutions, partial revolutions at the level of a field, and then we can remove the quotation marks; it is when we say 'the Impressionist revolution' without any notion of a field that it is absurd . . .) In order to show this, I shall have to explain on the one hand what academic art was and what its links with the academic structures were, and, on the other hand, show how the transformations of the academic structures and the specific crisis of the academic order provided conditions favouring a subversion of these academic structures.

To announce the thesis that I shall develop: the specific revolution driven by these kinds of heretical, heroic liberators finds the social conditions needed to make it possible in a specific crisis of the academic order, in a manner analogous to May 1968, that is, in a specific crisis which owes its form to the specific structure of the academic subspace. The thesis that I wish to advance is that the Impressionists would not have managed to impose their heretical definition of painting as painting with no purpose other than to be painting, as nothing but an interplay of colours (Zola, influenced by Manet, says this very well), if the very structure of the academic universe that underpinned their opponent, academic painting, had not been shaken by a crisis specific to the academic universe. That is my thesis.

My first point: academic painting, the painting we call '*pompier*', owes its properties to the logic of the university institution. It is the pictorial production of *homo academicus*. If *homo academicus* paints, he paints like a fireman, and even when he doesn't paint . . . he still

34 *Lecture of 14 March 1985*

plays the fireman [*laughter*]! As we could draw an (interesting) analogy between *pompier* painting and writing a doctoral thesis, it is not so simple for me here to speak of *pompier* painting. Here I am exaggerating somewhat, to show how the obstacles to sociological thought are nearly always social. Certain things are not intrinsically difficult to think about, the difficulties in thinking them through are social, since you often have to consider yourself as part of the object that you are studying, and especially since this is unpleasant to contemplate . . . if you see what I mean. This means that we must think these things through all the more because we would prefer not to consider them . . . (What we do like to think, is: 'I am a person', 'I am unique', and so on).

I am slightly embarrassed by my formula: 'the properties of the institution = the properties of the painting', it sounds rather dogmatic . . . The first property of academic art, and more generally, I believe, of any institutional aesthetic or product (it goes much wider than *pompier* art – it could easily, for instance, help us to understand Zhdanovism), is that the cultural producer, whether an original, individual person or a temperament (remember Zola's formula invoking the idea of a temperament as opposed to *pompier* painting, in a phrase that is still set as a baccalaureate examination question)[41] must efface himself in front of the subject – 'subject' being understood as 'what is to be painted'.

This leads us right to the heart of the problematic of vision; everything I have said this morning about the struggles over vision applies to painting, which is also involved in the struggle to gain a vision of the world and to establish the principles legitimising that vision. In a sense, when the painters live their lives as revolutionaries, they are not wrong, and in fact these specific revolutions (whose 'specific' nature I have explained) play a much greater political role than people believe. We should remember that we are dealing with a relatively autonomous field, although the ideology of the avant-gardes of the relatively autonomous fields assimilates their specific revolutions to a general revolution. High fashion is a good example: when we make high fashion go down into the street, this is a revolution.[42] Despite this propensity of the avant-gardes to identify a specific avant-gardism with a political avant-gardism, a propensity that leads to alliances (this is very important: Mallarmé was closely linked to the anarchists, surprisingly enough . . .), we should remember that we are dealing with a specific revolution in a relatively autonomous space.

That said, having expressed this reservation and defined the limits of the validity of a specific revolutionary action, we may judge that it is nonetheless much more revolutionary than a hard-line Marxist, say, would believe, thinking: 'they are spinning a yarn; it is a revolution

Lecture of 14 March 1985 35

in a superstructural space that does not touch on anything important'. If you think of what I was saying this morning, a revolution concerning vision and the principles of vision and the division of the social world is always much more important than people think . . . and ultimately the painters are much more revolutionary than they realise. Which explains the extraordinarily reactionary reactions that these specific revolutions inspire. Something we find difficult to understand if we visited the Orangerie museum as a three-year-old child, is that Impressionist painting could have provoked such furious passions. The fact of painting a simple tree could inspire incredible texts of an extraordinarily terrible violence, as in May 1968. This violence and its connections with positions in the social space as a whole would be inexplicable if these revolutions, however partial and specific, did not connect with mental structures, with visions of the world. Ultimately, saying that painting can exist without being in the service of some cause or other (which is basically what was being said), is a much more formidable revolution than you would think.

To return to my argument. The subject to be painted is itself the product of the whole specific history of the field. At any moment, a field is characterised by saying what you should see, what is worth looking at. The essence of a field of cultural production of any kind (it would be true of the sociological field today), is to tell us what is worthy of being studied, researched, painted or photographed. Telling people: 'That's worth painting, that's not worth painting' means saying 'That's worth looking at and getting people to look at it', and getting people to look at it is establishing it as being worth looking at, and more, being worthy of being represented. Now 'being worthy of being represented' is fundamental: this is the monopoly of defining legitimate symbolic reproduction. This is a typically sovereign power: the kind which says that in the last analysis the only thing worthy of being represented is the king. In fact the academic field says first of all that you must have a subject, and then that there are good subjects and others that are unacceptable or insignificant; what the painter is being asked to do, then, is to efface himself as a subject in the face of the designated subject, that is, in the face of the social rules that at a given moment define legitimate objects and the legitimate way of treating them.

Academic artists

Well then, what are the *pompier* painters? The *pompier* painters are school painters. They learn their profession for the most part through

36 *Lecture of 14 March 1985*

copying. If you think about it, the copy is both a designated object and an object already painted: the object is designated simultaneously both as subject and as style. Trained in the school of the copy, raised to respect the masters, the school painters are basically performers, in the sense that one speaks of a musician as a performer and one praises his performance ('The performance was magnificent'). To understand this painting (which could be judged by different criteria), to understand why it is what it is, we need to understand that theirs was entirely an art of performance. All the honour of the painter was concentrated in the virtuosity of the performance. The accent was placed on the performance, the pictorial act required an enormous effort to attain perfection in the performance, with no concern for originality or invention. The problem is not to invent but to perform well. That is, I believe, a universal property of any educated, academic tradition: the subject does not matter, what counts is the impeccable manner of treating it ... The academic arts are nearly always arts of virtuosity devoted less to showing something than to showing their excellent manner of showing it. It other words, they are formalist arts.

I'll give you some examples. Ultimately the painter only counts if he is a master who perfectly possesses a mastery that should never be surpassed (to surpass it is not even thinkable ...). His only aim is to rise to the level of the greatest masters and show excellent mastery of the skills he has inherited. In a famous book, Levenson, a specialist on China, describes something in Chinese painting that matches what I am saying here.[43] He speaks of a sort of expressionism in performance which can lead to playing academic games with the academic rules, and he speaks of 'anti-academic academicism': being anti-academic is part of academicism; which is why it is very difficult to subvert university institutions, since they allow for it in certain circumstances and situations, to a certain extent ... The academic painters then do not seek to exist as original subjects through new subjects or new styles at all; they want to excel through their excellence of manner.

Evidence of what I am saying: they themselves produced copies of their most successful works. A typical case is that of a certain Charles Landelle, a very well-known painter of the time whose works commanded astronomical prices, who produced I believe thirty copies of a painting, the *Femme Fellah*, which had been a great success at the 1866 Salon. This is a kind of proof of the fact that scarcity is not identical with the originality and above all the singularity of the painting. What the heretics invented was the idea that it is the unique work that counts, whereas for the academic painters, the execution of copies is not an inferior activity at all, but a highly valorised activity, and there was a market for copies just as there was for originals. They could be copies of original works by contemporary painters, but also copies of classical works from the past, which had pride of place in private collections, museums and provincial churches. A good copy was considered the equal of the original. On this subject, Lethève's book, *La vie quotidienne des artistes français au XIXe siècle*, is a good source, although rather anecdotal.[44] The book lacks a structure, but is a mine of information of the kind that I have just given you.

We see then that the invention of the artist as unique artist and the invention of the work as unique work go hand in hand. As I have tried to show in a different piece of research, this is relatively important, insofar as what makes for the rareness of a work today is not its unique status (although its unicity is part of the implicit definition of the work of art) but the unicity of the artist constituted as unique artist creating unique works.[45] In other words, to produce a work of art as a rare object in the modern sense of the word, we have to produce the artist as rare object. The social conditions of the production of the work of art are coextensive with the social conditions of the production of the artist, in the modern sense of the term. I believe that this thesis, which I have elaborated in connection with contemporary painting, finds clear validation in the fact that it was necessary to invent the unique artist in order to enable the invention of the unique work.

Further proof (I don't want to submerge you with endless evidence but it is important to illustrate the relation between the artist and his object) is the fact that the majority of the works by the *pompier* painters are commissions, and extraordinarily detailed commissions. Once again, I can cite Lethève, who shows that an absolutely unknown, second-rank painter who was asked to represent the Fête de la Fédération was obliged to rework his picture several times to take account of remarks made by [*inaudible name, doubtless the Empress Eugénie*], who thought that he had not respected the historical truth. Another example: a painter commissioned to paint a picture entitled *Le Génie de la navigation*, for a monument that Louis-Joseph Daumas was commissioned to erect in Toulon, received an extraordinarily precise programme whose opening lines I have noted: 'Her right hand grasps the shaft of the tiller which steers the seashell on which the statue is standing, her left arm, raised in front of her, holds a sextant, etc.'[46] There is no place for free experiment here. All that the painter can do is execute the programme the best he can. These analyses show that to be a painter is to accept this definition of his role, where the only thing he can do is execute a performance.

38 *Lecture of 14 March 1985*

These analyses are also important for the eternal problem of knowing when the artist was born (in the *Quattrocento*? In the *Cinquecento*, for instance?). We realise that the idea that the artist appears at a certain moment and distinguishes himself from the artisan once for all time is nothing but a myth. Another example, the same Landelle whom I mentioned just now was commissioned in 1859 to record the visit of the Empress to the Saint-Gobin glassworks; since he could not get the personnel to pose, he was obliged to work from photographs, and at the last moment he had to change the composition, because the Empress didn't like it. This was in 1859, not during the Renaissance . . . The artists had not won their autonomy at all.

To take this a little further . . . Insofar as their art is one of performance, the location of any originality has to be in the technique. What distinguishes one performance from another is virtuosity, or technique. This explains a property that Gombrich (speaking of the *pompiers*, I think) refers to as the flaw of the 'too carefully finished'.[47] The flaw of the 'too carefully finished' is that kind of pathetic search for a perfect finish in the quality of the historical treatment, but also in the sheer technique of the treatment. The flaw derives from the fact that technical virtuosity is the only way of affirming mastery. We can easily see that the school exercise is the extreme case of the situation the painters find themselves in: there is the subject imposed ('Write an essay on . . .'), these kinds of school problems that exist only to be solved, these difficulties entirely fabricated by the school culture which means that ways of transcending previous problems are written into the whole history of previous problematics. I think this is very important if we want to understand what an educated, academic culture is, for instance when we wonder why the humanities are not scientific. At this very moment I am constantly speaking in metaphors, by analogy with things that you know very well . . . I am speaking by analogy with 'art history' above all, which uses the canons of academic painting that it did not study but is starting to study.

School exercises, for instance, owe their existence entirely to a tradition of school exercises, and can appear as problems only to someone who has passed through the school, so that the autodidact can sometimes have an advantage, from not being aware of them. This was one of Manet's virtues – he had had the least training possible as a painter; in such a conjuncture relative ignorance can be an advantage. It is true also for the connoisseur: for instance, if the great majority of Impressionist paintings are now in American museums or private collections, it is because the Americans, lacking connoisseurs and collectors, were less submissive to the academic canons and their tastes

Lecture of 14 March 1985 39

were in a way freed from the school canons, so that they were able to be ahead of the times, by default. This is very rare, historically, but it does happen that the absence of capital can be an advantage.

The flaw of the too carefully finished defines the *pompier* style, with the icy perfection that we find in Couture's famous painting in the Louvre, *The Romans during the Decadence*, with its coldness and unreality born of an excess of perfection. The painting is a brilliant display of impersonality and insignificance. To suggest an analogy, I refer you to a very important work by Pevsner, *Pioneers of the Modern Movement from William Morris to Walter Gropius*.[48] In this book there is a description of works and objects presented at the Crystal Palace in 1851 by people who used this *pompier* style. Pevsner describes an extraordinarily illusionistic carpet which gave a three-dimensional illusion – you felt you were walking on a real building . . . Instead of playing with the flatness of the surface, it created a volume, a kind of extraordinary space . . . This kind of prowess, these pieces of bravura, are school exercises born of school exercises. Ultimately the work of art is always a school exercise, and one of the properties of the *pompiers* is that they are still at school. They have never left. In the first instance they have spent years there, taking competitive exams year after year, then they become teachers in the classes preparing pupils for these competitive exams, and then later still they are members of the examining boards for these competitions, and they set the examination topics, and so on.

Before I finish, I would just like to point out some very striking analogies with music. There is a character whose name at least you all know, Ambroise Thomas. In the music competitions, there were cantatas . . . It is the equivalent of the *pompier* style: there are conventions for the subject, the rhymes and the rhythms . . . This is what a very polite [that is, academic] *History of Music* says of Ambroise Thomas (who was a pupil of Lesueur, Adam's successor at the Institute):

You could say that he was a sage, embodying everything that this word suggests: with reserves of prudence, authority, useful knowledge and moderation. During his life he was already a man of the past, while around him art was being boldly and strikingly renewed [he was a contemporary of Delacroix and Berlioz, for instance . . .]. On the compositions he sent from Rome, the Institute delivered a judgement that could equally well apply to all of his work: 'his melodies were novel, but never bizarre, expressive but not excessively so [*laughter*], his harmony always correct, his orchestration written with elegance and clarity'[49] [*laughter*].

40 *Lecture of 14 March 1985*

That is what I wanted to show; the same causes produce the same effects; the academic structure produces the same effects in relatively different fields.

I haven't finished exploring the properties of *pompier* art, I shall do so next time.

Lecture of 28 March 1985

First session (lecture): going beyond perspectivism and absolutism – Scientific categories and official categories – The struggle over perspectives – Practical logics – Political creation – The theory effect and the master thinkers
Second session (seminar): the invention of the modern artist (2) – Perhaps the writers should write about nothing? – The master and the artist – A symbolic revolution – Historical painting – A lector's *painting – The de-realisation effect*

First session (lecture): going beyond perspectivism and absolutism

I would like to follow on from what I was arguing during the last two lectures, and try to show how we can go beyond the opposition between a perspectival vision and what we might call a realist, objectivist or absolutist vision, to create a true synthesis.

I was saying that social agents in the social world could adopt an infinite number of viewpoints. I also argued that in the objectivist tradition, these perspectives are reducible to the point from which they have arisen, and may therefore be considered null and void and as it were dismissed, in favour of the single, legitimate perspective established by the scholar. We have then on the one hand a kind of relativism and on the other hand a scientism that claims to establish itself as the only legitimate viewpoint. This poses a very difficult problem: the relation between this scientific viewpoint and the legitimate viewpoint as it is expressed in the social world itself. The problem is difficult (and yet, obviously, since I believe that I have found the solution, I find it difficult to formulate the problem without announcing the solution).

42 *Lecture of 28 March 1985*

I would like to refer to a text by Durkheim that I read a long time ago. (Unfortunately I have not managed to find where it is located, and if by chance one of you might be able to find it, they would be doing me a great favour. . . .) What Durkheim said is more or less this: faced with the social world, social agents have biased and self-interested viewpoints, that find their limits precisely in the interests and presuppositions that the agents have invested in the social world . . .[1] To these irreducible viewpoints Durkheim opposes what seems to him to be the viewpoint of science, a sort of absolute viewpoint that is distinct from the viewpoints of ordinary individuals, precisely by being a viewpoint onto these viewpoints, and – since this seems to me quite Spinozist I shall speak the language of Spinoza – thus avoids the constituent error of these individual viewpoints, which is the privation of a global overview of the viewpoints. In other words, according to Durkheim, the error is a privation (if we may use Spinoza's own terms here) and the individual view of the individual agents comes from the fact that they are localised and yet are not aware of this. You will find the same affirmation in Samuelson's treatise on economics:[2] investigating the difference between a scientific economist and economic agents, Samuelson says that both employers and union members, for instance, are situated, have individual viewpoints and *eo ipso*, because of this very fact, are biased, whereas the scholar himself is placed at a sort of absolute viewpoint from where he can perceive the individual viewpoints as viewpoints.

As I said at the outset, there are then two different philosophies adopted in the face of the social world. We might call the first approach a Nietzschean type, since Nietzsche is in fashion[3] (a few years ago, we could not have said this, but now we can, because everyone thinks they have some idea of Nietzsche's thought). This Nietzschean viewpoint (in the sense of Nietzsche's theory of knowledge) is perspectivist or phenomenist: there is no absolute truth of the social world.[4] For Nietzsche, that kind of ontological or even critical (Kantian) ambition is a theological hangover, an illusion of the 'Great Chinaman from Königsberg' (as he called Kant):[5] in matters of truth, no one should ever claim absolute knowledge. Of the social world, we can say exactly the same thing: the perspectivist or phenomenist perspective would argue that there is no absolute knowledge of the social world, only perspectivist visions. Against this position we could oppose the Spinozist vision, which turns up again in Durkheim, the 'technocratic' or 'epistemocratic' vision – I shall return to this – according to which the learned economist can use his equations, calculations and statistics and the models he constructs to escape these perspectives by establish-

Lecture of 28 March 1985

43

ing them as such. It would in fact be fairer to qualify this viewpoint as Leibnizian rather than Spinozan.

(These philosophical references are useful because they draw attention to the difficulty of knowing the social world as a specific entity, and I think that it is always beneficial to subsume a specific problem into a more general problem, especially when this has been as lengthily and as powerfully considered as the problem of knowledge [. . .].)

According to the absolutist viewpoint that I am calling Leibnizian, there is a 'geometral of all perspectives' (which is a term from Leibniz that Merleau-Ponty often quoted),[6] a geometrical focus of all the perspectives, a viewpoint from which all the perspectives are aligned in perspective. Someone situated at this viewpoint has a kind of absolute knowledge of the world and of perspectives on the world.

It seems to me that this vision haunts the unconscious of the social sciences. This epistemocratism is flaunted quite innocently by the economists, who are the least neurotic of the specialists in the social sciences: they think that with mathematical tools in particular the scholar can make a radical break with the naive viewpoint. Obviously the theme of the epistemological break[7] that opens up a gap between the layman and the scholar – this kind of initiatory break that founds the success of Althusser's philosophy – is part of this epistemocratism. As philosophical traditions so often do (and this is what I dislike about them), Althusserianism strongly flatters this feeling of being of another essence, another nature: the *vulgum pecus* lives in illusion and error, whereas he who has operated the initiatory *metanoia*, break or gap sees the world as it is, and sees others therefore as committing blunders. That is the adolescent charm of philosophy: it allows us to feel of another nature.

This temptation is present in the unconscious of the sociological vocation, and the utopia of the sociologist-king, who is merely an alter ego of the philosopher-king, is inherent in this epistemological vision. In fact, if there is a viewpoint from which all viewpoints appear as viewpoints and which is at the same time the only true viewpoint, it is obvious that whoever occupies this viewpoint should govern. According to Benveniste the *rex* is etymologically the person called on to *regere fines*,[8] that is, to define boundaries, for example between groups – he says whether a particular agent is a senior executive or a middle manager. He has the power to *regere fines* and to *regere sacra*, which comes to more or less the same thing, insofar as the *sacer* denotes the separation; on one side there is the distinguished, on the other the vulgar; on one side there is civilisation, on the other the uncivilised; on one side the scientific, not on the other. This claim to

44 *Lecture of 28 March 1985*

absolute knowledge that is inherent in the epistemocratic vision relies on a confusion of legitimate perspective with power: epistemological absolutism goes hand in hand with a claim to power. Whence the question – and it is here I think that we are moving on from what I was saying last time: how does the scholar situate himself in relation to the institutions which, in the social world, lay claim to this absolute vision? Are there not in the social world institutions which are conceived or which act in such a way as to exercise an absolute power of classification?

To my mind there is a difference between the reflexive scientific position that I wish to defend and the Durkheimian type of position that I have described. The epistemocratic, technocratic Spinozist optimism of Durkheim amounts to saying that the scholar knows more than the social agents; in particular he transcends their conflicts, since he sees their source and therefore their limits. Against this position I would argue that the scholar is not someone who is situated at the absolute viewpoint. He is someone (who may well be super-absolute, but that is nonetheless very different) who takes it upon himself to describe the social world while including in his description the fact that the social world calls into question the truth of this world. This world is a site of confrontations between social agents who constantly strive not only to take power over this world, but also to have the power to state the truth of this world, which is one of the fundamental dimensions of power. By the same token, social science can not only objectify the temptation to take power over the world that is inherent in scientific activity, but also objectify the institutions that do hold power at a given moment in this struggle for the right vision of the social world.

One of the most important projects for a comparative sociology of civilisations then would be the aim to define at every moment in every society the place from which there is the best chance of imposing one's vision as the legitimate and right vision. This exceptional project would need to review the history of the internal struggles of the dominant class in each society, since one of the aims of the internal struggles in what I call the field of power is to establish who has the power to state the true nature of the world. I think that we can extend what Duby says of the conflict between the *oratores* and the *bellatores* in the Middle Ages to include all of Dumézil's three orders.[9] One of the fundamental aims of these struggles among the dominant is to establish who has the right viewpoint, and for every historical moment we can make an objective scientific assessment of the place where we find the people who, in Weber's terms, have the best chance of imposing their own viewpoint as *the* viewpoint.

Lecture of 28 March 1985

Scientific categories and official categories

Now that I have sketched an overview of the problem, I shall go back over it more slowly and choose a simple example. In the social sciences, the problem that I am posing does loom very concretely in France today, in the relation between institutions like the National Institute for Statistics and Economics (INSEE) and what we might call independent research studies. Recently INSEE revised its socio-professional categories, drawing very closely on the classifications that I had produced in *Distinction*.[10] What happens when categories produced with scientific intent, for the purpose of understanding and explaining the practice of social agents, become official categories? Those who make the transfer do so in all good faith because they respect science. That said, if an institution which publishes powerful truths on the social world (when I wrote in *Distinction* of a 'new petite bourgeoisie', I didn't think that it would one day be printed on someone's ID card . . .), an institution imbued with the specific power that is symbolic power or authority, lays claim to these classifications, it makes them undergo a change of status, and it gives them a sort of force of law; these classifications take on a juridical quality, liable for instance to confer eligibility to draw a pension, take early retirement, or benefit from a bonus, promotion or mortgage.

Here we see the difference [between the scholar and the institutions which claim to have an absolute vision]. It seems to me that social science does not use criticism for the sheer pleasure of it, and the Frankfurt people,[11] whom I sympathise with in many respects, often annoy me with this kind of critical bias. (There I made an allusion, which is contrary to my pedagogical principles according to which one should not make allusions that are not comprehensible by all, but there are times when an allusion is the true measure of what needs to be said because those who don't understand are not missing anything [*laughter*]. My warnings are addressed only to those in the know [*laughter*]! In fact allusions are still not defensible pedagogically, they are a symbolic *coup de force* . . . but I can never mount a *coup de force* without admitting it straight away . . .!) The Frankfurt people tend to annoy me because they act as if there were a kind of critical choice that laid the foundations of an ethical-scientific posture. In my view, the viewpoint of the scholar is not distinct from the others because of what it decides, but because it must not stop being scholarly when dealing with itself, or when dealing with the relation between its own activities and those of other institutions.

What I want to find out is the difference between two agencies that appear to do the same thing, which is to classify, and then publish,

46 *Lecture of 28 March 1985*

elaborate and objectify their classifications. This means that the scholarly classifications made by those in power need to be challenged sociologically, and that the question of the epistemocratic temptation which I mentioned just now is no longer an ethical question. It becomes the following question: is there not, in the epistemocratic temptation that underlies many sociological vocations, the principle of a scientific error which consists in trying to endow a scientific classification, motivated by the search for knowledge, with a social power? Is there not a temptation to turn the sociologist into a sort of king who states where the right distinctions are situated? We could say the same thing for the relations between sociologists and economists: in fact in our contemporary world these are relations between the expert and the intellectual or scholar. An analysis both of this opposition, which I find crucial, and of the social role of economists and sociologists should start by making the question that I have put explicit, and it could be studied empirically, that is, with the usual arms of science.

The struggle over perspectives

I shall now pick up from where I left off last time. This kind of third-way science that I am arguing for is opposed both to the perspectivist illusion and to the Spinozist absolutist illusion and it includes among its scientific tasks a study of the struggles over perspectives and the forms of domination prevalent in these struggles. What advantages does one need to dominate in these struggles, and what is the specific logic of the balance of power?

It is not for the pleasure of making things complicated that I feel the need to reintroduce the objective space (which corresponds to the second level), the space of positions that not only forms the basis for the agents' strategies towards the legitimate vision of this space, but is also what is at stake in their strategies towards that objective vision. In fact my analysis is opposed to the perspectivist vision which is in fashion today, like so many excessively radical positions . . . There is always a facile radicalism tempted by extremes, with the paradox of course that extremes meet, like all radical positions. Nowadays, in the sociology of science, one sort of antiscientific philosophy consists in turning any scientific discourse into a sort of symbolic strategy destined to promote the interests of the scholar.[12] Briefly, this argues that science is merely a product of the impulse of the scholar who, through working to dramatise, publicise, revalue and celebrate his discoveries, manages to get people to believe in the scientific nature of his work, in a conjuncture where having science on your side is one of the most powerful weapons in the struggle for symbolic power. I was saying just now that we could do with a comparative history of symbolic systems and struggles for power: it is certain that in our societies, having 'science on our side' is tantamount to saying what people used to say in the days when they said 'God is on our side'.[13] The sceptics and the anarchists of epistemology would say then that scientific strategies are showpiece strategies of symbolic rhetoric designed to impose belief in the scientific value of the discourse concerned.

Against this position, which corresponds to a kind of exaggerated Nietzscheism, I maintain (and I believe that we must continue to maintain) that there is at all times a structure to objective space: you cannot simply say whatever you like about the social space. Since I argued this point at length last year, I shall not return to it. Obviously this objective space changes from one moment to the next, among other reasons from the viewpoints that agents take towards it, since their perception of this space is one of the factors that transform it (when I say 'one of the factors' it is because it is not the only one). This objective space intervenes twice over in the symbolic struggles. It intervenes firstly as the basis and foundation of the perspectives, since the social agents perceive the world from their viewpoints, and secondly as the target of these perspectives. By this token, one of the things at stake in the political struggle (since in fact this third level that I am now defining is the level that you might call political) is the transformation of the objective space. The political field is in a way a subspace of the social space, within which there are debates over the structure of the social space: Are there classes or not? Are there two or three? Are there the dominant and the dominated? Is the principal domination that of 'bourgeoisie' over 'proletariat', or 'masculine' over 'feminine', with one opposition masking another, and so on?

The struggle within the political space for the right vision of the social world is not an epiphenomenon. It is not what the old distinctions between infrastructure and superstructure (although I hope you have understood that I find these divisions into strata sinister) would call a place of symbolic conflict, that is, one of little influence and importance. It is a place where the imposition of the right vision can call into question the very nature and structure of the space. There is then a paradox: the structure of the space determines people's standpoints and at the same time these standpoints are not without effect on the space. One fundamental problem in sociology is to understand how the specifically symbolic forces that only exist insofar as they are rooted in forces of another kind manage nonetheless to take advantage

48 *Lecture of 28 March 1985*

of their autonomy and follow their own logic to produce effects that are real and not symbolic. Reintroducing the space as both foundation and stake in the struggle is therefore restoring the truth of the political universe as a place where people fight over classification. I could express this in a maxim, saying that the class struggle is perhaps fundamentally a struggle for classification,[14] insofar as it is by making classifications that we make classes: by getting people to believe, for instance, that differences exist, we help to make them exist, and the political struggle is a struggle to make things visible ('theory', *theorein*[15]) and to make people believe that what we make visible really exists.

That said, we can see what one of the most traditional objects of sociology consists of, and moreover it is something close to the idea that people have of it. Sociology is often identified with opinion polls, and people think that asking: 'What do you think of the prime minister?' is sociology. In fact it is a political act, typical of the political field. It amounts to asking: 'How do you see him?' 'What is your point of view?' Without realising what they are doing, sociologists frequently ask their respondents: 'How many classes are there, in your opinion?' This is astonishing, and if you reflect on it, even absurd. I did once deliberately put this question to someone who really had no symbolic defences . . . He replied: 'But it's you who should tell me, you are paid to know!' [*laughter*] . . . It is not necessarily absurd to ask in questionnaires 'How many classes do you think there are?', 'Are they hostile to one another or not?', but you need to know what you are doing. You should not believe that what you are measuring in this case is the real existence or non-existence of classes. What you are measuring among other things is the degree to which previous discourses on classes have been broadcast or have filtered through; it is the strength of the 'Marx effect', a theory effect (a notion that I shall return to).

What we call opinions are essentially explicit discourses on the social world. I could quote Plato: 'To opine (*doxatsein*) is to speak',[16] which means that opinion is coextensive with discourse. Opinion is a view on the social world written explicitly, spoken out loud, which makes us ask whether an opinion that is not expressed is an opinion or if there exists something that without being expressed is nonetheless a vision of the world. This leads to an extremely important question: What are the different forms of perception of the social world? Is there one single manner of perceiving the social world? Does the political illusion according to which there is only perception of the social world in an explicit state not make us forget a crucial state, not of opinion, but of the vision of the social world in the practical state (in the practical

Lecture of 28 March 1985

49

sense of being somewhere in the social world)? I shall now deal with this point.

Practical logics

It seems to me that a sociologist of the third way must be a sociologist of the perception that distinguishes between implicit and explicit forms of perception, identifying the implicit ways of saying that we know where we are. Goffman spoke of 'the sense of one's place'.[17] This is the sense of our own place in the social world, which leads us to say 'That's not for the likes of us', 'That's a place I can't go to', 'I'm not well dressed enough to go there', or 'I'm not educated enough'. In these extreme cases the feeling is enunciated, but in many cases this sense of position, this feel for the game, this sense of 'where do I stand in the game?', is expressed in an entirely tacit fashion, by avoidance, by keeping our distance, or as the saying goes 'voting with our feet', that is, keeping away from certain places that we are not officially excluded from but from where we are excluded in fact. The most radical exclusion is obtained with the complicity of the people who exclude themselves: 'This educational establishment is not for the likes of me.' Often it does not even have to be stated . . . This sense of position is one of the forms of our knowledge of the social world. It is a practical knowledge, existing as a practice, and like all practical knowledge, it is implicit, imprecise and not very logical.

Here I refer you to the analyses that I made of an object of study apparently very different, Kabyle ritual, but these things can be correlated.[18] When ethnologists (Lévi-Strauss, for example, for those who know something about him)[19] describe the systems of classification used by primitive societies, they describe the equivalent of what we mobilise in order to perceive our own social world, with oppositions of the type 'right/left', 'high/low', 'distinguished/vulgar', 'rare/common' and the like. When we judge a painting, a work of art, a hairstyle or someone's demeanour, we bring into play on a practical level very simple classifications, most often encapsulated in a couple of adjectives ('great/little', 'fine/base', 'fine feelings/base feelings'). These extremely simple oppositions enable us to apply some order to the world, to perceive it, and criticism in the arts is very often nothing more than the rather imprecise readjustment of practical taxonomies of this kind.[20] Like all practical logics, these taxonomies are obviously not coherent beyond a certain point. We can easily see that 'high/low' has something to do with 'unique/common', but whether you prefer to use the first

50   *Lecture of 28 March 1985*

pair rather than the second will depend on the domain. The opposing pairs with their partial overlap give very structured universes, sometimes violently so, all the more so because, since they do not have to be made explicit, they are not made explicit. They do not even have to be justified. They are constitutive of our vision of the world. These practical schemas have an extremely important classificatory power, to which their vagueness contributes. This is extremely important: it is their vagueness that allows these classifications to operate as universals . . . more or less.

A parenthesis here: the logician's temptation that haunted the structuralist ethnologists and which consists in formalising these systems of classification, seeing as it were a kind of algebra in them, leads them to destroy the very logic that they claim to discover. This paralogism is very common in the social sciences: the social sciences deal with practical logics, historical logics, logics that are 80 per cent of the kind that I have described, and the propensity to logicise, to appear 'scientific' (the theory of science as 'dramatic production' is not completely false, there is an element of 'staging'), leads them to destroy what is most specific in the practical logics, which is the fact that they are never completely logical – which is why they are practical. If practical logics are practical, in the sense that we call some clothes practical, it is precisely because they are logical only up to the point where it would be absurd for them to take it further. These are things that common sense is well aware of. Philosophers have thought on this, but very poorly, because philosophers in general only speak of practice in order to highlight the distinction, the Platonic break or divide, between philosophy and the *agora*, with its *clepsydre*:[21] the philosopher has time, he takes his time, he is in charge, he verifies the logic, he knows what he is talking about, he is answerable to the critics. This is all progress, but mindlessly applying the most powerful strategies of science – game theory, calculation of probability, etc. – to the human sciences destroys exactly what they allow to be expressed.

In other words, I think that the enlightened way of applying logical logics could be to grasp the mismatch between practical logics and logical logics. If, for instance, you amuse yourself by following an exercise that has been and still is practised by philosophers, formalising the proofs of the existence of God in Aristotle, or some chapter of the Logic of Port Royal,[22] you can have two aims. One would be to open up these pre-logical discourses to logic, while claiming to practise a truly scientific philosophy. The other would be to use formalisation to discover what is out of place, and thereby to show up, by their very disparity and by reflection on that disparity, the specifics of these practical

Lecture of 28 March 1985 51

logics that are only logical up to a certain point. But since, in a universe where the dominant science is 'hard' science (according to a stupid opposition [. . .]), in the sense of a formal, formalist and formalised science, the profits to be gained from logic are so great that people are tempted to destroy objects rather than understand them. (This is one of my missions in the scientific field: I think that we should, not always but often, be prepared to sacrifice some of the gains in scientificity in favour of practising social science. That was an aside.)

In particular these practical logics are practical precisely because they do not waste time questioning their own logic. They rely very little on reflexivity or self-verification, they function approximately, to a certain extent, within the limits of what is reasonable [. . .] but we should see that Lévy-Bruhl's 'primitive mentality'[23] or Lévi-Strauss's 'savage mind' are not the privilege of 'primitive' societies. The savage mind is our way of thinking when we normally think, when we are not playing at being logicians. In everyday life we spend our time thinking in the ways that Lévy-Bruhl says primitive peoples think. Eighty per cent of everyday thinking uses inexplicit and therefore not logically controlled categories of classification.

To open another parenthesis, which is important: sociologists are obliged to draw on codification. If they cannot classify at least masculine/feminine, young/old, there is no more science. But their codifying operations resort to an absolutist philosophy. Here we find what I was saying just now: I create a code, I am a scholar, I have to give an account of it to the community of scholars, and I therefore tend to think that my code is *the* code. When we codify 'masculine/ feminine', we imagine that there are no other possible categories. It is very rare, because it would be almost physically unbearable, to create a code while saying that it is only one code among others, that it is linked to a particular problematic, or that it does no more than reproduce a code that already exists in reality. I developed this at length in the first chapter of *Homo Academicus*: the easiest things to codify are those that are codified in reality, that is, codified by legal acts which put boundaries in places where there is a continuum (as at the airport they create a division by saying: 'No more than 30 kilos of luggage').

In real life most distributions are continuums, but sociology has to divide, according to Pareto, who is not to be suspected of subjectivism and is constantly cited by the supporters of hard science. Pareto asked where the frontier between rich and poor lies, where old age starts and youth comes to an end.[24] In every epoch there is a struggle to find out where old age starts and youth comes to an end.[25] In general, age has privileges but youth has advantages, and it is in the interest of the old

52   *Lecture of 28 March 1985*

to make the young believe that the young are too young to enjoy the privileges of age. There are some very fine historical studies of these questions.[26] For instance, during the Florentine Renaissance the young were told: 'You are young, you have virtue . . . that is [sexuality(?)], stop going on about power!' [*laughter*] . . . The theory of the three ages that we constantly find in philosophers is rooted in this. Alain rehearsed a naive version of this ideology: youth is love; age is wisdom.[27]

The most banal frontiers then are always *coups de force*. There is always someone who draws a line through the middle of what was a genuinely continuous distribution. You have to divide . . . Since in general the divisions exist in reality (as with the age of military service, or retirement, for instance), they are easy to codify, and the Spinozist vision is reinforced: I find everything codified, no problem, I reproduce the code . . . But if we want to codify, say, the degrees of scientific celebrity, things become very complicated.[28] There we have no code. And for good reason: so many people find it in their interest for there to be no code for this, that there isn't one; and perhaps there never will be. [*It has not been possible to restore the passage here exactly: Bourdieu seems to explain that the sociologist then creates a code, but that the code should not be considered at the same level as a code founded on differences existing in reality*]. In one case the codification is scholarly, produced by someone who has no involvement other than the desire to understand. He needs to create a division in order to be able to find differences, relations between differences, systems of relations between systems of differences: this is what scientific study is all about. In the other case a boundary has been imposed, usually after some struggle, to establish relations of domination, and the divisions are never like the pans of a scale: there is always a good and a bad side of the line. This is another property of practical logics: they are useful and practical, not too logical, so that they can remain practical, but they are also charged with practical functions, and in particular functions of domination, one fundamental consideration being that social agents have to be persuaded to accept the divisions that classify them, accept for instance that masculine/feminine is a legitimate division or that 'high/low' is an ethical definition independent of the properties of those who just happen to be high or low themselves (that is, for example, rich or poor).

Our ordinary perceptions of the social world are then structured according to patterns of perception of very general applicability, which serve just as well to classify social agents as they do works of art, books or any other objects . . . These principles are practical, pre-reflexive, unconscious, implicit, almost bodily schemas, which is I think most

Lecture of 28 March 1985   53

important: our most deeply rooted schemas are those that are incorporated. Our systems of classification, for instance, are expressed in our style of deportment: crossing our legs or not, standing upright (the right is the masculine), right and left, looking people in the eye (in Kabyle society a respectful woman lowers her gaze). The right/left division is translated into bodily postures. These incorporated principles of division are no doubt the most powerful constituents of the social world. As I was saying last time: the structuring principles of the social world are to a considerable extent an incorporation of the objective structures of the social world. If in Maghrebi societies, for instance, the opposition between the feminine and the masculine is a determining opposition from which all the others (high/low, dry/wet, hot/cold, east/west, etc.) can be derived, it is basically because the fundamental division of these societies is the masculine/feminine divide, which is to be found at every level of practice, and first of all in the division of labour. If we bear in mind that these divisions are in harmony with the objective structures and that they enjoy an incorporated state, in the state of quasi-reflex postures, we see the reproductive force of these principles of vision and division.

Political creation

This correlates with what I was saying about politics just now. The political field is the place where we speak of the social world, where people argue about the right classification, where they say, for instance, 'the class struggle is out of date', 'today the confrontation is elsewhere', or even 'that's an archaic opposition, this is a modern one'. Politics can, I believe, do two things. It can bring this practical logic of the perception of the social world out into an explicit state, and perhaps the essential task of politics lies in this kind of ontological promotion, transforming practical bodily schemas into explicit oppositions that articulate what was pre-reflexive and non-thetic. Politics can also (and usually simultaneously) work either at reinforcing or at transforming these structures through explicit celebratory or critical articulation. The essence of the political mission (in which we should obviously include religious undertakings, such as prophecy) resides, I believe, in this kind of creation, which consists in taking things out of their implicit state and making them explicit. You will ask: 'But why do you use the word creation, which often carries ideological overtones ('creative people', etc.), why this concession to the vocabulary of creation?' In fact, our practical schemas are essentially blind to themselves.

54 *Lecture of 28 March 1985*

In a way, the person acting according to practical schemas does not know what he is doing, and one of the difficulties of anthropological or ethnological study comes from the fact that the ethnologist, whether he realises it or not, is in a quasi-Socratic position; he has to make his informant give birth to principles of classification that the informant is unaware of and can only deploy in practice. Whence the major progress achieved by certain currents of ethnology, such as ethnobotany, using indirect techniques which give social agents the opportunity to put into practice their patterns of classification, and at the same time try to make these schemas explicit: they place herbal medicines or objects on little pieces of card and ask the informants to classify them and then to give a name to each category and finally to work out the principle of classification and the principle of the production of the different categories. I have transposed this exercise onto politics; you write thirty names of politicians on pieces of card, you present the little cards to the agents and tell them: 'You have the cards, classify them however you like.' Then, once they have classified the cards, you ask them: 'What do you call this class? And this one?' You do of course have to think about it, for you mustn't forget that the situation is artificial (the classic pitfall is, once you start conducting an experiment, to forget that the situation is experimental).

We do have to realise that the situation is artificial, that it is an exception for most social agents, who in their daily lives are never exposed to the kind of situation where they have to classify a whole set of agents and then articulate the principles behind their classification . . . But having made this mental adjustment, it remains the case that the experiment gives an idea of the way in which people classify in their everyday lives. One interesting thing [in an experiment where the respondents had to classify cards which each bore the name of a profession] is that these taxonomies often have extra-political principles, for instance the masculine/feminine opposition. I talked about it a few years ago in these very same rooms:[29] one of the subjects participating in the experiment [. . .] had created two categories: a higher one, at a level above qualified workmen, and a lower one, below, and for the higher one, typified by a television presenter, he said: 'They're all a bunch of queers!' . . . [*laughter*]. That makes us laugh, but these things are complicated, you could analyse it for hours: his answer meant that social divisions are sexually overdetermined, that the high/low in the social space is connected with something like the problems of virility.

Social agents then put into practice practical schemas, which we can try to reconstitute by indirect means. These practical schemas are not

Lecture of 28 March 1985 55

explicit, they are not organised. They do not have the consistency and coherence of logic: we classify, but time passes and in time we forget [which practical criteria of classification we deployed at the start of the operation], and you don't have to be a Socrates to say: 'But just now you were saying that . . . Make up your mind . . .' Practical logics function approximately, imprecisely.

The theory effect and the master thinkers

Here I need to slow down because these are things I think that we understand too quickly. The person who comes along with a classification has a fantastic advantage over someone using a practical logic. If you come along and declare 'There are two classes' to someone who has never thought about it, and he tells you 'They're all a bunch of queers!' or something similar because he is disturbed to have to find some kind of justification, you have an absolutely fantastic force of imposition. It is what I call the 'theory effect', the effect operated by any theoretical discourse as discourse that reveals things and makes people believe what they reveal . . . The formula is rather abrupt, but Marx (who of all the theorists of the social world is the one who has exerted the most powerful theory effect because he has managed to make people believe almost universally that his vision of the social world is the right one, even when they fight against it . . .) included everything in his theory, except the theory effect. When today we play with little pieces of card to measure opinions on the social world or visions of the social world, we are measuring the 'Marx effect'.

This effect that I am in the process of describing is the effect initiated by someone who is following a practical logic, who knows when they should keep a low profile, and when they can strut their stuff, etc. These things are entirely bodily. The social world performs a kind of dance. People also have a social shape and volume which have been much studied: it transpires that the more important people feel, the more room they take up, both in physical space and in temporal space. In a meeting for example, unless they have a specific mandate to speak (as I do here), where there is a struggle for the monopoly of speech, people allow themselves a time proportionate to the idea they have of the time that the group will allow them, and this can be sensed from their tempo, rhythm and rhetoric. Of course there are always people who calculate badly [*laughter*] and poor souls who take up too much time (so the others start chattering), but what is interesting is that people are less foolish than you might think: by and large the time that people

56 Lecture of 28 March 1985

allow themselves in a meeting is a good measure of the time that the group is prepared to allow them. It is in a way their representation of their own volume, of their social weight. When I say 'social weight' I mean it quite bodily: it becomes a way of walking, a style of speaking, a tone of voice . . . We could do with a sociolinguistics of importance, starting out from the feelings of importance that the subject thinks the group will allow him.

Imagine that someone who follows a practical logic, with a sense of orientation and practice in the social world, and of their own place in that world, is confronted by a theoretician (I use the word in a neutral not a pejorative sense) armed with a classification. This may, for instance, be a classification of a religious nature, such as pure/impure. But it may also be a political classification, as today. The theoretician confronting the pre-constructed and pre-reflexive, everything that I was explaining just now, almost automatically exerts an effect of imposition, and it takes an awful lot of symbolic force to resist someone who offers you a classification. Another example: imagine a game where you ask people: 'Take a sheet of paper and draw me the social world.' They wonder whether the social world is round or square, whether it has three dimensions or four, then someone shows them a little schema. This is the theory effect. Here you have it: the theory effect is the creative effect exercised by the simple fact of speaking explicitly ('I call belief a statement'), of being in a position to pronounce on the social world. The prophetic effect ('You would not seek me if you had not found me') thus lies fundamentally in this act of ontological promotion, which consists in telling people something that they already know in terms of practice, but that they are dazzled to discover in the objective form of a quasi-systematic discourse (because prophetic systems are never systematic in a logical sense), things that they were aware of in their senses.

The theory effect then acts as an explanatory effect. That said, practical schemas have a certain flexibility: they are compatible with several opinions (I apologise for accompanying my discourse with a meta-discourse, but I think that this is a very important point). Experience shows us that the same system of practical categories can be accounted for by relatively different explanations. This flexibility is not absolute (you cannot tell the 'bunch of queers!' interviewee that Yves Mourousi[30] is a hard labourer), but it is much greater than you might think. This is what makes political action possible. (You may sometimes have found this whole long discourse rather complicated, and I could have said everything that I have told you in a couple of minutes, but as I have said several times, sociology can be explained in various ways. For instance, I spoke in abstract terms last time, but to understand things a little better, I think that we need to move on to analyses that link the most abstract to the most concrete.)

One of the most important political effects then lies in this capacity to bring into existence through expression something of what was latent in these practical schemas, classifications and principles of the vision of the world, which means that the political struggle may become in part a struggle for explicit recognition – 'recognition' in the sense that people recognise themselves in the explicit discourse, and they recognise the explicit discourse because they recognise themselves in it. This is the prophecy effect . . . They recognise themselves with the feeling 'That's exactly what I was thinking.' They use the past tense, showing that it is over: we can no longer know what they thought before. Once you have heard someone tell you what you are supposed to think on some matter where your thinking was based on practical schemas, you will never know what you thought before. This is why we have to pay attention when we listen.

A lot of ink has been spilt over the master thinkers, or masters of thought (it was the fashion a few years ago),[31] but the position of master thinker is much more prevalent than people realise. The master thinker is someone who has elaborated a little more than most people some principles of vision of the world (whether ethical, religious or political, etc.), and who, by the simple fact of presenting an explicit product claiming to be coherent (it doesn't actually need to be coherent), produces an irrevocable effect and makes people think that they were thinking what he has just said.

If this effect is real, and if on the other hand, as I said last time (but there I would have to repeat a long demonstration), what the social agents think of the social world helps to reinforce or transform the social world, you can see that symbolic power and symbolic violence do have a symbolic strength. It is not from a taste for radical chic that I use the expression symbolic violence. My whole analysis shows that there is a violence inherent in making things explicit. Revelation is violence, because you must not forget the unequal distribution of the capacity for explanation, the capacity to have access to opinion, that is, to formulated, explicit discourse, liable to be pronounced because it is liable to be listened to. This comes back to what I was saying about social volume. If I don't speak it is often because there is no one to listen to me, and because in any case I will be a voice speaking in the wilderness. Given that the capacity to produce such explanatory discourse is unequally shared, you can see how political violence is inherent to the social structure.

58 *Lecture of 28 March 1985*

Now if it is true, as I said last time, that our perception of the social world helps to structure, maintain or transform it, we can see that the holders of the monopoly of pronouncing an explicit vision of the world – that is, the intellectuals, the writers and speakers, the theoreticians, the holders of the monopoly of discourse on the social world – are endowed with a considerable force. It is no accident if in most societies there is a struggle between the king, the *bellator*, the person who fights, and the *orator*, the person who prays and speaks and who can nonetheless hold his own against the king, saying that the world is other than the way he portrays it. It is interesting, moreover, to see the differing modes of expression that the king and the *orator* may use: the king can say how he sees the social world without resorting to words. He can express it, for instance, through the plan of a city. I am thinking of a study by Gérard Fussman,[32] who shows how in ancient India the social philosophy of the sovereign was expressed through town planning. Of course there is also the name of the city (everyone knows of Stalingrad),[33] and this is important because giving names is the alpha and omega of rendering explicit, since naming is saying how you should perceive, see and believe.

So we can pronounce discourses without words in the shape of the plan of a city, for instance, which is an ideal distribution of the social space, with divisions into castes, separate neighbourhoods, and processional circuits which follow an order which is the ideal order of the hierarchy. A procession, for instance, can be a political discourse: the Panathenaea are a fantastic political discourse,[34] especially when there is a sculptor to reproduce them . . . We can see that according to this logic, art is a political discourse. I certainly don't wish to reduce art to politics, but there is always a political dimension in an artistic discourse, insofar as it is one of the ways of speaking of the social world. As the portrait of the king shows, one of the definitions of the dominant is that among other things he is able to impose the right way of seeing him, the dominated being the person who cannot impose the right way to see him. One of the goals of the political struggle (I said that I would try to analyse the specific logic of the symbolic struggle, the political struggle) is to be able to impose on everyone the view that one has of oneself, which is after all in general fairly indulgent: it is the right profile. I shall return to this. [. . .]

Lecture of 28 March 1985

Second session (seminar): the invention of the modern artist (2)

I shall deal in this second session with the problem of the social history of the birth of the artist in the modern sense of the term. During the last seminar I tried to spell out the principles of *pompier* art, trying to show that they could in a way be deduced from a sociological description of the academic institution. I did rather overemphasise the deduction; there is a rather scientist aspect to the approach I am using. But it is a fairly exemplary situation where describing the institution is in a way describing the corresponding cultural production, which approach is much more relevant than you might think. The methodological interest of the exercise is to show that, in certain cases, a sociology of works, for instance the sociolinguistic study of an intellectual work, must be based on a sociology of the institution where the producers of the discourse under consideration are producing it (or are themselves produced), to avoid becoming mere descriptive waffle. This is true for the history of art, but also for the history of literature and science.

I am now going to say something rather wicked, for such an approach may sometimes be useful. Literary history in France today is in a state of advanced, almost tragic crisis: an indication of this crisis is the fact that each producer feels obliged to invent a logo to characterise their own production, such as 'socio-critique'. If you wanted to produce a rigorous sociology of works you would have to relate them to their place in the space of production of those who have produced them. This has been the alpha and omega of my teaching for years, since in studying institutional or academic productions, for example doctoral theses or *normalien* writers, you would deprive yourself of a capital instrument if you studied the works of say Julien Gracq or Giraudoux without studying the social conditions of their production, that is, the institution that has produced them, in their case the École normale supérieure. The sociology of works is inseparable from a sociology of the institutions in which the works are produced . . .

I want to say this formally because it is relatively important and very badly understood, to such an extent moreover that what I am saying on *pompier* art, although it may appear trivial, has never been said. *Pompier* art has suddenly become fashionable, but what seems to me most obvious about it has never been said; people behave as if it were a kind of art which had aesthetic properties which you could discuss, but they do not affirm strongly enough that what is needed to understand this art is to understand not only those who produced it in the sense of individuals – that is another error when people try to produce social histories of literature or painting, they believe that it is enough to study

60   *Lecture of 28 March 1985*

the producers, with their biographies and so on – but also the position
of these people in the space of production, and in this particular case
their institutional position, since the academic painters were supported
by an institution dominating the field, which led them to paint in the
way that they did. They had the power then to define the right version
of the world (the link with the first session of my lecture is obvious),
what you were supposed to see, what there was to see, that is, to paint,
and what not to see, what was odious (to paint it would be fatal), as
the definition of legitimate painting gave a pictorial definition of what
could be painted and how it could be painted. All of that is written into
the institution.

Perhaps the writers should write about nothing?

To recapitulate: I started last time by quoting you two texts, one by
Laforgue the other by Courbet, where we read that the history of
painting in the nineteenth century was the history of the liberation
of painting from the academic institution. What I am doing here is a
history of a movement of liberation, that is, the history of the conquest
of a collective, institutional autonomy, the right to do certain things in
a certain way, that is, the right to paint in a pictorial mode. I went on to
say (this was the plan of my analysis) that in the struggle for liberation
that marks the history of painting since 1830 the painters were only
able to triumph with the help of the writers, who afterwards used the
example of the painters to accomplish their own liberation. There I am
anticipating my overall argument considerably. If I wanted to keep
you in suspense I should not act in this way, but I wanted to give you
the general outline before launching into the details.

I would like to quote you another text. I was saying the other day that
Zola had a strange, individual role as an unconscious historical agent, a
situation that we could find echoed in other domains. He was Manet's
spokesman par excellence and the defender of painting as painting, that
is to say a painting which has no justification other than being pictorial,
and which has no need to justify itself through the quality and more
especially the historical importance of the object that it represents. I was
suggesting that, astonishingly, Zola did not take advantage himself, as
it were, of this liberation for which he was the spokesman, the liberation of the painters. Their aesthetic had nonetheless found its formula
in words spoken by him. In fact, all the historians say that Zola is likely
to have worked, if not under Manet's dictation, then at least after
listening to Manet, who had a capacity for articulation superior to the

average painters (which links up with the topic that we were discussing just now), particularly at this time. This must obviously be linked to the social characteristics of the painters who, as research has shown, had lower social origins and were less well educated than the writers. It is said that in the café where the Impressionists and the writers met, Renoir and Monet stayed silent and that often people teased them a little because they were rather unsophisticated and not very eloquent, etc. There are three great exceptions to this relation between painters and writers, this balance of power: Delacroix, who wrote, and wrote well (I think that he had passed his baccalaureate or the equivalent), Manet, and the one I find most exemplary, Duchamp, who was the first to explicitly denounce the formula 'Dumb as a painter'[35] that was often used by writers. It's the same thing in university circles where the saying is 'dumb as a geographer'.

These are classificatory formulae which reflect social differences: the hierarchy of disciplines which leads from mathematics to geology or from philosophy to geography corresponds to a hierarchy of social origins . . . 'Dumb as a geographer' implies that the social characteristics and conditions producing geographers mean that from the viewpoint of the dominant in a determined space they appear 'dumb'. 'Dumb as a painter' would mean the same thing: thus Monet had to leave school at the age of twelve and studied in studios in the provinces. As a manual worker with little education he was not at ease in aesthetic discussions with the writers.

After this parenthesis within a parenthesis, I return to Zola. He was the spokesman for a painter who was distinguished by his own eloquence, which meant that he expressed an aesthetic that he did not transpose into his own practice as a writer. The problem seems to me to be very well put in a text by Gide that I came across recently. Once again, I give it as a kind of epitaph:

I have often wondered by what miracle painting has gone so far ahead, and how it happened that literature has let itself be outdistanced? In painting to-day just see how the 'motif', as it used to be called, has fallen into discredit. *A fine subject!* It makes one laugh. Painters don't even dare venture on a portrait unless they can be sure of avoiding every trace of resemblance. If we manage our affairs well, and leave me alone for that, I don't ask for more than two years before a future poet will think himself dishonoured if anyone can understand a word of what he says. Yes, Monsieur le Comte, will you wager? . . . Illogicality shall be our guiding star. What a fine title for a review – *The Scavengers!*[36]

62   *Lecture of 28 March 1985*

Gide wrote that in *The Counterfeiters*. I don't want to launch into amateur literary criticism, but you could say that *The Counterfeiters* is a book which poses in practical terms the problem of the expression of discourse: should the novel say something or should it be a pure novel that says nothing but the fact of expressing itself? As always in such cases, it is a novel on the novel, with the self-reflexive effects of a *mise en abyme*. A novelist says that he is writing a novel on the novel: the novel becomes its own end, it becomes explicitly novelistic, as painting had become pictorial. You see how spontaneously Gide finds the comparison with painting: how could the writers lag behind the liberation that the painters had accomplished in affirming their explicit refusal to submit to a motif? In fact the poets that he is alluding to, despite what he says, had already accomplished their version of this revolution. The novelists, however, had not reached their goal (we would have to wait for the 'nouveau roman').[37]

The story that I would like to tell is the history of the liberation of the producers of discourse from the obligation to say something. This brings me back to my description of *pompier* art. One fundamental imperative of academic art was that it had to have meaning, and what Zola said in the text that I quoted at the start of the previous seminar was: 'But why do they expect these people to signify? Painting is not a language.' Zola did not say it yet, but [he called into question the obligation] imposed on the linguistic arts, that is, writing, to have meaning, to say something that transcended the manner of saying it: why shouldn't writers start to speak to say nothing, speak for the sake of speaking, and refocus their aesthetic intentions on the expressive ambition, the expression itself, instead of subordinating expression to the content expressed? That is what seems to me to be at stake.

The master and the artist

Now I shall very briefly run back over the principal characteristics of academic painting that I have already mentioned. I shall return to them at a later stage in my lectures when I come to discuss the criticism that the critics have subjected Manet's work to. There we will find, albeit in a practical and implicit state, the principles that I have been finding in academic art. Today it is through a reflection on the academic institution and its discourse that I am elaborating the principles that constitute *pompier* painting. We shall see some evidence of the logic that I described just now in the way these principles are expressed in practical terms as 'I like/I don't like', 'it isn't finished/it's too pol-

Lecture of 28 March 1985 63

ished', etc. I should point out moreover that, in my studies, I started by analysing the practical taxonomies that the critics deployed in their scandalised perception of the Impressionist painters, since practical taxonomies are much more clearly expressed in the presence of something they dislike. Indignation in fact brings the implicit to the surface, which is an important technique, by the way: if you ask someone what makes a 'good marriage', they won't know what to reply, but they will reveal their practical principles much more explicitly if you ask them to describe some scandalous marriages. Here it is the same thing: the academic painters are not very explicit if you ask them what it takes to make a fine painting, but the kind of scandal created by Manet's *Olympia* makes them explain why the nude is so fine when Couture paints cold and glossy nudes but scandalous when the nude is *Olympia*. Faced with *Olympia*, they lose their inhibitions, and gradually express their deepest implicit feelings. I had started to spell out these taxonomies, starting with an analysis of the critics; it was only later that I returned to the more dogmatic form of analysis that I am offering you today.

One major principle is that the academic painter is essentially a master as opposed to an artist. He is a master with all that this implies: he is canonised and consecrated by an academic institution. He has institutional authority. He is a mandarin and a delegate, whereas when the artist as character comes to be invented his personality will count as much as his work and his status, and it is with the Impressionists that we first find an interest in the biographies and the real or imaginary eccentricities of the painters. The master on the other hand does not have a biography. He has something very different, a career, a *cursus honorum*: he has studied in the studio, passed the competition to enter the École des beaux-arts, been to Rome, become professor at the Beaux-Arts, won a place at the French Institute in Rome, then become a member of the board of examiners there, has been awarded the Legion of Honour. Even now that the artistic field has become completely anonymous, there are still painters with this career: a few years ago in the article 'The Production of Belief', I gave some examples of contemporary painters who have an academic kind of CV, and a clientele of the same type.[38] They are painters guaranteed by the State, which raises a question that I was already asking implicitly just now: is there not in the social world a vision guaranteed by the State?

The only definition of the State that I am sure of at the moment is the following: the State has the power to grant certain visions. Thus an academic diploma guarantees that you are intelligent, that you know your maths. A few years ago I even said that the State holds the

64 *Lecture of 28 March 1985*

monopoly of legitimate symbolic violence[39] – it says: 'You are such and such', and this has the force of law. By and large, people believe what the State says. Even in times of acute protest such as May 1968, when people think they are protesting against everything, they do not really attack the fundamentals, because these are lodged in their minds in the form of structures of perception, etc.

A symbolic revolution

The master is an artist whose prices are ultimately guaranteed. Just as the Banque de France acts as fiduciary to guarantee the currency, so the State acts as a bank guaranteeing academic diplomas, protecting them against devaluation. Here the State guarantees the exchange rates of the painters, so to speak. It is quite extraordinary: the artistic revolution that I am describing is at the same time an economic revolution. In fact there are painters whose names you don't even know who are very expensive. In one famous sale, one of them sold a painting for three times more than a Titian; five years later, he was worth nothing. This links up with my first session, which might have seemed rather gratuitous and abstract: symbolic revolutions, that is revolutions in the principles of vision and division, in the principles of classification, have very real effects, such as a collapse in the exchange rate. *Mutatis mutandis*, you could see in what I have been saying an analogy with the upheavals that occurred despite everything in May 1968: the exchange rate of certain disciplines collapsed. Philology collapsed in favour of linguistics, which was not quoted at all before 1968.

These revolutions in vision have very real effects, economic effects. At the same time they affect the principles of vision which – as I explained at length just now – are part of people's bodily being, they are particularly painful revolutions. In fact they can almost be more cruel than the political revolutions that deprive social agents of their possessions, because depriving social agents of their vision of the world tears their mental structures to pieces and tramples on everything they believed in. That is why revolutions like those of May 1968 or 1848 can drive people mad. You could re-read Flaubert's *Sentimental Education* in that light.[40] Since they aggress the social agents whose interests are bound up with the categories of perception that are called into question, symbolic revolutions provoke absolutely heart-breaking dramas, analogous to those that are seen in pre-capitalist societies when the elderly, traditional peasants are faced with technical revolutions that are at the same time symbolic revolutions: their way of ploughing,

Lecture of 28 March 1985

moving slowly, unhurriedly towards the west, for instance, engages so many categories of perception (east/west, masculine/feminine, standing/lying, virility, and so on) that when the young generation starts to plough at top speed in the interest of productivity, it is not simply an economic change, it is the collapse of a vision of the world that represents in a sense what these people treasure the most. It is a kind of symbolic murder. The Impressionist revolution is of this ilk. People, including the critics, cry out in despair: 'If art is *Olympia* then I'm a stupid old fool . . .' The world is falling apart, it is all over.

The great religious revolutions and the great heresies are in the same way complete transformations of a vision of the world. We can understand why they are so murderous. If we are surprised that the Irish are fighting without any economic motive[41] it is because we have lost touch with this kind of thing. In the name of a kind of economism, we consider that a revolution with no economic issues is not serious; it would be merely a 'partial revolution', as Marx would say.[42] You could think of Iran.[43] I'm worried in saying that; I am making these connections because I didn't want you to think that I was retelling stories from nineteenth-century history, but obviously I am afraid that these connections may make you think: 'Hang on, he's mixing everything up, what is the connection?'

To help you understand what a symbolic revolution is, I can describe what I believe was the structure of the world and the vision of the world of those who produced this academic art. The painter was not an artist, he did not have a biography, he had a career. (A word in passing on the opposition between professors and artists. Even today the statistics, however crude, show that professors are more often married and have on average more children than unaffiliated intellectuals or artists;[44] they are more conventional, they are more likely to have the Legion of Honour. This structural opposition is still very strong and it matches up with the oppositions between critic and painter or critic and writer.) The master is opposed to the artist. He must take a back seat, because he is important not as an individual person but as a delegate. He is similar to the priest as analysed by Weber: whereas the prophet has an ego and has no guarantor but himself (he is obliged to say: 'Because I say so'), the priest is always a delegate and is condemned to take a back seat. There is a kind of structural hypocrisy of the delegate (we might also think of the spokesmen of the political parties[45]). When the priest or the master says 'I', it is a collective 'I', for otherwise they would be guilty of usurpation. This structural discretion explains why the copy is given the same value as the original work and why the accent is placed on the execution and on the virtuosity of the performance. Whence

66 *Lecture of 28 March 1985*

the technomania, the technicism and the cult of the prodigy, as well as the submission to the urgent insistence that the discourse should carry a message, and everything that I have been saying: the cult of the finished, the primacy of line over colour, etc.

Historical painting

We should add one last important property, the one that is generally emphasised because it is the most striking: the academic work must have a historical subject. There is a link between academic painting and history painting. It is said that the Impressionist revolution consisted in rehabilitating landscape, which was at the lowest level of the hierarchy: right at the top were political history painting and religious painting and then you came down by degrees to the lower form of the landscape, especially if it lacked any historical significance (you could paint *Phocion*,[46] but the Barbizon painters, for instance, produced pure landscape; they did have a clientele, but they were considered to be the lowest of the low in the hierarchy of painters).

Why is it that *pompier* painting and history are integral to the position of academic art? It is because history painting is also recommended in the name of a hierarchical relation: the relation between discourse and painting. It is the famous formula *ut pictura poesis*. A well-known book by Lee[47] bears this title and the theme has often been rehearsed: painting can only earn its titles of nobility by imitating literature or history and by appropriating historical subjects, that is, a discourse, a historical discourse. Academic painting, then, accepts this hierarchy that places discourse above painting and considers the noblest painters to be those who adopt historical subjects, which are the noblest subjects, and require the spectator to have the noblest attitude, that is, a historical culture, the humanist culture which was acquired at the time in the Jesuit schools or the *lycées*. The imperative to signify, which is central to academic painting and which governs, for instance, the primacy of line over colour (the line spells clarity and readability), is combined with the imperative to signify noble things, in an academic way. Now, what is noble in academic terms is what is historical. The more ancient it is, the more beautiful, and that is still true today: disciplines are all the more noble, the further away from us they are in time; thus medieval history is much more noble than modern history (not to mention the history of Assyria . . .). The farther away in time it is, the more beautiful it is; this is a very profound mental structure. This hierarchy of nobilities according to the degree of antiquity is combined with the imperative of readability to produce programmatic paintings that can only be understood by reading the caption [*la légende*], which is always some historical information: it is a *legendum*. It says that you need to read the painting and read it on the basis of what the painter says in the legend (and not otherwise). The painters' ambition is to rival the historians, and some of them undertook detailed historical research to reconstitute the details of the buttons of the lancers of the regiment they were painting, or the form of the chair that the hero was sitting on.

So the painting must say something and offer a meaning transcending the play of form and colour, the pictorial. It must say something and say it clearly. To quote Boime – who like the majority of the great historians of this painting, writes in English – 'The painting is a historical statement demanding a clear exposition.'[48] The painting then is a historical discourse in which the techniques of expression must be subordinate to what is being said. The form is not independent of the message, and to say 'What matters is the manner of expression' will be a bold wager. To borrow another quotation from another author, Sloane: 'For the academic painters as for the conservative critics [*Bourdieu points out:* they nearly all were], literary values are an essential element of great art, and the principle function of style is to render these values clear and effective for the spectator.'[49] This is the same idea again: technique, even if it is valued in the logic of a virtuoso performance, remains always subordinate to the expressive intention. This is what I was saying just now about the word 'legend': this painting is made much more to be read than to be seen. It is made to be deciphered just like a literary message and the proper reading is a historically informed reading that takes pleasure in discovering and reading a whole page of history.

A *lector*'s painting

As I was saying the other day, the metaphor of reading, much used when semiology was in fashion, is not neutral. It is typical of the academic vision, the professorial vision. In the Latin language, I think that it was Gilbert de la Porrée, a scholastic, who, following a distinction that it always gives me some sadistic pleasure to repeat,[50] opposed the *auctores*, that is, the authors and creators, to the *lectores*, the professors who read things written by others.[51] As I have demonstrated a hundred times over, the *lector* has a kind of bias that drives him to conceive all perception as a reading, that is, an act of decipherment. Treating things

68   *Lecture of 28 March 1985*

that were not conceived as such as things made to be read, he commits some very important theoretical errors. I take one example, to link up with what I was saying in the lecture just now, which is that a ritual is more akin to gymnastics than to writing. We can in fact 'read' a treatise on gymnastics while forgetting that it was written in order to get people to move, or read (in the sense of a 'reading' from the 1960s) a treatise on dance while forgetting that it was written in order to get people to make gestures. 'I turn seven times from right to left, I pass under the left shoulder, I pass under the right shoulder, with the right hand, the left hand': a ritual too is gymnastics. Painting also has its gymnastic element, a labour that has its own logic, but I don't want to rehearse the literature of painters on painting that accentuates this gestural and sensual side – I would merely suggest (since a scholarly discourse on the subject would be much too long-winded) that it is the poor man's aesthetic discourse, written by the painter who, with his limited linguistic resources, takes refuge in stubborn defiance, saying 'I wallow in painting' [*laughter*].

Academic painting, then, is a *lector*'s painting which is addressed to *lectores* and is made to be read and deciphered, like a document. Ultimately, you might wonder, as Zola did, why the painters don't write [rather than paint]: in telling their story, don't the painters lose the specificity of the pictorial work which is after all to make something visible in a two-dimensional space, in colour, etc. This academic painting made to be read works to reinforce the culture that it informs (Jesuit culture, classical antiquity, and to some extent the biblical tradition) and to reassure the guardians of that culture, who are made to feel legitimate readers. In designating the legitimate painters as masters, the academic institution by the same token designates the masters' legitimate audience . . . you do not enter unless you have a qualification, the *licentia docendi* [. . .]. This is a crucial function that is still the role of the museum nowadays: when I enter a museum, I express my right to view. I shan't continue, but I could justify my sally by catching you out with innocent questions, like: 'Do you prefer to visit a museum on your own or with somebody?' – to which I know the statistical answers! [*laughter*]

The right to read is then a recognition of this right, and we can see that the goal of the revolution will be to deprive these *lectores* of their right to read: they will not understand the language of these illiterate Americans (as they saw them) who wade in and fall in love with and buy up the Impressionists. There is a revolution, a collapse of the value of titles: until then, to enter a museum, you needed academic diplomas, you had to have studied the classics and know who Phocion was.

Lecture of 28 March 1985 69

Suddenly, the first transatlantic barbarian walking in off the boat to see *Olympia* had rather an advantage; with no preconceptions, he saw her more clearly. This was something of a cultural revolution, and the Impressionist revolution is also interesting in giving an idea of what a real cultural revolution would look like: it is a kind of scale-model revolution, which, like all variations of the imagination achieved in history, gives us an idea of everything that we invested in our culture, in things that we are so accustomed to that we are ready to slaughter someone because they are not in perfect agreement with us over Mondrian. Symbolic struggles are very violent. (I am in a decidedly prophetic vein today, I don't know why, but more than usual, I want to make you feel the implications of what I am saying.)

Academic painting then requires a historical reading supposing a knowledge of history and sensitive to allusions, rather than a specialist knowledge; you can be ignorant of all the techniques of painting and yet be able to respond; in this sense the painter qua painter is entirely dispensed with. The critics probably had some awareness of certain exploits favoured by the École, foreshortening, for instance. The syllabus, like most school syllabi, was arbitrarily hierarchised: why are things taught in one particular order rather than another? Why do we study *The Adventures of Telemachus* before *Athalie*, and *Athalie* before *The Charterhouse of Parma?* The syllabus then defined a hierarchy of exploits, and in producing them the masters performed feats designed for fourth-year students, for readers who knew the hierarchy. This produced an entirely fictitious and private set of features, formidably arbitrary because founded solely on the logic of the institution and its training. This is a typical example of the cycle of reproduction: objective hierarchies generate mental structures, with subjective hierarchies that match these mental structures, and everything seems completely natural, to such an extent that if someone turns up and asks: 'Why should we copy plaster casts. Why not place an easel in front of nature?', he is destroyed.

The de-realisation effect

The picture then must say something and say it clearly. What it says must be worth saying and be highly placed in the academic hierarchy, where historical reference is a guarantee of authenticity. At the same time it is very interesting to see how astonished and scandalised everyone was by *Olympia*. There had been nudes before in painting. In fact the scandal was due simply to the fact that she is not a historical

70   *Lecture of 28 March 1985*

nude. People immediately declared: 'She's a little tart from we all know where' – she was a contemporary nude. If you make the link with what I was saying just now about the hierarchy of disciplines, you will understand why sociology is always seen as scandalous (here I plead my own cause), whereas ethnology, and history even more so, are so well accepted: it is the '*Olympia* effect'. When you produce a nude of the type of *Phryné devant l'Aréopage* [painting by Jean-Léon Gérôme (1861)], there is no problem, because history 'de-realises'.

We need to think about this very mysterious thing called 'historical realisation'. One text that illustrates this well is an article on Amiel's journal where Luc Boltanski describes 'academic eroticism'[52] [*Bourdieu smiles*]. It is a long article which analyses among other things our attitude to erotic texts written in Latin, a very special kind of eroticism that consists in accepting the erotic only if sublimated and euphemised through Latin. Do you know that even fifty years ago when people wanted to describe something rather risqué in an ethnological article they wrote in Latin? Latin was the instrument of euphemisation par excellence. Which leads me to say that historicisation enacts this euphemising function: it distances things and at the same time transforms them into culture. This is another thing which has not been sufficiently thought through: what is the cultural destiny of something? You say something, it creates a scandal, and when it becomes 'Pascal against Voltaire'[53] you can write a dissertation on it, whereas you only need to relate it in a non-dissertational manner for it to become 'public against private'. What then is this de-realisation effect which accompanies history and which goes hand in hand with the academic institution? Think for example of the rule that prevents you from writing a doctoral thesis on a living author: what is the point of this neutralisation effect?

Historicisation, the historical character of a subject, is implicit in the whole system, and is surely a most overdetermined property. History is what you should say, it is what you can say because it is legitimate. It is also what allows you to say almost anything, to go as far as possible. There is the famous example of Couture: the subject of Roman orgies[54] is a thousand times more scandalous than Manet's *Olympia*, but it is a historical subject, the very manner of painting invokes historicity. Its very technique has the eternal and transhistorical aspect that characterises academic art, for the academic arts are eternal, they go hand in hand with this sentiment of eternity, of humanity as eternal. In a very fine passage in *The Evolution of Pedagogy in France* Durkheim contrasts what opposes the teaching of the humanities to what ethnology does: he says that the Greeks and Romans are taught in such a

Lecture of 28 March 1985 71

way that they are immediately confined to a sort of eternity,[55] even if they are at the same time treated as our contemporaries, through all those dissertation topics on the theme of 'The eternity and the eternal significance of the work of Racine', 'Racine lives'. Durkheim contrasts this kind of transhistorical humanity to the humanity that we would find in an ethnology of Greece or Rome: the eternal characters with eternal sentiments on whom we can eternally write dissertations would become real characters with real problems.

Consequently, academic historicisation renders sacred (because what is ancient is noble) and unreal, and with its technical formalism helps to produce that impression of cold externality that renders the most burning subjects cold. The coldness of form and its formal associations mean that you have to be really academic to get any eroticism out of it (this is the Amiel effect). Here I quote Baxandall, who is certainly one of the greatest living art historians. We have published in *Actes de la recherche en sciences sociales* a translation of nearly all of his book on the *Quattrocento*, which will soon be published by Gallimard.[56] In a recent lecture on David,[57] Baxandall describes the perception that the German Romantics had of French academic painting, which was still dominant at the time. Schlegel, quoted by Baxandall, said that this painting had two properties: one which he calls 'pantomime' and the other 'haberdashery'. 'Pantomime' is the theatrical quality of the characters, who obey a concern to depict noble subjects worthy of being represented (therefore in historical clothing and settings), who must always adopt heroic poses. Schlegel sees clearly that this is also linked to the idea that it is the soul that is the most noble attribute: to represent the soul when you can paint only bodies, you need to paint those bodies in lively, inspired, theatrical postures, resulting in grandiose gestures (which also derive from the fact that the subjects must be moral and edifying). As for what he calls 'haberdashery', this is the concern for historical truth, whose reconstruction is so clumsy and exaggerated that all we see is the costumes and the decors.

I shall conclude here: this painting de-realises, through its reference to a distant past, but also to a distant present. We often speak of their interest in the Orient, but the Orient was not interesting as Orient. It was a highly selective Orient of the bazaar. It was interesting because on the one hand it produced an effect of distance and nobility, and on the other hand it enabled the painters to resolve what was an important problem for them, painting the contemporary world with its modern costumes: the Orient allowed them to have contemporary characters dressed in biblical or Roman costumes. This is extremely important: introducing a character wearing a top hat was an extraordinary intrusion; it was a violent solution to the problem that the academic painters resolved with the Oriental or Orientalist approach.

The Oriental question is also important as a field effect. Obviously it is tempting to connect the interest of the painters in the Orient with things like the renewal of colonial conquest. But analysing in terms of relatively autonomous fields leads us to see it as a solution to a specific problem in a specific space. It is possible that Orientalism was overdetermined by directly political and other preoccupations, but it was above all a solution to a specific problem in a specific space, one that is pictorial.

Lecture of 18 April 1985

*First session (lecture): the sociological relation to the social world
– A materialist vision of symbolic forms – Perception as a system of
oppositions and discrimination – Investing in the game of the* libidines *–
The passage from action to discourse on action – The political struggle
for the right vision
Second session (seminar): the invention of the modern artist (3) –
Writing the history of a symbolic revolution – The surplus of educated
men and the academic crisis – The education system and the field of
cultural production – The morphological effects – The effects of the
morphological crisis on the academic field*

First session (lecture): the sociological relation to the social world

Do not hesitate to ask me any questions for me to answer. I invite you
to do this, in order to allay somewhat the impression of arbitrariness
that I inevitably feel every time I enter this hall, especially after a break.
This arbitrariness consists in imposing on people who have come here
on fixed dates a subject that they have not chosen, and making my
own choices in giving a certain number of replies to questions that
they may not have thought of asking. I say this essentially to counter
an impression that I feel, one which always makes beginning more
difficult for me, because I can never avoid wondering what my reasons
for speaking are. This is not simply anecdotal. This kind of anxiety
concerning the reason for a communication tends to be forgotten,
because we have an institution, and the institution is normally designed
to enable us to forget the arbitrary: the scholastic term for arbitrariness
was *ex instituto* – on the grounds of an act of institution.[1] For example
the initial act of institution through which a course of lectures at the

74 *Lecture of 18 April 1985*

Collège de France was created goes back so far and has been confirmed so often and for so long by successive agents, by successive relations between speakers and listeners, that the arbitrariness of the thing gets forgotten. That said, the arbitrariness remains, and the paradox of an institution is that its arbitrariness is constantly misrecognised, and recognised only insofar as it is misrecognised. If we have in mind a kind of Durkheimian, objectivist definition, which lends the institution the quasi-reality of a thing, we forget that an institution is also a certain relation between this objective thing, the institution (which is, moreover, very difficult to define) and the agents who come to inhabit it.

What I am saying at the moment provides an opportunity to test what is the relation between a habitus and an institution, between a habitus and a habitat, between a habitus and a habit. A habitus is something social: for an institution to function, people must find it normal and natural, they must have noted in their diary 'Lecture at the Collège de France' and meet up at the given time to make that certain something happen: a lecture at the Collège de France – with its portrait of Bergson, its table and microphones, all those sorts of things which make an impression whether we realise it or not.

What I have been saying just now is not normal, it is not institutional at all: the institution is designed to prevent us from saying this kind of thing, to remove any need for saying it, and even to make it slightly indecent and too personal to mention it. But we should also ask ourselves why this concord between habitus and institutions so strongly solicited gives way sometimes to a sort of discord. Is the discord that I feel at this moment due to sociology, does it spring from the relation between sociology and the institutions? Is it the anxiety of a sociologist, aggravated by sociological study, which leads us to be sensitive to these things, or is it the anxiety itself that drives the sociological gaze? In fact I think that there is a mutual trade-off between the two. This raises the question of whether the sociological relation to the world is a normal social relation and whether communicating this relation is legitimate; the fundamental question being whether it is socially acceptable to have a sociological relation with the social world. Those were the questions that I wanted to raise at the outset.

These questions are reasonably justified because they dramatise the canonical scholarly question of what an institution is: what I have just briefly outlined could form the basis of a reflection on the nature of the institution. I should say in passing that people often attribute to the sociologist – through a misunderstanding that he finds quite embarrassing – the vision of the social world that he produces in his studies, without seeing that this vision may owe its existence to his distance from the social world. He may need to be ill at ease in the social world and experience a lack of immediacy and obviousness in his relation to it, in order to see what normally escapes our attention; it may perhaps be the case that we grasp something better when we find it less easy to tolerate. The reader often supposes that the author operating a sociological objectification is expressing his own vision of the world, whereas he has perhaps had that vision only because this world for him is not self-evident, and he is like a fish out of water there. This might explain a number of things; I am not speaking for myself, but of something much more general which is valid I think for the great founding fathers of sociology and which would no doubt help us to understand the social factors influencing someone adopting a career in sociology or ethnology.

A materialist vision of symbolic forms

I would like now to take this sociology of the perception of the social world further, since it seems to me to be an indispensable component of any sociology. To solve the problem I might evoke the new alternative in which I believe the social sciences have for too long remained trapped. (I think – as far as I can see – that sociology has for a long time been enclosed between alternatives that were imposed on it because they were so strongly imposed in our ordinary experience of the social world.) The alternative that I am going to suggest is extremely powerful and does not completely overlap with any of the others that I have evoked so far. It opposes a kind of materialist vision to an idealist vision. The first places the accent on the thingified, reified aspect of institutions, on the objective structures and the material or objective bases of social operations and relations. The second places the accent on representations and visions, on the subjective aspect of the social world. I find this alternative in which sociology is currently caught sinister because it tends to leave out or to misunderstand a certain number of fundamental mechanisms. If the metaphor had not been misused in so many different ways, I would present the analysis that I have been trying to offer for some years now, and whose results I am trying to condense here, as a sort of materialism of the symbolic, as an attempt to make a materialist analysis of symbolic forms: symbolic forms have an objective existence and objective effects, and in particular very direct economic effects.

In my last lecture I was saying that the social space is at once a basis and a goal for struggle: it is perceived, it is an object of perception

76   *Lecture of 18 April 1985*

and visions, and at the same time it is the source that constitutes those visions. The social world then is an object of knowledge: it is known and recognised, and we cannot discuss it without questioning the practical knowledge that takes it as an object and without taking into account this permanent dialectic of knowledge, recognition and misrecognition. Applying to the social world such ordinary language terms, whether they come from Hegel or elsewhere, that are so familiar and habitual, makes us end up forgetting their common root: the idea of knowledge. What I would like to pursue today is the idea that in the social world there is both perceiving and 'being-perceived'.[2] Our visions of the social world are perpetual subjects of struggle insofar as being-perceived and the manner of being-perceived are a fundamental target of struggles for perception.

Political struggles aim to preserve or transform our vision by transforming or preserving our principles of division, and in particular the principles of the division of the social world, because what is at stake in this struggle to preserve and transform the principles of division is the being-perceived, the *percipi*,[3] that is, the being of the social agents who play these games of perception in the social world. If perception of the social world is so important, it is because being-perceived is one of the fundamental dimensions of the social agent. To exist socially (I have said this in an earlier lecture, but I shall now rework the theme in a different context) is partly to be perceived, but it is also – we must not forget this second, materialist dimension – to own things, to possess objective and objectified goods, etc.

We would be forgetting something essential about social struggles if we forgot that, since my social being is always to some extent defined as being-perceived, the struggle to impose the right categories of perception, those most favourable to what I am, is a crucial engagement. If my being-perceived is so important to me, if it is so important for me to be rightly seen, it is obvious that I cannot be indifferent to the struggle to establish what is the right vision. If you think about it, you will realise that a considerable part of social, and particularly political, conflict concerns the right vision of the social world. We might even say that 'being-rightly-seen' means 'being-seen' and 'being distinguished' as opposed to 'common'. If, among the structuring oppositions of the perception of the social world and other people, the opposition between the unique and the common, the ordinary and the extraordinary, the banal and the distinguished is so fundamental, if it plays such a prominent part, it is precisely because, behind the 'being-rightly-seen', there is quite simply the 'being-seen', that is, the concern to 'not go unnoticed', not be dismissed as a common, obscure member of the

Lecture of 18 April 1985

'other ranks'. We must not be expelled into outer darkness, we must be one of the forms that stand out against the background. This is what needs to be said from the outset, that being distinguished[4] is not being expelled into the blind spot of perception that is 'going unnoticed'.

Perception as a system of oppositions and discrimination

How does our perception of the social world function? Like all perception, it operates through divisions: we cannot posit a class without positing its complement; we cannot posit whites without positing blacks. As a result, in its spontaneous form, perception of the social world is almost inevitably diacritical:[5] there is no social judgement or *crisis* that is not a *diacrisis*[6] and a reference. We cannot posit a class without referring it negatively to other complementary classes; we cannot posit a group without positing the non-group, without positing the excluded. Perception, as well as being diacritical, is discontinuist: it introduces discontinuity where there was generally continuity. Take the example of the young and the old, or the rich and the poor that I mentioned last time when talking of Pareto: whereas statistical analysis exposes continuities, social perception introduces discontinuities. What Pareto said of age (there is always someone else we will appear old to, but social perception says that there are the young and the old, establishing a frontier between them) is applicable to all the fundamental divisions that we perceive in the social world. Perception of the social world then is diacritical, discontinuist and dualist. Ultimately it uses largely dichotomous and coherent systems of classification that function like languages, in that we cannot understand the signification, sense and value (in Saussurean terms) of any one element of the system of classification without reference to the other elements of the system.

The structure of a system of classification is its true origin. Here I merely repeat something that has been repeated over and again by the whole structuralist tradition: each element of a system takes its meaning from its relation to the other elements. In this sense it is in a way rather futile to look in objective reality for the foundation of judgements that the system of classification enables us to establish. For instance, our ordinary perception sees the opposition between distinguished and vulgar in realist terms and seeks in objective reality those properties capable of founding the judgements produced by the application of this dichotomy. In fact the simplest comparative history shows that what was once 'distinguished' later becomes 'vulgar'.[7] And what is more, we have here one of the fundamental sources of change:

78 *Lecture of 18 April 1985*

the 'distinguished' becoming 'common' or 'vulgar' – to become distinguished, you need to change. The search for a transhistorical essence of the 'distinguished', which our common perception pursues, is quite hopeless. It is in the system of differences that resides the source of each of the differences, rather than in some kind of substantive relation of a semantic element to a referent.

That does not mean – and this is a problem that I shall return to later – that the question of the referent is not raised and that ultimately the social world is completely reducible to the representation that can be given by a particular system of classification. This fundamental problem is common to linguistics, sociology and even art history, as I was explaining last time. Can we take this as far as a purely idealist theory of systems of classification, where they would contain their own truth, and the question of the referent would not arise? Some critics, like Barthes or Kristeva who always like to go to extremes, have gone so far. Can we go so far as to say, for instance, that the structure of the system of representations of the social world and the structure of the representations of classes are the truth of the social classes? I do no more than raise the question, but it is crucial. Some of you may have it in mind while you are listening to me, and I am aware of it.

Our vision of the social world is diacritical, which amounts to saying that it is systematic. Saying that it is diacritical means that each element is only meaningful in relation to the system and that – I follow Saussure once again – it is only within the system that each element assumes its distinctive value. It is then within a system of oppositions constituting a vision of the world that each element of this vision is constituted. Saying that our perception of the social world is diacritical and distinctive is to say that what we call 'discrimination' is both the capacity to discriminate and also the virtue that consists in knowing how to discriminate in the proper fashion. The discriminating man, who is discreet, and goes unnoticed because he is discreet, has so well internalised the appropriate systems of classification in a particular universe that at every moment he does what is needed to remain within the norms, which is the best way of going unnoticed. This is why it is never simple to play with the norms. Think of the problem of whether to wear a tie, for instance; you are caught whichever way you turn, there is no right solution. In some cases discrimination may consist in discovering and applying to the world the very categories that structure it, the principles of division that divide it, and thereby acting appropriately, as it were signing on the dotted line.

What we call discrimination is the possession of categories of perception, diacritical structures so adapted to the objective structures that we

Lecture of 18 April 1985 79

do what we are supposed to do without asking questions, as when we say: 'He did what he had to do.' In a way, one of the universal forms of excellence consists in being the person who at every moment does what they are supposed to do without even asking the question. This is not unconnected with what I was saying at the beginning. Discrimination enables you to pass unnoticed, to avoid standing out as someone trying not to stand out, and excellence clearly consists in doing what you are supposed to do in an ostentatiously discreet manner. [. . .]

(I think that the way I am resorting to playing with words today has a sociological basis insofar as language conveys a social philosophy that needs to be reactivated if we are not to let it function without our knowledge. One property of institutions as I said just now is that they function continuously: the features I mentioned in my opening remarks on the lecture course – 'course', 'Collège de France', 'Bergson', 'ancestors', 'François Ier', etc. – continue to function at this very moment although everyone has forgotten them, and that is the reason why they work so well. For words it's even worse: the reserves of social philosophy that are contained within words and the potential power to structure the social world that is contained within words never cease to function. As I have often said, this is why sociological writing is so difficult: we may inadvertently use words that say the opposite of what we want to say, because they bring their history with them as they continue to function in the ordinary world and the philosophical world. Very often the principle function of a philosophical, theoretical or historical culture is to be a bit more aware of what we are saying, without needing to constantly say: 'Danger: Hegel!'; we know that at a certain moment we are using a certain theoretical register by the simple fact of using certain words.)

The link that I am establishing between the words *diacrisis*, diacritical, *crisis*, judgement and discrimination might be perceived as a kind of etymological game. But to my mind this kind of analysis reminds us that our perception of the social world involves not only a capacity to see, and to see rightly, but also a capacity to be rightly seen because we see rightly. In this way the person who knows how to be rightly seen because he goes unnoticed when he ought to is the person who exercises discrimination. Indeed, the 'show-off' is the person whose categories of perception are entirely maladjusted, for example because he has not acquired the structures at the right time. In general, he has acquired them too late: the show-off is the upstart, the late start, the false start [*laughter*]; [. . .] that was not my own pun, it is well worn, therefore culturally legitimate [*laughter*]. By importing into one world categories that have been acquired in another, generally inferior,

80   *Lecture of 18 April 1985*

world, the show-off is doomed to vulgarity. He forgets, for instance, that supreme distinction lies in disguising distinction. Being seen to be rightly seen is to be a show-off (which is the absolute opposite of being distinguished); there is no other definition of vulgarity. Supreme distinction, which must be natural, consists in having discrimination so deeply ingrained that we forget ourselves as we do what has to be done in order to be distinguished without looking as if we are trying.

The sociological argument that I am offering here is very far from the thousands of texts that you will find in literature. Paul Valéry and so many others strive in vain to define distinction because they define it in substantialist and celebratory fashion. I for my part situate myself in a logic that is neither celebratory nor non-celebratory, but Spinozist ('neither rejoice, nor detest, etc.'),[8] which entails taking things as they are, which is I believe the logic of sociology. This is why I needed to make that detour through language [. . .]. If we reflect on the nature of discrimination, we can find a concrete link with the word 'discreet'.[9] This is a first point.

Investing in the game of the *libidines*

So these visions of the social world are divisions. They divide. We cannot see without dividing: seeing is seeing the difference, making distinctions. We might say that blindness in any particular domain is being deprived of the ability to tell the difference. To be lacking in taste is to be deprived of the ability to tell the difference. There I make another link between discrimination and taste.[10] Good taste is discrimination, that is, the ability to see the differences that we are supposed to see at any given moment, and of course – because the complementaries are always present – to avoid seeing those that we are not supposed to see. Good taste is knowing how to close your eyes to what you should not see, how to see what you should see and tell the right moment, neither too soon nor too late, to see what you should see (the moment is in fact very important: the latecomer is always doomed from the start because he always sees something too late, when it is no longer of interest because it is no longer exclusive). Thus visions are always divisions, and the link with taste is crucial in seeing the right divisions: to tell the difference you must not be indifferent.

Here again I seem to be playing with words, but this appeal to etymology has its advantages, and I think that I can justify my analysis. I refer to a very fine analysis by Guilbaud[11] on game theory, where he says that the basic but difficult notion of interest depends above all on an exercise in comparative thinking: being interested in something is to reject saying: 'It's all the same to me, I can't tell the difference, I don't see the point in distinguishing.' If I see no interest in distinguishing something, it is because I am not interested, I have no need of it, because I'm uninterested in what is at stake in the game in question, or, having started to play too late to acquire the principles of differentiation that make the game playable, I fail to see the differences (for instance, I don't see why people will kill to obtain some particular post in a universe that does not interest me).

To take Guilbaud's analysis further: interest is investment in a game. In fact it is synonymous with *illusio*, which, if we stretch the etymology a little,[12] designates the fact of engaging with a game and investing in the stakes that constitute the game. In other words interest, as opposed to the indifference that is the inability to differentiate, supposes two things. On the one hand it supposes a propensity to invest and grant importance – interest is what is important, and important to me. On the other hand it means granting enough importance to the game to want to know what is important and what is not. In other words the precondition for any judgement on a game is acknowledging the importance of the game: for instance we need to acknowledge the importance of the literary game before we come to wonder who is the best literary prize winner of the year; if literature does not interest me, I am uninterested in telling the difference, I have no interest in the question of the difference between the important and the unimportant, between what is interesting and what is not. There is then a basic interest, which is the precondition of a search for what is interesting and what is not.

The problems that I have so often had with some of my commentators, who are largely critical of me (in other words, they criticise before they understand what I have to say, or, worse, before they wonder whether they have understood me or not), show that all this is not as trivial as it might seem. Because of what we might call the 'Bentham effect',[13] the notion of interest is very often identified with economic interest, that is to say, reduced to a very partial definition, linked – for those who have attended my previous lectures[14] – to the establishment of the economic field as a relatively autonomous field ('business is business'). There is, however, a much broader, more fundamental and important definition of interest, which is the one that I refer to: interest is what interests me, what leads me to want to tell the difference.

So my first point is that this fundamental kind of interest is the propensity to invest, in the economic and also the psychoanalytic sense. The propensity to invest time and money, toil and trouble, but also

82 *Lecture of 18 April 1985*

emotional and libidinal interests in every sense of the word, and in particular the libido produced in a particular field. For there are plural *libidines*. The only thing that we can reproach people who generalise psychoanalysis unreflectively with is not seeing that *libido* is a particular case of the universe of *libidines* and that the nature of the social world is to establish extremely different things as *libido*: at the extreme it can establish almost anything as *libido*. It can make people take an interest in quite extraordinary things, which, for anyone not in the game, seem to be small potatoes: the social world can play crazy games and make people go crazy for things which, for anyone not in the game, are really crazy. The people seen as normal are those who are mad about something which is recognised as worthy of interest in a determined field.

Fundamental interest, which is established by a game and through playing that game, is then the propensity to invest, to grant interest, and thereby to discern differences: granting importance means asking yourself what is important and what isn't, what is most important. If you grant importance to a game you are already starting to play the game, you are ignoring the question of whether the game is worth playing, and the nature of any successful game is to make you forget that you could ask: 'But what is the point of playing?', 'What makes a baseball player (or a prime minister or a professor . . .) compete?', 'Why does he compete rather than not compete?' The nature of the game is to suppress indifference and the very question of indifference, along with the questions of rationale and sufficient reason.

With this question suppressed, the question 'What is most important/least important?' arises, and takes on as many forms as there are games. The principle of discrimination and judgement, the fundamental *diacritics*, will be different for the games played in the academic, the economic, or the political fields. Where some people will see differences, others will not. Where some will find an interest and discover the process of being interested, others will not even notice what is not interesting but will remain indifferent, which is very different. Interest then presupposes a fundamental investment in the game and a propensity to invest.

Secondly, almost correlatively, it supposes discrimination, that is, the ability to differentiate, to distinguish. In the social game, the little mechanism that drives this process is what we normally call taste. Taste is a propensity to consume (as in: 'have a taste for' – women, fruit or flowers, for instance), but also an ability to consume with discrimination: the two dimensions are always present. That said, this ability to differentiate, to tell the difference rather than be not indifferent, does

Lecture of 18 April 1985 83

not come from nowhere. It is – and this is one of my fundamental hypotheses – produced by the incorporation of objective or objectively recognised principles of differentiation in a given social universe.

One thing that I have not yet said in this analysis of interest is that in a way there is no such thing as a disinterested practical perception. Perception notes differences but, if everything that I have been saying is true, all perception is an investment. No perception is neutral. By the same token the categories of perception and in general the systems of dualist concepts that in all societies function as fundamental principles structuring the social world are always suffused with values: there is always a good and a bad side. Since these systems function as systems, each of the oppositions implicates all the others. In a pre-capitalist society where the fundamental systems of opposition are mythical systems, there is a whole cosmology: in masculine/feminine there is hot/cold, sun/moon, east/west, etc. In this way, to change a structure like masculine/feminine, you have to change everyone and their whole vision of everything. This is why these systems are so powerful. But it is just the same in our own societies: to change 'the one and the many' (a classic dissertation topic), the rare and the common or the vulgar and the distinguished, you have to change a whole world view and all those who have produced this world view. By the same token, there is necessarily an iconoclastic and symbolically revolutionary aspect to any revision of these structures.

'Telling the difference' is done by people who are insiders. This was implicit in everything that I have been saying: you only tell the difference if you are not indifferent, and if you are not to be indifferent, you have to be on the inside, you have to be involved in the game. Therefore *interesse* is always *inesse*.[15] For instance, the person who notes the pertinent differences in the academic field knows how to distinguish between the 'admissible' candidate, who passed the written exam but not the oral, and the 'bi-admissible', who did this twice running, between an *agrégé* of the old régime and one of the new, between a State doctorate and a third-cycle doctorate.[16] All these extraordinary distinctions have fantastic social effects, but seen from the viewpoint of someone who is not in the game, who has some sort of detachment of any kind, they are the work of someone who belongs. 'To belong' is to make distinctions.

Which brings us back to discrimination: anyone who seems not to recognise these distinctions, or worse still, not give a damn about them, is utterly excluded. It seems to me that the greatest subversion is the one that consists in handling the structures of discrimination in such a way as to show that not only do we not discriminate, but that

84 *Lecture of 18 April 1985*

we don't want to know. There may be two degrees of interest: there is interest for the game and interest in the game. The fact of accepting the fundamental axioms of a game or a field, the fact of participating in a collective illusion which is the kind of collective belief that is the real foundation of a field, this belonging, this fundamental investment, is thus the condition for the acquisition of the just and legitimate vision. Which means that *discrimination* is the condition for the real entry into the game.

The passage from action to discourse on action

What I have been describing so far is practical vision, and in my last lecture I insisted on the fact that [. . .] the passage from practical knowledge to scholarly knowledge, the passage from a vision expressed at a sub-linguistic level – or, to use my favourite metaphor, from a feel for the game – to discourse, is a dangerous leap, a very major discontinuity. This is one of the topics that I developed at length last time: you cannot move from a feel for the game to a discourse on the game in a smooth and continuous fashion. There is a change, a 'passage to another kind of nature', as Plato might say, a threshold, a major change of register. I emphasised last time the fact that the same habitus, the same ethos, with their system of implicit, practical patterns of appreciation and their materialisation of a practical moral code, can figure in various different ethics: practical visions of the world have a certain elasticity.

This is one of the main problems that arise in the struggle for the *percipere* and the *percipi* that I am now describing, in the struggle over the way to view the world and impose the legitimate vision of the world, which is the political struggle. In the political struggle, one of the principal points of action, one of the Archimedean points where political action can insert its lever, is this articulation of practical vision with objectified vision. I remind you that the same practical vision can figure in various different objectified visions: there are misunderstandings, the effects of *allodoxia* that I have so often described. You can mistake one discourse for another: I may believe that a discourse expresses what I really feel, on, say, birth control, or it can seem to me to have an affinity with what I think, at a pre-discursive level, of the matter in question.

I come now to something important. Political visions, as I have been saying, are linked to interest. They are linked to a position in the social world, they are therefore subject to the reality principle, which means that each practical vision is adapted to the position of the person pro-

Lecture of 18 April 1985 85

ducing it. One of the most striking things shown by empirical analysis of the practical action of social agents is that they are not mad: they nearly always act with discrimination, which does not mean that they could describe what they are doing – doing something and saying what you are doing are not the same thing. This is a problem that affects the drafting of the questionnaire fundamentally: depending on whether you put the questions at a level requiring verbalisation or at a level closer to the practical choices of everyday life, you can discover different things, since social agents know better what they should do, given their position, when they just have to act, as opposed to having to say what they should do. I think that this distinction is important for those among you who have to produce questionnaires.

What I am going to say is quite elementary, so elementary and fundamental that it is often overlooked when questionnaires are drafted (those who conduct opinion polls don't even think of it): a fundamental question that you need to consider is what level you are aiming at if you are trying to capture the practical vision (which goes without saying, but since we often proceed by means of questionnaires instead of observation, we are already working in the discursive order). When we proceed using set questionnaires with pre-packaged answers, we assume that we have solved the problem of the passage from practice to discourse, since we act as if the agents would have been able to produce the response that they are able to recognise. But pointing at a given reply is really not the same as producing a reply on reflection. [. . .]

In an enquiry led by a pollster of any kind there is an enquiry effect that we constantly need to examine in order to see if the question is formulated to appeal to a practice or to a discourse on that practice. If we formulate our questions very carefully and indirectly, or use techniques like the one I mentioned last time where we provide little cards for classifying,[17] we can try to use discourse to place the person as nearly as possible in situations where their feel for the game can function. We can approach the conditions of practice (those who experiment on animals know the problem: it is the natural situation versus the experimental situation, the cage or the jungle), but on condition obviously that we never forget that the situation is experimental. Now the sociologist has a vested professional interest in forgetting that the situation in which he is working is artificial (if only because he spends his days in this artificial situation, and it is his whole life), and when he asks questions of his colleagues, they don't want to know that the question that figures least on the questionnaire is the question of what it means to question and how artificial is the act of questioning.

86 *Lecture of 18 April 1985*

That said, as long as we bear in mind how arbitrary it is to question, we can question in the least arbitrary way possible; we can try, within the limits of a situation that questions the situation, to approach situations where the practical sense and the feel for the game function, below discourse, below questioning even, because in fact the practical sense is something that makes us constantly answer questions that we do not think of asking – which does not mean that we don't give the right answers. This implies revising an old prejudice. We all have in mind the old Cartesian formula ('I doubt', and so on); the analysis of the practical sense that I am presenting you with – which is in fact not a case of rehabilitation, which would be ridiculous, there is nothing to rehabilitate – amounts to saying that the practical sense is a form of knowledge that operates below the level of language, theory and argument, but is nonetheless not ill-adapted. We may then, within the limits of a survey situation, approach real situations and grasp practical visions. That said, as a consequence of the distinction that I have just been making between practical vision and objectified or explicit vision, we cannot pass from practical vision to explicit vision without a radical break, which is the passage into discourse, the *logos*, where the speaker's expressive faculties, the linguistic traditions, the verbal and conceptual systems at his disposal, everything that I mentioned just now, play their part.

The political struggle for the right vision

To continue these analyses, I would say that our visions of the social world are divisions, that these divisions are linked to our interest, that they are practical, pre-explicit, sub-linguistic, 'non-thetic' as the phenomenological tradition would say, that is, not proposed as theses but lived as self-evident. Another point: since these visions are linked to interest, they are obviously interested and linked to the holding of a position in a social universe and to the interests linked to the holding of a position. There is no neutral world view: every vision divides, but they are already divided. They divide the social world, because to speak of white means that black exists, just as to say that there are good people means that there are also bad.

In pre-capitalist societies there are many dualist systems of this kind. We manage to understand systems based on kinship, but there are very bizarre systems that have always intrigued ethnologists, because they seem to have no economic or genealogical basis (although these are the two main principles of vision that we imagine in these kinds of society). Most often they are associated with the names of colours, we find yellows and greens, east and west, high and low. These oppositions, which have virtually no intrinsic content, are always linked to a position in space that we need to see. There is then no neutral vision: practical visions are always visions in a practical state, but also have a practical function: I always see in the social world what it is in my interest to see. In other words, visions divide the world, and divide it according to principles of division that form the very structure of the world. There are necessarily divided opinions on the visions: a consensus of visions is unthinkable – this follows from everything that I have been saying: divisions are always ethically or politically coloured, which means that we need to return to the notion of interest.

I now need to explore [. . .] all the properties that separate practical vision from represented vision. I have reminded you of the autonomy of the representation and the gap between praxis and the discourse on praxis, between practical discrimination and discrimination in explicit discourse. In the next session I shall try to show how we can use what I was saying about the existence of visions and divisions to understand the specific logic of the struggle to impose the right vision of the divisions. In every society one of the fundamental struggles is the struggle for the right vision of the division into classes: are there classes or not? To conclude this session I shall try to sum up everything that I have said on social classes and the theory of classes. To illustrate the argument that one of the major subjects of struggle is the struggle to impose the right vision, the legitimate vision or viewpoint of the divisions, I remind you that the word *nomos* [. . .], which means 'law' (and which by the way is related to the word *numisma*, which means 'money'), comes from *nemo*, which means 'to cut', 'to cut up'.[18] What I want to show is that the political struggle, the struggle for the right, that is for the right (or right-wing) vision, which translates as orthodoxy, is a struggle to impose the dominant vision, not recognised as such, and so recognised as legitimate. It is the struggle for the right vision, the struggle for the right *nomos*, that is, for the right dissection.

Second session (seminar): the invention of the modern artist (3)

I return to my analysis of the symbolic revolution introduced by Impressionism, and more generally the question of the birth of the modern artist. During the previous sessions I looked into the question of the social conditions that favour a specifically symbolic revolution and what makes a revolution symbolic as opposed to political. I also

88 *Lecture of 18 April 1985*

started to describe the structure of the academic institution and show that the aesthetic principles that are manifest in so-called *'pompier'* art could in a way be deduced from the principles of the institution within which academic production was defined, so that I think the right concept to describe this art would be [. . .] 'academic art': this art finds its source in the structure of the academic institution. I reminded you that we can transpose this manner of seeing very widely: whether in literature, painting or criticism, for instance, it seems to me impossible and scientifically intolerable to study a discourse independently of the institutions within which it is produced, which does not mean that the internal study of a language has no justification (I am repeating this because, as we always have alternatives at the back of our minds, as soon as we insist strongly on one of the terms of the alternative, we appear to be denying the other term, as I was arguing just now).

We should take seriously Spinoza's dictum that we nearly always have 'two translations of the same sentence', one from an institutional viewpoint, the other from a discursive one.[19] When I said: 'It is scientifically intolerable . . .' it is because choosing [between studying the discourse and studying the institution] is scientifically absurd, unjustifiable and stupid. When we have two translations of the same sentence, it is best to study both, as Champollion knew. If we want to understand what was being said in the university in May 1968 – I always take this very simple example – we can note the speeches (collections of speeches from May '68 have been published)[20] and make an internal analysis, or study the system of agents who produced these speeches (that is, the academic institution), and it is true that they are two translations of the same sentence. But the formula 'two translations of the same sentence' also means that they are not using exactly the same language: if it was the same thing twice over, we would notice. So we need to study both things to notice that what was not explicit in some May 1968 discourse can be detected from the properties of the person who wrote it (for instance, he was a socialist in his youth, etc.). All that is very important from a purely methodological point of view.

In the case of a sociological study of the discourse of a poet, critic or politician, it is vital to know that what they say explicitly is only another manner of saying what they express through what they are, not in the ordinary biographical sense of the term, but in the sense that they are a position in a space, where their position says the same things that they say in their discourse. I have already said this at least three times [in the previous sessions], but I know that resistance to sociology is very strong; some of the things that I am saying here, taking advantage of the situation that I described at the beginning, some of what I consciously formulate, springs from my awareness of the following: since sociology encounters resistances analogous to those encountered by psychoanalysis, making sociology comprehensible means exploiting social techniques to circumvent these resistances and be understood by people who are hard of hearing, in the seventeenth-century sense,[21] because they don't want to understand, because they don't want to listen or because they understand only too well.

Sometimes changing the way of saying something does finally drive people to understand, or at least I hope so. What I am saying here is trivial, but the social forces that are behind the internal reading are so powerful that when we escape internal readings we fall abruptly into the most reductive kind of external reading, as a kind of recantation. (This is yet another very classical law of intellectual biographies: we escape one dogma only to surrender to the contrary one, whereas we should perhaps think of escaping the absurd alternative itself.) Despite the fact that we have had in France fifteen years of rampant, semiological internalist analysis, I am tempted to say that we should stand up for internal reading [*laughter*], because the same people who [in the 1970s] swore only by formalism, in an absurd reading of the Russian formalists (who weren't formalist at all),[22] are now going to launch into amateurish socio-critique which I shall find even more annoying than their previous formalism. I shall therefore be doubly heretical – which has happened to me more than once before. I am saying things that we are not supposed to, but they underlie so much of what I have to say, that in a way it is only honest to say them out loud.

Writing the history of a symbolic revolution

Analysing this symbolic revolution, I tried to describe the structure of the dominant symbolism against which the Impressionist rebellion, or more precisely the rebellion led by Manet, was directed. For this, I showed first that there was a structure, an academic institution, with its laws of operation, its syllabus, its modes of recruitment and training, its manner of shaping peoples' minds and therefore world views, and I went on show that you could in a way deduce from the institutional structures – which I exaggerated somewhat for the purposes of my demonstration – the properties of academic paintings that most clearly arise from an internal reading. In other words, the most specifically stylistic properties that tend to attract an internal reading – I cited Gombrich: 'Pompier art is the art of the finished' – seem to me to be directly linked to the institution where they are produced.

90   *Lecture of 18 April 1985*

This tentative demonstration was itself one phase of an ongoing argument where I was trying to answer questions that I myself had raised. I needed to make this detour through academic painting and its institutional foundations because the Impressionist rebellion is defined in part by the opponent that it defines itself against. Here again, this is a major law of social fields, and intellectual fields in particular: we are defined as much by our adversaries as by our own position, insofar as positions are diacritical. When people tell me that my vision of the social world is 'determinist', they forget that knowledge is liberating in its own right. To know, for instance, that there is no position in a field that is not defined diacritically by its opposition to other positions, whether immediately neighbouring or spatially distant, no position that is not defined objectively and therefore subjectively and symbolically, opens up an epistemological strategy: beware, not of your opponents, but of what your opponents impose on you through their very existence. This is an epistemological principle.

(In the history of thought, all the great Cartesians became Cartesian from fighting Descartes. This proposition may appear crude and cavalier: if there is a philosopher in the room, I shall be torn to pieces . . . But I think that it can be demonstrated, in particular in the case of Leibniz: what is most Cartesian in Leibniz comes from the fact that he spent his life disputing and making marginal annotations to the works of Descartes [. . .], and therefore being motivated by Descartes' problematics.) A field is a space where people exist in relation to one another, and the space itself is one problematic. From the moment that someone intrudes into the space, even a 'new philosopher', their existence creates a problem and provokes thought, although that thought may make people think askew, not to mention the fact that it may cause people to burn energy that could be more usefully employed elsewhere [*laughter*], which is something we always tend to forget. (On this subject, one of the major functions of a certain number of institutions is to divert attention from our true interests, to make us waste one of our most valuable resources, the time we have at our disposal. [. . .] In politics, any politician who masters the logic of the field – we see examples every day – knows that, to do something different, it is enough to direct your attention to a problem that they have concocted for the purpose. In intellectual circles, likewise, there is even a whole series of debates whose principle effect is to divert your attention away from the real issues. I might remind you of what I said last year[23] about the effects of the intrusion of journalism into scientific life; it is a perfect illustration of my argument [. . .].)

Lecture of 18 April 1985 91

In their very intention to subvert, then, the Impressionists were defined by the structures of the institution against which they took up arms, so much so in fact that that a whole 'enterprise' in the study of academic art and *pompier* art has taken its inspiration from the idea that the Impressionists were much less revolutionary than we think and that finally the *pompiers* had done practically everything that the Impressionists did, ultimately leaving the Impressionists with the sole achievement of passing off as art what for the *pompiers* and the academicians were merely sketches.[24] This thesis, developed by a certain number of people, is based on some very interesting research, such as that of Albert Boime which I have already discussed,[25] but they distort the evidence. This distortion is due to the fact that they are not asking the same question as I am: they are not recomposing the space in which an intellectual form operated – this is the great anachronism to which historians, who are the most anachronistic of scholars, frequently succumb.

Literary historians in particular believe that by far the best thing you can do for an author is to resuscitate him, make him live again, which is one of the pedagogical principles that also inspires philosophers, who try to show, for instance, the contemporary relevance of Plato. For Plato it occurs at an elementary pedagogical level, but this is no longer the case when people today talk of a 'return to Kant' or a 'return to Fichte'.[26] There is a tendency to think that the best way to approach a thought system from the past is to rethink it as we would think it in the present, which is to make it function in a field that does not concern it and can even be entirely different from the one that produced it. In fact, since such thought systems can function [in the contemporary field] through structural homologies that we are unaware of [. . .], rehabilitating a past opponent of the homologous ancestor of our contemporary opponent is a means of attacking a contemporary opponent. Struggles for rehabilitation then are of great importance. A whole book by Haskell (who will be coming to the Collège de France and who is really worth listening to) is concerned with rediscoveries in art.[27] Rediscoveries in art to my mind are always based on the present interests of the field: we only rehabilitate Caravaggio in terms of our present interests, in our present struggles against homologous or contradictory painters from the past. The source of these rediscoveries and rehabilitations then lies in the present.

We can see how anachronism is linked to the scholar's ignorance of his own interests, while he himself is situated in a field with its own issues and struggles: it is not neutral to rehabilitate Simmel today,[28] when all the specialists had already read him twenty-five years ago, or

92   *Lecture of 18 April 1985*

to call on the Frankfurt School now (here too I could speak at length).[29] As long as they are not made explicit, the aims that lie behind our strategies towards the past affect the very past that is being rehabilitated: the person dealing with this past does not know what he is doing in dealing with it, he does not know that the very source of his perception of the past is the transposition of structures of perception linked to one state of the field onto a field that was not structured in the same way and which therefore was not accompanied by the present structures of perception. [. . .] Any literary historian will say: 'We are perfectly well aware of all that', but re-read your average literary history and you will see . . .

So this work of recomposition is necessary. My own work on Manet and the Impressionists is obviously not exemplary. Since I am not a specialist and have not spent twenty years of my life studying the Impressionists, my research can do no more than give an idea of what you would have to do to answer the methodological requirements that I have myself established. But in formulating such requirements we are faced with an alternative: either we make all sorts of empty, ideal and abstract recommendations or we make a start on putting them into practice even though this will inevitably be partial and imperfect [. . .].

The surplus of educated men and the academic crisis

To come to my argument for today. To understand the Impressionist revolution, it seems to me that we need to understand the true structure of the organisation of the field of painting before this revolution, and investigate the specific factors that made it possible to call this structure into question. The idea I have in mind is that the field of painting has a structure of domination. In academic art there is the domination of a certain system of reproduction of the legitimate painter and his training, for instance. This structure had to be in a state of objective crisis for the symbolic questioning to succeed. This is the thesis that I have in mind, and it enables us to understand how difficult the symbolic revolution was. I said it at the outset: the Impressionists' vision of the world is so obvious to us that we are even tempted to say that it was not as revolutionary as all that, which is what conservative historians of painting are the first to say today; there is a series of exhibitions at the musée du Luxembourg and elsewhere along the lines of: 'Pompier art was not so bad, and after all is there such a great difference between such and such an academic painter and another, Impressionist painter, when one was the other's teacher?' We can wonder, without wishing to

Lecture of 18 April 1985

be at all polemical, why the conservative art historians have an interest in saying that the difference between the so-called revolutionaries and the so-called conservatives was not so great. I leave you to draw your own conclusions, but it is closely related to what I was saying just now.

To escape anachronism, we need to avoid projecting onto the past our present categories of perception and above all the interests linked to these categories of perception. There are no categories of perception without specific interests. I am not speaking of class interests, but of the very specific interests that are those of the art historian or the literary historian, in the individual subfield where they are involved and where the goal is to be distinct and distinguished, to claim, say, the name of a school, to call oneself a 'socio-critic', for example. For instance, over the last twenty years not a single literary critic or literary historian has written without claiming membership of some school. Take Roger Fayolle's book, *La Critique littéraire* (1964):[30] practically everybody is attached to a school (one of which is 'socio-criticism'). In this universe there are interests and issues which are not political: when I say 'conservative', I mean in relation to the specific logic of a field. Nonetheless, the question of the homology between the conservative position in a given field and the conservative position in the political field cannot be avoided. [. . .]

What I want to show, as I was saying, is that the possibility of a crisis in the art of the School is predicated on the possibility of a social crisis affecting the School itself, a condition that is necessary but not sufficient, empowering but not conclusive. The School had to be in crisis for the enterprise of symbolic subversion led by Manet to have any chance of succeeding. In other words the success of a symbolic revolution is conditional on the conjuncture of an objective crisis of the institutions on which the previous symbolic order was founded, and on a subversive enterprise able to articulate against these institutions the possibility of a different manner of creating. What I am saying here has a fairly general import and could be applied equally well to religious or philosophical prophecy, for instance.

I shall not repeat what I was saying finally about the properties of the academic art that Schlegel described in the texts that I quoted. I shall simply mention the crisis in the school system. Here I refer to studies by historians of education showing that in the years 1800 to 1850 the whole of Europe suffered from a crisis that we sometimes call 'an excess of educated men'. I refer to studies by Lenore O'Boyle, in particular in the *Journal of Modern History* of December 1970.[31] In the same review there is a whole series of studies of the surplus of graduates, the 1848 Revolution and the rise of a democratic left in

94 *Lecture of 18 April 1985*

Germany. This is, moreover, a topic whose traces we find in literature, in particular in Balzac: in *Un début dans la vie*, there is this theme of the surplus of graduates, with all the people who arrive in Paris, found a small review or a newspaper, etc. The topic was present then in the minds of the agents themselves (the equivalent today would be a topic like 'the young can't find employment').

In fact one problem in avoiding anachronism when analysing a period in the past is how to reproduce that kind of confused awareness that the agents had of the state of social affairs. This is extremely difficult because it was often subconscious. We can only grasp it through its literary expression, and therefore often already transposed into the form of a literary model. Yet it is very important to try, because the strategies of the agents, although they are driven by their sense of practice and their feel for the game, always owe some part of their complexion to diffuse and confused representations such as 'the word on the street' (for instance when we say today that professional opportunities for young people in electronics are 'dead and buried'). This was a problem that confronted us full on when Monique de Saint Martin and I were working on the bishopric in France.[32] In order to understand what moved someone to become a priest and then a bishop, for example in the 1930s at a time when recruitment to these vocations was at its lowest, we had to recompose not individual states of mind, not lived experience, but that kind of vague, diffuse perception, confusedly shared among a whole milieu, which is a real social factor. Moreover, one of the goals of the political struggle that I was discussing just now is to manipulate these diffuse 'representations'. This kind of record left by representations is not what historians call a 'mentality', nor is it a lived psychological experience, it is something very difficult to situate, for which I don't have a very precise term, but whose existence I think that we must at least acknowledge and which we must keep at the back of our minds, in order to understand, for instance, what is entailed in a choice, like a choice of vocation or the choice to become a writer.

This phenomenon of a surplus of educated men was then an objective fact that historians can reconstruct through statistics, and one which started to appear before it became an ideological theme. I think that the theme of the 'unemployed college graduate' only appeared in the 1880s. It became a very strong ideological theme in the period when compulsory schooling was being discussed. What had been merely a mood became a political issue. In fact the best term for it would perhaps be 'a kind of ideological mood'; Lovejoy, a great literary historian, spoke of the ideological *mood* of an era. *The Great Chain of Being* is a very great classic in the history of ideas.[33] In it Lovejoy

Lecture of 18 April 1985 95

studies the progress of the idea of a chain of being leading from the tiniest 'animalcules' right up to God. And thus he speaks of a *mood*, with all that this implies: moodiness, optimism, pessimism, 'things are going well', 'things are going badly', in fact everything that is in the air at the time, the *Zeitgeist*. This kind of mood is not a psychological construction but the product of a social process which is the object of the political analysis that I described this morning.

The education system and the field of cultural production

The surplus production of graduates has been studied by historians and I would like to comment on this: in this particular case my own research consists in making connections between things that have never been connected before. It seems to me that this raises the question of premature specialisation in the social sciences. Social scientists believe that they are acting scientifically when, imitating the more advanced sciences, they specialise, albeit, it seems to me, with entirely social motives (more popes need more divisions . . .[34]). But social science in specialising too early loses its links and connections. In this particular case my task is to make connections between the social history of the literary field and the social history of the academic and university field. Now since there are specialists of one and the other, who neither know each other nor read each other's works, and since there is no procedure for linking the two, the history of the university system is practically absent from literary history – which is quite astonishing, although I would of course be delighted if anyone could show me detailed proof to the contrary. They just don't make connections . . . well, yes, there are people who make connections, there are three of them in the lecture hall here, I know their work well (and to prove it, I shall constantly quote them), but I mean that normal people [*laughter*] practise literary history with no mention at all of the history of the education system. Pierre Louÿs, for instance[35] – it may have something to do with the fact that the leading subject studied by the children of the bourgeoisie ceased being exclusively the law and came to include the humanities as well. This is a crude link that I offer only as an example, for things are much more complicated.

I would simply like to say that, if we want to look for specific determinants, we could locate one of the basic foundations of the history of the literary field in the history of the education system. The education system produces a greater or a lesser number of producers (and I believe that it is through numbers, morphology, that specific evolutions

96 *Lecture of 18 April 1985*

in the fields of cultural production occur) and it produces them with properties of different types: it will variously produce lawyers, men of letters or scientists. This already gives us two forms of intervention in the process of production. The education system also intervenes in the process of consumption: the more school pupils there are, the greater the number of potential readers. It produces a potential public and this function must be acknowledged. And finally it also produces effects through the simple fact of having a relatively autonomous history in relation to strictly economic history: it can create effects of surplus production from simple inertia. The country needs engineers, for example, but the system continues to produce classicists . . .

This is the specific effect of the education system; there is a much longer period of transition, a time lag, a kind of structural delay compared with the changes in other universes. Which then introduces specific contradictions of a particular type. To summarise this topos, I should say that, among the major factors of change in the universes of cultural production, the specific contradictions of the university and school systems, as a space producing both producers and consumers, are no doubt the principal factor of transformation, in any case the principal mediating force of transformation which we have to take into account in order to understand the relation between economic changes (for instance economic crises) and specific crises, between economic revolutions and specific revolutions.

To continue: the transformations of the education system, under the influence above all of the changes in volume and social character of the student community, constitute one of the principal historical determinants of the fields of cultural production. The determinants operate principally through the direct effects that they exercise over the volume of the public – I refer you to another classic, Ian Watt's *Rise of the Novel*:[36] Ian Watt shows that the development of the novel cannot be understood without the changes in schooling in England which provided a mass, and particularly female, readership for the novels – and in the volume of producers, the surplus production that I just mentioned generating a number of innovations such as the creation of new genres or new disciplines. To enter these fields, these surplus producers had to create new positions that did not previously exist: they had to create new journals and new reviews. In thus creating positions that did not previously exist, they transformed the field. The relative overproduction of graduates which can be seen all over Europe in the first half of the nineteenth century, and which is the result of a growth in the proportion of children enrolled in secondary education, then sees its effect on the labour market multiplied by the mismatch between the dispositions instilled or reinforced by the education system and the new positions available in industry or administration. In other words, to understand this overproduction, we need to take into account the relation between the specific logic of the academic field, with the inertia that I have just noted, and the logic of the new economic space being constituted, where there is a demand for people different from those produced by the education system. These people are surplus, not absolutely, but relatively, because they have not been trained to meet expectations – all the historians have noted this.

This phenomenon was particularly striking in France, for three specific reasons. First, the youth of the administrators recruited during the Revolution. This was a situation analogous to the one that we have today:[37] there was a phase of massive recruitment, but once the young men were in place their successors had to face a long wait. The youth of the administrators recruited during the Revolution, the Empire and even the Restoration prevented the children of the petty and middle bourgeoisie from accessing careers in the army, medicine and administration for years to come. Individual biographies may help to make sense of this very general proposition (you might think of Stendhal, for instance). To which we may add competition from the aristocrats, who regained control of the administration and blocked the rising talents of the bourgeoisie. We can see already how specifically political factors came to intervene in the labour market: the Restoration allowed the aristocrats back into the race and they blocked the career paths of other people. This meant that a proportion of the young were jostled from rejection to rejection towards the literary field. Here we find Sartre's theme in *The Family Idiot*: 'You will be a writer, because you weren't able to be a doctor, etc.' We find the equivalent at the structural level of what Sartre describes at the level of a personal biography within the logic of the domestic group. Among these factors in France there is then the effect of the youthfulness of the administrative executives.

The second factor is centralisation, which concentrated the graduates in Paris, giving the phenomenon a particular intensity and visibility. This Parisian concentration is at the heart of the emergence of Bohemia and its associated institutions: the café, the innumerable little reviews. A third factor is to be found in another characteristic peculiar to France, that is, the elitism of a grande bourgeoisie particularly shaken by its experience of revolutions. There is no need to invoke some 'national character', but there is a national history that gives national traditions and which in France [led them to perceive] all forms of social mobility as a threat to the social order. In a famous

98   *Lecture of 18 April 1985*

speech to the Chamber of Deputies in 1836, Guizot denounced the teaching of the humanities as a threat to the political as well as the economic order. This grande bourgeoisie tried to reserve the leading positions, notably the upper echelons of the administration, for their own children, among other things by trying to preserve a monopoly of access to the *lycée*.

The morphological effects

These then are the structural conditions affecting the relations between the academic field and the economic field. This all results in a surplus production of graduates. Business and public administration cannot absorb this excess number of intellectuals, entirely nourished with the humanities, Latin, Greek and rhetoric, especially the most needy, those who entered the education system because it expanded, but who lacked the social connections tacitly required in the previous state of the system in order to obtain a position matching their qualification.[38] This is an extremely important point, because you mustn't believe – as sociologists commonly tend to – that social effects are a mechanical expression of morphological effects. The morphological effects, that is, the effects linked to volume, in Durkheim's language,[39] are only exercised when they are transformed into the terms of the specific social constraints of a given social space. One is only 'superfluous' (think of emigration) in relation to the often unspoken requirements of being present, of being there, of belonging, of being accepted as a member. Which means that the morphological effects are retranslated into the social effects of being an unwanted, abusive excess, of 'not being supposed to be there', leading to the *numerus clausus* and racial laws.

   It is very important not to indulge in morphologism. I am a Durkheimian, but I bring Durkheim up to date. I think that this is what makes sociology a cumulative science: using the best of everything that has been done in the past, but trying to improve on it, which is not always easy. Even doing as well is extraordinary. I always say that if all sociologists were as good as their predecessors, our sociology would indeed be great. We must do at least as well, and if possible, better, not at all to distinguish ourselves, but simply to make progress in research and see what in fact were the limits to the thinking that we are reactivating. In fact Durkheim set up his morphology in opposition to Marx: when Marxists invoke economic factors, they forget to take into account factors like the size of the population, their awareness of their numbers, and the problems associated with the density of social

Lecture of 18 April 1985 99

groups. For instance, in placing the morphological phenomenon at the origins of the division of labour, in *The Division of Labour in Society* (it is with the increase in numbers that the division of labour appears), I believe that Durkheim tends to turn the morphological effect into something natural. There will certainly be a Durkheimian to show us that Durkheim on at least one occasion did not say what I have just said; which does not mean that he did not do what I am saying most of the time [. . .].

This marks out the difference between the history of ideas or philosophy, and the historical use of concepts from the past: I do not study Durkheim for the pleasure of reading him, but in order to do something with him. There is a fundamental difference between the *lector* and the *auctor*. Durkheim tends to act as a demographer, he is the unacknowledged philosopher of the demographers; it seems to me that he is the one who tells the truth about the demographers' usage of demographic factors. Demographers, who are the nearest to natural scientists of all the specialists in the human sciences, tend to treat demographic factors as almost physical and inevitable factors which act in an infra-social, infra-historical or even a-historical fashion. I am talking about a crucial theoretical issue. Those who are not in the know may say: 'Whatever is he talking about?' But that's what a field is: when you belong to one, you know what the crucial issues are. Those who are not entirely at home or who are newcomers can say: 'Why is he lingering so long over a problem that seems of no consequence?' Yet it is a crucial issue. It is, for example, something that would separate me from people whom I otherwise greatly appreciate, like Emmanuel Le Roy Ladurie,[40] or certain demographers with a demographic-morphological and naturalistic vision of history: it is a history with no history that obeys the quasi-natural laws of demographics.

Despite appearances to the contrary, biological reproduction is not at all natural. Firstly, the effects of demographic phenomena are always retranslated. As facts, they are virtual: an increase in natality, a *baby boom*, has an impact only when socialised and historicised. It has to be relocated in a given context: people want more children and they don't get them, or they don't want any and yet they come [*laughter*], these two things don't have the same significance. It's very simple: if we find that there are 'too many', it is because we didn't want them. We cannot judge the effect of a demographic factor without knowing the field within which it comes to pass. It is the same with morphological effects: if we say that there are too many literary graduates, it is because we didn't want so many. In fact this is what Guizot says, but others might delight in the surplus of men of letters: if you think that men of

100　　　　　　　　　*Lecture of 18 April 1985*

letters will cause a revolution and that we must have a revolution, then you can never have too many literary men!

To sum up this argument, which I hadn't prepared, since when I was writing I assumed that it was well known, and didn't even refer to the argument: it is important to study the morphological factor, to pay attention to these numerical phenomena, while simultaneously remembering that the morphological effects are subordinate to the structure of the field where they operate ('correcting Durkheim', as I called it). Consequently, we can only predict the result of a morphological effect if we study both the history and the structure of the field within which it operates.

The effects of the morphological crisis on the academic field

To continue, briefly. The surplus of graduates was retranslated in the field of painting in the shape of a multitude of fanatical *rapins* (daubers) and the emergence of *la vie de Bohème* (the bohemian lifestyle). We could say that the fields of painting and the academic field responded to this morphological explosion with the creation of a whole series of studios: there was the 'Suisse' studio (after the name of its founder, not the country), and more generally all sorts of unknown or barely known painters set up training studios. There are then what ethnologists call secondary institutions that replicate the functions already fulfilled by the more official institutions. There is a whole crowd of more or less unsuccessful *rapins*. When we talk of an 'unsuccessful *rapin*', we are referring to a *rapin* already transformed by the laws of the field: an unsuccessful *rapin* is not simply a superfluous *rapin*, it is one who has tried to obey the laws of the field only to be rejected by the field. One of the effects of the field is to transform an aspiring *rapin* into an unsuccessful *rapin*, that is, into a potential specific revolutionary. Unsuccessful *rapins* are in this way a potentially destructive force.

I have been interpreting the morphological effect in sociological terms, but we still need to ask in what way these unsuccessful *rapins* are defined even in their own self-image of their rejection by the institution designating their failure. In other words, in order to fully understand these supernumerary, temporary, part-time extras of the painting world, we need to understand both that there is a surplus of production, and that the system has expanded, because a system that sees a crowd of new entrants arrive always wants to profit from them: they generate careers, and buildings and masters. But not everyone in the field has the same interest in the *numerus clausus*. I refer you to my

Lecture of 18 April 1985 101

analysis of the university:[41] within the university field people whose interest it is to subvert the system have an interest in seeing numbers increase. One of the allies of the dominated in every field is the sheer quantity of newcomers, because these are potential clients who, since they are imperfectly socialised, can be satisfied with inferior products that are disqualified in terms of the dominant norms of the field at the time. We see then that the treatment of these superfluous candidates will depend on the position that people hold in the field as it was previously constituted. The treatment that they will be subjected to will in fact depend on their fate in the field: will they succeed? Will they slip in through the back door? Through the side door? Or through the main entrance? If they fail, will they internalise their failure and live their lives as rejects or will they assume and claim rejection as their identity? In other words, will they transform their mark of shame into a badge of honour? [. . .]

What I have been describing in a rather hesitant and confused manner are the enabling conditions: there had to be a morphological crisis and it had to be translated into a social crisis, there had to be surplus production. I have also said that a symbolic process was needed for this crisis – which might have remained a morphological crisis – to be socially transformed before it could become a symbolic revolution. There was a historic moment to be seized in order to have a symbolic revolution. The problem that I am trying to formulate is the classic problem of Napoleon, the great man, causality and so forth.[42] Even if people did not really experience it as such, there was something of an opportunity for a symbolic revolution at hand. There was an objective crisis that could become a revolutionary crisis, if only someone could invent a critical discourse capable of convincing the *refusés* [the artists rejected by the Salon for painting and sculpture, which exhibited the works accepted by the Academy of fine arts] to set up the Salon des refusés (Salon for rejects) in 1863. It was unheard of. Just imagine if the candidates who failed the entrance exam for the École normale or the École polytechnique had mounted a 'School for failures'! [*laughter*] But it is not so easy when you are Manet in a studio like Courbet's to go in for the Salon des refusés. The smartest and more resourceful of the rejects, with higher social origins, were very hesitant about entering a Salon for rejects, because they wondered whether they would look more like a Salon or more like rejects [*laughter*], they were not sure whether to participate . . . Everyone was aware of this: Manet and Cézanne and others said they should be wary, because of the likelihood that creating a Salon des refusés was constituting a class that immediately designated everyone else in negative terms; and joining

102   *Lecture of 18 April 1985*

that class might be like wearing a bell round your neck for your whole career. All the more so because of agents like the critics who flocked to try to define the Salon des refusés as the Salon for genuine rejects. The issue became whether the refusés of the Salon were genuine rejects, [and if so], whether accidentally or on purpose: were they refusing to participate or were they refused entry?

This is a major problem for all symbolic strategies: how to be a heretic without appearing to have failed to be orthodox? Are heretics merely failed priests or can they manage to redefine their mission in such a way as to make orthodoxy appear to be a humdrum and depreciated vocation? Here we see that the symbolic struggle for classification – 'What is that?', 'What do you call that?' – becomes crucial. Interpreted in this way, criticism ceases to be an exercise in deciding who is right or wrong; it becomes a vital element in the struggle to define what people are doing and therefore who they are. It seems to me that it was more or less unthinkable for the revolution to succeed, despite all these favourable conditions, if the smarter of the revolutionaries had not been skilled not only at painting but also at controlling the representation that people in a position to say what painting was and who was good at it could make of their painting, and of their identity as painters, one of the crucial issues being the characters of the painters, in case they might be ridiculous imposters. You can see this struggle every day: are they ridiculous imposters, failures attempting to transfigure their failure in order to make us believe that they have chosen their destiny? Or are they eminent figures who believe in what they are doing? It is here that the person himself becomes most important – people said, 'Monsieur Manet is a very distinguished gentleman, look at his portrait, for instance. He seems quite eccentric, but he's not one of the great unwashed, he is obviously bourgeois, he expresses himself well and he is very well dressed.' The link between symbolic revolutions and political revolutions takes this path. Because the conciliatory tone of 'He is very well dressed' implies: 'He conforms in other respects and he is not a threat to the political order.' We will follow the story next time.

Lecture of 25 April 1985

First session (lecture): thinking the already thought – The liberty and autonomy of a field – A question about symbolic power – The political struggle as struggle for the legitimate vision – Symbolic capital and gnoseological order – The law as the right way to speak of the social world – The verdict of the State in the struggle for identity
Second session (seminar): the invention of the modern artist (4) – The psychosomatic power of the institution – The symbolic work of the heretic – Collective conversion – The strategies of the heresiarch – A revolution affecting the ensemble of the fields of cultural production

First session (lecture): thinking the already thought

Today I intend to tackle the problem of symbolic power more directly than I have so far. But first I would like to briefly explain and justify my manner of presenting this exposition. I imagine that many of you are feeling lost as you wander down a relatively non-linear path, which is difficult to follow with its multiple twists and turns, its U-turns and repetitions. I would like to explain why, independently of determinants which are beyond my control, I allow myself to indulge in this manner of presenting the results of my research.

I think that one of the difficulties of thinking about the social world comes from the fact that what we need to think has always already been thought in the very world that we are trying to think, and, in particular, in the words that we dispose of to describe it, so that every silence, every gap in our reflection, is immediately invaded by something unthought by us. For instance this morning, reflecting on what I was going to say today, I intended to say that the socio-professional categories established by INSEE are statistical categories 'guaranteed

104 *Lecture of 25 April 1985*

by the State'. If I had put it like that you would have immediately understood. I am not quite sure what you would have understood, but you would have understood something. Perhaps that a whole part of my exercise today would be an attempt to find out what 'guaranteed by the State' means: we could say that a currency is guaranteed by the State, there are words that are guaranteed by the State, and there are people who hold the power to guarantee words, currencies or things. So these four words – 'guaranteed by the State' – were about to pass my lips without being sifted or rethought, and yet they would have functioned in my mind and yours: there would have been an apparent communication without the object of that communication having been thought through by anyone. It is something of a classic philosophical theme (the Heideggerian theme of 'they think',[1] the Lacanian theme of 'it thinks',[2] etc.). But simply, when we are talking about the social, we feel less driven to rethink in personal terms the totality of what there is to be thought.

It is, for instance, very striking that English and American sociologists, who enjoy a magnificent tradition of philosophical reflection on language,[3] hardly ever make active use of it in their own practices, but resort to a generally very elementary positivism which would lead them to see what I am doing, for example, as a typically European hangover from metaphysical thinking, which in their eyes is something pre-scientific.[4] Social science calls above all for the philosophical *epoche*; this type of disposition rarely extends to radical critique. This results from a number of social conditions. To make these explicit I could, for instance, make you aware of what someone is claiming when they call themselves a 'sociologist' rather than a 'philosopher': of a sociologist, we do not expect the kind of exercise that I am practising, and even when they do practise this kind of exercise, which in fact we would call 'philosophy', we would not credit them *a priori* with profound and radical thinking.

I would like to show today, among other things, how, when philosophers in the 1960s rushed in, like poverty assailing the lower clerical orders, to deal with the problem of power,[5] they analysed the problem very poorly in my opinion, particularly for all the reasons I have given. Their thought was lacking in method and above all in any radical intent. Which means that even in the best of cases – and you know who I mean[6] – their questions showed insights that are very close to what I have to say, but with the considerable difference that separates intuitive gesturing towards where the problem lies from an analysis actually dissecting the problem. This dissection is a long, slow and rather pedestrian process, and we need to grant the sociologist what

Lecture of 25 April 1985 105

we are only too ready to grant the philosopher – it is even a true philosophical mantra in some traditions, such as (to put it simply) the Heideggerian or Wittgensteinian traditions – that is, the kind of pedestrian repetition, inch-by-inch progress, U-turns and micro-mania that home in on the minutest details. We don't allow sociologists to do this, whereas, I repeat, they need it even more [than philosophers or other scientists]: when we think of mathematical problems, very little pre-digested thought comes to crowd into the gaps in our thinking, for the very good reason that mathematics exists in a pure universe: when we think about something social, as I showed with the example of the State guarantee, every fissure is immediately plastered over. Language itself rushes in to plug the gaps.

To return to my manner of proceeding: you can be sure not to leave here having heard a formal lecture. A formal lecture is the *doxa* formulated as dogma (the two words share the same root[7]), that is, a constructed discourse foregrounding its architecture, staging its own logical structure in a generally linear form: firstly, secondly, thirdly; the old structure that, whether you know it or not, is the plan of Saint Thomas Aquinas' *Summa Theologiae* and the plan of Gothic architecture.[8] The tripartite division is an old structure that is ingrained in our minds. I have no quarrel with this sort of thing, it has its uses, but I think that it is not suited to a lecture course; a lecture course is not an *ex cathedra* address [*laughter, no doubt because Bourdieu is placed in the situation of giving an* ex cathedra *address*]. To my mind, a lecture course is not a monolinear structure with an introduction and a conclusion, it is more a network of connections where we can travel in any direction, passing through the same point several times but starting out from very different points, and thus experiencing very different effects, with the most difficult task being to synthesise all the perspectives obtained from this journey through the labyrinth. To encapsulate this in a formula, we could say that the formal lecture contains its own formulation, and this is one of the things that I am going to discuss today: obeying the formal rules is always a manner of responding to censorship, it is also always a manner of imposing censorship while using form to hide aspects of the content that would not be speakable in a different form.[9] I think therefore that there is an affinity between a certain content needing to be transmitted and a certain discourse. (As I stated at the outset, I cannot disguise the fact that there is an element of apology and self-justification in what I am arguing; at the same time I think that our individual drives may be socially determined and sometimes have a social function that we are unaware of.) What I am saying is as old as the world: it is the old Socratic discourse on succinct

106 *Lecture of 25 April 1985*

dialogue as opposed to the verbiage of the Sophists. It seems to me that I could not say what I have to say using the ordinary forms – or rather, if I could say it, it would be something quite different. In fact what I have to say does exist, or I hope that it will, in book form.

Given that the social world is always pre-thought, I shall often refer to the notion of *nomos*, insofar as to think is to break the *nomos*, that is, not only 'takeaway' thinking, but compulsive thinking. The sociologist cannot be a 'nomothete'[10] who decrees a single mode of thinking. Since he is analysing the nomothetic effect, he is not well placed to exercise it. But things do not have a single meaning; it is perhaps also because he is disposed to hold a nomothetic discourse that he is more prepared to reflect on the *nomos* than the others are. That is what I had to say to start with, perhaps to help you better understand my teaching and thus be less lost, or at least differently lost, in the labyrinth.

The liberty and autonomy of a field

Now to deal with two questions that I have received. The first (which dates from two months ago) deals with the relation between the autonomy that characterises a field, and liberty. The question is very elliptical; opposing autonomy and liberty, it asks: 'What is liberty in a field?' I have to do something with that, it almost needs a dissertation [*laughter*]. I shall say what I understand by the question, while taking care to reformulate it. What would seem to me to be a very good question is: 'Is there a link between the autonomy of a field and liberty?' When I say that the artistic field obtains its autonomy (which is what I am discussing in the second session) or that a scientific field establishes itself as such, 'autonomy' means both independence and at the same time obedience to its own laws: the fundamental laws of a field are those that characterise it specifically; entering a field means obeying the specific laws that go to make up the field and therefore benefiting from a kind of independence from the external determinisms that are in force outside it.

If we put it like this, we can see that progress towards the process of differentiation and autonomisation in the social universes that I have previously mentioned can be seen, in terms of a philosophy of history, as progress towards multiple liberties (this would take too long to develop, so I prefer not to bog myself down with that). That said, the liberty won collectively by a field, for instance the artist's freedom from economic forces or the scientist's freedom from political forces, is linked to institutions which are themselves limiting. The truly stupid antinomies that people establish between liberty and determinism, liberty and obligation, are worth a dissertation: a field liberates through its obligations. The scientific field, for instance, imposes specific obligations, those of scientific competition and rivalry – and a law of the scientific field is that you can only be a winner there if you use the weapons of science, and so on. Liberty is simultaneously obligation. It is the institution of a specific obligation that grants freedom from determinism of other kinds.

I think that the more autonomous universes there are, the more numerous the liberties (you can leave one field to enter another, for instance). I shall say no more about this, but this should be enough to make things awkward for those who, when they call my work into question, start by telling me 'You are a determinist', and asking me 'Why are you a determinist?' (I shall stop here, for to continue would be to completely lose track of my argument, which is already tortuous enough.)

A question about symbolic power

The second question is too long and elaborate for me read it out in full. It has filled me with optimism because it proves to me that, despite the twists and turns of my labyrinth, I feel that I have been very well understood by a certain number of people in the audience. It is so good that it anticipates what I intend to say and I shall reply to it as I pursue my argument.

It deals first with the term 'symbolic': 'How do we define it?' On this point, I shall first make a scholarly reply, referring you to a paper that I gave in 1972 and which was published in 1977 ('Sur le pouvoir symbolique', in *Annales*).[11] This article should meet the expectations of those who wish to know what I see as the traditional theoretical, philosophical foundation of what I was arguing last time and shall be arguing today. In this article I try to reconstruct the field of possible theoretical positions on the problem of power, which is, I believe, an exercise that helps control our reflection, study and research: whether we realise it or not we are always thinking in relation to a theoretical field, and the fact, firstly, of knowing this and secondly of articulating it explicitly, instead of letting a few major references (such as Marx) impose themselves, does have its pedagogical value.

It is also, I believe, very important to distinguish the manner in which we conduct research from our manner of teaching, and often of philosophising (insofar as philosophy is closely linked to the practice

108 *Lecture of 25 April 1985*

of teaching). It is obvious that I did not think of symbolic power [in the way in which it is presented in the article], that is, I did not think: 'There is a Kantian type of position, where symbolic forms are instruments that compose the real (Kant, Cassirer); there is a type of structuralist thought that sees the symbolic as systems of difference imbued with significance (Saussure, Lévi-Strauss); and then there is the Marxist tradition, which speaks not of "the symbolic" but of "ideology", which is the instrument of power and its legitimisation. Given these three positions, could we not make a synthesis and construct a definition of the symbolic as the instrument of construction of reality, fulfilling its function of construction through its systematicity and exercising through this a function of legitimisation?' But it is obvious that we do not conduct research in this way: it is after the event that we can establish a somewhat mythical genealogy of our own thinking, as in biographies or in pre-capitalist societies where we invent more or less mythical ancestors to structure our social identity. Most often when they refer to the past, philosophers and sociologists or any other kind of thinker are involved in this kind of exercise. It is no accident if Anglo-American thinkers speak of their 'founding fathers': it is exactly like the mythical ancestry of a tribe. We have to take these genealogies seriously, with their social significance, but we must always be rather wary of their truth value. In this particular case, I think that what I did had a certain truth value, but it is not the truth of the research that led to what I am going to argue. That said, this is a way of answering the first question: if you want a rather scholarly, academic definition (what is the meaning that you attribute to the word 'symbolic'?), I cannot do better than refer you to this article.

And then, my questioner asks about the theory effect: 'You said that Marx had created the most considerable theory effect in the twentieth century. How do you explain the theory effect of Marxism and its importance?' I shall return to this (not today, which would take me too far; and I am already anticipating greatly what I intend to say later), but in discussing the theory of classes, as I have said on several occasions, we must go beyond the alternative of the realist definition, according to which the classes are the product of acts of social construction. In fact a construction has all the more chance of succeeding socially the more it has an objective base, the more it is founded in things themselves. I think that if the Marxist theory has such a powerful constructive force, it is because it followed, however crudely, the dotted lines that were out there in reality: it was not bad at all compared to what had come before it . . . So the exceptional theory effect that it has had derives in part from its relatively strong truth value.

Lecture of 25 April 1985 109

The third point, which is very important (it leads into two pages of reflection), is the problem of defining the State and the role of the State in the symbolic struggle. I shall quote just one sentence. After noting that I insisted on the legitimising function of cultural power, and in particular the way that the academic diploma acts as a guarantee on behalf of the State, the questioner asks: 'Should we not generalise this and show that the State guarantees much more than the academic diploma?' Then, taking this perhaps to the extreme, he writes: 'The State is absolute self-legitimisation, all States are totalitarian in their way.' This is not false, but I would never put it that way. Firstly, this is common currency at the moment: the word 'totalitarian' is in fashion this year and we are not at all sure what it means.[12] Those who like to use it are obviously trying to produce political effects disguised as scientific effects, or rather logical effects, that is, political effects that take on the guise of scientific effects: 'grammatology', 'archae-ology', 'semiology',[13] etc. This happens a lot in our own universe, and I believe that we must be very wary when we venture down that route.

The political struggle as struggle for the legitimate vision

To return to the political struggle which I was discussing last time, I shall do this by illustrating what I was saying just now about meta-discourse. I consider that to make progress in sociological reflection we need to pass several times through the same point. I would also say that we very often, it seems to me, have to repeat the same thing several times over, practising a sort of polyglot logic that consists in constantly changing our style of speaking, to realise afterwards that we have said the same thing in several different ways and discover all the properties that we revealed successively, because as we changed words we changed universes and saw different aspects of the object. I think that this manner of proceeding is fundamental. It is not simply a professional or personal tic, it is a method, it is a systematic manner of thinking. For instance, the usage that we can make of passing through Greek, Hebrew or Arabic and etymological analysis are part of this strategic method. Thus we can say in turn 'the political struggle', or 'the struggle for symbolic power, 'the struggle for legitimacy', 'the struggle for knowledge and recognition', 'the struggle for the imposi-tion of theory as *nomos*, that is, of vision as a principle of division', 'the struggle for the imposition of the principle of division and even of dominant division' or – and it amounts to the same thing, ortho-doxy

110   *Lecture of 25 April 1985*

meaning 'right vision' – 'the struggle between orthodoxy and heresy'. All these manners of speaking refer to theoretical universes that can be experienced as different, and I think that it is by combining them that we can produce an integrating effect. In fact it was clear just now, when I described this kind of network thinking, that one of the functions of this procedure, using multiple passages through the same point, was to try to multiply the viewpoints in the hope of achieving a certain type of totalisation.

The political struggle may be described as a struggle to impose the legitimate vision of the space within which that struggle takes place. In other words, it is a struggle to impose the right vision of the divisions of the space within which people are divided, among other things, by their visions of the right divisions of the space. This struggle would be absolutely gratuitous if changing people's visions and viewpoints did not go some way towards changing their world and their lives. Changing our vision of the social world is not a gratuitous or a ridiculous goal; symbolic struggles are not symbolic in the sense of saying: 'It doesn't really matter.' Symbolic struggles are not 'symbolic' in this sense of the word: there are real issues at stake because in changing our vision, and the theory that underlies that vision, we can change the real structures to some extent.

Why? One of the reasons – and there are many others – is because changing our vision of the divisions means giving ourselves some chance to change the way that all the agents view these divisions, and when that happens, the divisions themselves may change because the agents may form different groupings. Changing our vision is therefore a means of changing groups by changing the ways in which we recompose our groups and our alliances. That can operate at every level, for instance at the level of recomposing groups of classes: will the middle classes join a group with the proletariat? This was the problem for Marxists at the end of the nineteenth century, and changing the vision of the petits bourgeois – telling them: 'You are only . . .' (I don't know what they tell them in such a case) – is a way of encouraging them to join groups on one side or the other. There was a time when, in election periods, executives suddenly became solicited by candidates for election, who disagreed over how to address them, that is, in which direction to push them. This is a typical example: if you manage to convince them that their real position is on one side rather than the other, there is some chance that they may go where you want them to. If you change their vision and its rationale, the visions 'represented' can then help to change the real divisions. May I remind you that I explained last time that we don't pass automatically from practical visions to

Lecture of 25 April 1985   111

'represented visions' – the term 'represented visions' draws attention to the fact that representation is a process.

We can use physical demonstrations to change the visions represented ('Everyone to the Bastille!', 'Tradesmen: man the guns!'), or use theoretical, abstract demonstrations at a discursive level. In which case it will consist, for instance, in changing words, changing the way of describing something. There is, for instance, a whole struggle over whether we should speak of the 'working classes', the 'proletariat', the 'workers', 'social partners', 'dangerous classes' or 'humble classes' ('humble' [French *modeste*] is a splendid word: it is one of the finest euphemisms in the social language), and so on. Often in imposing a word we can gain a victory by winning over the people who recognise themselves in this word.

These strategies whereby a group uses demonstrations to transform its vision of itself and the vision that others have of it may be either individual or collective. I have been highlighting the collective strategies, but there are obviously individual strategies, for instance the strategies of self-presentation described by interactionist sociologists, particularly Goffman.[14] That said, when you read the 'births, marriages and deaths' column in the papers,[15] and you note the importance of the strategies of self-presentation and representation, you immediately see the political dimension that the interactionists, who rely on an inter-individual perspective, always forget. A political dimension is present in the most individual strategies, for example in those that consist in changing your name. (Here I am presenting only what you might call the theoretical aspect of my analyses, but it should be obvious, I must insist for those who might not be aware of it, that what I have to say is based on statistical and ethnographic research, and is not at all speculative.) Someone could make a major study of the changes: when did a particular category change its name, and what names did it move towards? Changes in first names (people who were called Nathanael at eighteen but are called Jacques at thirty) would also be very interesting, as would the use of pseudonyms in the literary domain. In many societies, the transmission of surnames and first names is a vital issue.

In pre-capitalist societies, capital is present above all in symbolic form. As the economic capital accumulated is relatively weak, and what can be transmitted and reproduced is essentially honour, prestige and esteem, there are strategies concerning the transmission of surnames and above all first names. I have described in *The Logic of Practice* the strategies that oppose brothers, in a family, in obtaining the name of a father or a grandfather for their elder son.[16] To show that my analyses are not based on speculation, I can give you an example: let us suppose

Lecture of 25 April 1985

that I am the elder son of a family where there is a very prestigious Abdeslam. My younger brother had a son first, I have only a daughter, which is a catastrophe – I cannot pass the first name Abdeslam down to her! (The fact that names are only transmitted through the male line is a problem: it would suffice for it to be transmitted through the female line as well for a whole lot of the fundamental strategies that guide our families to be transformed. If the names of the nobility were transmitted through the female instead of the male line, aristocratic strategies would be transformed; the stakes are very high.) But the name is transmitted only through the men, my brother's children were all sons, I have only daughters [*laughter at this excess of misfortune*], but I am the elder son (so I do have some advantage!). My brother appropriates the prestigious first name before me, by calling his son Abdeslam: this is a catastrophe, because biology is the one thing that we cannot alter. There could, however, be negotiations to agree that when the elder son eventually has a son, the younger brother returns the rightful first name. Since my studies of Kabylia, we have found similar things in the sixteenth-century Italian Renaissance and other very different societies.

Among the practical strategies there are obviously all the strategies of alliance. When I was talking just now of the petite bourgeoisie and the proletariat, I raised the question of alliance and misalliance in political terms. In the case of families, the question is: 'Who to marry?' It is a problem of *diacrisis*, of judgement, of correct perception (a particular alliance is good/not good). The matrimonial alliance is a practical procedure for constructing groups, it is a form of demonstration, and indeed a grand marriage is a moment for processions, that is, 'theories' – the word *theoria* also means that we make a display:[17] we show off our family relationship. If there are processions for funerals and marriages, it is because processions are theoretical acts whereby we show and make a display of our group; we are saying: 'Look at all the relatives we have here, coming from far and wide, there are the As and the Bs, and our cousins the Cs . . .' I have been speaking of tribes, which sounds exotic, but the funeral of Monsieur de Wendel that I analysed in my study of business managers follows exactly the same logic.[18] There was a hierarchy in a space: the hierarchy of the families was projected into that space in the form of the hierarchy of the processions.

In fact a 'theory' is a theoretical discourse. It has been thought through in order to be seen and the principles of its division must be carefully respected: you cannot take up any old place in the procession. Protocol dictates in what order the people will be on show. This is not

Lecture of 25 April 1985 113

its only function: protocol also helps to avoid conflicts over the order of display, because your position in a space gives an indication of your place in the hierarchy, you can't mess about with it, these things have been made visible and objectified. The Panathenaea and all those things that you know and on which you have unconscious opinions have got to be understood through the logic of what I have just said.[19] (I have deliberately proceeded as I said I would just now: I have tried to present you as rapidly as possible with an image of the network that I am now going to run through more slowly, because I think it is useful for you to have a global overview of the network constantly present in your minds, while I am exploring it in more detail today.)

To recapitulate, briefly. Political life is a struggle to preserve, change, or transform people's visions. This struggle is not gratuitous, because by changing visions we have an opportunity to change real divisions. If this is so, it is because there is a real and substantial link between words and things, between, on the one hand, the way we designate individuals, things and groups, and on the other hand the form and even the existence of these groups. Another consequence of this is that there is a political process which we might call 'worldmaking' (after the title of a book by Nelson Goodman, a contemporary American philosopher),[20] a process of fabrication of the world, or at least the visible universe. This process of worldmaking is a creative, poetic work, in the etymological sense.[21] I am not playing with words: in many archaic societies the 'chief' was the poet, the person able, using the most intense, elliptical and powerful language, aimed at the norms of reception of the given group, to state the right way of perceiving the world. He was in particular the person who could give meaning [to the world and its events] on behalf of the tribe, especially in those moments when the tribe no longer knew what to think or which saint to pray to. In a situation of crisis, for instance when there was a dramatic conflict between the rules and a situation which demanded the suspension of the rules, it was the poet who found an acceptable way for the group to say that the rules could be transgressed; in other words, he was the manager of their collective bad faith. In all groups – it took me quite some time to realise this – the management of collective bad faith is something crucial: an eminent function of many spokesmen is to tell the group that things which they are well aware of are not what they think and say they are, in moments when it is vital for the group to disguise what they know so well.

114 *Lecture of 25 April 1985*

Symbolic capital and gnoseological order

Part of the political process is a verbal process, and so discourse is very important. The spokesman is at once working with words and practising a symbolic manipulation of groups and practices, as I said when I discussed demonstrations.[22] We could establish a kind of lexicology of the language of power. Referring to Benveniste's magnificent book, *Dictionary of Indo-European Concepts and Society*, that I always quote with profound respect, we can see that what is at stake in 'power' derives from two roots: the root of 'to see' and the root of 'to say'.[23] This does not actually prove anything, since power tends to define itself anyway as the power to make you see and make you believe, but it is interesting. [In the previous lecture] I spoke of *crisis, diacrisis*, discernment, discrimination and decree. The crucial word is obviously 'sacred'. I shall return to this in a moment: the person who makes you see is someone who divides, and to divide is to separate, put to one side, put out of reach; you immediately recognise the theme of Durkheim's 'sacred', although in this context it takes on an entirely different function.[24] (In passing, I hope that this will confound those who see Durkheim and Marx as antithetical.)

Following the logic of a Durkheimian analysis of the sacred as separation, we can understand how power, including political power based on economics, can take the form of the power of separation and division described by the most traditional sociology of religion. One crucial notion is obviously the notion of the limit: the limit, restriction or definition, the boundary between groups. This is the theme of the *rex* – *regere fines, regere sacra*: the king defines the limits. Now the limit, *limes* in Latin, is the threshold which, in Kabyle society for instance, is the fundamental division: it is the house, the opposition between inside and outside, masculine and feminine, and these thresholds are immersed in ritual. Rites of passage are nearly always the crossing of a threshold, and it is no accident if Van Gennep, when he characterises rites of passage, defines periods such as preliminal, post-liminal and liminal, etc.[25] The word *limes* is a central word and clearly takes its place in the logic of the sacred.

The second root is the root for 'to speak'. To speak is to say, and Benveniste notes that the judge is the *iudex*,[26] he who states what is just, what is right, what is the law. He notes also the relation between *dico* ('I say') and *dike* ('justice'):[27] the judge is the person who says. To conclude this etymological game I shall make a link between the rule (*regula*) and the king (*rex*), as well as *regio* (the king it is who divides up the regions and defines the boundaries between those regions).

Although I shall not discuss them, there are also Arabic roots that follow this pattern ('a fraction', 'to fracture', to divide', etc.). I have mentioned this because I shall continue to explore this semantic field, and now that I have drawn your attention to these things, I think that you will constantly keep such important links in mind.

The political process, then, addresses the just perception of the social world, and I could define political sociology – in a way different from the Sciences Po definition – as a sociology of the symbolic forms of perception of the social world, and thereby as a sociology of the construction of groups. In other terms it is a sociology of the construction of symbolic capital insofar as it is categorial, that is, it addresses categories. I can make another series of equations: 'symbolic capital' can be equated with 'legitimacy' and 'social identity known and recognised', therefore with 'recognition, or acknowledgement'. According to this logic, symbolic capital would be both the principal goal sought, and the principal weapon and instrument of the political struggle as a symbolic struggle to impose the legitimate perception of the world. Symbolic capital is something that is 'seen to be seen'. It is the word *nobilis* that means 'to be visible' (as opposed to 'obscure'), to be 'noteworthy' or 'notable'. In the intellectual field, to have symbolic capital is to be known and famous; and to be known is to have credit, that is, to be credited with credibility, to inspire confidence. If I weren't afraid you might think I was just rambling, I would be tempted to take you through Benveniste's magnificent philological study of the root *fides* as confidence granted, but above all as confidence received by the person to whom we grant it, which is what Weber, in a different context, calls charisma; it seems to me that Benveniste's *fides* is an ethnological description, based on the Indo-European lexicon, of what Weber described with his notion of charisma.[28] (I am mixing the lexicons on purpose, but scientific study very often consists in taking words that are separated like the basins of a river by obstacles linked to our habits of thinking and conditions of learning, or to ritual antagonisms – such as Weber v. Marx – and making them communicate.)

Symbolic capital then is about being seen-to-be-seen, being known-to-be-known, being noteworthy enough to be able to influence our ways of seeing. Someone known and recognised as legitimate is credited with a power authorising him to pronounce on the nature of the social world. He is trusted to know the social world, people refer questions about the social world to him: he is its spokesman. To quote Benveniste again, he is the person that they give the *skeptron* to. The sceptre was in fact given to the orator when he was due to make a speech.[29] This symbol of statutory authority meant that his speech

116   *Lecture of 25 April 1985*

was authorised and that he was authorised to speak. And therefore his speech bore authority and would be performative, meaning that you had to believe it and obey: what he had to say was worthy of belief. There is then a link (and this is at the heart of the notion of symbolic capital) between being seen-to-be-seen, being-visible and making-visible. Symbolic capital, as the fact of being known and recognised, implies an ability to command knowledge, to impose knowledge and recognition of that knowledge. I should have said this at the outset: when you are involved in the realm of power, you are entirely engaged in the problem of knowledge. Deep down, the problem of power, and political power, is a gnoseological problem, a problem of knowledge. It asks: 'How do we know the social world?' And in the case of things social, the act of knowledge is necessarily a political act. We must then think of the political as a problem of knowledge, and those of a philosophical disposition must have realised that the alternative forms of knowledge of the social world that I have examined are the classic alternatives in the domain of knowledge of the natural world.

Legitimate knowledge, which is the privilege of the *nobilis*, the person known, and recognised and acknowledged, is a division that carries the force of law. This is the meaning of *nomos*, which is rendered as 'the law' in [Greek] dictionaries or translations, and which comes from *nemo*, 'to cut', 'to dissect'; it is in fact the same root that generates not only 'judgement', but also the fact of 'separating'. The French word 'cerner' ('to outline'), which we find in 'to discern', means both 'to see' and 'to separate'. The *nomos* is the discourse of power, that is, the discourse of the man in power, whose visions create actual divisions, and who has the power to put his visions into practice, so to speak.

I want now to explain what is the main issue in what I have been trying to say. The sociology of symbolic forms, then, becomes a science that studies power over vision, which is a power over the structuring of groups. The dominant vision is not recognised as dominant, but recognised as legitimate and orthodox. Orthodoxy is a powerful vision, expressed in words endowed with authority, that has the power to put itself into practice. Here I could once more cite Benveniste who shows in the case of the word *kraino*, which indicates the force and power of the king, that the power of the king is the power to make things exist merely by nodding his head in approval.[30] It is the king, when he says 'yes', who puts things into practice, making them exist. The word of power par excellence is obviously the royal command or edict, that is, the word that encapsulates the power to make the group exist. To use a Kantian metaphor,[31] it is not an *intuitus derivatus*, a descriptive vision, but an *intuitus originarius*, a vision which, like the divine vision,

Lecture of 25 April 1985 117

makes things exist. In other words, the analogy between the Homeric king of Benveniste's analysis and a god makes sense when we see that both have in common what Kant ascribed to God, that is, a vision with creative power: I nod my head in approval and I make a new region or a new country exist; I shake my head in disapproval, and I deny their existence.

The law as the right way to speak of the social world

Manipulating words is a trial of strength and is the quintessence of royal power – it is the ordinary sense of the word *nomos* – it is the law, which, as objectification and codification of symbolic power and powerful vision, is a kind of powerful sociology. The law is a sociology that has the force of law. Of course the sociologists will remind us that there is both law and custom: you cannot base a sociology of the medieval Church on canon law, although historians (and anthropologists too) often do. English and American anthropologists denounce as 'legalism' the propensity to treat the orthodox discourse on the social world as if it were social reality. This orthodox discourse may be the law, codified and written, or it may be habitual and customary, or even quite simply the discourse of the elders (the best informer is often an old man, that is, an official who delivers the official discourse, what they tell a stranger in public as opposed to what the women say, which in general is unofficial, secret and hidden, whether economic or sexual).

The law is a discourse made visible, public and publishable. It is an objectification, and in objectification there is the idea of publicity and publication, *Öffentlichung*, making visible and putting on display something that can be seen by everyone, and is openly announced to everyone. Similarly, ceremonies, theories and processions [make visible, put on display and announce openly]. We could refer to the Durkheimian opposition between the religious – practised in broad daylight, for everyone to see, in the presence of the whole group, men, women and children together – and the magical – practised by women at night, in order to dominate their menfolk, or to avenge themselves, for instance.[32] The orthodox, official legal discourse then is both objectified and published, the quintessence of publication being writing, and particularly the printed writing that renders the legitimate discourse on the social world accessible to all ('ignorance of the (printed) law is no excuse'). The discourse of the law is published and publishable, and in societies where a State exists, it is guaranteed by the State. Being guaranteed by the State, as is the currency, it enjoys a kind of gold

118   *Lecture of 25 April 1985*

standard. The State says: 'Behind this article of the law, there is public force, the power to sanction, imprison and physically punish.'

But the important thing is that the law is the way that society represents itself. (It's awful, I get the feeling that when I reach a certain degree of reflection I am making a confession . . . [*recording inaudible*].) The juridical vision is the vision that a social universe has of itself. The struggle between the sociologist and the jurist is absolutely fundamental to the existence of sociology: Durkheim fought all his life against philosophy on the one hand and on the other hand against the faculties of law, whose object of study he wanted to appropriate. In the eyes of the jurists, the absolute limit was, if you think about it, the sociology of law: since the law sees itself as the discourse of legitimacy there is no justification for trying to study how it comes to be produced, because the law proclaims how things should proceed. In its way, the discourse of law is the discourse of power. This is an approach that Goffman uses when discussing the psychiatric discourse in psychiatric hospitals. In his splendid book, *Asylums*, he says that the discourse of the inmates is a weak discourse, relying on ruses and defences (like the feminine discourse in masculine societies); it is a clandestine discourse, complicated and partial. It is confronted by the discourse of the psychiatric institution, which is coherent, public and official, published in books and validated by science.[33] The inmate cannot struggle; at the very least he is ill-situated to do so. In a way, the law is the proper description of the social world. It is the legitimate viewpoint, the dominant viewpoint. This is what the *nomos* means.

The verdict of the State in the struggle for identity

The law then is an objectified and consecrated vision, a codified perception of the social world guaranteed by the State: it is a verdict, *veri dictum*, 'something spoken in truth'. For those of you who heard what I said about Kafka:[34] it is the verdict of society, with the analogy between the social and God that Durkheim made explicit,[35] making Durkheim seem ridiculous although he wasn't really. The law tells you what you really are. It is your civil status. This is another giveaway phrase. Someone's civil status is what the State says of them, what the State notes in them. A social agent has many properties – physical, physiological and psychological – but their identity as defined by the State retains only a select few of them. What is written on an identity card is made public, official and universal.[36] It can, like a currency, circulate abroad to be shown to anybody, to be presented on demand.

Lecture of 25 April 1985   119

This sort of socially constructed identity is the verdict of the social world on the individual.

What I would like to show next time is that the verdict makes sense only in a universe where there is constant negotiation over identity: one of the means for the social world to put a stop to the permanent struggle for identity that consumes so much of men and women's time in certain societies is the verdict, the civil status. In a book that has just been published, an American anthropologist[37] shows that social units are a constant target of transactions by social agents who modify social units through representation, and through verbal action on representation and practices, for instance those that involve passing from one group to another or creating alliances between groups which should not be allied. Societies where the power of codification is less developed, where one's civil status is less brutally imposed, leave an infinitely greater place than ours for different strategies in the struggle for identity. This means that these societies are most instructive. Following this logic, ethnology becomes vital because it enables us to see close up something that is less obvious in our societies [and remains clearly visible only in certain quite specific places]. In Proust, for instance, the struggles in and around the salons are very similar to struggles over which tribe you belong to. But in our societies there is a State that states clearly what people are, which gives them titles, titles of nobility that are ultimately more or less guaranteed by the State (you only have to see the number of ENA graduates who are aristocrats), deeds to property or educational qualifications, which make up a civil status.

A State that does all this with a relatively strong symbolic force blocks our strategic games over good and bad visions of the world. That said, this play for identity still exists in our societies, particularly in the intellectual field. This universe has won its autonomy from the State: the State can still intervene (autonomy is always relative), but this interference does not have the force of law and can even bring discredit when they attempt to bestow credit, so that the freedom left to strategies of 'bargaining' over identity is greater than in other universes. The good places to study what I am talking about then will be societies like Kabyle or Islamic society, places where the codification of positions and social identities is relatively weak, the salons in Proust or the intellectual field. That said, this struggle is permanent and exists even in the most codified regions of the social space. We can, for instance, challenge the dominant codification of professions and say: 'Personally, I think that the principal codification is in terms of gender', or 'I think that the principal codification is in terms of regions', and then call for 'Free Occitania'.[38]

120 *Lecture of 25 April 1985*

Second session (seminar): the invention of the modern artist (4)

I shall start by making the connection [with the first session]. I was saying just now that there was a link between being seen-to-be-seen and the power to make visible. To experience it concretely we only have to take the example of the literary field where the consecrated individual, as we call him, has the right to consecrate, by writing a preface or one of the other many symbolic acts that are the daily bread of our intellectual life. He consecrates, for instance, by publishing or recommending publication in a prestigious place (a consecrated publisher consecrates, a minor publisher brings discredit). The word 'consecrated' is a crucial word that I shall return to.

I say this to make you realise that with the notion of power, we are following the logic of magic, knowledge and recognition (I shall return to this). This in no way means that it is not serious. Here again, it is one of the oppositions that we have at the back of our minds. We have at the back of our minds a social definition of magic as something that does not work – which is the Tylorian definition of magic:[39] magic is opposed to science, it is used by primitive societies whose people believe they can act on the world through language. But people gradually started to understand that you cannot act on the natural world through language ... Actually, I think that people always knew this, but they didn't want to admit it: it is one of the things that the group does not want to know, and with their authorised spokesman helping the group to act as if they didn't know, they continue to maintain their belief although they also know that it doesn't work. This is the great debate – in Malinowski et al. – about the role of ritual in the manufacture of canoes:[40] why do people take so much trouble over the construction of their canoes if they think that magic should suffice?

Our vision of magic leads us to forget that in the case of the social world magic can be an excellent technique. It is even *the* social technique ... No, that would be going too far ... It is a good social technique, an important one. In any case, to understand the phenomena of power, it is important to make the connection that I have already made several times between the tradition of domination and the tradition of communication, and put an end to that absurd opposition between consensus (in which there is 'sense', 'significance', 'cognition') and conflict, or domination. Just as earlier I situated Kant in relation to Marx, now we need to situate Durkheim in relation to Kant and Marx, without it becoming what Engels called 'a pauper's broth'.[41]

(I said this because [. . .] I had the impression that I had not really finished what I had started saying [in the first session].)

Lecture of 25 April 1985 121

To pass now to the artistic field. Last time, to put it briefly, I focused on the morphological conditions of a symbolic revolution, showing that the morphological conditions were never purely morphological but that they were redefined in each case in function of the specific structure of the given field. I showed how the overproduction of diplomas was retranslated in the artistic and literary fields and in the wider field of cultural production by a certain number of contradictions: the emergence of Bohemia and starving *rapins* who at first remained subject to the symbolic rule of the Academy. This follows the logic of what I was saying just now: the Academy holds the monopoly of the definition of the legitimate artist, it can say: 'He is an artist/he is not an artist', and the challenge of the symbolic revolution will be to ask 'Who can say who is an artist?' They say: 'But there are artists in the Academy.' But are they really artists? Should we not change the definition of the artist in order to change art?

Changing art means changing the definition of the artist and even creating the notion of the artist in the modern sense of the term, in opposition to the notion of the master that I referred to last time. So it means destroying the monopoly of symbolic consecration and creating, for example, a universe where the struggle for the monopoly of consecration is more equal. The situation at the start of the nineteenth century, marked by the domination of the Academy, relates to the artistic field just as the medieval Church related to the religious field: it is a situation where one principal, dominant agency of consecration concentrates almost the whole power of consecration, so that you cannot escape the orthodoxy of the right way of painting and being a painter (the two things being inseparable) without being immediately rejected as a heretic, that is, cast into outer darkness. This is the problem of all heresies: you have to construct the very possibility of heresy, the possibility of working differently, of existing differently, of being a different kind of artist.

The psychosomatic power of the institution

To understand the difficulty of starting a symbolic revolution, we need to realise that those likely to enter into revolt against the verdict of the institution do in a way belong entirely to the institution. The symbolic revolt against its verdicts supposes a sort of mental conversion, and we can think of symbolic revolutions in terms of religious conversion: it is a complete transformation of a vision of the world. You could re-read the autobiographies of the great converts (such as the famous example

122   *Lecture of 25 April 1985*

of Cardinal Newman)[42] to get an idea of what it is to say: 'But after all you can be condemned by the Academy and still be an artist.'

One important thing to note, whether in the case of mandarin competitions in China[43] or selection by the Academy, is the suicides that they provoke. There is the oft-quoted case of the painter [Jules Holtzapffel] who was chosen for the Salon one year, but not the following year – which is doubly painful (this is what we might call the syndrome of the runner-up in a competitive exam, the one who almost makes it through the door – it's Kafkaesque – and spends years waiting for the porter to open it again, until finally it closes for good).[44] He committed suicide, leaving a note saying: 'I have been rejected by the Academy, I am not a painter.' This symbolic power then is a very real power. It is a power over life and death, since symbolic life and death, in certain circumstances, imply physical life and death. I think that what has been said about primitive societies, where exclusion, excommunication and expulsion from the group provoke death or the equivalent, a sort of decrepitude, is valid to different degrees in our societies: think, for instance, of those excluded from political parties[45] or those failing competitive exams.

One question to explore is how groups manage to produce physiological effects, to act on the body. There are some, unfortunately rather uncommon, studies (in the case of Nazism, for instance) on the interaction between social bodies and biological bodies. There are also studies of so-called primitive societies and their symbolic manipulations that may have physiological effects: there is a sort of spontaneous and practical psychosomatism of the group, as if the group – here I am saying something linguistically suspect [in making the collective the subject of a sentence], although I did say 'as if' – possessed a sort of practical knowledge of physiological mechanisms and knew how to act on its agents, especially in situations of exclusion. It still happens today: to exclude someone from a firm, we resort to strategies of the same type; we cut all the strings around them, all the networks, everything that gives them meaning and defines their identity; we remove their personal files, then their secretary, then their chair. I am being schematic, because if I entered into detail, you would find me too melodramatic [. . .].

In the case of artists, the difficulty of struggling against the institution is that it is lodged in the mind: if the institution acts so powerfully, it is because it is completely incorporated into our patterns of perception, our manners of thinking and appreciating. We cannot think the world other than through the categories of the institution, which when it rejects one of our values, obliges us to deny ourself all value: 'I am no good', 'I am nothing.' There too we could quote post-failure confessions as evidence. It is obvious that the diabolical power that the education system wields nowadays – power of consecration, excommunication, lifelong election or condemnation, which also has its links with suicide – is a psychosomatic type of power that affects the body through its actions on our mental structures and perception of the world, and thereby on the self, this perception of the self being inseparable from a sort of corporeal posture. Just as studies in social psychology have shown that the more social importance and recognition you enjoy, the more physical and temporal space you take up,[46] so the person we see as 'found wanting' can only make themselves smaller and smaller, annihilate themselves and disappear, in a way. All of which is present in language.

(At the moment, people are starting to reconsider the problem of emotion – in all the sciences, from mathematics to sociology, problems disappear at certain moments in history; it seems to me that there is a revival of interest at present in the problem of the emotions.[47] One of the mysterious problems that confronts a theory of emotion is the correspondence between the words that express our emotions in a given situation and our somatic reactions, including the most unconscious, of the 'pain in the guts' variety. Things that science has only very recently discovered, levels of haemoglobin or adrenalin, are often related to the popular way of naming the corresponding emotion.[48] The hypothesis that we may advance – unless we assume a highly improbable infiltration of knowledge by the body – is that language, or society through the language that expresses its emotions, has the power to structure our bodily experience, including its most unconscious aspects. I close this slightly madcap parenthesis, I have overstepped my mandate, but only to indicate to what extent symbolic struggles go beyond the symbolic.)

The symbolic work of the heretic

Those people who, unlike the consecrated, are excluded, who are consigned to oblivion, but want to wrench themselves free of this condemnation and execration, can envisage – which is already an extraordinary act – creating a new agency of consecration, a Salon des refusés [Salon for rejects]. That said, and this is the whole logic of the symbolic struggles, for the Salon des refusés to become a consecrating Salon, it has to stop being defined negatively as the Salon for the outcasts. For this to happen, the people who compose it must wipe their minds entirely clear of the failure inherent in the very fact of undertaking

124 *Lecture of 25 April 1985*

this enterprise. In fact, in the very act of constituting a Salon excluding the Salon, they continue to drop a thousand hints revealing how they recognise the legitimacy of the Salon that excludes them. What is most difficult to exclude from the conscience of the excluded is the feeling of exclusion, and what makes the failed candidate pathetic is his resentment of those consecrated, his execration of the chosen few. There is a manner of denouncing the Salon that implies and includes recognition of the dominance of the Salon. One of the misfortunes of symbolic domination – which is true of all kinds of domination: social, sexual or cultural – is that the rebellion against symbolic domination, unless it is very self-conscious (and scientific study can be helpful here), includes recognition of the argument that condemns it. Common sense acknowledges this: extreme execration is a supreme form of recognition. I think that this is extremely important: if, for instance, you take the example of decolonisation, it has its share of this in what we stupidly call its 'growing pains'.[49]

The aim then for these outcasts is to eliminate their exclusion without validating the principle of exclusion through their form of revolt. They need to be able to leave the space, by creating a Salon des refusés that becomes a Salon in its own right. [. . .] At first, the heretical groups tend to gather in a subspace, creating sects ('section' or 'sect' again);[50] they split up and break away from the mainstream and see only their own kind, that is, people who have the same vision and who can act in such a way as to turn this negative vision into a positive vision and change this inversion of the sign into a positive vision so that this inversion or change of sign can be a lived-in practice: 'We are not heretics doomed to live in the catacombs', 'We are not the lowest of the low', 'the first shall be the last', 'We overturn, and we overturn in practice, because around us there are now only people who overturn.'

Avant-gardes are always 'mutual admiration societies'.[51] This appellation is a well- known joke and can only be used to describe a group satirically, but it does designate a social fact, and we can understand how vital it is: unless we are mad, we don't want to be a heretic living in isolation. In a collective of heretics, there is already a measure of support: when I say that I am the greatest painter, there is bound to be someone who does not think me mad, someone who believes me. In other words there is someone who accredits my vision and therefore recognises my vision and sees themselves in it. In general it is a case of: 'He is granting this to me so that I shall grant it to him.' Which may sometimes be difficult . . . This was a problem for Manet, who was surrounded by people who said 'Manet is great', 'Manet is doing

Lecture of 25 April 1985

something really difficult' (he was indulgent towards these people but got rid of them as soon as he could).

This then is the task facing the heretic. [. . .] In their descriptions of heretical movements people habitually talk as if there were *pompier* painting first, followed by Impressionist painting. In fact it is an imperceptible, interminable process: by his fourth year, Manet wants to show the studio masters how clever he is. In the studio of Couture, who is a semi-*pompier*, a rather academic but slightly marginal master, Manet paints some striking works, he attracts attention. At the same time, he has talent; he shows that he could paint conventionally if he wanted to, which is very important because the heretic is open to the suspicion that 'he is rejected because he is incompetent', 'he excludes those who exclude him, therefore his exclusion is unjustified'. The problem of the reject is to make people feel that his exclusion is elective, that he has chosen to exclude himself and exclude others; he has to overturn the relationship, which may oblige him to demonstrate virtuosity, to show what he could do if he wanted to. One of Manet's great problems is that one of his first paintings (I shall certainly make some factual errors, anyone who notices one would do me a favour by pointing it out to me) was a bullfighting scene with a very small torero and an enormous bull, and people said: 'The perspective is wrong, it's a disaster. He can't even paint . . .'. So all his counter-capital collapsed because he had made a strategic error: he challenged the dominant viewpoint on such a central point (the need for a painter to master perspective) that his transgression appeared to be a mistake.[52]

The heretics' strategies may on the contrary consist in concentrating their transgression on the weak points of the structure of the dominant vision (I nearly said the 'dominant ideology', but you should never say that!), that is, the relatively imprecise and uncodified aspects (such as colour). There are then sectors where they can make progress, flaunting their ability to accomplish a performance at the same time as the deliberate and free character of their transgression. That is the task of the avant-garde. (Here too I only use the term 'avant-garde', which has so many connotations, while putting it in mental brackets, because it already contains a philosophy of history: when we say 'avant-garde', we think of marching, they are the advance guard of an army, they are in the lead and we know in advance that they are going to succeed . . . We shouldn't say 'avant-garde'; 'heretics' is better already.)

Collective conversion

There are then the problems of self-confirmation of the heretics (they have to embrace a really different kind of faith), of mutual confirmation among the heretical group. And then there is the struggle between the view that the heretical group holds of itself and the views that it reads back from those around it. There is the problem of their relation with the critics and with the other painters, who are going to deploy strategies of disqualification. The heretics try to attract credit ('Trust in us'). One of the issues is the problem of sincerity: 'Does he believe what he's doing, or is he a cynic?', 'Does he really believe in it and can we trust his intentions?', 'If what people say is true, and he is acting intentionally, that is disturbing . . .'. The personality of the painter is important because it is the person in general, the whole person that has to be trusted: 'Is he credible, as a person?', 'Does he have decent values?' Then they look at his work: 'Can his work appear to be credible, even if you look at it in the light of the canons that it transgresses?', 'Does he look as if he did it intentionally or as if he could have done it differently?'

Luckily there are two or three splendid studies that contain collections of texts by the critics and which detail year by year all the criticism that Manet's work encountered. Here we can find the strategies of the holders of the orthodox viewpoint relayed by the critics, who are their objective allies (and certainly not 'at their service', because in the intellectual field the best servants of a cause serve their own cause by serving that cause; in other words, the field of criticism being homologous with the field of painting, it is by settling their account with the other critics that they best serve the painters who correspond to their position).[53] The struggle between critics is a struggle to determine the legitimate definition of this new painting, and the breakaway painters keep a constant watch over the progressive construction of this image. We find an infinity of small, individual judgements, re-situated in their context. As people walk by a painting at the Salon, they pass remarks on it. The critics relay these comments. Satirical drawings show the failed artist in front of his (absent) painting, noting the reflections of the visitors to the Salon. Then there is word of mouth, the word on the street: what people say about Manet. There are anecdotes. There is what is said by the rival painters with strong symbolic power: they can with a cutting remark destroy five years of symbol making. There are the critics who are the objective allies of the dominant who, without even having to refer to the authority of the dominant painter, see through his eyes because they share his outlook. All this takes time. But opposite is the heretical group, with the artist who speaks out, which is very important and which in my opinion is one of the major unspoken reasons for the painter's success. From the time of the revolution that I am in the process of describing, the cleavage between painters who speak or stay silent, who are educated or not, who do or don't have their baccalaureate, becomes very important. Manet, for instance, is distinguished in all these aspects. I think that if his symbolic revolution survived it is because he knew how to speak of his painting and he also knew who to speak to: he found the right spokesmen (Zola and Mallarmé together, which isn't bad . . .).[54] He knew how to contact them because he had a feel for the game and also because when he had found the right people to talk to he knew how to talk to them – he was not being cynical.

Destroying one image and constructing another is a kind of continuous, imperceptible process. Obviously it is very difficult for the social scientist to reproduce the infinity of small individual transformations that lead to a change in our vision of the world. Studying the changes in the Church around the 1960s[55] would pose exactly the same problem: it isn't a Council that at a certain moment in time decides to launch an '*aggiornamento*', it is thousands of minor individual conversions orchestrated by people who, being subject to the same movement of conversion as many others, are in addition able to express their conversion in such a way that those who are being converted find the rhythm of their own conversion accelerated through the discourse of these new converts. This phenomenon is very widespread yet very difficult to describe because it involves threshold effects: where is the tipping point? Théophile Gautier, who was not a progressive, felt at a certain moment that you had to be in favour of the Impressionists. When was the moment when the intellectuals moved from the right to the left?

This is a very interesting problem, and a perennial one: there are moments when the intellectuals are nearly all on the left; and moments when they all tend to be on the right. Of course there is always a political event dividing the two (such as the *coup d'état* of 1851–52), but it is never a collective conversion on a given day: it is a process, an orchestrated ensemble of individual conversions. This helps highlight the role of the exemplary prophets, the spokesmen who have the power of vision: there are people who, while following the same process of conversion as the others, have both the ability and the power (which often supposes access to effective media of expression) to express at a certain moment what is happening and, by the fact of expressing it, to make it happen. This does not mean that they create the minor conversions, nor that they do nothing. This is what 'consecration' means: they

128 *Lecture of 25 April 1985*

consecrate the minor conversions because they have the authority to say: 'Romanticism is dead and buried', '*Pompier* painting is dead and buried.' You find this staring you in the face all the time: there are all those articles in *Libération* and the *Nouvel Observateur* to the tune of 'Social Science is dead and buried', and the like.

The strategies of the heresiarch

[. . .] The life of this avant-gardist fraction, the breakaway fraction that I am describing here, was made difficult by the existence of 'failures' (as defined by society). Those who suffered negative verdicts did not revolt, or if they did join the rebellion, they did it so ineffectually that they compromised the chances of the rebels being recognised as accomplishing a positive rather than a negative revolt. Last time I mentioned something that was a great problem for the major leaders of the movement: deciding whether to participate in these 'Salons des refusés'. The first Salons des refusés were lamentable. They were so obviously the work of those 'failing' to meet the dominant norms that they reinforced the institution; everyone went there for a laugh, to say: 'It's unbelievable how awful they are', 'It's dreadful', and so on. 'They are not philosophers' (I am switching the genres for you to feel the impact), 'It's nonsense', 'They are stupid', 'They can't even paint.'

Little by little there started to be signs that things were looking up. That was the moment when the heretics needed heresiarchs. They cried 'Manet with us!' then 'Cézanne with us!' That said, Manet and Cézanne were not mad, they saw that these were drowning men clutching at their necks and likely to pull them under, and wondered whether they should join forces with people who were obviously failures in terms not just of the old categories but also the new. This is the problem of the heresiarch (which is never explicitly framed as such, it never appears in the texts, except through the surprise of the historians who say: 'Look, how strange, Manet and Cézanne weren't there'). We should not translate this into our own categories, for we now know that they were an 'avant-garde', we know who won the race. At the time they were not so consecrated, they had a special kind of prestige among the little sect which did nonetheless strike terror in the hearts of the critics, saying 'You are idiots, Manet is a great man.' The conformist critic knew that for these 'madmen' Manet was a great man, which was already a way of being rather consecrated ('There are those who say that Manet is a great man, but obviously nobody believes it').

Lecture of 25 April 1985 129

That said, Manet and Cézanne had careers and social origins with all that this entails: a feel for the game, a sense of positioning as in football, or placing an investment as in banking, which means knowing where you need to be and need to be seen, and where not to be seen. This is crucial for the present period: 'Tell me where you exhibit and I'll tell you not only what kind of painter you are but also above all how well you know the field of painting.' You need to know the field of painting to know where to place yourself. Cézanne and Manet had a feel for positioning which enabled them to avoid entering certain places, or to enter them only if appearing to do so out of solidarity with people who were ill-starred victims, but they always maintained the freedom to escape classification. Taxonomies are in fact the principal instruments of the struggle. If you are catalogued and characterised, that is, condemned as an 'Impressionist', and this is an insult – which was the case at first – it will be difficult to escape from Impressionism and go on to be a Manet.

That said (and I think I have now said everything I wanted to on the strategies of the group), why do they need a group? I have just explained the functions of the group from the point of view of the heretic's belief and ethics: the heretic must believe in himself in order to get others to believe in him. Hagiographies abound that are full of the heretic's doubts: Zola's novel *The Work of Art*, which alludes to Cézanne and Manet, is a very romantic account of such doubts. The group exercises a function of reassurance, but this is not its only role. It is also an important means of being perceived, *nobilis*, to break free of obscurity: it is better to be saddled with an insult, a label that will at least identify you as a participant in a category, rather than go unnoticed. This is very important for our understanding of how groups function, but also how they evolve.

In fact it is almost a law of artistic struggles: heretical enterprises start as a collective and finish with individuals. They are riven by schisms, partly because the (obviously specific) interest of belonging to a group diminishes as the group or at least its leaders find success and therefore have less need of the group. This is the first reason. The second is that as long as there is nothing to share but insults, the forces of cohesion (where your opposition creates your position) remain stronger than the forces of dispersion. A very fine study of the Impressionist group by an American historian gives an excellent account of the communal enthusiasm of its origins,[56] the moment when the group 'shared everything', and shows how the divisions and conflicts arose progressively, but paradoxically, when things were going well for the group. How do we explain the paradox that these groups split up when everything is going

130   *Lecture of 25 April 1985*

well for them, when they are starting to become known, when people are starting to look on them favourably, etc. There are the reasons that I have given. There is also the increasingly unequal distribution of profits within the group, since the symbolic profits collectively associated with the group are tendentiously monopolised by the heresiarch, the leader. This could help us to understand quite a lot: there has been a whole series of books, for instance the one studying the conflicts among the entourage of Freud.[57] I believe that if we follow a materialist logic (but obviously the kind of materialism of the symbolic that I am using at the moment), it is quite easy to understand things that are generally explained in a purely psychological logic of incompatibilities and drama that explain absolutely nothing: otherwise, why would these conflicts start in 1862 when these people had been together since 1840?

A revolution affecting the ensemble of the fields of cultural production

What they need to do then is manage to establish an acceptable vision of the world and impose it. They need in a way to overturn the dominant vision, to impose a new *nomos*, to arrange for the principles of division with which the universe of pictures presented becomes completely transformed on a certain day, in a certain exhibition. What was good has to become bad, and by the same token the old heretics must become nomothetes, who are consecrated and therefore endowed with the power to consecrate. Their first task, for example, may consist in consecrating painters from the past who were despised by those who were consecrated against them (Watteau, for instance, became a subject of contention). It's the same thing today: in the struggles for consecration, the strategies of rehabilitation are very important: Condillac is rehabilitated, there is renewed interest in X or Y, for instance.

To sum up, the morphological crisis of overproduction laid the social and even perhaps the economic bases for a symbolic revolution. That said, for an economic crisis (or even the specific form taken by an economic and social crisis within a field, that is, a morphological crisis) to become a symbolic revolution, it needs a specific process of conversion which has to affect groups, through individuals working on themselves, in a sort of collective *metanoia*, collective conversion. This conversion does not occur suddenly ('at the very same time on the very same day') – it would be just the same if we were talking about May '68 – it is an ensemble of collectively orchestrated conversions, because, since the same causes produce the same effects, the same positions in a field favour the appearance of the same dispositions in the holders

Lecture of 25 April 1985 131

of those positions. An ensemble of orchestrated revolutions changes qualitatively when they find spokesmen, when they find a language – even in insults proffered by others – and produce manifestos. Literary manifestos and programmes are important even if they are not decisive: for instance, with the Symbolists, it was one of the feeblest who wrote the manifesto;[58] the real leaders had something more important to do, they had poems to write.

A poetic revolution is, in fact, no more a programme than a political revolution is, but the existence of a manifesto and a programme that helps convince us that the political (or artistic) revolution has been thought through, and that the new nomotheist is an epistemocrat who is giving orders in the name of science, is very important for its credibility. Moreover, a manifesto makes what was implicit become explicit, so that dispositional revolutions, experienced initially as a mood, become conscious and systematic. What was a 'reflex', that is, the reaction of a habitus, becomes a rallying cry; a moody feeling is translated into a conscious, rational slogan; antipathies ('Hugo is an old fart') become theorised ('Down with lyricism', they say). Obviously if the terrain of art is interesting it is because things there are particularly visible, for the reasons that I have just mentioned: we are dealing here with experts in coding and exposition.

That is the point that I wanted to make: if this symbolic revolution came to fruition, it was because the painters, who with very few exceptions were hands-on practitioners, linked up with professionals of expression. I think that we cannot understand the revolution against academic art if we fail to see that the painters found spokesmen, people who undertook for them the work that I described of codification, exposition and theorisation, which rendered theoretical, conscious and explicit what had until then been a practical mood. We could say that the artists found in the writers ideologists ('-logists' meaning 'speakers'), or spokesmen to speak on their behalf. But you don't become someone's spokesman for the fun of it . . . Why did the writers become the painters' spokesmen? What did they gain from speaking their message? What impact did making these declarations have on them? How was the artistic field transformed by their words? In what ways did the fact of expressing these ideas affect literature and change the literary field? An anecdotal point that explains a lot is the fact that the phrase 'art for art's sake' was invented by a painter, who was called Jean Duseigneur.[59] The phrase came from painting, then. It passed into literature, where it was orchestrated, but in orchestrating it, the writer who preaches the new word cannot avoid applying it to himself partially even if he doesn't adopt it completely: I gave the example

132   *Lecture of 25 April 1985*

of Zola, who expressed Manet's ideas very well without drawing any consequences for his own practice. This phenomenon is very common in our story.

The consequence was to be this kind of permanent exchange of roles between the artistic fields and the field of literature, with the field of music ever-present – Berlioz et al. – but becoming more active, and not only as model of reference, I think from the 1880s onwards. Finally it seems that the history of the birth of the artist can only function at the level of the ensemble of the fields of cultural production which, although separate, autonomous and irreducible, each endowed with its own logic, can move to the same rhythm at certain moments, because their interests converge. Obviously they move to the same rhythm through misunderstandings. And it is this kind of cross-field exchange that engenders a true symbolic revolution, which I believe would have otherwise been impossible.

Lecture of 2 May 1985

First session (lecture): collective bad faith and struggles for definition
– Justification of a decision to buy and competing viewpoints – 'Taking
apart' and 'putting together' – Subjective manipulations and objective
structures – Managing the symbolic capital of the group – Effects of the
corps
Second session (seminar): the invention of the modern artist (5) – The
alliance of painters and writers – The artist's way of life and the invention
of pure love – Artistic transgression today and a century ago – The
mercenary artist and art for art's sake

First session (lecture): collective bad faith and struggles for definition

I want to reply to two questions that were put to me last week. I'll read
the first: 'Your theory of the social world poses the problem of the sincerity of social agents in a new way. Between the bad faith diagnosed
by philosophers and the like, and the good faith that people claim for
each of their social acts, is it possible to determine a middle way, [. . .]
and if so, what are the consequences of this [. . .]?' [. . .] It seems to me
that what I was trying to show is how I find the social world based on
the way that social agents work both individually and collectively at
disguising the sense of the social world from themselves. There is then
a kind of collective bad faith, in the sense of self-deceit, the difference
between Sartre's model and mine residing in the fact that, in Sartre's
case, bad faith is a relation between individual subjects, or between
the subject and himself, with the subject deceiving himself – which
is slightly improbable psychologically – whereas what I am trying to
show is that there is a collective enterprise of bad faith: when social
agents want to lie to themselves, so to speak, they draw support from

134 *Lecture of 2 May 1985*

the institutions. There are institutions of collective bad faith. The most obvious example in certain situations would be the religious institution, but bad faith is present everywhere all the time: we can find it even in an academic meeting and more generally in a host of circumstances where the individuals who want to deceive themselves find a collective complicity with people who need to share the same lies at the same moment. This is my argument. I am formulating it in a rather simple and abrupt form, but I wanted simply to reply to the question.

As for the second question, I feel that I may well express surprise at being asked it, because anyone who had been listening to me for long enough would have started by asking themselves why they are asking the question: 'What is your reaction to the suspicion or even contempt of Anglo-American social scientists who reproach European sociologists with claiming to have a hot line to Providence?' What is interesting in this question is the fact that, as I have very often suggested, scientific fields are battlefields, one of whose principal stakes is the legitimate definition of science. It is obvious, for example, that there are conflicts where Anglo-Americans and Europeans confront each other, often with stereotypes, calumny, insults or blanket condemnation. What do they mean by '*the* American sociologists', '*the* French sociologists'? (I personally feel much closer to certain American sociologists than to the French sociologists.) This kind of proposition is itself inherent in the logic of the struggles for symbolic domination in a specific field, which are struggles of intellectual imperialism. The only question that I would put [in the light of the question that has been put to me] is: 'Who has asked this question? How has it been formulated?' I can of course make a guess (without wishing to launch an enquiry); I think that from the fact that this question has been raised we can presume a certain number of things about the social position of the person putting it.

Justification of a decision to buy and competing viewpoints

To move on to my argument for today. [. . .] This morning I was reading the transcript of an interview that I conducted a while ago in the context of the housing situation.[1] We asked a woman who had taken a place in an estate of prefabricated houses of the GMF type [*groupe maisons familiales*/family housing group] to describe the conditions that influenced her decision. I have chosen to quote this interview in order to show you that what I said last time in a single sentence, which might have seemed like a theoretical hypothesis, is

Lecture of 2 May 1985 135

rooted in the most practical practice; if there is a secret to European sociology as I practise it, it is this combination of high theoretical speculation and immersion in the most empirical empiricism.[2] It is not always easy to hold these two aspects together, thinking of Kant, for instance, while listening to someone discuss the purchase of a house, but I think that this is the way for science to make progress today. I shall now simply read out a short passage (although the whole text would be interesting):

[The questioner]: 'How much is your house worth?'
'When I bought it, it was worth . . . but now it's a while ago . . . exactly 55,900,000 francs [about 10 million euros] . . . it's 600 square metres [about 5,400 square feet]'
(This already shows a certain attitude to the value, a 'hopefully')
'So it's a big house?'
'Yes, it's an F6 [a four- or five-bedroom house]. With four children, we couldn't take anything smaller!' (Now what does 'We couldn't take anything smaller' mean? Compared to what standard? Where does this standard come from? Who is the subject of this subjectively felt imperative?) 'Otherwise it's fine, really . . .' (There we have a very interesting word [French: *enfin*]. Oswald Ducrot has written a very fine article on the uses of the word 'but', and, if I have time, I'll write an article on the uses of 'really'. Here the 'really' signifies: 'That's my opinion, but there are others, I know that some other people' – other people might be my husband, 'they', or the vendors, for instance – 'don't think like me.') 'Well, really, it's the minimum, as my husband says . . . Inside, you can hear everything, the walls are so thin, and all that, but I'm happy in my house.'

In other words, her view of this house has become conflated with an external viewpoint that she has to accommodate, and the word 'really' introduces the switch in viewpoint. Having noted the 'really' at that point, I kept seeing it afterwards:

'It's nice, the bedrooms are small, the children are happy, and there's a loft.'
'You have an upper floor?'
'*They* call it an upper floor, it's a loft [. . .], *well really*, I call it an upper floor, but they say it's a loft.' (Listen, here things get interesting . . .) 'Rooms in the loft, they call them . . . But, *really*, for the council taxes, all of that makes an upper floor.'

136 *Lecture of 2 May 1985*

This is, I believe, a lovely story [*laughter*], which shows how different viewpoints collide. We can clearly see the conflict over terms, where saying 'upper floor' or 'loft' has very precise, legal consequences, for taxation for instance. The whole interview follows this pattern, and every time that it appears, the word 'really' introduces this change of viewpoint. Last time I was looking at the worlds of political or artistic and literary struggles, where we see the clash of viewpoints clearly enough, with the political arena being obviously the place where these things are most open. But I didn't want you to think that this was something extraordinary, that it was pure speculation: these things are at work at every moment, for instance in decision making, because that is what is happening, this is an enquiry into the process of decision making: what is it to decide? What are we doing when we decide to buy an F6 when we are living in an HLM [*habitation loyer modéré* – a council flat on a housing estate]. This kind of retrospective account of a decision enables us to see, among other things, that the subject telling the story is constantly confronted at the present time with rival viewpoints, and in particular, with all the viewpoints showing that they have made a bad purchase. This is a law that I think consumer specialists in the United States were the first to establish: people who have made a purchase find all the reasons they can to justify it. This is what creates, for instance, loyalty to a make of car: people are loyal to a make because it is important to justify their decision [. . .]. When we come to the purchase of a house, the number of free variables is enormous and (as the interviewee said) you are quite in the dark: the decision has implications for over twenty years of family life, it presupposes they won't get divorced, or have another child. In a decision of this kind, the subject is taking a leap in the dark, so to speak, and this kind of rather cruel retrospective enquiry obliges them to rehearse the story that they tell themselves in order to 'satisfy themselves' (using all the senses of the term: 'I find it satisfactory enough', 'I am satisfied' and 'I am satisfied because I find it satisfactory enough') with other viewpoints. The word 'really' marks each change of perspective.

'Taking apart' and 'putting together'

The important thing is that the juridical viewpoint, which is dominant and is expressed in terms of sanctions, taxes, deductions from salary, etc., the viewpoint that is able to impose itself, is the famous *nomos* that I referred to last time. The fact that I was speaking Greek does not mean that I was being abstract. The *nomos* is the principle of percep-

Lecture of 2 May 1985   137

tion and selection, which highlights certain aspects of reality and leaves others out. This principle of abstraction has more or less the force of law. It can impose itself as the right principle, the principle that has to be accepted; whatever the woman we interviewed wants to claim, she has not got a loft, but an upper floor, and this view has the force of law. Goodman, in a book that I mentioned last time,[3] insists on the fact that one of the fundamental processes of this fabrication or 'fiction' (taking the word fiction in its etymological sense)[4] of the world is what he calls 'taking apart' and 'putting together', two things which, by the way, do go together: 'taking apart'/'putting together' is what we would call in Latin *secerne*, the root of 'sacred'; it is placing things separately, and in putting them to one side, showing them to be separate. What is shown as separate is precisely the sacred, something that we have to treat differently, that we have to behave differently with.

Goodman indicates that this sort of composition and decomposition is normally operated, assisted or consolidated through the application of labels:[5] the operation of separation is accompanied by the attribution of a name, a baptism. In fact the act of baptism would be the exemplary act of consecration: to impose a name is to endow someone with a different identity. Goodman distinguishes other operations (I am not quite sure why he distinguishes them, since they seem to me to be implicated in the fundamental process that I have just described), including in particular 'weighting certain aspects' (which is already implied in 'take apart' . . .) and 'underlining'. (If you think about it, underlining in a text is an operation of imposition of a viewpoint. It would be interesting in fact to note the techniques of writing that are manipulations of the reader's reading, that try to anticipate and orient the reading in advance. Because there are a lot: titles, subtitles, capitalisation, or even the utilisation of notes that can minimise for maximal effect – we can place in a note, which appears to be a very modest form, things that are very important.[6] We could use this logic to deliver an exercise in the pragmatics of reading.) Other fundamental operations include 'ordering differently', that is, changing orders, overturning hierarchies (as the heretics do in the symbolic struggle), and finally 'deleting some aspects and supplementing others', 'deformation'.[7] (This distinction proposed by a philosopher of logic is not very logical . . .) The operation which according to him is fundamental to the construction of the world, and which is the one that I intend to use (and continue to use systematically [for the rest of this lecture]), consists in taking apart and putting together.

I would now like to briefly describe how, in the ordinary logic of social struggles, social agents practise these operations. Goodman, as

138 *Lecture of 2 May 1985*

a philosopher, describes them *in abstracto* as generic operations of abstraction. In reality they are operated in practice every day according to the demands of practical needs and in particular according to the demands of symbolic struggles. The divide between 'American sociologists' and 'European sociologists' that I was alluding to just now is a typical example [. . .]. A fundamental aim in what I call the struggle for classification is to impose a certain vision of the social world, and thus of the constitution of groups. Here I refer you to my study of Algeria, which is in fact the starting point for all of these reflections.[8]

In a society where all classifications are relatively uncodified, where social identities are relatively uncodified (whether in the shape of property deeds, educational qualifications or titles of nobility, for instance) – because of, for example, the absence of civil registry in the sense that I indicated the other day, or the absence of writing – the labels are oral and are obviously much more manipulable than in a society where you can say 'Let's go and consult the records', 'There are genealogies, we can check.' Things are the same with oral poetry for instance. As long as it is oral, poetry is open to manipulation: you can substitute one word for another without anyone being able to say, as a philologist would, 'This is the right reading.' One of the errors committed by philologists, as Bakhtin has clearly shown,[9] is to interpret societies where writing was still ancillary, as in Homeric society when Homer's texts were codified, through eyes fabricated in societies of writing. Jack Goody has drawn attention to the effects of writing:[10] writing, by fixing, changes the use of the things that it fixes, fixes the thing, and philologists for instance, looking at some word that had been quoted throughout Greek antiquity by everyone up to and including Aristotle, declare: 'This is the right reading: he said [x], he did not say [x´]'[11] (I have made up this example). In fact the philologists forget that this idea of fixity and certitude is linked to societies of writing, whereas in 'archaic' societies the use of discourse is such that there is no correct reading: the words or proverbs of the tribe are weapons in their everyday struggles; people fight to impose the right reading ('If he said [x], I'm the one who is right, if he said [x´], then you are right'), and in a way the last person to write will be right.

This introduces what I have to say today: these symbolic struggles that we see working effectively in pre-capitalist societies where the cultural capital is relatively un-objectified because of the absence of a school system and writing, where the economic capital is relatively un-objectified because of the absence of an economic structure, continue to function in our societies, but with more difficulty, for the reasons that I gave just now: the town council will always be right ('You may

Lecture of 2 May 1985 139

well think that it's a loft, but I say that it is an upper floor, and I am right'). This raises the question of the position of the State in symbolic struggles, of the State as having the last word, in pronouncing the 'verdict' on problems of definition of identity.

I refer you to my study of the Kabyle to show you that there is absolutely no discontinuity between the reflections that I offered on kinship groups[12] and the reflections that I am offering today on social class.[13] In societies where the dominant principle of structuration and categorisation is the domestic one, with the model of the family and kinship, there is a permanent struggle to know where you belong. This game is partly verbal. You can play with words, with the family name or the first name (I gave examples last time), but also with the common names of social units: the names that serve to denote the clan, the sub-clan and the tribe are contentious because, in fighting over these words people are fighting over what links people, and their ways of being united and separated. What is at stake in the overall struggle is finding out how we are united and how we are separated; it is a fight for the principles of vision and division. These struggles are possible because there is some vagueness or fluidity in objective reality. For example in our society (but it is true for all societies) the word 'cousin' is extremely elastic: you can be a parallel cousin or a second cousin, through the male or the female line, and so on. There are loops in the genealogies, so that you can be related to someone in two different ways (I showed this in *The Logic of Practice* where I give an example of these strategies).[14] There are two routes: you can be a relative through the male line, and that's fine, it is a good relationship, or through the female line, and that is not so fine (I have to point out that these are not my own values). The agents can then exploit an objective vagueness that the ethnologist always ignores because he must present to his colleagues a neat genealogy (such as a 'patrilinear system').

Perhaps because I was closer to the indigenous viewpoint than ethnologists usually are, my work welcomed both viewpoints with equal seriousness, and it seemed to me that the ethnologist should not have to choose between them. He has no need to arbitrate and say: 'They are properly related, patrilinear, etc.', as his relations with his colleagues incite him to do. He should take account of the ambiguity inherent in certain kinship relations and at the same time note the strategies that aim to exploit this ambiguity. I have conducted a full analysis of the example of a marriage with a parallel cousin which can be either an ideal marriage or a wretched one: it is the very essence of the ambiguous reality – remember the 'well really' of a moment ago – in which the social agents can manage to believe, and get as many other people as

140   *Lecture of 2 May 1985*

possible to believe, that a wretched marriage, a forced choice imposed by circumstances, was a noble choice, following traditional conventions, establishing the slightly faded cousin, who had no value on the matrimonial market, as a parallel cousin.

The complicity is collective: the group is well aware of the game and can pretend to believe in it if the marriage with a parallel cousin is very important for it. As marriage with the parallel cousin (the daughter of the father's brother) represents the official model, someone who 'pays homage' [*in English in the text*] to the dominant model is well considered. The man who can say: 'I gave my son to my brother's daughter' respects the norm of the group, and even if we know the truth [that it was an obligatory choice], the moustachioed elders will say: 'That's good, that's good . . .', and it becomes a perfectly noble marriage of cousins. Such is the collective process. To achieve this you need a fine moustache, you have to know the ropes, you need status and distinction, or *arete* as the Greeks used to say; you have to have done your homework because the others are on the lookout, they know the truth. So there is on the one hand the struggle, the 'what will people say?', the 'word on the street', the 'they say' (and 'what people say is cruel', the Kabyle say), and on the other hand the norm, the official discourse. The social agent who has the rules of the game at his fingertips will be able in some way to disguise one thing as another and gain collective approval. Groups like people who do what they can to reconcile themselves with the group.

In other words, the ethnologists describe the rules of kinship while I describe the strategies used in coming to terms with the rules. Both exist: the rules of kinship are made to be transgressed. 'Every rule has its doorway', as the Kabyle say; otherwise it would be unbearable. This does not mean that the rule doesn't count: the rule is the official discourse that you need to hold in order to be legitimate, and when you transgress the rule, if you pay that sort of verbal respect to the rule (which is not hypocrisy), [. . .] if you 'pay with words', the group is satisfied because it is granted the essential, which is acknowledgement of the dominant values of the group. On the contrary, someone who marries their parallel cousin while saying 'She's an imbecile, but I have no choice' commits the worst transgression because he defies the rule and spoils the game. The action is the same but its sense is entirely opposite depending on the style of the action: and who is to judge the style of the action? We can tell from the word 'style': 'style' is something that is perceived by others; it is a relation between the person acting, their manner of acting in objective reality, and the view of the person perceiving.

Lecture of 2 May 1985   141

Subjective manipulations and objective structures

That is what I tried to show when describing Kabyle society. In our societies it is exactly the same. There is the everyday politics of manipulating our view of the distinctions verbally, saying: 'She is not a cousin on the male side, but a cousin on the female side.' They won't address her in the same way and they won't discuss the same matters with her. Similarly, you can say to anyone 'hello, maternal uncle'; this is a friendly greeting, as when you say 'hello, dear friend' to someone [*Bourdieu makes a gesture showing that you don't attach much importance to the person, which makes his audience laugh*]; but when you say 'hello, paternal uncle', that sounds serious. [. . .] These apparently insignificant everyday strategies are perceived by the others, who are also busy measuring distances: since in these societies everyone knows everyone else's genealogy, they know the real distances (they don't do the calculations that the ethnologist does, for which you need much paper and more time, but they have something equivalent in practice). They watch each other playing with the structures and the rules, while all the time they know the objective reality. That is how society works: things come together, then pull apart, then they come together again, in a mixture of freedom and necessity. If you ignore the fact that you cannot do exactly what you fancy, you are in danger.

And so, for reasons that have more to do with the sociology of the American field of academic production than with the objective truth of what he was studying, Rosen, whom I cited [in the previous lecture],[15] moves towards an ultra-subjectivist position where he sees social realities as pure constructions of the mind, as in a sort of process of continuous creation. Some interactionists, even Goffman himself, move towards a position where every social agent at every moment is creating the world; the social structures at every moment would be the creation of social agents through their work of negotiation and haggling, using strategies of the type that I have been describing. Against this type of vision we should at least argue that structures do objectively exist, transcending the aggregation of all the judgements. What we call 'public opinion' does not exist,[16] and yet at the same time it does exist as the totality of all these small differential viewpoints. You do have to take account of what other people are going to say. If I say: 'She's my parallel cousin', but everyone knows that it is not true, it won't work. There is then a daily political effort destined for others and yourself, and the more you convince the others the more you convince yourself: individual bad faith goes hand in hand with collective bad faith (the example I gave at the start shows this clearly).

142 *Lecture of 2 May 1985*

People who 'make up stories', as they say, for themselves, usually their life-stories (I should say in passing that I am very sceptical about life-stories, which are an old anthropological red herring, which has come back into fashion, once again for reasons more sociological than scientific[17]), those who make up life-stories for themselves or others are creating strategies for others and for themselves at the same time. Making up your life-story always serves some end. Confiding in someone does certainly have a psychological function, but it is also an attempt to construct an image, to seek out a witness who will validate the image we offer, and it is indeed quite extraordinary to be able to find a single person ready to listen – 'to listen' meaning: 'I accept that this is not madness.' This is one of the functions of psychoanalysis: listening without saying anything, without crying out, is granting the right to publicise, to say publicly and officially to everyone what was ultra-private and ultra-secret.

This daily political effort takes two forms: it is a playing with words, with their representations and designations, and, as I showed with the example of a marriage, it is simultaneously a playing with things, such as the realities of kinship. In this logic, the fundamental operation of union and separation is marriage, which unites and creates bonds, etc. I think that all the fundamental operations of social rituals (marriage, birthing rites, rites on the seventh day or the fortieth day after birth, circumcision rites, burial rites) or agrarian rites (rites of first ploughing) are always linked to problems of union and separation. Dualist systems (such as masculine/feminine, hot/cold, dry/wet) structure the dominant mythico-ritual vision of the world, but in practice you have to live in this world, divided into masculine/feminine for example. For order to reign, for the world to be intelligible, there has to be masculine/feminine, there has to be *haram*: *haram* means 'sacred' [*Arabic word*], 'taboo', the 'separate' that must not be touched, the 'house' – it is the house where there are women, that is, the sacred place it is forbidden to enter. To be liveable, this divided world must be reunited and marriage is the legitimate, official, visible, publicly displayed transgression of the absolute division between masculine and feminine. The agrarian rites are the same: the rite of ploughing is the transgression of the masculine/feminine divide with the plough/the earth.

For the world to have meaning, we have to divide, but for the world to be liveable, we need to transgress those divisions, and rites, whether agrarian or social, like marriage, are a kind of collective denial in the Freudian sense of the term: they are acts in which the group acts collectively as if it were not transgressing the limits that it had itself established. Since the group has established the limits, their transgression

Lecture of 2 May 1985 143

has to be legitimate, that is, collective, open to the public and seen to be organised by the group [. . .]. The more sensitive the boundaries the transgression affects, the more you need the totality of the group ('the whole group was present') to transgress them: only the group can give the group the authorisation to transgress the limits that it has established. Here we have the opposition that has always been intuitively drawn between religious rites, which are public, and magic rites, which are secret.[18] (Here I am adopting the same definition, but explaining its foundation, as I see it, in publicity: the marriage banns are what make the difference between what people now call 'juvenile cohabitation'[19] and marriage: it is an act that consists simply in rendering public and official – there is the publication of the banns, everyone knows about it, I announce it in public. I close this parenthesis).

Thus in their everyday social lives, social agents manipulate the words that designate groups, and in manipulating the words they bring into being cohabitations, alliances and actions that would otherwise be impossible. In societies where the fundamental principles that structure the social world and social reproduction are in the gift of the domestic unit, one fundamental problem is knowing who you can ally yourself with and who you can't – knowing what you can combine or, to use Goodman's vocabulary, what you can put together and what you must take apart. In everyday life, conflicts nearly always arise from the contradiction between the theoretical definition and the real definition of the potential ally. This is the opposition that I made between theoretical kinship and practical kinship, kinship on paper and usable kinship.[20] If kinship is thought of in terms of genealogy, it's easy, it's unequivocal: there is only one line linking one point to another. This is why rather formalist ethnologists adore genealogy: it is swiftly garnered, easily understood, you can put it through the computer and even make a standard template of it, for the links can even be mathematically analysed, they seem to be made for this purpose. But we know well enough that the word 'cousin' is a very ambiguous word. Most societies have very detailed and specific terms enabling you to give different names to the daughter of the father's brother, the daughter of the mother's brother or the daughter of the father's sister. There is then on the one hand theoretical kinship, kinship on paper, in the genealogy elaborated by the ethnologist, which everyone knows and which can't be tampered with; and on the other hand, real kinship, that is, the people whom we would really like to marry (not in the modern sense of the term), whom we need for reasons of alliance, or, in some societies, to consolidate the patrimony or to strengthen the group: it is what I call practical or useful kinship.

144 *Lecture of 2 May 1985*

While conducting this analysis I came across an old French term: 'The cousins that you enjoy cousining with';[21] there are cousins that you frequent as cousins, and others that you drop. To define these phenomena I took the analogy of a space where there are paths. There are theoretical paths, open routes. Thus for a Kabyle, the daughter of the father's brother is very important. Any son knows that she has a special name and that he is in a way predestined to marry her. Another example: the 'elder son' in certain societies is from childhood treated differently from the younger; he has better clothes, better food, and so on. He is constituted (an important word, the same as the one used in the Constitution of the Republic) as different, everyone tells him 'You are different', and so, given the Pygmalion effect, he becomes different. This theoretical kinship on paper, which also exists in people's minds through the mechanisms that I have described, is not always compatible with people's interests: they do not always follow the theoretical paths. There are theoretical paths sown with brambles that they never venture down. There are people genealogically very close whom we nonetheless never go to see: they gave us gifts but we never reciprocated; the last time they came we were not very welcoming, which made the grandmother cross. These people who are very close in terms of theoretical kinship can be very distant. On the contrary, a very distant cousin can be very close because we have 'cousined': perhaps we have previously asked him to arrange an earlier marriage with a wife who will advocate nourishing this relationship because it's in her interest (she gains support in her domestic conflicts if she imports a man or a woman from the same group).

All the stories that I am telling you and that the ethnologists don't talk about are part of real-life matrimonial strategies. Just considering the ideas that I mention supposes quite a different attitude from that adopted in recording the formal genealogies ('Aïcha, daughter of so-and-so, etc.') that are much easier to note. If we reason in terms of social classes, we face exactly the same problem as we do with the problem of theoretical/practical kinship: there is also a named space, there are 'colleagues' ('colleague' is an active concept, like 'cousin'), and we should note all the other words that designate loyalty or membership, which in general imply duties ('We ought to . . .', 'We really ought to . . .', 'We really ought to invite the so-and-sos', etc.). These obligations attached to appearances can exist on paper or in practice, and one of the great problems of sociological analysis is to put these two things together, that is, to construct a theoretical model of the distances on paper and to introduce into the model a knowledge of the strategies used by the social agents to manipulate those objective distances, to

Lecture of 2 May 1985 145

approach what is distant, or, as we have said, keep their distance from things that were close to hand, to keep up or drop relationships, often in accord with their interests. This is another extremely important difference from the genealogical model. The genealogical model acts as if there were a rule defining preferential relationships, and as if agents had simply to execute them (which is a technocratic vision of societies, easy when you survey them from on high – which is often the role of the ethnologists, who cannot do otherwise . . .). Moreover, these are the rules that are in general fed to the ethnologist. They tell him: 'Look, this is how we do things here'; they present him with the official truth. These rules are very important as a model but are at the same time targets for strategies, redefinitions and manipulations, obeying logics analogous to those that I was describing just now; people want to persuade others to believe them, they want to make themselves believe.

Once again, I have not even started beginning to say what I wanted to say, but I think that I have clarified some very difficult questions. For once, I am quite pleased with what I have done, because I think that I have communicated something important that was very difficult to communicate in an official teaching situation, because I needed to reawaken forgotten experiences.

Managing the symbolic capital of the group

Now I am going to try to be more formal and say something of what I originally intended to say. In all social universes – and this is easier to see in societies where things are less formalised and codified – social relations are subjects of dispute. The names that designate them are subjects of dispute, and in these struggles people invest very important symbolic interests. One dimension of social identity that influences us in striking up an alliance is the symbolic capital held by the person concerned: if the person concerned has very high social prestige, our interest in becoming closer to them is greater than if their prestige were faded or waning. In these societies, then, the social world, like the natural world, is subject to permanent games of classification, of struggles to classify, tending to separate what was joined or join what was separated, to increase distance, to keep our distance from the risks of misalliance or on the contrary to approach and to join, to make connections and establish alliances.

Social agents manipulate names and the corresponding realities and connections, creating new alliances, and they also manipulate the image of the effects of these manipulations. For instance, there is what

146 *Lecture of 2 May 1985*

I mentioned last time: the theories in the Greek sense of the term, which means the principle of vision, but also a procession.[22] A theory is also a procession, a cortège. In Kabyle society and in many other societies, marriage processions are very important because they are a way of displaying family relations. They are a practical as well as a theoretical genealogy displayed for all the world to see. When town-dwellers say: 'You have to be mad to spend so much money on a marriage', they fail to see that, in the logic of symbolic profits, it may be absolutely crucial to spend a lot showing off your family relations because this capital will come in useful for the next marriage. This is another small point to make against traditional ethnologists or genealogists: they act as if each marriage were a self-sufficient unit, whereas it is obvious that each marriage is part of the ongoing history of all their marriages; a failed marriage is not only a failure for the person responsible and for the specific logic of one particular matrimonial exercise, but also for all their successors, who may take three generations to make up for a failed marriage: they have wasted their symbolic capital.

We can understand in the light of this logic that what Weber called 'status groups'[23] (there are whole shelves of mostly American dissertations on Weber and Marx, on *Stand* in Weber[24] and class in Marx), that is, a nobility, an 'order' in the sense of the *Ancien Régime*, are basically a class, in the sociological sense of the term, one that takes in hand its own symbolic representation, the collective representation of itself. All the properties that Weber associates with the notion of *Stand* are of this type;[25] they include control of misalliance, of *connubium* and *commercium*, control of all the relations that can contaminate, compromise or annihilate the founding *diacrisis*, the separation that constitutes the *Stand*: we are different, so we need to mark out that difference. Strategies of distinction, in the active sense of the term, include all the symbolic expenditure that we term 'conspicuous consumption',[26] clothing, adornment, furnishings, glamorous residences, in other words everything that a group may use in order to be noticed, to have a *percipi* matching the image that it wants to project of what it is.

This is not at all unique to the *Stand*; I see it as a property of all groups, which as soon as they are established have to take account of the image of themselves that they project in composing themselves. This is obvious in the case of clubs which take such pains over their conditions of membership. Take, for instance, the role of sponsors or guarantors, which, if you think about it, is as eccentric and archaic as anything that I have described in the marriage with a parallel cousin; its function is to control qualifications for membership and avoid mis-

Lecture of 2 May 1985   147

alliance, that is, the acceptance of someone whose sole presence will discredit them in the strongest sense of the word, and destroy the credit of the whole group. If so-and-so can be a member, then so could I: remember the famous quip by Groucho Marx, 'What kind of club is it if it would accept me as a member?',[27] which splendidly reveals a fine sociological paradox. In defending their boundaries, groups are defending their sacred. It is the same with secrecy – we ask: 'Why is power linked to secrecy?' There is in many situations a deliberate cultivation of secrecy [. . .]. Something that ethnologists have often said is also valid for important clubs and many exclusive establishments: they make us believe in the exclusiveness of their existence by maintaining a wall of secrecy around what happens in their enclosed space. There would be more to say about this . . .

To resume. There are manipulations of personal identity that the interactionists, especially Goffman, have largely helped to map. But the strategies of self-presentation, the strategies we use to project a favourable image, are only a minor part of these strategies and in general are indissociable from collective strategies of presentation. I could say that we should combine what Goffman did in his book on self-presentation with what he did in *Stigma*,[28] where he was much more sensitive to the role of collective identity. The manipulation of personal identity seems to me to be nearly always linked to a manipulation of collective identity insofar as personal identity is the intersection of a certain number of collective identities. To my way of thinking, this banal observation then seems to take on a certain value in explaining the strategies of display and self-display, of showing one's worth without being a show-off, of polishing one's image, etc.

Effects of the corps

This is a shame because, once again, I have the impression that I have not given my argument unity and coherence. I shall return to this point next time, but I would simply like to say a few words on the relations between the effects of the field (I have constantly referred to the field as a space where, when we are in the same section of the space, we have a lot in common) and the effects of the corps, that is, the effects that result from the fact that, as I have just said, people near each other in space add a specific effect by composing themselves into groups.[29] What happens when people who are, for example, at the bottom of all the distributions in the social space, who have the least of all the rare forms of property in a given social space (the least economic

148 *Lecture of 2 May 1985*

capital, the least cultural capital, etc.), join up to constitute themselves as consciously organised classes, provided with delegates, proxies, representatives and spokesmen?

The phenomenon is much more general: the corps effect is not only valid for a class, but also for a corps (the corps of mining engineers from the École des mines, the corps of highway engineers from the École des ponts et chaussées, the corps of the alumni of the X [the École polytechnique], etc.) and for a family. A family is the corps par excellence, it is the model for all the corps. A family is precisely the product of that alchemy that consists in transforming proximity in a given space into elective proximity, into alliances, bonds proclaimed, professed and announced in the public arena, with all the corresponding strategies that I have just mentioned with regard to Weber's *Stand*, that is, strategies of conspicuous display and theatrical representation, by which the group strives to impose the right perception of itself. [. . .]

The effects of the corps as I have just described them pose many problems for empirical sociological analysis. Last year I invoked the notion of social capital, which I had created to account for those things that you can't grasp when you work only with individuals.[30] In empirical enquiries, the unit of analysis, except in exceptional cases, is a respondent, an individual. You can ask him about his profession, his partner's diplomas, his parents and grandparents. That said, he is still a unit, although we know perfectly well that, for an explanation of certain social effects, for instance decisions about housing, the singular consumer is not the real unit. These decisions are collective. Often it is the couple, sometimes the extended family, who are implicated in these important decisions. If, for instance, you want to distribute people in the social space, you need to take account of those effects that depend on the fact that the individuals are inserted in relationships, and are members of networks. The notion of social capital enabled us to say that, in addition to what they possess in their own right (income, salary or shares, economic and cultural capital, more or less codified in terms of an educational qualification), there is everything they garner from the fact of having relations, of belonging to a family, etc.

What I was trying to describe is something that I shall now name as an 'effect of the corps', located within the limits of the effect of the field and the effects linked to holding a position in a field, but that has an added impact, which is the properly social product of the operations of the type of symbolic factors that I have mentioned, which tend to constitute – in the full meaning of the term – groups as such, through acts of alliance and consecration, and the consecration of alliances, whose paradigm is marriage, because marriage, as I said the other day,

Lecture of 2 May 1985   149

is an act that makes a practical relationship official, that transforms practical kinship into theoretical kinship and consecrates, in the sense that it makes legitimate, displayable, publicisable and public, something that until then was private, secret and even slightly shameful, depending on the conventions of the moment. The 'corps effect', 'corps solidarity' and *'esprit de corps'* are very important things.

A corps has a spirit (we could discuss this for hours . . .), which means among other things that agents' interests as a corps are not equivalent to the sum of their individual interests. They also have symbolic profits as a corps. The clubs are most interesting because they are an almost perfectly rational form of the composition of a corps. Within capitalist societies, it seems to me that they show what I have described for Kabyle marriage: the almost conscious and controlled constitution of separate, sacred groups. Someone might write a major monograph on the Jockey Club in the nineteenth century or the great English clubs, which are absolutely extraordinary: they are separate and sacred groups who affirm their difference at the same time as the homogeneity of all their members. This homogeneity is often manifest on the symbolic level in a jargon, a private language, and signs of distinction, but also through a solidarity much more fundamental than that pertaining within a family. The honour of all is engaged in the conduct of each and every one: just as it is with Kabyle society. It would have been very grave in the nineteenth century for a member of a chic club like the Jockey Club to marry a Jewish girl: the club extends its control to cover the whole person. Whence the need to have sponsors: the sponsor guarantees the whole person, he guarantees his habitus, that is, his appearance but also his behaviour and manners, his generative grammar, enabling them to anticipate his every move [. . .]. The corps is something extremely powerful. It would be the same for the alumni of American universities or most of the *grandes écoles*, to varying degrees.

We might well argue that people are less tied to these associations than they would be to an economic enterprise, but they are much more committed to aspects that touch on those much more vital values that we call symbolic, such as honour and dishonour, those things which people are ready to die for and which engage us collectively. Everyone suffers from the discredit affecting any member of the group, but the group also benefits from the credit earned by any member. Whence the importance of ranking lists for all the clubs: all clubs (as you can see from the annuals published by the *grandes écoles*) celebrate their members' good fortune; it is one of the only situations in which men celebrate other people's good fortune [*laughter*], because it contributes

150 *Lecture of 2 May 1985*

to their collective capital and enhances the group's prestige. It would be very interesting to read *La Jaune et la Rouge* [The Yellow and the Red], the review published by the X [the École polytechnique]. It is extraordinary: it works in a completely Kabyle fashion, with the same sort of goals.

The corps then is a space of collective identity that becomes an object of collective concern and strategies and is collectively managed (the problem with a club is that it cannot have a spokesman, for this would create complications and offend sensitivities . . .). Collective identity is socially known and acknowledged. It is generally indicated by a name. It has boundaries, which is very important: a corps can be counted, whereas it is absurd to count the members of a class (although this was done in the hard phase of hyper-Marxism, with people counting the petits bourgeois down to the last man[31] – which shows that all things are possible in the world of science). Since a club is countable, we can say at the same time that a club is a *numerus clausus*: it comes to the same thing because you need only one black sheep, so to speak, for the whole corps to suffer. Here we could also consider which professions are a corps (this would seriously rejuvenate the whole American theory of 'professionalisation';[32] although I have not said so, 'corps' is certainly a better term than 'profession') – why do we say: 'There are black sheep among lawyers'? I think that there are professions for which we would not say that (you would not say 'There are black sheep among the O.S. [specialised workmen]' [and this almost defines the O.S. (?)]). All this is discussed in moral terms but in fact it is a question of accounting.

I should have said at the outset that this capital is subject to rational accounting and management, whether in its accumulation – through a series of good marriages – or its dilapidation – through misalliances introducing agents who bring discredit or who spill the beans (this is a classic case, people who spill the beans are the worst of all: they say that there is no secret, whereas the whole existence of the group is based on making others believe that when its members meet they have extraordinary things to say! [*laughter*]).

I shall go deeper into this next time. If you will allow me a moment to salve my [group (?)] conscience: [. . .] I have made as strong a connection as possible between the strategies of accumulation of symbolic capital, the management and manipulation of social identity and honour in pre-capitalist societies, and the everyday strategies of our own societies, but there remain considerable differences, due to the way in which our societies are so much more codified. We have a State, and I would like to analyse in what ways the existence of a State

Lecture of 2 May 1985 151

changes the rules of the game. At the same time there should be a way of using this perspective to say what the State is; in other words, using this perspective to say what it is that the State does. So I shall discuss what the symbolic strategies of display and representation become when the symbolic capital becomes institutionalised in titles (titles of nobility, academic qualifications, etc.), and at the same time discuss the specific role of the State. I want to look into the role of the State scholars: the demographers, the INSEE statisticians, most of the economists and obviously the jurists (there are newer forms of State scholars, but the jurists are the classic form) announce the nature of the social world publicly and officially ('officially', 'publicly', 'in your face': it's just like the Kabyle . . .) without being challenged by anyone because they are incontrovertible: their methodology – which is in fact positivist – is such that it leaves no place for disagreement. I shall return to this. These people are able to pronounce on the details of the social world to the public. They can say: 'This is the correct figure, there are 1,500,000 unemployed, you cannot deny it.'[33] Although actually the unemployed are even more complicated than your cousins! [*laughter*]

Second session (seminar): the invention of the modern artist (5)

[*Bourdieu starts by reading out a question that he has received during the interval:*] 'You said: "We wouldn't say that the O.S. have their black sheep as we say that lawyers do." It seems to me that the O.S. are neither a corps nor a profession, but a level of classification in the hierarchy of workers.' This is quite true. I agree immediately. It is obvious, and it is what I thought I had said. I was saying implicitly that they are not a corps.

I shall now continue my lecture on art and the history of art, but I shall move back a little because in the meantime I have read a text by Jacques Thuillier. I hesitate to mention it because Jacques Thuillier is a very good friend and colleague[34] who happens to write on the problems that I have been discussing (I was aware of one lecture that he gave here in the Collège de France, on *pompier* art,[35] but I only discovered the present text recently). I shall discuss it, however, because I think that it will help you see the *quid proprium* of the sociological manner of raising an issue. The text is the preface to a book that appeared on the occasion of an exhibition of prix de Rome paintings between 1797 and 1803.[36] This book includes reproductions of the paintings that were classified among the first three or four in the competition for the prix de Rome in those years, and gives an extraordinary overall vision

152 *Lecture of 2 May 1985*

of what painting was at the time: it was like a dissertation exercise for an entrance examination. Most of these paintings are now to be found in the École des beaux-arts or in provincial art galleries. They were assembled for the exhibition, and Philippe Grunchec, a specialist in this kind of painting, wrote the catalogue. In his introduction he explains the workings of the competition, the recruitment of the judges and the composition of the successive juries very well. It is a first-rate document.

Last time I said *in abstracto* that what I was saying was useful in helping us to avoid anachronism and a synchronic kind of ethnocentrism. Ethnocentrism consists in projecting onto another civilisation the categories of perception inherited from membership of a different civilisation, using a code inherent to one civilisation in order to decode a different civilisation. This is the strict definition of ethnocentrism. The anachronism consists in applying to a past civilisation the categories of perception and principles of vision and division that constitute our present condition, with a peculiar effect that I have already briefly mentioned: as the historian studies a civilisation more or less immediately preceding his own, he risks adopting towards it the viewpoint provided by a civilisation that is a product of the civilisation studied. We have not reflected sufficiently on this problem: when I observe the Kwakiutl[37] with American eyes, I produce a certain type of distortion; when I observe the *pompier* painters with the eyes of a Frenchman in 1984, that is, with eyes formed by the perception of paintings born of the revolution attacking the paintings that I want to study, the danger of anachronism and ethnocentrism is of a very special order; there is a genuine logic of error at work, because I am obliged to see things that my viewpoint was based on rejecting.

That is what I said, and it might have seemed somewhat abstract. I myself felt that this kind of anachronism was rather unlikely. But in fact Jacques Thuillier presents himself as a sort of revisionist of what people say about *pompier* art. He says: 'We are in a kind of anti-institutional period, where institutions are not liked, and this leads us to misunderstand pompier art.' I would like to say by the way that when I came across the reference to this article and saw 'The Artist and the Institution', I realised that what I had been telling you last time, hoping to be original, was in fact not original at all. This always causes a little pang and yet at the same time we are pleased: since Thuillier is a major specialist in this area, it is rather comforting [to see my opinion confirmed]. So I read the text very willingly. (I can speak confidently of this text, not at all to show off, but to show you how a sociologist works.)

Lecture of 2 May 1985 153

Thuillier says implicitly that since the institution is unloved he is going to rehabilitate it: he says that he is *in favour of* the institution at a time when it is viewed unfavourably. He does thus reveal the principle of his vision, but without taking it as an object of study as such. When I say that we need to make a sociological analysis of the sociologist who is making the analysis, you might think that this is a spiritual point of honour; you might think that it is 'very European', that it is some vestige of philosophical theory. In truth what we see at work is this: Thuillier says that the principle behind his whole analysis is that he is *in favour of* institutions: 'Here I am dealing with an institution. I am myself the product of an institution of cultural production.' I drew the analogy: to really understand, in a non-anachronistic way, what the Impressionist revolution was, you have to think of the *grandes écoles*, and imagine that we had a salon for the leading candidates rejected by the entrance examination for the École normale supérieure.[38] But this conscious, controlled analogy supposed a conscious, controlled relation with the institution, whereas the driving force of Jacques Thuillier's analysis turns out to be a non-analysed relation with what I would call the 'anti-institutional mood'. For those of you who know my work, I recently finished a study of the anti-institutional mood as a generational phenomenon of the period of 1968.[39] I try to show how a certain kind of relation to the family and the education system, combined, is a general disposition in a certain generation, 'generation' being understood in the social sense of the term: the generation of people who have a certain relation at a certain moment with a certain education system.

When I work on the notion of the institution I cannot be unaware of the fact that our relation to the institution is not neutral nowadays – and maybe never could be; we cannot speak well or ill of an institution, or simply analyse it, without inviting a reflexive doubt on the relationship that we are investing in as we analyse this institution. What is involved in the revision of *pompier* art suggested by Thuillier is a paradoxical kind of posture, non-conformist to the second degree. Since nowadays it has become chic or even banal to oppose institutions, since there is a kind of anti-institutional mood and the academies of painting and the fine arts are institutions, Thuillier considers that, to understand or rehabilitate the institutional painting that *pompier* painting is, we need to rehabilitate the institution. Thus he assumes a normative and judgemental function, which is always the role of the critic: the struggles for rehabilitation that I have mentioned are concerned with changing the hierarchy of values, with inverting the order of values.

154 *Lecture of 2 May 1985*

In his text, Jacques Thuillier defends the competition and makes an explicit comparison with the École normale: 'The kind of artistic "cagnes" [khâgnes = preparatory classes] formed by the studios of Léon Cogniet, Ingres or Gleyre, simple preparatory classes with no official link to the École des beaux-arts, were probably more important for the fate of French art than the teaching of the École itself or the prize winners.'[40] This is quite true: I totally agree and am delighted that he says so, but his failure to self-analyse leads him to use as instrument of analysis a relation with the object of study that is not only unanalysed but metaphorical too, since – and this is the heart of the problem – it is the unanalysed relation of the analyst to the École normale which serves as the unanalysed principle for understanding the relation of the analyst to the structural equivalent of the École normale that is the École des beaux-arts. This means that this is an apologia rather than a scientific discourse, and surprisingly, the article which apparently intended to understand and describe *pompier* art has nothing to say about art itself.

Without wishing to score points, I argue that my own approach showed that it is only if we analyse the institution as institution and keep in mind the transhistorical invariants – not of any institution but of the institutions of cultural production and reproduction (for instance, the fact that the producer is anonymous and impersonal, a master and not an artist) – that we can in some way use the analysis of the institution, once defined in its specificity, to interpret the properties of the artistic work (for instance, the fact that it foregrounds virtuosity). Something very surprising is that, in analysing the works, Thuillier does at least refer to the institution, which is most welcome, but he does not use this to help understand the work. This is because his intention is not so much to understand the work as to rehabilitate the institution, and in the last analysis to rehabilitate the institution whose values he has inherited.

I need to say that because this is a common problem. I came across the article only this week: it is likely that if I cast my net wider I would find many more anachronisms of this kind. I should say in passing that Thuillier's text contains a quite astonishing rehabilitation of the democratic side of the institution of the Beaux-arts. It appears – an opinion that I shared[41] – that the *pompiers* suffered a major handicap in their rivalry with the leading Impressionists: being of lower-class and often provincial origins, they were not very adept at managing the strategies of self-display that are part of artistic production. Indeed, as soon as the artist is invented and produced as such, he no longer needs simply to produce material objects, but also to produce the representa-

Lecture of 2 May 1985　　　155

tion of the artist that contributes to the value of the material product; and in order to produce the artist as artist, he has to produce himself as an artist, he has to dress and speak like an artist, and frequent cafés for artists; and these skills are not equally distributed across different geographic and social origins. This has been verified a hundred times: the provincials with their local accents are not good at the self-representation and display that are part of the implicit definition of the painter as soon as he becomes constituted as an artist. Thus they were handicapped in the competition. That was my analysis.

In Thuillier there is a kind of defence of the institution that draws on our contemporary 'left-wing' thinking which focuses on its democratic character: its members were very poor; moreover, the masters protected the poorest, dispensing them from paying their studio fees. You can understand now why I underlined the fact that accomplishing a descriptive sociology that isn't positivist, or a neutral sociology that isn't axiologically neutral in Weber's sense,[42] and understanding an institution through its own logic and operations without value judgement (even if, like everyone, I am obviously more sympathetic to the values of the Impressionists), are only possible if we are capable of analysing our own relation to the object of study. This is why after hesitating at length I broke the rule of not criticising a colleague, who is also a friend, without giving him the opportunity to defend himself. I could have given many another example. If I feel free to say certain things that otherwise would be *ad hominem*, it is because my argument is not pitched at the level of struggle, rehabilitation and rivalry ('They are better', 'They are no good').

I believe that the condition for this sort of objectification, which is not social neutrality at all, is the objectification of the position we hold in the social space (and more precisely in a certain state of the social space), with hidden interests, which in the case of a historical phenomenon may depend on effects of homology. (I have, for instance, quoted philosophers who, in order to make a past way of thinking appeal to modern tastes, often refer to the present day. Sometimes they do it consciously. When they say: 'It is like so-and-so, today', 'A Sophist today would be [André] Glucksmann', they are scoring points, or planning strategies.) So I think that it is very important to make the space and our position in that space an object of attention, and to be on the lookout for the homologies that may create relations of hidden interests with people dead and buried long ago, with whom we apparently have no connection. In my eyes, this is how to have true epistemological control of historical study. (I have taken my time over this, but I do believe that it is important.) 'This is a lecture for the

156 *Lecture of 2 May 1985*

present moment', 'The story that I am telling is something that I am still involved in': most historical narratives are still issues in struggles between historians, and even beyond them;[43] otherwise they would not be told . . .

The alliance of painters and writers

Now to return to the main issue. Last time, I insisted on the fact that the symbolic revolution operated by the artists was important as a sufficient condition, when the necessary condition was the objective crisis of the institution: for this objective crisis to become a symbolic revolution, it required the symbolic work of transforming names. It's like changing the name of a street, [. . .] they needed to name things differently, what was positive had to become negative. In their strug-gle, the painters were accompanied by the writers as objective, and also active, allies. Without the help of the writers, they would not have succeeded. As I said last time, the collective conversion manifested in the transformation of the representation of paintings, of the painter, of the process of painting and exhibiting, of the place of exhibition and the relation between painter and critics – this symbolic revolution of the whole machinery of symbolic production supposed a whole host of small, individual, objectively orchestrated conversions.

Another important thing is the fact that we tend always to posit the alternative of the individual and the collective, whereas impor-tant historical phenomena are in fact individual changes, objectively orchestrated in line with the affinities of habitus, and reinforced by the explanation given by the professional commentators who, in saying out loud what is happening in people's minds (because it is in people's minds that these things happen), accelerate the symbolic transforma-tion that we call, in a very poor term that should be banned, the 'awakening of consciousness'. Here we are talking about a very general model: I think that this type of mechanism should be invoked to under-stand, for instance, what happened in the French Church between 1950 and 1970, or what has been happening in French universities over the last twenty years, providing a good illustration of the relation between practical changes and changes in the discourse accompanying a move-ment, which it accelerates by the fact of enunciating it.

The painters did then find allies in the writers, but to understand what happened in the nineteenth century, we need to see the move-ment in both directions: the painters were a great help to the writers by assuming the role of 'exemplary prophets'.[44] This is Weber's concept,

Lecture of 2 May 1985   157

where there is a form of prophecy which is not so much a prophecy through the word but a prophecy through the example. This would be, for instance, the martyr who speaks through his acts, his *praxis*, his exploits or his virtues, and who creates an effect of symbolic transformation though his very existence. The painters for the most part were bereft of language, since in general (with the few exceptions, such as Manet and Delacroix, that I have already mentioned) they were of inferior social origins and less well educated than the writers. They did nonetheless incarnate the whole pathos of the life of the artist, up to and including death. The theme of the death of the artist seems important to me. Once again, you are likely to see that as a kind of hagiography ([Alfred de Vigny, in] *Chatterton*, and other great Romantic authors, narrated the tragic adventures of artists who died from their love of art).

For myself, I identify it as a social fact; insofar as there is no greater attestation of the value of something than the fact of dying for it (this is I think a social fact that we may accept as a proposition), the fact that many artists, many painters, died for the love of art is a social fact which people were very struck by. For instance, contemporary memoirs are full of anecdotes on this subject. There is one that I have already told you about: the one where the gravedigger, seeing some starving *rapins* arriving at the cemetery poorly dressed in rags and threadbare black felt hats, says: 'I've seen that lot already, and they are back again' (they had buried one friend and had come back to bury another). In other words, people were dying like flies and they were dying for the love of art. The struggle against the academic system that I was describing the other day was paid for by real sacrifices and the painters figure a sort of exemplary realisation of the antinomy that was being formed between art and money, bourgeois and artist, the artist placing the values of art above all else, and even above life itself.

The artist's way of life and the invention of pure love

We need to look again at all these very familiar things. First, the writers and the artists did meet. For instance, Théophile Gautier, who was very important, was originally a painter. This is usually mentioned by critics who draw attention to the pictorial nature of his poetry, but there is another very important aspect: Gautier knew the life of the painter very well and he contributed not just pictorial metaphors and the taste for Spain that were in fashion among the painters, but also that kind of *art de vivre* which is the art of living in poverty with all that

158 *Lecture of 2 May 1985*

this implies: the artist's way of life is, for example, the art of finding little restaurants where you can eat for almost nothing. The artist's life then becomes a chic way of life. This is actually an interesting historical phenomenon which is still with us: the artist discovers little bistros that become chic and that they then have to avoid because they can no longer afford them. The role of explorer in this kind of lifestyle has been very well described by Flaubert and Balzac and in all the novels of the nineteenth century. It also is part of the role of the exemplary prophet.

One important book is obviously Murger's *Vie de bohème*,[45] where we see that the artists are at once inventors of the pure love of art (that is, the love of art unto death) and the pure love of love. The two are closely linked: the artists were at once the inventors of pure love and of eroticism. This is a very important social fact. They are closely linked in Murger. It has been said, for instance, that 'love is an invention of the West',[46] but I think that the modern forms of love, as opposed to money, are an invention of the artists. The opposition between love and money, between pure love and venal love, becomes one of the fundamental structures of Flaubert's *Sentimental Education*, where there are, for instance, the two characters: the venal woman who offers herself freely to the artist, and the pure woman who does not yield but who is not paid either, the two being opposed to the bourgeois love that is either domestic, mercenary love, or extramarital love, which is also mercenary.[47] The concept of the 'mercenary' is very important. It underpins a modern mythology of love that goes hand in hand with the modern mythology of the love of art; it's more or less the same thing whether you sing the praises of a perverse relationship with art or of a pure relationship with art . . . We could say that there is an aesthetic kind of eroticism and a kind of aesthetic angelism.

You can see the analogies, but I am not just playing literary games. What I am describing is the invention of social models of the art of living, and in *Sentimental Education* – which is an extraordinary novel because it is a virtual sociology, however disguised, of the universe it describes – Flaubert associates our relation to art with our relation to love: the two are inseparable, the invention of pure love and the invention of the pure love of art are contemporary. Murger's book is very important for this reason, even if it is quite tedious and uninteresting [from a literary point of view?]. In every period there is a highly influential book that everyone reads but is then forgotten by literary history. This is true of philosophy too. Whence the falseness of histories of philosophy; they record only the outward signs and they forget that Hegel – who said it himself, which is why we remember it[48] – and all

Lecture of 2 May 1985

philosophers in general read the newspaper every morning. Just like all of us, they read things that are completely stupid (for example, I don't know, the equivalent of *Science et vie*),[49] and we assume they have spent their whole lives reading nothing but Kant [*laughter*], which rather distorts our reading of these authors. When Hegel walked down the street, he saw all the same signs and masses of ordinary things that we all do, and they remain in his mind when he philosophises.

It's the same in the domain of art [*short silence*] . . . I hesitate because there the common opinion is that sociologists, unlike literary men, rehabilitate minor authors. This is an absolutely unanswerable way of disqualifying the sociology of art: 'We literary men support the elite, with our selections and extracts' [*laughter*], which is historically true (the authors who have lasted are those who have been preserved in the published extracts). For any of you who are looking for a topic: a brilliant and historically important study would be a social history of ranking lists. How was the roll of honour that we now find self-evident composed, given one or two fashionable rehabilitations from time to time, reintroducing, for instance, [the seventeenth-century dramatist Jean de] Rotrou or [his contemporary, the poet Honorat de Bueil de] Racan? Haskell, who is at the Collège de France at the moment (I recommend him: it is a unique opportunity, you mustn't miss him), has written a splendid study (which I have already mentioned [in the Lecture of 18 April 1985]) on rediscoveries in art. It is a kind of social history. He makes a fantastic analysis of a painting by Delaroche, who was a professor at the École des beaux-arts and who figures clearly in my universe of academic painters. In about 1880 he painted his vision of a pictorial Olympus.[50] Who figured in it? We note that there are people like [the *Quattrocento* painter] Piero della Francesca, for instance, whom we would definitely include in a chart of this kind but who are not included at all. Comparing different lists, as Haskell does, is to compare and study categories of perception: 'Tell me who you include in your chart, and I'll tell you how you see painting.' It is very difficult. How can we reconstruct the categories of perception of people living in the twelfth century? We may of course feel 'Einfühlung' [empathy] with the texts, but we still need strategies. One strategy consists in looking for indirect clues: we know what these people painted and we can hypothesise that they painted what was considered worthy of being painted, what it was honourable to paint. We can then, from what they painted, form an idea of their categories of perception, especially when there are several painters to study.

This process should be followed in exactly the same way for what in my jargon I give the theoretical label of 'the process of canonisation

160 *Lecture of 2 May 1985*

of authors': as with saints, who are the authors that we accept as 'classics', that is, as worthy of being taught in class, who are the legitimate, that is, sacred and consecrated, authors? There are the classics and the non-classics: the classics are allowed to enter the classroom, they can cross the threshold and the priest of culture may legitimately speak of them, even if he says that there were authors who were better, or worse. It is not at all the same for the non-classics: they are excluded from the class, they are consigned to hell. One of the most powerful effects produced by an academic or school system is precisely to create a boundary accepted as being self-evident: it makes us believe that the tiny universe of the classics inculcated in the classroom is coextensive with the real universe. So you can imagine how interesting it would be to explore the limits of our contemporary French and Western minds[51] by making a historical analysis of the process of canonisation: how did this kind of list of consecrated, sacred authors, that we accept as self-evident, compulsory reading matter, come to be composed? For it does indeed imply obligation, but also a right, the scholarly right to ignore some authors and to know others ('Let no one [ignorant of geometry] enter here . . .'),[52] etc. Haskell has done this work and we should by a similar logic study the history of such boundaries to see that authors who may have been very influential at one time have disappeared from the roll, often for sociological reasons. For this reason, our whole perception of the period is false.

To return to what I was saying before I started discussing the process of canonisation: the sociology of literature, seen by its opponents (and God knows there are some), is accused of reintroducing the masses. It relies on statistics, it levels down. Here we have the opposition between the one and the many: statistics are on the side of the many, the vulgar, the middling and the average – all this is in Heidegger[53] – and sociology, by reintroducing the masses, is destroying literature as such. I don't mind admitting that the sociology of literature associated with the name of Escarpit[54] does rather match that description: it seems to me, beyond all value judgements, that it should be discounted since it is not really scientific. The sociology of literature as I conceive it also reintroduces – but in a different way – the totality of people who at one moment or another created some effects in a field.[55] There are people whom it is vital not to forget to reintroduce, because they created effects in a field, and this is the only acceptable definition of membership of a field: somebody belongs if it is impossible to understand certain things happening in the field without taking their existence into account. Murger is the type of character who, however we rate his value according to our categories of perception, has produced enormous effects.

Lecture of 2 May 1985   161

As a position in the literary space he must then be reintroduced, and that has nothing to do with statistics (which does not mean that the statistics are not useful).

The properly sociological analysis of a universe like this one must then take into account the people who have helped fashion its world view, for instance by representing one of the positions in relation to which the people we remember today constituted themselves. Thus Flaubert and those around him who constituted the position of art for art's sake, and whose only common factor was to hold this position, are only intelligible in relation to people whose names you have completely forgotten,[56] who are not even mentioned by literary historians and who represent on the one hand the pole of bourgeois art (what at the time was called the 'theatre of good taste', with boulevard authors who are occasionally revived on television in *At the Theatre Tonight*[57]) and, on the other hand, what at the time was called 'social art', that is, people, some of whom, like [Pierre] Leroux, are still remembered because they had some political role, but who for the most part are completely forgotten. The point is not to reintegrate them to make up the numbers, to include everyone, but because their existence was one of the structuring principles behind people's perception of the field: anyone living in this field had their eyes structured through this opposition between social art and bourgeois art, and could then constitute themselves as being neither one nor the other; 'art for art's sake' was to a great extent constituted in this way.[58]

Artistic transgression today and a century ago

After this new parenthesis, I return to my topic: the artists and the writers were linked by a sort of alliance of mutual interests. The writers found a model in the life and death of the artist and in return gave the artists what they most lacked, that is, a celebratory discourse helping them to identify themselves as artists. That said, the celebration of artists very soon became determinant in the role of the intellectual and the writer. Today for instance, in order to expand the limited role of the author, artist or philosopher, an intellectual may go in for politics or write on painting. It is part of the unspoken definition of the intellectual that he needs to write on painting – even if in general he writes rubbish. This is yet another historical invention that might not have happened; it is linked to a certain state of the field.

Thus the artist found a spokesman and an ideologist in the writer. The writers did not merely say: 'It's good to be an artist', but also

162   *Lecture of 2 May 1985*

'This is what the life of an artist, or the love of an artist, etc., is.' The writers invented it and found the words for it. The term 'sentimental education' is extraordinary. It is as if Flaubert had become aware that an entirely new role had appeared and he needed to learn it. To give a novel such a title implied: 'This is an edifying novel, composing a new genre and a new character', and Frédéric [the main character in *Sentimental Education*] is a type of character who, when he can't manage to incarnate one of the two roles tenable in the given space (those of the banker and the artist), wavers between the two, wandering from one point to the other without ever managing to establish himself – the role of the 'artist' was no doubt all the more difficult to fulfil for being so recent.

This is another thing that we forget when we fall into ethnocentric anachronism. Today certain well-known Parisian imposters have no problem in acting the part of the artist (as long as they don't take their imposture too far) because it is ready-made. They know what they have to do and the public is ready for it. Part of the role is to accomplish a certain number of tasks that had to be invented: to be in certain cafés at certain times, write about their transgressions, write on eroticism, rehabilitate Sade[59] . . . The role play is established and is not open to criticism . . . for the critics themselves have been formed by past experience. Since they know that their predecessors committed historical errors that are universally mocked today, they have a kind of favourable bias towards the avant-garde. This is another example of the anachronism effect: the role has already been created, but is now played by people different from those who created it. I am not simply saying that the revolutionaries are not the same as their epigones (a well-known little historical law), but that the invention of the role, the invention of art for art's sake, were formidably difficult, and the people responsible for inventing them had social properties different from their successors: in general they had more capital; you need more capital to create a role than to act it out once it has been created. We need to bear this simple law in mind. Since it takes more capital and also more energy, describing the social properties of the holders of these roles will reveal differences that we cannot account for if we merely note the homology, and forget that although the avant-garde in a field where the avant-garde is a hundred years old is homologous with the avant-garde in the field where it first appeared, there is the enormous difference of historical precedence.

In other words, our avant-garde today is a secondary avant-garde; we inhabit a universe where everyone knows what it is to be 'avant-garde', where institutions exist that imply recognition of the avant-

Lecture of 2 May 1985   163

garde. The Salon des refusés itself was unheard of: that is what we need to bring into the equation, we need to de-familiarise our perception and try to feel astonished that there could have been a Salon for rejects.

The mercenary artist and art for art's sake

In this sort of alliance, the writers and the artists had their interests, but I ventured on this digression to prevent you from projecting into your understanding of the interests of the writers of the past the interests of the writers of the present. (I deplore having to fly this kind of kite, but it is unfortunately necessary in order to stop you launching into your own spontaneous sociology . . .) Although it was in the writers' interest to ally themselves with the painters, this does not have the same implications as what Sollers is doing today . . . It is something quite different. They had an almost constitutive interest, they too were in the process of constituting themselves. We need to take the word 'constitution' in the sense that I was using it just now: they were in the process of constituting themselves, that is, engaged in the process of self-constitution; they needed to know who they were, and what they were there for. For instance, as has often been noted, one obsessive theme of all the art-for-art's-sake writers was the comparison between the writer and the prostitute.[60] This kind of solidarity – which was also shown in paintings like *Olympia* – should in my opinion be taken very seriously. It is not simply a literary theme, even if it did become one later. It is about being 'mercenary': mercenary love and mercenary art are created as objects for sale. This is a point that I shall develop.

Paradoxically, the artists broke free from the Academy by using the market. This is another thing that has not been properly understood: when someone makes a rather impressionistic sociological study (on 'capitalism', or the artist in the service of 'high capital', etc.), they tend to say that the artist hates the bourgeoisie. In fact there are revolutions – which we might call anti-bourgeois (although this is not much help) – which can only be started with the help of the bourgeoisie and a bourgeois market. For instance, the Impressionists mounted a revolution against the Academy with the ideological help of the writers (who to some degree play the part that we say that intellectuals do with the proletariat) and with the objective alliance of a market of consumers which allowed them to live with new forms of commission and acquire freedom from the Academy. There too they were in the process of inventing something very strange: doesn't the artist discredit himself

164 *Lecture of 2 May 1985*

by making money? It is the old problem of Socrates and the Sophists: the latter ask for payment, the former does not.[61] The only difference, often – think of the difference between a healer and a doctor (sometimes I say things very quickly because I know that your innate intuition will cut in) – is in rejecting money or at least not handling it personally.

The problem of the artists and writers was heart-rending: are we not mercenaries too? Are we all prostitutes? Do we all write in exchange for money? Is it sufficient not to write for money to be an artist? This poses a terrible problem because, if all those who don't earn a penny are consecrated as artists, I am obliged to recognise all those who fail as equal. This was Flaubert's great problem. Not earning money then is a necessary but not a sufficient condition. Voluntary rejection is different from obligatory rejection. This problem is still with us: there are those who refuse to attend colloquia and those who are not invited; there are those who refuse to appear on television or in the media and those who are not invited – those who are not invited are the most virtuous, of course . . .

This problem was posed in concrete terms. The painters who were dying in their attics while singing songs for Mimi[62] were very important as models ('It must be worth living like that because there are people who are dying for it'). At the same time they needed new words to describe it. In rooting for the artists, the writers were obviously rooting for themselves. At the same time as they were writing serials, most of them were also in the process of inventing the artist who, in order to create pure art, exploits the market and the consumer, and in their most basic form: you need to accept writing serials paid by the line in order to create ambitious novels elsewhere, which will be read only by a few.

This is a fantastic contradiction. You must recognise in what I am saying many things that you already know, but if we put them all together systematically, we get a very different view of what an artist's work was. For instance, we understand that *Sentimental Education* is a novel that Flaubert wrote for Flaubert. We cannot just say that 'Frédéric is Flaubert'. That is an absolutely stupid question, even from the viewpoint of rather trendy literary canons (in fact, we would not put it that way now: Barthes has had his say and we know that it isn't *chic* [laughter]!). But it is nonetheless true that it is Flaubert, that the whole space projected into *Sentimental Education* is Flaubert's vision of the world, and that in constructing Frédéric's failure, Flaubert, a psychoanalyst would say, is solving his own problem symbolically: What is it to be an artist? Is it worth the trouble? 'Mightn't I have

Lecture of 2 May 1985 165

done better to study medicine like my brother?' 'Maybe my father was right?' This is something very difficult, which haunts the greatest minds. We forget that such problems arise, and yet I believe they lie at the heart of the work.

Lecture of 9 May 1985

First session (lecture): certification and social order – The principle and justice of distributions – Private charity and public welfare – The three levels of analysis of a distribution – Where is the State? – Verdicts and the effects of power – The field of certification
Second session (seminar): the invention of the modern artist (6) – Academic painting as a theological universe – Institutionalising perspectivism – The invention of the artist as character – The painter–writer couple

First session (lecture): certification and social order

[. . .] I shall pick up from where I left off, that is, with the analysis of the phenomenon of legitimate categorisation summed up in the word *nomos*, as an operation consisting in dividing, but with authority and the force of law. I could have pursued this analysis in the direction that I took last time, studying the effects specific to the judicial divisions of social space. I had indicated simply that social divisions, like divisions into corps (for instance, the corps of the engineers of roads and bridges) and in particular the divisions into families, tended to confuse the analysis of the social space and the distributions within it. I shall not develop this point, I shall return to it if I have time, but I shall rather follow the logic of my discourse, and now turn to the essential. What I intend to do today is attempt to show how the legitimate division and the agents socially mandated to maintain it exercise a function that constructs the social order.

To give you an immediate idea of the drift of my argument, I propose to reflect for a moment on the idea of the certificate. There are certificates of competence (at all levels) delivered by the education

Lecture of 9 May 1985   167

system, and there are certificates of incapacity, so to speak, such as those delivered by doctors. In our society doctors are socially mandated to certify that someone is sick, that they have such and such an illness, that they are an invalid, that they have such and such a degree of disability, the handicap being measurable in percentages corresponding to socially recognised benefits. The idea of the certificate is I think extremely important, and if I had to sum up in a word the analyses that I have expounded I would no doubt use the word 'certificate': someone certifies that something is true (the Latin spells it out: *certus-facio*), and this act of certification, of consecration of something said to be true, is guaranteed by the State; it is a judgement of quite a particular kind, that philosophy has never analysed. The doctor who issues a sick note certifies that you are not an imposter, or at least that he has not detected any imposture, which is a crucial problem: the question facing those mandated to deliver certificates is how to know whether they are dealing with an imposter or someone genuine. They are obliged to detect cheating and all forms of dissimulation. For instance, one problem for the doctor delivering a certificate is how to know whether he is dealing with someone who has mastered the procedures needed to enjoy his rights, or someone who has mastered the procedures needed to make the doctor believe that they are in the right.

We find ourselves in the universe of belief. Firstly, the certifier must be certain that he is certified to certify. This is very important, because he might have his doubts. For instance, when there is a crisis in the Order of Doctors,[1] the doctors may start to wonder whether their power of legal certification is really included in their power of medical certification, and whether they shouldn't distinguish between certifying that a person has an illness and certifying their right to the benefits arising. This concerns the medical certificate as it does the school certificate (a comparative study of the two forms of certificate would surely be very significant: one is a positive certificate, certifying aptitude, the other a negative certificate, certifying incapacity – one question to consider then is whether it is easier to certify the positive rather than the negative). The authorised person signing a medical certificate wields the acknowledged power to confer extra-medical privileges, privileges of two orders: the positive ones (a medical certificate may grant the right to welfare benefits) or negative privileges (which dispense you from obligations – for instance, a medical certificate may dispense you from the obligation to perform military service,[2] from paying your debts or, in extreme cases, from judicial sentencing – this is a problem for the legal experts . . .).

168 *Lecture of 9 May 1985*

We can see right away what is at stake. I have said several times here that there are fields within which the truth is a matter of dispute. Here this is very obvious. The question as to whether the person concerned is genuinely ill or simulating is central: there is the whole system of the expertise of the patient's doctor, the counter-expertise by the medical authorities, etc. Part of the approach of the medical system is based on the idea that there may be simulation and cheating: the diagnosis (we are always in the logic of perception, of correct perception) or medical *diacrisis* can be abused by the strategies of the potential client for the benefits associated with a recognised disadvantage. The question then is how to know who can say that someone is disabled, and to what degree.

One important aspect of what I have been saying concerns these notions of handicap and invalidity. The whole lexicon ('handicap', 'handicapped', 'invalid', 'invalidity', 'incapacity', 'incapacity for work') has historical origins. This process of legally guaranteed social categorisation has a social history, and to understand it completely, you would have to go back I think at least to the eighteenth century and the politics of poor relief. A considerable part of the discourse of the 'philanthropists', as they were called, consisted in asking whether someone poor was genuinely and legitimately poor. 'Is he poor because of some vice, or poor because of some misfortune or fate?' This central problem of political theology is still at work behind our contemporary discussions of the Welfare State:[3] what is debated is still always the distribution associated with the fact of categorising people as socially disabled (which often – but not always – means 'disabled by the effect of the action of society') – which is in fact the principle of legitimate redistribution.

The principle and justice of distributions

In other words, what I have been discussing so far is the question of distribution: in any social space (such as the university field, the political field or the religious field), there is a certain distribution of scarce goods at issue, and a certain representation of the right distribution of goods is always in play at the heart of this space. The question of the just representation of the distribution within this space, the just distribution in the *nomos*, that is, the right and legitimate distribution, is part of the struggle (which occurs in every social space or field) to transform the distribution within this space. To have the *nomos* on your side, as the Kabyle have 'the rules on their side',[4] to have with you

Lecture of 9 May 1985

the representation of the just distribution, is to have a symbolic power, and one of the goals is to be able to say: 'The distribution that we presently have is just', 'Our present mode of redistribution, our means of giving to the poor, through charity or public welfare for example, is legitimate.' There is then a double discussion: a discussion over the adequacy or the justice of the prevailing distribution, and a discussion over the adequacy or the justice of the current mode of redistribution ('The Welfare State is too expensive',[5] 'Charity is humiliating, we should replace it with public forms of assistance, mediated by the State'). In the ever-present debate over the transformation of distribution, the representation of distribution then is one of the weapons that may be used.

The person with the power to certify has considerable power in this struggle. If intelligence, for example, is one of the legitimate principles of justification of distribution or redistribution, the person with the power to certify which men are intelligent disposes of an important power (I was saying just now that we can certify aptitude or incapacity; in general – I have only just thought of this, I haven't had time to check – it seems to me that positive principles need to be invoked in order to justify principles of justification, and negative principles to justify redistributions. We need to check . . .). The person who certifies that someone is intelligent according to the social norms in vigour at a given moment in time (it is obvious that intelligence is the object of a social definition at a given moment: there are if not an infinity at least a great number of forms of intelligence, but the education system, for instance, tends to favour one and only one),[6] the person who makes a quantitative evaluation of intelligence using external criteria, has a considerable social power of justification of distribution.

Based on this analysis of the certificate, we can see how a practice like medicine has a curious status. I referred to this briefly in *Homo Academicus*: in making a distinction between academic departments with a judicial dimension, like law and medicine, and the humanities and science faculties, I was referring to their property of infusing intellectual acts with judicial values.[7] The whole group of faculties accomplishes such acts of judgement at the time of academic exams (which, like a medical examination, involves a diagnosis accompanied by an effect of certification), but the faculty of medicine has a supplementary capacity: it can also certify incapacity, with the various social benefits guaranteed by the State. In this sense the faculty of medicine functions like an expert: it is a social agent whose viewpoint is socially recognised, and whose verdicts have the force of law.

170   *Lecture of 9 May 1985*

Private charity and public welfare

Although they apply to individuals, these verdicts are not individual verdicts. They are categorial verdicts, and the whole problem is to know whether the individual concerned is really eligible (the word 'justified' would say it all), if he fits into a category suitable for me to grant him a certificate of invalidity. This is where these judgements differ from actions of charity, whose judgements are strictly individual (*idios*)[8] and singular, and performed on the spur of the moment: the beggar holds out his hand, I judge ('Is he an imposter or not?'), I am perfectly free to decide. This would be worth analysing . . . If I had to pronounce an axiom that defines the State, I would say: 'The State is what establishes the difference between a beggar and someone entitled to official welfare benefits.' The beggar appeals directly in person to another person, from one individual to another, and he obtains something like what Weber called *Kadijustiz*, an act of justice by the *kadi*, which is founded on individual intuition, not on anything universalised. It is the justice of Sancho Panza or Solomon: if Sancho Panza is in a bad mood or has not eaten well he does not give alms; if he is in a good mood he does. It is totally variable. It is based on the ethics of sympathy and sentiment that was criticised by Kant.[9]

Social welfare, on the other hand, although meted out by an individual, is administered by an individual officially mandated by society. He acts not so much as an isolated individual, he is sworn in and accredited. His good or bad moods may obviously influence him, but within limits foreseen by the law: he will be checked. If he has a personal relationship with the patient an official specialist will verify or challenge his act . . . He is then a bureaucratic individual, that is, interchangeable, substitutable, accomplishing universal and therefore formal acts.[10] Bureaucratic morality, like Kantian morality in fact, is based on the principle of universalising the singular act:[11] it is an act of which we suppose that any other individual placed in the same circumstances and presenting the same statutory guarantees in the eyes of the State would do likewise.

Thus the act of justice, as opposed to the act of charity (this is an old *pons asinorum*, but we often need to think about these basic problems, for well-worn examination questions often hide important social problems that need to be rethought without prejudice), is a categorical judgement that assimilates a singular individual into a general category which is socially constructed and has a social history. The category of the 'handicapped' for instance, was created by a decree in a particular year, after struggles among doctors, philanthropists, sociologists and

Lecture of 9 May 1985   171

historians, among others, to define it; it is written into the statutes, it has a name that was fought over. Similarly, some people fought to be called 'mail officers' instead of 'postmen',[12] for instance. The application of these generic categories to specific individuals is the monopoly of certain agents whom we suppose to be capable of perceiving the category and recognising specific examples. To a certain extent the clinical act of diagnosis which consists in assimilating an individual into a class and making them members of that class coincides with the legal act of categorisation, since in both cases it is a question of assimilating an individual into a class, but a class is both scientific and juridical. Here we touch on an important point: this class is both a *nomos* in the sense of division (*nemo*, I separate; I say 'this is this, that is that') and a *nomos* in the sense of a law ('this has merit, that does not'; and if I say, for instance, 'This man deserves to be exempted from military service, and that man is a simulator', their social destinies will be totally different: one will end up in hospital, the other in prison).

The three levels of analysis of a distribution

The problem of legitimate perception (which I shall return to in the final lecture, to show you a sort of theoretical genealogy since Kant and other founding fathers) might seem rather speculative to you. With this analysis it seems that it is also concrete [. . .]. It seems to me that the sociology of perception that I was proposing leads us to understand the elementary perceptions of classification, that are at the same time operations of codification. In fact, behind the notion of *nomos* that I mentioned there lies the whole problem of distributive justice in moral philosophy. The distribution that statisticians speak of seems objective: the sociologists or economists study the distributions, they look for the primary explicative principles of the distribution and they note its structures. Most social structures are in fact manifest in the guise of distributions, and this is the easy way to grasp them. As I have so often said, the structure of a field is the distribution of specific capacities giving power over what matters in the field: for instance, to find the structure of the university field, I must determine the relevant properties that give power in this field, and then see how they are distributed among individuals. This structure will provide the structure enabling me to explain the attitudes of individuals: someone who has a lot of what you need in order to dominate will tend to behave in a certain way, different from someone who has very little, etc. This is what distribution is: it is the *nomos* realised, it

172   *Lecture of 9 May 1985*

is the fundamental law of a field that has become a space of unequally distributed goods.

We should keep in mind the metaphor of gambling: some players have large piles of chips, others have none, and the game continues ... Analysing the structure of a field means stopping the game at a moment in time and observing the structure of the piles of chips. From this structure, I can understand what has been happening (who has won, and so on) and also anticipate what is going to happen, because there is always a connection between the distribution of the piles and the strategy that the agents will use in order to preserve or subvert the structure of the piles. This is what a field is like. The sociologist, then, is in a way the equivalent of a Roman *censor* (I am using the word on purpose, I shall return to this: the *censor* was charged with conducting the *census* – as we use the word today – and seeing how wealth was distributed in order to determine how individuals should be taxed). He conducts the census in positive terms (what is the distribution?): he does not pass judgement, he describes the distribution, he says who has not very much, who has a lot, and who has something in between.

In general the people who stop at that (saying: 'My work as a sociologist requires simply conducting a *census*') are the State sociologists (I shall return to this) who conduct official censuses. Their work is to designate statistical categories, which (since they are State sociologists, official scholars . . .) are often *eo ipso* judicial categories. The bureaucratic censor at INSEE and the official demographer are ultimately closer to the doctor (they deliver certificates) than to the autonomous sociologist (I shall return to this question of autonomy). Limiting yourself to the census, that is, to the study of a real distribution, grants you all the appearance of scientificity; if you want people to say: 'Your work is truly scientific', you should leave it at that. To give an extremely simple example: when the sociology of education started, it established the laws of distribution of success in the education system while immediately offering hypotheses explaining the determining principles of this distribution, which is obviously a contentious issue, and open to dispute.

A book by Monsieur Thélot entitled *Tel père, tel fils*[13] [Like Father, Like Son] has given a bureaucratic account of this in the guise of an uncritical report, and it has become a kind of reference work of indisputable authority. He says more or less what had been said by the sociology of education – and you can be sure that, without this sociology of education, he would never had said what he said, it would never have occurred to him – but, couching it in bureaucratic terms, backed by a bureaucratic guarantee, and drawing no conclusions

Lecture of 9 May 1985 173

about the whys and wherefores, the determining factors and the possible consequences, gives him the bureaucratic patent, and he can be taught throughout the land with a kind of bureaucratic guarantee of scientificity. I shall return to this point, which I find very important in settling the problem of deciding who is scientific in the social sciences and who isn't.

Distribution, then, can be the object of a positive statistical analysis ('This is how things are distributed'). We should not stop there, but what has to be done next is not to ask whether the distribution is fair or unfair. This is not really the business of the sociologist, even if he may have his opinion. He can say: 'In relation to the norms of equal distribution, it is unequal.' In order to measure the strength of a relation, we often compare the distribution we observe with the theoretical distribution, other things being statistically equal. This comes down to making a hypothesis. Physicists do the same thing, but since they deal in particles, nobody says to them: 'You have an egalitarian bias.' When we are dealing with individuals, the scientific operation consisting in comparing the distribution observed with the theoretical distribution that you would obtain if the variables were independent is obviously perceived as political: the independence of variables is an egalitarian hypothesis . . . There we have something important for understanding the particular difficulties of the sociologist. In describing the distribution as very strongly asymmetrical, or as bimodal, the sociologist expresses an attitude, whether he likes it or not, towards the value of this distribution and whether it is fair or unfair. At all events he provides weapons for those who struggle to find whether it is fair or unfair. This is why the most objective report is necessarily an object of dispute. There will be people who will say that it is not true, even when it is as plain as the nose on your face. In the social world, you don't convert anyone by quoting statistics. A scholar can never have the last word if at a given moment the social truth is stronger than the scientific truth. I think that this is also extremely important for understanding the peculiar status of the social sciences.

A first level then involves making an assessment. At a second level we say: 'I am neutral, I do not take sides in the struggle.' That said, this neutrality is a fiction, because, whatever we do, the result, the right number, so to speak, is an object of dispute. What we need to include in our model is not just the fact that there is a distribution, but that there is also a struggle over this distribution. At the third level we find in the object of study a struggle to discover whether the distribution is fair or not, and whether the mode of redistribution that aims to correct this distribution is fair or not. The positivist sociologist who records a

174 *Lecture of 9 May 1985*

distribution (of soap, shaving cream, motor cars or whatever) always records both a state of the distribution and the result of struggles to change the distribution and transform the principle of distribution. In other words, the distributions recorded conflate the result of struggles for the legitimate distribution with the legitimate representation of that distribution. I am becoming rather repetitive, but it is because I believe that it is important: the idea of a fair distribution is one of the factors that determine the distribution, and the struggle to transform or preserve the distribution involves struggles over how to determine the legitimate representation of the distribution, the *nomos*. You only have to think of Social Security: to avoid repeating myself, I shall let you think this through on your own, and you will see that this is what is at issue in all our discussions on Social Security and its various functions.

Where is the State?

What is the central question in this struggle? If we think of the problem of disability, which I raised when discussing the medical certificate, the fundamental questions are as follows. First, in the case of the legitimate redistribution to people who are entitled to benefits because they have socially recognised physical or mental disadvantages, this question takes two forms. It concerns primarily the basis of the distribution and the legitimate redistribution: is it merit (which in our societies is, *grosso modo*, work) or need? This is the old Marxist distinction: 'From each according to his merits/to each according to his needs.'[14] Once this question is resolved (it will not be resolved in the same way at different moments, but if we say, for instance, that the blind should receive social benefits, we are acknowledging need), there is a struggle to displace the frontier defining the categories of those entitled to compensatory social benefits. In other words there will be a struggle between those who seek, say, to broaden the category of invalidity and those who try to restrict it.

We can, for instance, consider the medical certificate again. Someone who delivers a certificate pronounces their diagnosis in the light of a whole host of parameters not always consciously brought into play. They may have received instructions (the government governs through instructions) or injunctions. These kinds of injunction may or may not be accompanied by sanctions [. . .], their execution may or may not be verified (instructions have recently been sent to primary school teachers:[15] is it possible to check whether they have been executed or not? There are inspectors general, but do they check, do they even

Lecture of 9 May 1985   175

want to?). The social agents who deliver certificates have to take into account the existence of instructions, but also their patients, who have their own strategies. In the particular relation between the patient and the doctor, the doctor may be led to give an elastic interpretation ('You have backache, so I prescribe twenty sessions of physiotherapy') or a restrictive interpretation ('The State has problems enough, you are a simulator . . .').

A full analysis would be long and take more time, but suffice it to say that the author of the diagnosis is faced with someone who is suffering and who can express that suffering in terms that may be simple or elaborate. They may have only their non-verbal body language at their disposal or they may use the legitimate technical language (which may impress the author of the certificate) or a quasi-legitimate jargon aspiring to legitimacy (which may exasperate the doctor). So we see the symbolic strategy of the person trying to convert their complaint and their suffering into symptoms that the doctor will recognise and acknowledge. He attempts to meet recognised criteria and enjoy the benefits of that category (if he wants, for instance, to be exempted from military service). He is faced with the doctor and his clinical categories. The doctor pronounces his diagnosis, [. . .] converting an individually defined need into a legitimately and socially sanctioned need with legally guaranteed benefits on the economic plane.

Transactions of this type are rehearsed over and over again, and in very diverse fashions. They can, for instance, be conducted by a physiotherapist who may say: 'But the doctor has sent me a simulator whose back is no worse than their feet and who just wants to take some fitness classes or take the waters at Vittel', and will react in different ways, depending on their relation with the doctor. I may be starting to sound anecdotal, but the subject of my remarks is the State . . . (There was a period when philosophers discovered the State, and as so often when philosophers discover something, it suddenly becomes enormous: the State with a capital S. They don't even worry to find out whether it exists: since the word exists, the thing must exist . . . My foray into anecdotal immanence is very important, it enables us to recognise the State where it is and not to put it where it isn't.)

The State, then, is the physio who may perhaps not say that the doctor is an imposter (or the accomplice of an imposter, or an imbecile duped by an imposter, etc.), which would call his legitimacy and his socially guaranteed competence into question . . . Rather than denounce the doctor, there is a kind of inter-legitimisation: a certifier who, conscious of his reputation, but also his personal interests (keeping his clientele rather than losing it – 'If I don't prescribe, he will go and ask someone

176 *Lecture of 9 May 1985*

else', etc.), may send them to another certified certifier [. . .]. Which gives a kind of circular process of certification. Then we may have the intervention of the person charged with verifying the procedure and validating the expenditure, etc. From one phase to another there is a series of acts of vision and revision and legally guaranteed benefits which, through the accumulation of a whole host of decisions, give us what we may call a 'politics of social security'. Usually when we think of a 'politics of social security', we immediately think that there is some principal agent of the State[16] who legally authorises the benefit.

Verdicts and the effects of power

What I have just suggested in this analysis, which I shall not develop further here, is that the subject of this politics is not a minister or a cabinet or even a government, but an ensemble of agents who are competing for the monopoly of the legitimate exercise of the act of certification and the delivery of the rights to social benefits and exemptions, etc. It is a system of rival agents, a kind of subjectless system, where each subject intervenes within the limits of the statutorily recognised power attributed to him and the specific interests he follows in competition with the other agents. In other words, specific interests come into play at every moment. Consequently those who say that my arguments are determinist are seriously mistaken. My analyses are very different from those visions in terms of an 'apparatus' (the word 'apparatus' is a mechanist term) that describe the dominant agencies as kinds of machines that lead somehow to a sort of delegation reaching beyond the acts of responsibility exercised by singular agents. If we want at all costs to insert moral arguments into the analysis that I am proposing, we see that each single agent cannot do very much, but he can do some small thing, within the limits of his position in the field and the interests associated with this position. That was a small ethical aside. I don't offer these very often, but [. . .] this one could be developed.

These universes of expertise have a very special property: they have the capacity to deliver verdicts, that is, judgements of truth, which at the same time have the effect of power. Looking at it from my viewpoint here, my analysis tends to replace the idea of the State with what we might call the field of expertise, or the field of agents in competition for the power of social certification, that is, for the power to say what is what in the social world, with authority and power and judicial consequence. The judge, for instance, has the power to determine the condition of a person, with the consequence that they will go to prison

Lecture of 9 May 1985   177

or be set free. But doctors and professors also belong to the same category. These agents decide in a way that may be irregular, that may be idiotic,[17] that may seem idiosyncratic, yet will not be considered as any such thing, but will immediately be perceived as universal. They have to resolve problems of discrimination (*dia-crisis*[18] ...), problems of truth: 'Is the disability that I am going to certify real or simulated?' The analysis on the medical certificate and the act of certification provide a reply to the question: 'What is the dominant class?' We might say that those who are dominant in this field of symbolic power are those who have the most publicly recognised authority to say what is what in the social world.

To fully develop the phenomenological implications of this proposition – 'The truth of the social world is a subject of conflict' – is not easy, I think, but I want to return to it for a moment. Whether it is a question of poverty ('Is this poverty authentic and worthy of assistance?'), or of a physical or mental handicap ('Is he mad or not? Is he responsible for his acts or not?'), these social acts are entrusted to agents who have in a way been detached from the private sphere. But singular individuals without a mandate continue to pass judgement, and this is very important. Everything that I said last time remains true: each one of us retains the power at any moment to say: 'That man is really mad, he should be put away', or contrariwise, 'It's a scandal, he should never have been put away.' Moreover, insofar as each agent retains his power, he contributes to the definition of the *nomos*. At a given moment people have a certain feeling of fairness or unfairness, and when, for example, pressure groups want to fight in favour of the expansion of a category of disability, they say: 'It's not enough to place tuberculosis in that category, you should also include bone tuberculosis', resorting to their sense of a broader definition of fairness. (Today unfortunately they rely on opinion polls which are supposed to register an opinion but which in fact produce it.)[19] They rely on something that at a given moment is a feeling for justice and which is itself a product of a host of all our everyday dealings with the definition of justice ('I must say it's really outrageous, X has spent the last fifteen months at home, fed and watered by the Social Security ...'). This kind of permanent work by the individual citizen goes to define something most undefinable, a sort of implicit *nomos* (Antigone is said to have spoken 'unwritten laws'),[20] a sort of vague feeling of what is just or unjust, that the lawgiver must negotiate in order to transform this sentiment of what is just and what is unjust into public laws.

The act of expertise with judicial repercussions is specific to our societies, where science becomes a dimension of most judicial acts, as we

178 · *Lecture of 9 May 1985*

see in the case of the medical diagnosis. The judicial act with scientific implications, or inversely the scientific act with judicial implications, is an official, public and visible act, broadcast by the media and controlled by the State, which leads to titles being granted. Just as there are positive titles that give the right to professions, there are negative titles that give the right to social benefits: a certificate of disability is a title that 'entitles' someone to something, 'gives them the right' to enjoy official benefits, which are privileges assigned to a category, not the individual. In other words, this establishes a certain mode of perception. For instance, a category for those with 'motor handicaps' is an established and recognised perception, a socially accredited perception, implying the differential treatment of people who fall into this category. We can easily see that these categories are in opposition to the private categories of the singular individual, the one who says: 'I am giving alms to this person because he doesn't smell of drink.' This is a daily-life diagnosis, it is private, and its implicit, confused and diffuse principles remain invisible: they are not published, they are completely in the hands of the individual, who decides whether or not to give, without having to render accounts to the State . . . unless he wants to apply for gift aid deduction in his tax declaration. (This passing remark shows how difficult it is to define what is public and what is private: there is a kind of border dispute constantly in play there.) This act then is an individual attribution, which has no consequences. In the other case, we have a completely codified attribution, but which does have consequences. It is what we call an institution.

You could apply to social identity the same method that I have applied to disability. The problem is the same. Someone who usurps an identity cheats perception in the same way as someone who simulates an illness, and we find a smooth continuum from the strategies of bluffing in everyday life, strategies described by Goffman,[21] which consist in passing yourself off as better than you are, to the strategies of simulation through which you gain exemption from military service when you are perfectly healthy in mind . . . and in body.

The field of certification

Legitimate social verdicts are, then, the monopoly of a certain number of agents, and ultimately, in my way of considering these things, I would replace the notion of the State with the space of agents in competition for the monopoly of social violence, with some reasonable chance of success (which is what characterises them, since all agents

Lecture of 9 May 1985

are engaged in a struggle). This is a generalisation of Weber's definition of the State: 'The State is the holder of the monopoly of legitimate violence.'[22] Weber was obviously thinking of the violence involved in foreign policy (the power to declare and wage war) and in internal law enforcement (the power to use violence to coerce individual agents). What I am introducing is a sort of generalisation of the concept. This definition by Weber marks a considerable step forward, but it is obvious that the State has the monopoly of coercion. Modern, rational law is a verdict accompanied by the power to execute it: it is justice plus the police. Simply speaking, this is what Weber says.

What I am introducing is important and much less apparent. It is the idea that the State has the monopoly of legitimate symbolic violence, that is, the monopoly to decree, to discriminate, to divide and separate, to say: 'You are this, you are that, you are good, you are bad, you are neurotic, and so on.' The monopoly of legitimate symbolic violence is the monopoly of 'nomic' [normative] acts, acts of division accompanied by legal sanctions and social effects. What should be described, [. . .] is the subfield of struggles within the field of power for the determination of legitimate claims to incapacity. There are social agents who are moved by a sort of judicial sentiment and an approximate knowledge of their rights to tell someone: 'You know, you have the right . . .', 'You should go and see a doctor.' The individual in question goes to see a doctor, tells him that he has backache, and employs the strategy that makes the best use of the means at his disposal to claim his due rights, real or imagined. Who will say whether this claim of incapacity is legitimate? Look at the subfield that I have just mentioned. One of the problems of this empirical study will be how to define the boundaries of this field: who today has the power to say whether the claim is legitimate? Is the faith healer one of them? We will immediately see simple definitions of licit and illicit medicine (you periodically get debates on television where you see doctors confronting faith healers) that are easy to understand using the analyses I am offering here: take my categories of 'public' and 'private'. (I am saying all this in order to insist on the value of my categories, because otherwise you are likely to say: 'My God, he does go on, and for something so simple.' In fact it is not as trivial as all that.)

So on the one hand we have singular individuals who take up arms to make their invalidity known, and on the other hand a universe of agents who come and go. At any moment there are new arrivals: the psychoanalyst, the psychiatrist, the child psychologist, and so on. These new arrivals will struggle to find their place and define their competence. The word 'competence' is very important because it is a technical word

180 *Lecture of 9 May 1985*

with judicial implications. The expert has a 'competence', that is, a recognised capacity (one problem for otherwise 'capable' people is that there are aptitudes that are not certified). Someone who issues a certificate must be certified as qualified to issue certificates, and he is certified to issue certificates by others who themselves . . . Think of the Order of Doctors.[23] There was a whole debate at one time, because some doctors who were technically certified by the faculty refused to join the Order of Doctors; the Order of Doctors promptly excluded them. They were still certified technically but not socially (if you think about it, you will see that things are not that simple . . .).

Who then are these certifiers who certify that others are legitimate certifiers? A mathematician is someone whom mathematicians call a mathematician. All the universes of expertise are of this type. That said, in the case of the experts and competences that I have been describing, the certification is the work of the State, it belongs to the order of the State. It is a legitimate symbolic violence because it involves sanctions. The fact that one mathematician says of a second mathematician that he is a mathematician changes nothing in the social order, and confers no power, or very little, to the second. When one doctor certifies another as qualified to certify, it is an act of a judicial type which makes this doctor's act of certification part of the order of the State. We should analyse the field concerned with the elementary diagnostic act of a clinical diagnosis: who belongs to this field today? Does a physiotherapist belong? Does a nurse? Does an anaesthetist? This raises a whole series of questions, with arguments about where to draw the line. The boundary lines are vital because the certification of the certifier is called into question by the definition of his right to certify. Does the anaesthetist need the presence of a doctor to certify his act of certification? All these struggles over the monopoly of legitimate symbolic violence are eventually decided by the State. Some are winners, and manage to have their definition of the boundary recognised as legitimate.

The State is not a single entity with a capital S that possesses its own will, thoughts and feelings. It is the structure at a given moment of the balance of symbolic power between agents claiming legitimate certification in a fight for their advantages and disadvantages, in various domains of their practice. Ultimately, making a sociological study of the State means making an analysis of struggles to define the legitimate principle of distribution and redistribution, seeing them as struggles to transform, by extending or restricting them, the categories of perception of the legitimate divisions of the social world, which are at the same time the legitimate categories of distribution and redistribution

Lecture of 9 May 1985 181

of the social advantages at stake. Changing the categories of disability will have effects on welfare benefits: a certain number of people who were not eligible for benefits will now become eligible. Consequently the nomic boundaries, the boundaries that have social effects, will be transformed. Obviously the attempt to change the boundaries often leads to a change in terminology.

How does the sociologist deal with this? Although it is not the aim of my analysis, one thing I wanted to show is the quite unique position of sociological analysis when it is absolutely consistent, when it avoids sacrificing its theoretical liberty in order to gain the status of an expertise (this is not a claim for the singularity of sociology itself). There is a trade-off: if you have been following my argument you will immediately see that acquiring the power of certification means taking part in the struggle for symbolic power. Another strategy consists in describing the struggle for symbolic power as it is, which supposes stepping back from it, at least for as long as we are describing it; moreover, this distance is necessary for us even to have the idea of describing it. [. . .] One problem to investigate is the position of sociology as a science whose work on divisions and their representation inevitably participates in the struggle for the legitimate representation of these divisions. But, as I shall demonstrate next time, it stands out from [. . .] that space of experts struggling for the monopoly of legitimate symbolic violence: it attempts to analyse it, while being situated within it, yet being constantly situated within this space is a way (and the only way) of separating from it. I shall return to this next time.

Second session (seminar): the invention of the modern artist (6)

I find it difficult to start the second session devoted to the sociology and social history of the artistic field qua field, and the artist as the character we recognise. I often find when I return from the break between sessions that I am suffering from what psychologists call the [Zeigarnik] effect, describing children interrupted in the middle of a game that they want to continue playing. Rather than launch straight into the artistic field, I would like to make the link between what I was saying just now and what I am intending to say next. At the end of last session I was saying that what we call the 'State' is a certain state of the balance of powers in the field of certification. The State's verdict will impose its judgement on some object or aptitude that is at issue in the struggle for definitions in the social world. In the case of painting, this is quite simple.

182 *Lecture of 9 May 1985*

I always put the question of legitimacy in simple terms: who is to judge the legitimacy of the judges?[24] This is the question of legitimacy itself, that I raised when discussing Kafka.[25] I hope that any of you who might have been surprised to hear me invoking Kafka as a sociologist will understand more and more what I was trying to say. Usually when we say 'Kafkaesque' we are thinking of an oppressive and overwhelming bureaucracy, and so on. But I think that Kafka is describing rather the very logic of the bureaucratic universe, that is, the universe where everyone struggles to be the supreme judge, to be able to say: 'X is guilty, Y is innocent.' Obviously when we are talking about justice, where the verdict may decide between life and death, it is much more striking. But a medical certificate or a certificate of exemption from military service is a mini life or death sentence, just as is a diploma granting qualification for teaching in primary or secondary school. We always return to the same question: who is to judge the legitimacy of the judges? And under what conditions can the judge make people forget to put this question?

We tend to think that this question no longer arises when there is a State and that it takes someone strange and slightly perverse like Kafka or a sociologist to make it reappear. This is why I am led to wonder whether sociology should exist, which is a perfectly legitimate question. Should sociology exist *independently of the interest that sociologists have in existing as sociologists?* This last reservation is important. For instance, a few years ago a philosophical congress[26] started with discussions on the interests of the field of philosophy, but nobody raised the question of why we are interested in philosophy. It is nonetheless extraordinary that none of the powerful and radical thinkers in the room thought to say: 'But might our interest in philosophy not be interested? Would we be interested in philosophy if the professors of philosophy were not interested in its ongoing existence?' This is a question that I would answer in the affirmative, but I think that the [question of being interested in philosophy merits being raised].

When sociologists remark that the existence of an expert raises the question of having the right to exercise expertise, they generally find that the question rebounds upon them, and it is true that, paradoxically, sociologists often forget to direct the question back at themselves. This is because so often they practise sociology in order to put embarrassing questions to others. Basically, the sociology of knowledge in its spontaneous form is a sociology of the social foundations and therefore the limitations of other people's knowledge. We are all spontaneous sociologists of (other people's) knowledge when we say: 'You are saying that because you have a grudge, etc.' We cannot

Lecture of 9 May 1985   183

avoid the more general question that this raises: 'Who shall judge the legitimacy of the judges?' It is applicable to any judgement: 'Who shall judge the legitimacy of the judges, and therefore of my judgements?' Is there an ultimate agency that can deliver verdicts on verdicts? The verdict in its [etymological (?)] logic is *veredictum*, that is, a judgement claiming to have a reasonable chance of being the truth, like any judgement, in such a way that we do not think to question its foundation. A judicial verdict is a verdict that is not only accepted but also makes us forget to question its foundation, that is, the foundation of the very act of judging without having to justify its foundation.

Academic painting as a theological universe

Now that I have relieved my feelings, I can move on to discuss the Academy, but you will see that what I have just been saying was justified. In fact, when there was an Academy, there was a legitimate agency qualified to say legitimately who could legitimately call themselves a painter. Saying who is truly a painter and who shall judge the legitimacy of the painter is a permanent bone of contention. Similarly who shall say that X is a genuine sociologist or Y a genuine historian? In the case of the painters, today, this question of legitimacy is a running sore; the universe of the painters is one of those where the question that I raised at the outset – 'Who shall judge the legitimacy of the judges?' – is least surprising. The universe of painting is a place of charismatic ideology, of discovering the truly great painter, of conviction, vocation and predestination (everything that defines charisma), but the world of painting is riddled with doubts over its legitimacy. Perhaps it is only so charismatic because painters have to live in a state of high anxiety over their legitimacy. There are in fact fields where a greater or lesser insecurity over their legitimacy reigns. In the judicial field it takes a very great crisis for the judges to raise the question of the legitimacy of the judges (but it can happen, as in 1968, for instance [. . .]). The field of painting today is in a state of permanent uncertainty over knowing who will say that X is a painter, apart from X himself.

The general theory of fields that I am trying to propose has the merit of enabling us to subject every field to general questions that can only be answered by specific replies based on empirical studies in each field. I have just raised a general question: we may wonder in each field how far the question of the legitimacy of the specific domination exercised there is consciously present in the minds of the people. What I am going to describe is the passage from academic painting to modern

184 *Lecture of 9 May 1985*

painting and the modern artist. Academic painting corresponds to a phase of pictorial production where there was a State monopoly over what we may call legitimacy: there was a place that assembled the whole group of people recognised as qualified to say who is and who is not a painter, what is and what is not painting. There was a god out there somewhere, a last judgement to which it was possible to resort.

This is not Kafka's universe at all. If you remember,[27] I said that analysing Kafka raises an absolutely fundamental sociological problem. It is perhaps quite simply the universalisation of the question that faced the writer at the time that Kafka was writing, that is, a period when the independence of the literary field was quite advanced: 'Am I a writer, and who can tell me whether I am a writer?' 'Is it my publisher? Is it my friends?' 'If I give public readings, my friends will tell me that they are good, but is this a purely honorary award, designed to humour me, or am I really certified, and who can certify me?', 'And as for me, would I certify the person who certifies me? I'm not so sure . . .' We have an infinite regression: we end up with God . . . or nothing. What Kafka universalises is a possible state of any field, as he draws on his experience of the artistic field at a certain moment in its history, at the end of the period that I am talking about.

The academic universe was a field of disputes over the legitimate definition of painting and the painter, over the certified definition of painting and the painter, where there was an agency holding the monopoly of certification, an agency dominant in the domain of certification of the validity of the act of painting. We may compare this situation to the state of the religious field in the Middle Ages, where one agency, the Church, held the monopoly of certification of the legitimate religious act. The break between 'he is a true believer' and 'he's an imposter, a faith healer, a magician or a sorcerer, and he must burn' was relatively simple and straightforward. As there was an agency that held the monopoly of the definition and was universally recognised, the heresies arose within the agency of legitimisation rather than outside it,[28] and did not call into question the idea of certification itself.

You will see that my topos on the *nomos* was not simply a play on words: if you have a sociological background, you will immediately find the opposite of *nomos*: it is Durkheim's anomie.[29] Durkheim invented the word anomie to designate states of the social world in which there are no longer any dominant norms – not Durkheim's own terms, but no matter. I shall not elaborate the notion of anomie, I presume that you are familiar with it. We may say that in the period of academic painting, the field was 'nomic': the Academy collectively held the monopoly of certification in stating, discriminating and dividing, of

Lecture of 9 May 1985   185

saying who was a painter and who was not. This collective monopoly was a statutory monopoly, which each individual member enjoyed only in delegated form – the academic painter, as I have repeatedly said, was mandated or delegated, and could not exercise his act of *diacrisis* ('He is a true painter!') in his own name, or, as defined by charisma, in the name of his inspiration, conviction or sincerity; he exercised it in the name of the institution, not according to a personal judgement of the type: 'I don't grant it because he smells of drink', but after a socially grounded examination, a competition that was prepared according to established norms and accepted only candidates already preselected as qualified to compete. In other words it was an institution that legitimised itself collectively and was capable of legitimising each of its members, within the limits of their allegiance to the institution. Which means that asking the question: 'But what is a painter?' was not even considered.

Here the analogy between sociology and theology that I evoked when discussing Kafka is obvious:[30] they are theological universes where there is a god. We know that truth abides there, and the institution is the temporal equivalent of God. It is what Kant calls the *intuitus originarius*:[31] it is the vision that makes what it sees exist – 'I perceive you as painter, therefore you are a painter', and there is no cause to look further. You would be amazed at the analogies I could draw . . . Recently someone important in the Ministry of Education said to me: 'But I am well aware of the difference between the *agrégés* and the *capésiens* [those holding a 'Certificat d'aptitude au professorat de l'enseignement du second degré' (Capes), and so qualified to teach in secondary schools rather than universities]. There are some in my family and I can see the difference straight away . . .' [*laughter*]. He didn't see that it is precisely the function of the education system to create the illusion of a difference by establishing itself as an *intuitus originarius* producing the difference, and thereby making us perceive it. The force of the social institution is to make you see a difference produced by your regard as pre-existing your action of looking. I think that what I am saying here is important.

I may shock your sensitivities, but we must always raise this question of competence. It may well be that there is a difference of technical competence between people who are also defined as unequally competent in social terms, but we must always ask whether this perception of difference may not be a difference of perception, socially established in the eye of the perceiver, through his dominant gaze, with the nomos telling him: 'He is different, therefore you are bound to see him differently.' In other words, a joke made by an *agrégé* will sound wittier than

186   *Lecture of 9 May 1985*

a joke made by a *capésien* [*laughter*] if your eyes are trained to see them differently . . . That's what the *nomos* does to us.

Institutionalising perspectivism

To pass from the *nomos* to anomie is to pass from a field with a monopoly to a field where symbolic power has become fragmented. I think that the best example of anomie is the field of painting today, where any one can say of anyone else, without excluding themselves from the universe of the painters: 'He is not a painter.' In other times, to say that Ingres was not a painter was really to exclude yourself. Today you can say it of almost anybody. In the literary field it is almost the same. It remains the case that the manner of saying it has changed (for those who have the categories of perception to perceive these differences, of course . . .). This is what happened according to my history of the artistic field: the collapse of the academic monopoly was the death of God. At a certain moment in time someone wrote 'God is dead', 'Man is dead',[32] and although I don't much like these ontological or theological metaphors, in this particular case the analogy seems to me to be perfectly justified, and not just a philosophical witticism or even a philosophical thesis. Since I think that the spontaneous vision of the social world is a theology, it is perfectly normal to use theological language to describe the relation of social individuals to their social identity and the social verdict that will tell them who they are.

To conclude this point: the state of anomie of the field is the moment when the *nomos* has broken down, where there is an infinity of *nomoï*, to each his own *nomos*, there are only *idioï nomoï*, individual idiots' points of view. Everyone can say to his neighbour: 'You are an idiot', with no danger of looking like an idiot, whereas, in a universe where the objective structures and the structures incorporated into the perception of the social world are strongly guaranteed by agencies that are themselves strongly guaranteed, you cannot denounce the institution that condemns you without condemning yourself, which is a problem. As I was saying last time, the problem of the rejects was how to reject their rejection without rejecting themselves. The problem of the avant-garde is, how am I to exclude the institution that excludes me without excluding myself through my very intention to exclude, without showing in my very revolt against the institution how I resent that institution? This is the great problem with a heresy: how to avoid betraying the love–hate I feel for the institution in the violence that I denounce it with. There are denunciations that take on the very shape

Lecture of 9 May 1985 187

of recognition, and that was the problem of the artist confronting the Academy.

They had to move into a sort of society with no God, a universe with no privileged viewpoint. There is an analogy that is difficult to describe between the constitution of a field of painting with no privileged viewpoint and the evolution of painting towards forms of production like Cubism, which destroys any privileged viewpoint over objects or the social world, and where ultimately several viewpoints of the object are offered at once. Once the dominant viewpoint, that is, God, is dead in the field of painting, there is no longer any privileged viewpoint, there is no longer the traditional, central perspective that was the viewpoint through which everyone saw what the painter had painted; that was what perspective was for. The kind of perspectivism that establishes in the eyes of the world what makes a painter also engenders the perspectivism that establishes our view of the natural world. Having lost the possibility to say who is a painter, the painter can no longer claim to say what is the proper viewpoint over the world . . . Perhaps the sociology that I am offering is slightly Cubist [*laughter*] . . . (I am not saying that to spoil the suspense, but to make you aware of what you are letting yourselves in for so that you can defend yourselves; if I were a cynical strategist it is the last thing I would tell you.)

The invention of the artist as character

I had got to the point where I was discussing the misery of the rejects faced with the problem that I was describing [. . .] I had shown you, I think, the determining role that the writers played in what we might call the work of rehabilitation of the rejects: they had provided a discourse capable of legitimising the existence of a painter with no purpose. I shall sketch this rapidly, because it is all very familiar. The whole Romantic period, from Chateaubriand via Musset (*Lorenzaccio*), Théophile Gautier et al., had worked towards inventing a new social character, the character of the painter or artist, capable of living for goals different from those of the ordinary man. The opposition that we now find banal between the artist and the bourgeois, between the sordid financier craving profit and the artist ready to die for the love of art, took some time to develop. There are of course the *Mémoires d'outre-tombe* [written between 1809 and 1841], where Chateaubriand exalts the endurance and sacrifices of the artists. There is also Musset. I am thinking in particular of *Lorenzaccio* [1834], where the character of Tebaldeo makes this extraordinary statement: 'It is he [the painter]

188   *Lecture of 9 May 1985*

who exorcises evil, temptation and corruption, and who accomplishes the dreams of ordinary people by breaking with the meanness and baseness of everyday man, alienated through submission to material satisfaction.'[33] This construction of art against money, of free art against mercenary submission to commissions, was established only very gradually.

I shall not develop this further, but to understand the emergence of a market for art, which could be an absolutely extraordinary source of profit and had its own specific logic, we need to understand the initial process needed to constitute works of art as priceless objects. Today if we say that something is 'priceless' we mean that it is very expensive, which is the case with works of art . . . the price of priceless things . . . the existence of priceless things is made possible by the emergence of a break between things that have an immediately assessable market price and artistic works which are of such a different order that we neither calculate nor count, for fear of slipping into base bourgeois materialism. The break between artist and craftsman is one of the acid tests of art history, which is determined at all costs to find the moment when craftsmanship became artistry. I should say briefly in passing that I believe I have solved this problem (there are problems in social science that it is possible to solve . . .), but there is obviously not one instant t when a certain number of characters appear having all the properties of an artist.

The emergence of the artist is an ongoing problem that sees no end. It concerns the emergence of an artistic field autonomous enough for the criteria defining the pictorial production socially recognised as legitimate to be completely different from the criteria defining ordinary pictorial production. To use a brutal contrast: in order to understand the difference between an artistic painter and a house painter, you need to study the field, otherwise you can't. For instance, historians have shown that there was a time when painting was evaluated – as still happens today – by its weight or the surface covered or the cost of the paints employed.[34] For the painting to be judged on its pictorial value, treating it as a material object (that is, as colour on canvas), the whole artistic field needs to be established as such, with a universe of critics and a whole system of evaluation, etc. [. . .] The process of establishment of the artist as artist was not completed in the nineteenth century; it is much more advanced today, but it can always revert. There is not a linear progression with clear breaks.

The Romantics set the artist against the craftsman by a whole process. For instance, they invented the character of the artist. They endowed him with a passionate and energetic nature and an immense,

Lecture of 9 May 1985 189

inordinate kind of sensibility, a sort of faculty of transubstantiation: the artist is someone who transforms and transmutes things in an alchemical logic. This occurs as part of a permanent association between specialists of the various arts. In the preface to the first edition of *Jocelyn*, in 1836, Lamartine says: 'Fine verse, a fine painting or fine music are the same thought in three different languages.'[35] This text gives explicit expression to a conviction that arose in practice in this period, that is, the unity of interests of the corporation of artists. The artists frequented the same cafés, attended the same concerts, met up in the same places and used the same subjects (one example among many was *Mazeppa*, which travelled from music to painting), there was a circulation of themes, preoccupations and representations . . . In the case of *Mazeppa*, there are obviously Victor Hugo's poems in *Les Orientales*, but also paintings by Louis Boulanger, Horace Vernet and Chassériau, followed by Liszt, who composed a piece for the piano and then an orchestral work, for instance.[36] This kind of unity is attested in the artists' everyday productions, and also in the representations that they variously gave of one another's activities. We know the exemplary figures such as Delacroix or Berlioz because they were more cultivated in the traditional sense of the term than the others, and made this kind of interpenetration of the arts more visible. But in a more general fashion much more obscure people, engravers and lithographers like Johannot, more or less unknown sculptors and really minor painters met up in the same cafés and shared in the collective ideology of the artist. The word is not really right, but there came to be a sort of 'club' or syndicate of artists. An association or union of artists who forged an ideology for themselves.

Within this society of artists, the painters, who are quite special because they incarnate suffering and a spirit of sacrifice to the highest degree, discover the discourse that they needed to justify their way of living their art. I have already told you that the notion of 'art for art's sake' was the invention of a sculptor, Jean Duseigneur, who exhibited at the 1831 Salon. He was the first to use the expression, and then it circulated among the group that was called the 'Petit Cénacle' [small clique] that comprised people like Nerval, Borel and Gautier. The theory was expressed essentially in poetry by Théophile Gautier, who played the part of exemplary prophet (there is a very fine article by Rémy Ponton on the subject):[37] he embodies both the character of the artist and the discourse of the artist capable of defining his requirements independently of any external solicitation. It is his famous preface to *Mademoiselle de Maupin* [1835] that defines the principles of what is at once the life of the artist and the work of the artist. Generally speaking,

190 *Lecture of 9 May 1985*

it sets those who receive commissions in opposition to those who freely develop their intellectual creativity, even at the risk of shocking good taste, that is, flouting the dominant definition of taste, and seeming barbarian in the eyes of the Academy.

This idea of liberty is inseparable from the idea of transgression that became constitutive of the definition of art (I'm afraid it wasn't Bataille who invented the idea of transgression):[38] whereas the philistine respects the conventions and the rules, the artist defines himself as the transgressor who detests shopkeepers and the bourgeoisie et al. This intellectual transgression is at the same time sexual transgression. (There too, this was not invented by Bataille ... I don't say this for the pleasure [of targeting those who refer to Bataille] but because it is important for intellectual research: I find that a lack of historical culture is sometimes so extraordinary that it leads to relatively major errors; it is quite something to attribute to Bataille something that existed in 1830, or to attribute to the Frankfurt School something that pre-dates it.) Transgression becomes the avant-garde act par excellence. Transgression of the bounds of ethical propriety is inseparable from transgression of the bounds of taste. That is understandable, because, as I was saying, the Academy was an agency that defined good taste as a code of behaviour; good taste was inseparable from etiquette, aesthetic virtues were ethical virtues. To defy the philistines, then, was to glorify love, whether pure love (Murger, *La vie de Bohème*)[39] or its erotic form.

Another side to the definition is anti-utilitarianism: art against money, conventional morality, religion, duty, responsibility and the family, in fact, ultimately, art against the moral order, that is, everything that might suggest any kind of service to be rendered to society. This is important if we want to understand why it is so difficult to make a sociological study of art: this sociology has to describe activities that are established in opposition to the sociologist's object of study ... This is the paradox: the reductive sociological model is denounced in advance by those that it reduces. This is why a rigorous sociology can only be a sociology of the conditions of sociological reductionism. We need to make a sociological study of the field, otherwise a sociology that reduces an art erected against reductionism, especially of a social nature, is disqualified in advance.

Lecture of 9 May 1985　　191

The painter–writer couple

All of this [anti-utilitarianism (?)] is to be found in Théophile Gautier, who is not known as an avant-garde author, and it was then developed by the Goncourts, Flaubert, Leconte de Lisle and Baudelaire, who all celebrate painting as the supreme art, the superior art. This was the period that established the painter–writer couple, which, with occasional breaks, has remained absolutely unchanged until the present day. For instance, at some moments in the artistic field, the leaders of the school were impresarios-cum-writers: the leader of the school was a non-painter who established the group by discussing it in public, giving it a name, writing prefaces and catalogues, performing all the ordinary acts of consecration that impose legitimate perception. This was the moment when the couple was composed and when admiration for the painter became an unavoidable facet of the role of the writer. It was also the time when the figure of the artist as saturnine character was invented. (I say this because there is a relatively important book by Wittkower on the saturnine theme that I thoroughly disagree with.[40] He offers a description, completely anachronistic in my opinion, of the emergence as early as the sixteenth century in Florence of the properties of the saturnian artist. He also notes the artists' high rate of suicide, sexual liberty and licentiousness. In other words, in a classic effect of retrospective illusion, Wittkower finds traces back in the sixteenth century of the properties which were invented as such during the Romantic and post-Romantic period.) Taking their model from the painters, the writers described the saturnine character, doomed to misfortune and despair. They describe the painter as an eccentric, irrational character, but also as a social misfit whose words and actions are entirely unpredictable. He is an absolutely unpredictable character, incarnating the absolute liberty, or even irredentism, of the intellectual.

In tracking the process of construction of the image of the artist, we should go back to Baudelaire's writings, which contributed not only to this creation of a doomed artist, but simultaneously to the demolition of the character of the academic painter, described as a bourgeois artist. This is very interesting: the academic artists, who tend to be of lower social origins than the non-academic artists, are perceived as 'bourgeois' because they seem academic in the light of the tendency to assimilate membership of a stable institution with the status of the bourgeois. This is a very common error of perception: even today the opposition between the art teacher and the artist reproduces the opposition between academic painters and avant-garde painters.

192   *Lecture of 9 May 1985*

The opposition between musicians trained in the *conservatoire* [music academy] and those who follow deviant paths also reproduces this opposition. If a small fraction of art teachers manage to gain recognition as avant-garde painters, the artists still perceive their teachers as more bourgeois, whereas in fact they are art teachers because they cannot take the social risk involved in becoming an artist. Their membership of an academic, university or school institution creates a kind of identification with the bourgeois dispositions of regularity, stability and status. In fact there exists a kind of chiasmatic relationship: it is the painters or writers of the least favoured social origins who choose the safest refuges because they can't afford the luxury of a spectacular break. This kind of chiasmus is extremely important for understanding the conflicts within the field of painting – just as for the conflicts between critics and writers during the whole of the nineteenth century, between teachers and writers or between teaching philosophers and unattached philosophers.

Baudelaire denounces as 'bourgeois' the academic painters who are in fact much more petit bourgeois. He describes them as worthless inheritors (whereas they are academic, not social inheritors) who possess only 'the art of sauces, patinas, glazes, gratins, gravies and stews'.[41] His description pours scorn on the way the whole of academic art is 'cooked up'. I could continue at length, but I simply want to say that one of the properties that mark the specificity of a profession is the possession of a tradition, this is 'the glazes, sauces and stews, etc.', a certain manner transmitted hereditarily which has a relatively autonomous history; the history of pictorial techniques is in fact the history of the autonomy of painting from other manners. But how can anyone affirm their autonomy by refusing their heritage? If the Impressionist revolution takes a very radical form, it is because breaking with the Academy is in a way casting off all the moorings that can guarantee autonomy [. . .], it is obviously abdicating the competence socially guaranteed by the Academy and it means breaking with competence in the technical sense of the term. Not only do I no longer recognise the verdict of the Academy (when it says 'X is a painter', I can say that it is absurd), but, even more, I reject the technical justification for this verdict, that is, the existence of a specific technical competence defining the true painter, the art of applying complementary colours or accomplishing some other technical feat.

Given this, how can I found an autonomous art if I don't even have the possibility of basing my claim on competence? Painters who have broken away find themselves in a way at the mercy of the literary men. In the following period, Odilon Redon, according to Dario

Lecture of 9 May 1985 193

Gamboni,[42] was the first to have denounced the submission of the painter to the writer. He was the first to say: 'We've had enough of people writing poems at our expense.' Huysmans created virtual paraphrases of Redon's paintings and then went on to publish them as poems: the painter was the pretext for an autonomous literary exercise, and he became doubly dependent on the writer, because on the one hand the painter was a foil for the writer and on the other hand the writer created his own values independent of those of the painter. Odilon Redon denounces this kind of contract which was useful in the phase that I have just been describing but finally became odious afterwards.

What Umberto Eco calls the 'open work'[43] is a historical invention that fits in with the logic of Odilon Redon. We could say that there are as many views of the work as there are perceiving subjects and that the work then is objectively polysemic, but I think that we are entitled to say that the invention of the open work, as a work conceived and created to be the object of a multiple gaze, might be connected with this problem of the relation between painting and its commentators. If the work is really polysemic, then there is no right commentary, there is no God of the commentary, there is no longer any absolute point of view. In this case the painter leaves all the commentators to contradict one another and remains master of the truth of his work which is to have no truth.

Duchamp pushes this to a further degree. So we have interviews with Duchamp where he is asked why he gave some strange title to one of his works and he replies: 'I don't know', or he says to a commentator 'Oh, yes, I was thinking of that', then to another [who suggested a different interpretation] 'Yes, yes, you could say so.'[44] In other words, he endorses all possible interpretations, which is one way of remaining the absolute master of interpretations and interpreters. This strategy is echoed in philosophy, notably by Heidegger. The open work is the painter's mastery of his work: he is the one in the last instance who can give its true meaning, or declare that it has no meaning. In general he says that there is nothing to be found, which sends university scholars running back to their ridiculous academic search for concepts. This is an important move in the conflict between agents.

[*Long moment of silence*] What I wanted to discuss is the paradox of the conquest of autonomy when you are depriving yourself of what commentators see as the most essential foundation of autonomy, that is, technique. The artists protested to the writers: 'You don't understand at all. You turn it into literature. There is a technique.' The writers must obviously have understood this early on, because

194   *Lecture of 9 May 1985*

the painters told them, and Zola, for instance, says: 'Don't look for meaning, you can see it's about colour.' It starts to get more difficult to get rid of the writers when they adopt your legitimate discourse, and we end up with Odilon Redon, who says: 'I reject all discourse, including technical discourse. . . .' But I have moved too quickly to the break between painters and writers [. . .].

For the painters, abandoning technique as the foundation of the autonomy of art means abdicating any possible legitimisation of the status of the painter. Now this is the paradox of the break with the Academy: to break away was not only to denounce the claim of any agency whatever to say what painting is and who is a legitimate painter, it was also to deprive themselves of everything that the Academy represented, that is, a technical tradition, an agency charged with preserving, perpetuating, reproducing, inculcating and consecrating a technical tradition defining painting as a specific activity, in contrast to writing or sculpture. Thus the break with the Academy represents a sort of absolute void which in a way throws the painter into the arms of the writer, who is the only person able to provide an outright justification ('You are a painter because . . . you incarnate painting'). The writer can say, for instance (and here we see the invention of the artist as character), that it is painting that makes the true painter, meaning someone who has the true behaviour of the painter, who lives as they say the artist should live, who is ready to die for his painting, is not a conformist, has extraordinary love affairs, and so on. It is all in Balzac's *The Unknown Masterpiece*,[45] which follows the Romantic logic perfectly. This is not a modern text at all, despite what we might think. It is a text that is entirely typical of its period: it is a paean to the painter as a character who is in search of the absolute and is justified as a painter by this kind of simultaneously exemplary and desperate ethical posture.

What I wanted to show afterwards is how the emergence of an 'anomic' artistic field, in which any reference to an absolute, any last resort (or ultimate agency), is excluded, involves a complete redefinition of the notion of the artist, of painting itself, and of what is worthy of being painted, by enabling the coexistence in the same state of the field, if not of an infinity, then at least of a multiplicity of rival manners of painting that consecrate one another mutually through the very fact of struggling to be consecrated. In other words, what remains of academic absolutism is the struggle for the absolute, to be absolute. The only proof of legitimacy, the only proof of the existence of God – the pictorial God – is this claim by each and every one of them to be God. But this claim is necessarily frustrated in a universe

Lecture of 9 May 1985

where there is no place from where one may say: 'He is the true painter.' There is no divine place any longer. This is what I shall try to describe next time, by showing how I find that this changed the very work of the painter.

Lecture of 23 May 1985

First session (lecture): Paul Valéry's insights – Amateur and professional – Bureaucracy as a massive fetish – Categorial mediation – Validated perception – Science and the science of the State
Second session (seminar): the invention of the modern artist (7) – Polycentrism and the invention of institutions – The false antinomy of art and the market – The collective judgement of the critics – The three reproaches

First session (lecture): Paul Valéry's insights

[*We were unable to restore the beginning of the lecture. Bourdieu is answering a question somebody had put to him.*] I would like to read you briefly one or two texts that I find interesting and which relate directly to the problems that I have been discussing during these lectures: they are from the chapter entitled 'Teaching' in volume 2 of Paul Valéry's *Notebooks* in the Pléiade edition. The author of our question was citing some passages concerning the teaching of philosophy, and here Valéry formulates a number of remarks on the education system that are astonishingly modern. I'll read them briefly: 'What could be uglier than philosophy, or what passes for such, since it has been taught as a career qualification and a professional specialism?'[1] 'Philosophy when taught – as a specific subject, an object on the syllabus, controlled and controlling through examinations and grades, a means of livelihood, subject to remuneration and distribution – with all that this implies of platitudes, summaries, dissertations and obligations to imitate – psittacosis and the like – rabbiting on[2] – aping the positive sciences, ceasing to be the product par excellence of the *individual*. "Complete Course in Philosophy"! Whence the fatal degeneration into "History", and comparative studies! – etc. All this encouraged by the State – subservient philosophies.'[3]

What I have been asked is this: 'The authority of the author of these reflections forbids anyone from suspecting his motivation (followed by a quotation extracted from one of my books). This implies that we should not reproach Valéry with being inspired by resentment. In which case how should we place our reading of this discourse within the dialectic of the struggle for the legitimate representation of visions?' I think that this is an important question. It is connected with the problem of the struggles over the imposition of an image. Meanwhile, I have come across a very fine definition of bureaucracy, written by Valéry. I would like to comment on all this. Paul Valéry's text is obviously polemical. It is the vision that a writer has of a philosophy teacher, at a certain moment in time. If you turn the pages of the volume you will find that the headings of the sections ('Science', 'Bios', 'Theta', 'Eros', 'Affectivity', 'The Self and Personality', etc.) are philosophical subjects, and even topics set for the baccalaureate ('The Self and Personality', 'Attention', 'Consciousness', etc.). It is plain to see that there is a competition for the legitimate definition of philosophy, and it is a fact that these texts were written at a time when the struggle for the dominant definition of the legitimate discourse called 'philosophy' was intensified, with the professionalisation of the philosopher and the increasingly strict definition of the role of the professional philosopher as opposed to the amateur philosopher represented by the writer.

On this process of professionalisation and the emergence of a sort of professional corps after 1900, I refer you to research by Fabiani, some of which has appeared in *Actes de la recherche en sciences sociales*.[4] Kantianism, for instance, marked out the difference. Valéry and Alain (who happened to write on Valéry) were separated by the claims of the professional philosopher to know his authors, to be a repository of canonical knowledge, to show mastery of the canonical authors. Which is one of the traditional definitions of religion. For Weber, the opposition between the priest and the prophet turns on the problem of the canonical authors: as soon as prophecy becomes routinised, a finite corpus of authors is composed,[5] a kind of pantheon of legitimate authors. And the *lectores*, the professors, are established as the legitimate commentators on the legitimate texts, and on these alone. What Valéry expresses illustrates what I have often said: in the struggles within their field, everyone sees the position opposite to their own clearly enough (we are always good at sociologising others, we find the right viewpoint to survey their viewpoint and interests from). Valéry

198 *Lecture of 23 May 1985*

touches on absolutely essential things: the prophet's tendency towards 'familiarisation, 'simulation' and 'usurpation of identity'. He touches less on more [sociological?] things: 'In the order of the intellect the University represents the same timidity and pettiness, the same petty doubts and the same qualities, as the French petit bourgeois does in the order of his life.'[6] [. . .] 'The habit of using the powers of the mind as instruments of control, torture, trial and measurement – as a practical end, a means of earning a living, etc. – Making a living from sacred things – Is abandoning everything noble – everything.'[7]

In other words, Valéry reproaches the professional philosophers with making philosophy their profession, with transforming philosophy into a livelihood and thereby endowing it with a utilitarian function: this is the opposition of 'art for art's sake' and 'art for social ends'.[8] It is obvious that I shall not take up a position in this debate (although I'm worried that one may be lurking somewhere in my argument), because what is at issue are two representations of which we cannot say that one is true and the other not. We could also find contradictory texts: when philosophy becomes professional, it tends to discredit the philosophy of writers by denouncing its more platitudinous maxims. When Valéry, says, for instance, that 'time is a weary clock', this is not extraordinary, he clearly hasn't read Kant, 'he doesn't know how to formulate a problem'. He answers this criticism in advance, by saying that philosophy teachers do not pose the problems that they are faced with, but problems that they know must be put, and in so doing they undermine their audience's likelihood of raising real questions, by imposing issues that are irrelevant to them.[9] These are exceptional arguments, and they make sociology question what it can use them for. This is extremely difficult: you can study them at the first degree or place them in an epigraph (an epigraph is often a phrase that anticipates a whole argument [. . .]).

I would like to take this a little further and introduce a quotation from Valéry that I find very important in the light of what I was saying last time about the certificate or licence effect. Valéry says that Napoleon made rather a mess of the conception of the education system: 'Napoleon, having slept rather rapidly once or twice with Minerva, left her the University to suckle.' [*Bourdieu comments*: a professional philosopher (not to mention a historian) would never write that [*laughter*], which is a shame . . . But it has an intuitive force.] 'That great man, truly great because he had a feel for Institutions, sensed how their fiduciary nature was organised and driven by automatisms and independence from the individual, yet this singular character attempted to reduce the role of personality, whose inconstancy he knew too well.'[10]

Lecture of 23 May 1985   199

The style is somewhat Mallarméan, Lacanian or neo-Mallarméan, but here we have Weber's whole theory of bureaucracy in a single sentence. I'll read it again: Napoleon 'had a feel for Institutions', and what is an institution? It is something 'fiduciary', that is, it holds things in trust (faith). It is even, more precisely, an 'organised fiduciary', not the spontaneous fiduciary that we see in the case of the charisma of the singular prophet who asks you to believe in him in person. There is delegation to an organisation; faith is organised, and the fate of that faith is to become an organisation: that's what a bureaucracy is, as opposed to a prophet.

The formula 'fiduciary nature organised and driven by automatisms' is very interesting; 'driven by automatisms' is the opposite of what I was describing last time: Weber's Sancho Panza or *Kadijustiz*, where you react as the spirit moves you. Whereas the 'organised fiduciary' reacts in the same way every day of the week, whether he is in a good or a bad mood, the bureaucrat reacts by and large in a consistent manner. In any case the bad mood of the bureaucrat is catered for. In Valéry's words: 'driven by automatisms and independence from the individual'. Bureaucracy exists beyond the individual, it is impersonal, which infuriates the defenders of the authentic:[11] it de-personalises, it is a 'they', it is anonymous. This can be a nuisance, but from a view of consistency of reaction, of reliability over time, it does provide guarantees. Valéry continues: 'This great man [. . .] who was so individual, trying to reduce the role of personality, whose inconstancy he knew too well.' In passing, he underlines a paradox: Napoleon, who was so individual, 'tried to reduce the role of the individual'; the inventor of rational bureaucracy, who is charismatic by definition, tends to reduce the role of the individual, whose inconstancy he knows too well. We can relate that to the ethics of Kant rather than those of the Scottish philosophers, who wanted to ground ethics in the inconstancy of sentiment.[12] The good bureaucrat, like the good moralist in Kant's view, knows that you must not rely on sentiment. In order to ensure constancy, you need an 'organised fiduciary'. Therein lies the paradox of bureaucracy.

Amateur and professional

My aim was not only to comment on this text and to make a transition from what I was saying last time. I also wanted to show the difference between an amateur philosopher and a professional philosopher, and one might add a scholar of the social world working in a cumulative

200 *Lecture of 23 May 1985*

tradition. An amateur can provide maxims and formulae that may have the power to stimulate striking insights, but somewhat at random. Valéry made some extraordinary reflections, for instance: 'Diplomas – spirit of defiance which is answered by the spirit of simulation – naivety – immediately forgotten. The State uses them to allow us to forget – to stop making an effort. Advantages – a certain education, however misunderstood.'[13] Here this is really *homo academicus singularis* who returns, and says: 'Diplomas are not great, but they are a guarantee.' He has not thought about it very deeply, and he should have taken it further. From time to time he hits on a felicitous formula. We could analyse that. In fact behind these antagonistic visions, there are often genuine problems in defining the position: what is the right way of obtaining the post? We could, without any value judgement and in an analytic spirit, bring Valéry, Alain and Max Weber to confront each other (there are many books with titles such as 'The Scholar and the Politician') in order to understand the academic positions, as if we were describing the occupations of a storekeeper, a baggage handler or a pedlar.

I shall, albeit very quickly, look at the differences. Comparing Valéry and Alain, we see straight away that Alain would not have spoken of bureaucracy: it is not on the syllabus, Plato does not mention it, neither does Kant . . . With Hegel, he might make a small excursus in which he could insert his ordinary experience of the social world, not scientifically sublimated. (It is something interesting: philosophical texts always operate on two levels. There is the manifest architectonic level of the manifest discourse, and beneath them runs a hidden discourse, that occasionally erupts. I can refer you to my critical analysis of Kant's *Critique of Judgement*,[14] which has infuriated the professional philosophers. My analysis of Kant was analogous to Karl Schorske's analysis of Freud in his book on *Fin-de-Siècle Vienna*.[15] Schorske submits the dreams that Freud describes in his *Introduction to Psychoanalysis* to a sociological analysis, and beneath the overt discourse noted by psychoanalysts he discovers another discourse, where Freud speaks of his relationship with his father and the University, of his fear of not having a university career, etc. It depends on the terrain, of course – there are terrains where it is more relevant than others – but I think that philosophical discourse, however carefully controlled, often hides a covert social discourse whose coherence can only be detected when read as a whole. It is as if there were holes in the overtly coherent discourse through which the social thrust suddenly erupts; little scraps, examples or notes through which social fantasies escape . . .) In short, Alain would most probably not have discussed bureaucracy.

Now for Weber. I have said that Valéry unwittingly formulated a 'Weberian' definition. The difference between Valéry and Weber is that if Weber hits on this definition, he knows what he is doing, he knows that he is talking about bureaucracy, he mobilises his theoretical and empirical resources, he proceeds using a comparative method, he tries to build on earlier knowledge, he has read Hegel and everything relevant to what he is trying to understand. He *elaborates* his construction, firstly because he sets it up explicitly as an object, but also because, having taken it as an object, he develops all its properties, instead of leaving it as merely a passing remark that would only make sense to someone who had read Weber. (Another trivial remark but perhaps mildly defamiliarising: what is a re-reading? Re-reading is frequently practised and used as a weapon in the struggles between positions. If you practise literary semiology, being able to say 'Valéry and I' is a strength; in another universe on the contrary it might be a handicap. In a re-reading the re-reader often imports his own categories of perception. Thus Weber says of Luther that he 'read the Bible through the spectacles of his whole attitude',[16] with his whole habitus. Obviously re-reading enables an extraordinary reconstruction, and when Troeltsch compiles the readings of the Gospels over twenty centuries[17] it is quite extraordinary, it is a projective test of the first order. Another important question is quotation: what is a quotation? Someone who places between inverted commas on the same page the words of a person he has interviewed and the words of Hegel only rarely asks himself what it means in both cases to quote these words: is it an attestation of truth, a certification of authority? Quotation and re-reading have an effect of re-creation.) Weber, reading Valéry's text, would obviously have seen everything that Valéry was saying and that Valéry himself in a way was unaware of.

I shall stop there, but I take this opportunity to thank the author of the question, and in general, everyone who asks me a question. I don't know if the explanations that they lead me to give are useful, but these questions are very useful for me psychologically because they give me the feeling that I have a better idea of your expectations.

Bureaucracy as a massive fetish

I return to my argument. The connection is easy to see. Last time I was speaking of the certificate and the effect of certification, the effect of attestation guaranteed by the State. It would be useful to compose the whole semantic field of bureaucratic words of this kind ('licence',

202 *Lecture of 23 May 1985*

'certificate', 'attestation', etc.), which all follow the logic of the fiduciary. 'Attestation' means: 'I was a witness, and I attest that . . .', 'I declare, offering myself as guarantor, that this man is genuinely capable and worthy', one of the problems being to know who guarantees the attestation. Who guarantees the guarantor? The bureaucratic guarantor's credit is institutional. It is as a public servant that he attests. It is through his impersonal function that his personal guarantee is guaranteed, enabling him to sign – or not to sign, perhaps. The debate 'Should public servants sign or not?' is a very important theoretical debate: does the personalisation of the bureaucracy not create a sort of soluble fish, a sort of institutional contradiction? (I don't want to develop this, because you will think that I am drowning in anecdotal current affairs and that I am losing touch with the theoretical heights.)

If you think about it, all these notions ('title', 'licences', certificates', etc.) designate extremely mysterious, ultimately magical, social acts. Imagine, for example, the importance of the guarantee of authenticity given by an art critic, often without seeing the painting. Someone phones him from Tokyo telling him, 'I've got a Monet.' He knows the person, he trusts him, takes him at his word, and signs. But in signing to say that Monet's signature is authentic he is countersigning a signature which itself multiplies the value of the painting a hundredfold. Because if, as Duchamp once did, I grace a urinal with my signature – which is a real example[18] – I multiply its value a hundredfold. Those who study commodity fetishism in archaic civilisations find phenomena of this type before their eyes every day. Very often we have a magical act which works to state that things really are what the person who signs says they are. The problem obviously, as always, is who guarantees the guarantor. If the signature attests that the painting is really a Miró, why is it important for it to be signed by Miró (It is the question: 'Who created the creator?'). We need to believe that Miró is important for the signature attesting that it is Miró who painted the picture to be important, for the signature of the person attesting that it is Miró who signed to be important, and so on. The artistic field is a series of signatures, and we never know who is at the origin [. . .].

For instance, there is a much-quoted phrase by Benjamin (Benjamin was very useful twenty or thirty years ago, but as so often, these things arrive in France too late . . .): 'One should fight the fetishism of the name of the master.'[19] This is relatively important: for instance, one kind of sociology of literature is a hostage to the fetishism of the name of the master, which renders it unable to analyse. That said, what I am saying is that the name of the master really is a fetish. In other words, we should first say: 'Beware the fetishism of the name of the master!' – it is a mistake to study Victor Hugo as Victor Hugo. But a second mistake is the illusion of demystification, which makes us forget that the name of the master is really a fetish, and that what we need to understand is how such a fetish is made. How in our societies do we make a fetish, how do we create a Renoir exhibition?[20] What is the process whereby, adding credit to credit and signing blank cheque after blank cheque, we produce some enormous objective reality with economic effects? (This would require a very long analysis, but I believe it would be of fundamental importance.)

The analogy with the artistic field that I have just drawn is not chosen at random. The artistic field is a fertile terrain for studying the fetishism of the signature, the licence, the certificate, the expert or his expertise, but everything I have said could be applied *mutatis mutandis* to bureaucracy. Bureaucracy is perhaps an enormous fetish that guarantees the magic acts that guarantee the fetish. Which does not mean that it doesn't exist. Nothing exists more strongly than a fetish, since everyone believes that it exists, and that is what is important. The notion of what is 'important' needs some thought; it is, as [Husserl][21] might have said, the 'noematic correlate' of interest: interest is what gives importance. Philosophers of language have recently studied this notion of importance, which indicates what is socially constituted as having value, unanimously recognised value.

Categorial mediation

I return now to what I was saying last time. I looked at the problem of those acts, that we might call 'nomic', where a socially delegated expert performs an act which may, for example, impose a classification. To recapitulate briefly: I chose the example of private charity as opposed to public welfare. I recalled that this opposition between a private act of charity, where I give alms to a beggar, and an act of public welfare, where a doctor issues a certificate of invalidity to someone who becomes an authorised beneficiary, is the opposition between acts [. . .] left to individual initiative and acts controlled, guaranteed and mediated by the State.

We may note in passing that this provides a pattern for rethinking, in quite a surprising new light, the debate that has much exercised France in the last few years concerning the opposition between public and private.[22] (My manner of working is designed to offer a way of thinking, rather than asserting a thesis.) I shall not develop this fully, I am just giving you the idea. With the education system, the propensity inherent in all groups, especially family groups, to ensure their own reproduction, not only biological but also social, their sort of *conatus*, or tendency to persevere in their being which is the characteristic of those who want to perpetuate themselves, in identical or augmented form, comes up against something entirely new. In the case of peasant or aristocratic families, primogeniture, for instance, was a way for the family to remain in charge of the transmission and retain complete mastery of certification: the father could consecrate or disinherit an heir. The introduction of systematic schooling introduces a force of impersonal mediation controlled and regulated by the State, so that families have to take account of a verdict that no longer depends on themselves alone. Globally speaking, we note that there is a statistical relation between the cultural capital possessed by families and what they obtain from the social system. Since by and large the education system statistically reiterates the given distribution of capital, we can say that this is a statistical figure, and people always object to my analyses because they do not allow for the fact that many polytechniciens do not send their sons to the École polytechnique. In fact a polytechnicien does have a much greater chance of his son becoming a polytechnicien than a non-polytechnicien would, but this is not a certain possibility. Which means that there is a measure of doubt, which has considerable social effects. It helps to disguise the whole mechanism and it has very powerful psychological effects. We find an opposition of the same type as the opposition between private charity and public charity (or welfare): in the one case I am in charge of giving or not giving, I have complete control over the operation; in the other I am abandoned to the verdict of an institution that may globally fulfil the function that I am seeking, but in such a way that my particular case is not satisfied. In other words, satisfaction is given to the class, in the logical sense of the term, without all the members of the class obtaining satisfaction.

This is a contradiction that arises from the detour through categorial mediation. This is closely linked to the opposition between bureaucratic judgements and pre-bureaucratic judgements which, like the judgements of the *kadi* or customary law described by Weber, always concern the individual and the particular: it sees an individual woman who bears a specific child[23] and passes a particular judgement. When Weber describes bureaucratic judgement or rational law as being subject to mediation by the universal, there is some ideological bias (we are all liable to be subject to this . . .): the theme of 'bureaucratisation = rationalisation' is one of Weber's great ambiguities (he was in fact aware of this, since he distinguished between formal rationality and material rationality). But it is true that bureaucratisation introduces

Lecture of 23 May 1985   205

a new type of judgement. The *nomos* is a judgement, a categorisation and a separation, for instance between those with disabilities and those without, but it is a categorial *nomos*: it no longer applies to one or other individual; it is designed to distinguish the genuinely blind from the simulator. As always, there is a continuum, but the *nomos* cuts through this. Using the simple example that I always use: at the airport check-in anything over 30 kilos is excess baggage, there is a simple cut-off point . . . Another example is a joke by Alphonse Allais: 'What should I do if I take the train with my child and half-way through the journey he has his third birthday [and is no longer eligible for the reduction for children under the age of three]?'[24] [*laughter*]. The imagination of comedians often packs a sociological punch. Bureaucracies accept that people are unlikely to stretch their honesty to such limits, but they may well anticipate the case of the child [who becomes three years old during the journey]. Bureaucratic judgements, unlike judgements by the *kadi*, are universal. And they are universal because they are categorial. And being categorial, they become statistical: they can be valid for the category without being valid for the individual. We find the same paradoxes that I was discussing just now.

Validated perception

Basically, I am considering the nature of an institution (which is the question that Valéry was posing). Institutionalising a validated social perception constitutes a *nomos*. The term 'validated' is extraordinary, if you think about it. It is typically bureaucratic. What does it mean to 'validate [*homologuer*]' a record-breaking performance? The Greek *homologein* ['speak in agreement with', 'be in agreement'] implies that everyone will speak in unison, as long as they have proceeded with all due caution, consulted four timekeepers and taken the average of the times measured. Another example: the validation of a diploma or a title which is one of the major issues disputed in our societies. As I said last time, in our societies someone's civil status can be defined as the sum of their bureaucratic attributes: our social identity is the sum of those categorial attributes which are granted us by the entity we call 'the State' and which figure on an ID card for instance. The attributes that have been chosen for validation have been the object of considerable discussion. Collective agreements, for instance, are struggles to establish what it is to be called this or that, what they imply. These are logical struggles that are also social struggles, that is, socio-logical struggles. Saying 'I have the right to wear a uniform' or 'I am entitled

206   *Lecture of 23 May 1985*

to wear a white overall or a grey overall' means taking sides in a struggle. If I am entitled to wear a white overall, I am entitled to be paid the
wages of those people who wear white overalls. Thus there are logical
games that employ social logic to arrive at unexpected implications. If
I change my title and instead of calling myself an 'assistant lecturer'
(*assistant*) I call myself a 'lecturer' (*maître-assistant*),[25] everything
changes, because my rank in the hierarchy of salaries changes.

All these struggles for validation bring us back to the problem that
I have been discussing obsessively all year: how can we come to agree
to say the same thing about the social world? As I have said, we have
only points of view. Which is why I find certain Husserlian forms of
theoretical and lived phenomenology irritating: the philosophers of
communication who ask us to 'put ourselves in other people's place'
are extremely naive: we can never take the place of anyone else![26]
If there is some truth in my sociology, we cannot put ourselves in
[someone else's] place, unless we perform the theoretical act of constructing the space of places. Through such a theoretical work, we
may have a virtual intuition of what it is to inhabit a certain place, and
I have sometimes found that through this kind of work, discussing
with people working on milieux that I had no knowledge or native
experience of, I could anticipate their observations by constructing
an intuition of what such and such a place in some particular space
might be. This has nothing to do with intuition – the word is generally
pejorative: [in the social sciences it tends to mean] 'It's not bad, but
really, he'd do better to write a novel . . .' (Remark that on the other
hand they might say: 'It's fantastic, he could even turn it into a novel'
[*laughter*]. Compliments can cut both ways! Sociology can help us to
live [*laughter*] . . . You can always turn an insult into a compliment if
you know where it's coming from . . . [*Bourdieu struggles to continue*]
When I say things like that, I always lose the thread of my argument
[*laughter*]!)

Institutional perception is a validated perception: it is taken as
given that everyone must be in agreement with its propositions. I have
already expressed this in different terms: the State is the monopoly of
symbolic violence; the State has the power to say what you are ('You
are an *agrégé*') in such a way that nobody can contradict it, that everybody must accept it, with all the rights, duties, claims and obligations
that it implies. This validated definition is something quite extraordinary from a sociological point of view, and I am surprised that people
don't seem very surprised by it. This is a difficulty with sociology: we
spend our time enquiring into what we all think about people, whilst
crediting institutions with the extraordinary right to say what they

Lecture of 23 May 1985   207

really are, yet such phenomena are so blatantly obvious that they don't surprise us.

The philosophers of authenticity are important because they represent a certain category of agents who claim the monopoly of legitimate symbolic violence against what they see as the 'illegitimate' symbolic violence of a bureaucratic type. Nobody has noticed it, but I think that Heidegger is in fact in dialogue with Weber, and that his famous passages on 'they', *das Man*,[27] which people comment on as if they were metaphysical, are sociology transformed into ontology. Heidegger represents the professorial claim to be treated as an individual: 'I myself have the right to be the composer of my own identity', 'Who is this nobody to tell me who I am?'

I can illustrate this very concretely: in an enquiry into the relations between a bank and its clients, we analysed clients' protests against their treatment by the bank,[28] and a sizeable proportion came from teachers, and rather more from those in higher education, including professors of law. We might suppose that this is because they have a greater *libido protestandi* than others, insofar as composing oneself as a person, claiming to be the subject and founder of one's own definition (the problem of foundation could be studied further in this light . . .), is part of the definition of their function.

Science and the science of the State

To conclude on the subject of validation. In fact the bureaucratic effect is extraordinary: it manages to present a perspective that passes for neutral, trans-individual, trans-perspectival, for being a verdict on verdicts (to use an image from Leibniz, who said that God is the 'geometral' of all perspectives, the geometric locus of all viewpoints).[29] When the State says that a profession is validated, this shows that there is a consensus on its meaning, giving a trans-subjective and objective meaning to social objectivity. The struggles for validation, for the *nomos*, are struggles for objectivity. This raises in concrete terms the problem of the position of the scholar in this struggle. What is the specific position of the sociologist? If I want to tell the truth about the social world, must I be challenged by those who are empowered to deliver verdicts? One of the main reasons that leads someone to become a sociologist is very similar to what leads someone to become a philosopher: it is the aim to reveal the legitimate truth of the social world. This means that the main adversary is the holder of the power of certification: the bureaucrat, the senior civil servant or the technocrat

208 *Lecture of 23 May 1985*

who can produce certainties that can be validated, that are socially recognised as unbiased, objective, and not delivered from a particular point of view.

The problem (raised by Valéry, again) is that of a State science as opposed to science as such: are not philosophers who are State philosophers, State bureaucrats? Is a sociologist paid by the State necessarily a State sociologist? In general this question is only raised in order to formulate the equation: 'sociologist paid by the State = State sociologist'. This is most often a way of avoiding the problem. There is in fact a way of giving a pseudo-radical turn to questions which consists in taking them to extremes – for instance, to move on from acknowledging the fact that 'the School system tends to reproduce inequality' to the radical position 'We must abolish the School': most often these ways of radicalising a problem are a way of avoiding it [. . .]. On the question of State philosophers, there is a commonplace attitude that manages to avoid the issue: it offers a thumbnail sketch of Hegel and German bureaucracy, etc. [. . .], whereas in fact we need to ask what is meant by 'being a State scholar'. Now, we have the answer: a State scholar is someone whose verdicts are validated and who is empowered to validate, someone who can be said to be 'neutral and scientific', someone who doesn't prompt us to ask where they are coming from (someone like the INSEE researcher, for instance). It is someone who 'signs' anonymously (which is an interesting oxymoron).

I could say a lot about the relation of bureaucrats to their signature: there are things that a bureaucrat cannot sign, except by a pseudonym. In this case we speak of simulation or cowardice, but it has nothing to do with psychology; these individual variables do no more than disguise structural relations and effects. As soon as you see a publication, check whether it is signed or not, and if it is signed by name, whether there is an acronym or not. A name plus an acronym means 'State science', 'science guaranteed by the State'. The theory (in the sense of a 'vision' or a 'viewpoint') is legitimate, that is, arbitrary: it is delivered from a viewpoint, but it is misrecognised as such, and therefore recognised as legitimate. In other words, it comes from a viewpoint the social conditions of whose production are such that its individuality and arbitrariness are dissolved and disappear. That is the condition for this theory to become powerful and legitimate, to gain the force of law and confer rights. INSEE's taxonomies have been revised to a large extent (three quarters or four fifths, or perhaps more) on the basis of my own work, but in becoming INSEE categories, they [my categories] have completely changed their status.[30]

Lecture of 23 May 1985   209

The difference between the sociologist and the State scholar is that the sociologist who wants to make a scientific study of the social world must raise, not as an epistemological point of honour, but as an absolute critical preliminary, the question of his position in the space of positions. He needs to realise that the social world is a subject of struggle, that there exist all sorts of incompatible standpoints and that there is a particular position, the State position, which is given – or manages to pass – as a position-less position, as a quasi-divine position (the social world does have its God). As an individual, the sociologist exists in this space (he views things through its eyes, faces its challenges, etc.), but he takes this space as his object of study. This means that he takes himself, inhabiting this space, as his object of study, and he objectifies (or at least sets himself the task of objectifying, with the means at his disposal) all the forms of objectification that he encounters. This is what is special about his objectification. Thus he renounces certification by the State and can then be paid by the State without being certified by the State. (It is obvious that I don't dream of having the State sign everything that I have said about the social world, thanks be to God!) The sociology of expertise is what marks the difference between the sociologist and the expert, and what means that the sociologist will never be an expert. People say (I have even said it myself – we don't always know why we are saying what we are saying . . .) that sociology is necessarily critical, but this is not a choice, it is a constituent part of its approach. I think that if the sociologist does his work properly, objectifying every objectification, especially the most powerful and legitimate, he cannot avoid establishing a distance. The scientific study of scientific power is what characterises the specificity of science.

In my next lecture I will give you in a rather artificial form a sort of theoretical perspective on all the theories on offer dealing with what it is to think of the social world. This will be rather academic: I shall speak of Kant, Hegel, Weber and Durkheim. If I had done this at the outset, you would perhaps have had an exalted idea of my thought, but I think that you would not have understood things as well as you will understand them after first hearing the tales I have been telling you and then seeing them crowned by what Kant and company said . . .

Second session (seminar): the invention of the modern artist (7)

[. . .] As an introduction to this session on the history of the Impressionist revolution, I would like to discuss a rather extraordinary painting that is on show in the Renoir exhibition:[31] its title is *Monet Painting in His*

210　　　　　　　　　*Lecture of 23 May 1985*

Garden [1873]. In general, painters painted themselves painting. Here the painter is painted in the act of painting by another painter. What is amusing is the fact that we don't see what it is that Monet is painting (but of course we know: he is surrounded by flowers, he is painting a garden, etc.) and the fact that Renoir is painting what Monet is not painting. Monet's painting at the time was a very closed universe, a universe of gardens. This was the moment in Monet's life when he was assuming a petit bourgeois lifestyle in Argenteuil. For the first time in his life he was becoming relatively settled and tranquil, he had a garden that he was very proud of, and enjoyed some good cooking. In short, he had arrived and he felt a kind of euphoria which we find expressed in terms of a happy, sheltered environment. Yet what we see on the horizon of Renoir's painting is a background of very ugly suburban houses. In contemporary photographs – for instance in the book *Monet at Argenteuil*,[32] which is where I got this information from – we see an industrial environment of factories under construction. The flaw, so to speak, implied by Renoir's viewpoint (every viewpoint is a viewpoint from one particular point and implies something unspoken) concerns a whole ensemble of things that make up modernity (when we say 'Manet and Monet, painters of modernity', we are referring to only one certain kind of modernity).

With this opening anecdote, which I would of course like to tie in with this history of a viewpoint, I wanted to raise the issue of the relation between aesthetic revolution and political revolution. It is an issue that I believe has been very poorly treated. The notion of the field has the advantage of enabling us to place, better than we usually do, the problem of the relations between the changes in world view introduced, for instance, by a cultural revolution (what I am studying here is a cultural revolution) and social changes. In the traditional logic of the social history of art, these problems are not always treated with the simplistic logic of reflection used by Goldmann[33] (who at least has the merit of taking that logic to its limits). But most often critics implicitly postulate a relation between social changes and political changes, for instance through divisions into periods that, like school textbooks, reproduce the moments of rupture within political history (like the break of the '1848 Revolution'), which introduces a highly contestable philosophy of history.

The notion of the field enables us to take our distance from the tired clichés of the infrastructure/superstructure problem[34] that is past its sell-by date, and pose the problem in a more realistic manner: the revolution occurs in a relatively autonomous subspace – where a specific balance of power is based in a specific type of capital, etc. – and

Lecture of 23 May 1985 211

what we need to discover are the conditions that need to be met for a cultural revolution to succeed. For there are cultural revolutions that fail. Marx spoke of 'partial revolutions',[35] and there are partial artistic revolutions. As people said after May '68, the revolution was 'hijacked' (but this is an absurd term, as if there were a hijacker exploiting it for advertising or for an avant-garde literary review to be read by busy executives[36] [*laughter*]). I think that this idea of a 'specific revolution' is extremely important. We are scared of using the word revolution, believing that 'the only true revolution is one that upsets the infrastructure', but true revolutions do exist that are specific to the level of the superstructure (which absurd language I use only for the purposes of communication). Since fields are relatively autonomous social spaces that have their own specific power relations, a change in those relations brings with it profound changes in our view of the world. When the principal function of the field is to produce an objectified view of the world, a 'theory' in the sense of a vision objectified (which is the case for paintings, but can also be the case for language, and discourse on the social world), transforming these power relations in the field means causing a cultural and theoretical revolution.

We may wonder whether this theoretical revolution is not limited by the social characteristics of those who lead the revolution, because of the pre-existing balance of power within the field and the fact that the autonomy of the field, being relative, does not exclude dependence on other social factors. But we may also wonder why a cultural revolution is felt as being tremendously revolutionary, in the most political sense of the term (as if to say: 'Hands off my vision!'). The critics of the time spoke of Manet with extraordinary violence. Why did they react with such violence if in truth all the man did was change a superstructural vision? Courbet and Manet were hated more than any politician had been; they must have touched on something extremely important. I think it is because changing our vision is in itself something extremely revolutionary. A fortiori, the sociology of vision as viewpoint, the sociology dealing with the type of object that I have taken this year, is I believe intrinsically disturbing.

I have no ambition to play the part of the intellectual driving history forward, and I don't harbour many illusions about the impact and limitations of the discourse I can deliver, but I think that it is as subversive as possible because it touches our internalised *nomos* with its 'a-nomic' nature. It is formidably anomic because a successful *nomos* is one that manages to avoid detection in terms of the *nomos* as I define it: 'recognition' is in fact misrecognition of the arbitrary. This has all been said for years now, but through empty formulae which have no

212 *Lecture of 23 May 1985*

impact ('The dominant culture is the culture of the dominant class',[37] etc.), whereas what we need to discover concretely is the fact that the struggles over the perception of the social word have a certain functional logic, that they can only be divided into segments historically, and that the only truth to be found through these struggles is that they are struggles for the truth. Sometimes I wonder whether the only truth that we can deliver on the social world might not be that the social world is the site of struggles for truth. You may be thinking that I am proceeding by identification with my topic (it happens so often that we choose a topic in order to give ourselves a pretext for talking about ourselves . . .)? I say this to give you leave to think it, but I don't really think it is the case! [*laughter*] [. . .].

Polycentrism and the invention of institutions

To recapitulate. I finished off last time with the paradox of the cultural revolution that the Impressionists were in the process of launching; to conquer their autonomy they were obliged to fight against the institution that guaranteed their autonomy, insofar as it was charged with transmitting the specific competence, inherited from the past, that is the most distinctive property of any professional agency, [. . .] and what enables it to affirm its difference. I reminded you that in order to become a successful cultural revolution, their break had to take advantage of objectively favourable conditions (the crisis in the Academy born of the overproduction of diplomas, etc.), and also that it had been obliged to constitute a specific new infrastructure, that is, to establish a new institution. I don't want to enter into detail because these are familiar stories which have been told in all the books. What I want to add is simply the process of modelling: the artistic field in the modern sense was established through the constitution of an ensemble of competing institutions, in other words by a sort of institutionalisation of anomie. This is the paradox that, when I started to discuss the artistic field and said that 'the artistic field is the site of a struggle for legitimacy, they are all fighting each other', led me to add 'But I am not saying that there is legitimacy, I am saying that there is a struggle for the monopoly of legitimacy, which is one way of recognising legitimacy.'

There are states of the field in which there is an orthodoxy, that is, a viewpoint that manages to impose itself as dominant. For instance, if what I said just now is true, we might imagine, in the field of sociology, that for economic, social and political reasons, INSEE, as the certified science of the State, would gradually come to hold the monopoly of the production of data socially recognised as scientific, and that there would be a real monopoly of scientific legitimacy, such that anyone saying what I said this morning would appear to be a retarded philosopher, offering unfounded criticism without any statistics to back up their claims. That said, even if, in some of its states, the field can be the site of a dominant legitimacy, it is essentially a place where people struggle for the monopoly of legitimacy. In the field of painting, after the cultural revolution operated by the Impressionists, there came a state of institutionalised anomie: an ensemble of institutions was created and none had the monopoly of the *nomos*. In other words, even for anomie to exist, you need some institution.

This idea has guided my politics in the domain of the social sciences for some time now: the more sources there are producing social science, the more chance social science has of being scientific; anomie is the condition of scientificity. (What I am saying here is very serious, it is neither a joke nor an empty paradox . . .) It is very important because, as I said a long time ago, sociology is a subordinate science, it is constantly tempted by what I call the 'Gerschronken effect',[38] that is, the temptation to ape the more advanced sciences, to adopt an air of consensus (saying: 'The physicists are all in agreement, they are not like you sociologists who haggle over everything'). There was a phase in the field of world sociology when there was a sort of 'working consensus', in Goffman's words,[39] to designate that sort of fictitious consensus between people who don't know each other very well and want to avoid conflict: you meet up, you don't quite know who it is you are meeting, you size each other up, you take mental notes ('He has the Legion of Honour'), you don't discuss the army, the State or the clergy, but you comment on the weather . . . The social sciences experienced such a movement of consensus in the United States in the 1950s:[40] they said that sociology had become a respectable science and that there was general agreement. Parsons described the social world for us, Lazarsfeld was more empirical, but basically they were in agreement, and Merton arranged everything by saying that what was needed were 'medium-range theories'; and this kind of Capitoline triad of the gods[41] of the world's social science was able to create the illusion that sociology was a science because it was consensual.

The domination effect exercised by the other sciences is evident. Firstly, things have never functioned this way in any state of the most advanced science. Next, this simulacrum of a consensus is a parody of the social conditions favourable to science – and also, it seems to me, to artistic production. The institutionalisation of consensus is a process

214 *Lecture of 23 May 1985*

that leads to the existence of a multiplicity of places of production and evaluation – yet none of them exercises a definitive, lasting domination, none having the power to impose its own, particular *nomos*, that is, its individual viewpoint as the universally validated viewpoint. Sociologists are perpetually torn between two naive extremes. The naive autocratic vision (sociology has a pope and a Mecca and a verdict deciding who is a genuine sociologist and who is not) is opposed by a spontaneous, anarchic vision, arguing that anybody can say anything ('my judgement, after never having conducted an interview, seen a survey or a statistic, never read Weber, Marx or Durkheim, is just as valid as anyone else's . . .'). The anarcho-spontaneous vision is a perfectly logical error; it is sociological. The homologies between the political field and the scientific field depend on the fact that there are homologies of structure.

In fact, what I am saying amounts to this: the institutionalisation of autonomy was a kind of polycentrism; each time that a new pole of development emerged, socially constituted as capable of producing something likely to be recognised, even if only in discussion, as science, the chances of scientific progress increase. This is a normative proposition, but I believe that it is inherent to the analysis of the process of institutionalisation and the sort of paradox that I was formulating: the institutionalisation of anomie. Anomie, in the case of nineteenth-century painting, signals the absence of a dominant place of certification or consecration, that is, the collapse of the Academy as a place where someone could say who was a painter and what painting is. The history of Impressionism is the history of a series of inventions: the invention of galleries, the (enormous) invention of the notion of group exhibitions, the invention of the idea of the Salon des refusés, the invention of a new definition of the critic, the invention of new journals, etc. This collective effort was obviously not orchestrated, it was not guided by some sort of end of history; it was the product of often warring interests. Gradually things became organised in such a way that a field started to function, these rival institutions generated conflicts that made things change in this direction. (I don't know if I shall discuss this, because I don't know if I will be able to describe it in a sufficiently nuanced manner . . . I think that this struggle for the monopoly of legitimate painting leads in practice to a kind of purification of the definition of painting, something like an essentially historical analysis . . . I shall say no more, but I might return to this . . .)[42]

We should look into the process of the birth of this specific infrastructure, of all these institutions. Of course there are names, even simple words. I already told you one day that the invention of the

Lecture of 23 May 1985 215

word 'jogging' was extremely important. Similarly, in the nineteenth century, they needed to invent words, they needed to invent words for the artist, they had to invent the 'café', the café as a legitimate place, as a place for painters, musicians and artists to meet . . . there are then social uses for institutions that already existed . . .

The false antinomy of art and the market

Here we see another paradox that undermines reflection theories: very often when people raise what they call the problem of the relation between 'art and society' (a problem with strictly no meaning, except the conjunction of two words), they wonder about the meaning and form of the dependency and they inevitably ask art suspiciously: 'Are you not compromised by society?' Behind the sociology of art, there is always a suspicious question (which Valéry would have called 'petit bourgeois'): 'What if they were fakers?', 'What if they were having us on?', 'What if they had sold out to the bourgeoisie.' This backstage scrutiny is one of the subjective charms of a certain kind of social science (Wittgenstein denounces it very wickedly; I recently came across a text where he says in apocalyptic tones: 'What a joy to say "that's all it is"'). There is a subjective satisfaction in simplifying every-thing and saying, for instance, 'The Impressionists are just petits bour-geois', on concluding the kind of study I have mentioned, like *Monet at Argenteuil.* The theme is fashionable in the United States – even in *Time* magazine we may read: 'These people who have been presented as revolutionaries are in fact petits bourgeois who are showing off their gardens'. [*laughter*] This suspicious vision, which can be directed anywhere, disguises some very important things. To the alternative 'does art serve society (which we should often understand as "does art serve the bourgeoisie") or is it independent?', we can oppose some very simple questions: 'Can we not make use of the people that we serve?', 'Might one of the ways of gaining freedom not be to borrow the means from those who have stolen it from us?' Said in this way, it looks like a paradox, but it is perhaps the principal thesis of my analysis.

I no longer fully subscribe to the famous argument by Raymond Williams that I have often presented in my teaching. In *Culture and Society*,[43] Raymond Williams shows that the modern theory of culture (meaning the 'humanities', in the academic sense of the term) was constructed by the English Romantics in their reaction to the indus-trial world, and more precisely to the industrialisation of literature and the fact that art and culture were becoming just one commodity

216   *Lecture of 23 May 1985*

among others. He draws on numerous documents to show the revolt of the great English Romantic poets against this kind of 'massification' of production: finding that he had become a type of specialised workman in the culture factory, the cultural producer developed a sort of charismatic definition centred on the personality and the singularity of the producer, against the objective truth of his implication in the creation of an industrialised literature. According to this thesis, the cultural producers react against the domination that the economic powers exert through the press. But the history of painting and in particular an analysis of the Impressionist cultural revolution show that it is in a way by making use of the market that the Impressionists were able to escape the Academy: it was by making use of the freedom ultimately afforded them by the existence of a market and a clientele of aristocratic origins that the Impressionists liberated themselves from the kind of bureaucratic demands of the Academy.

An analysis of the Impressionist revolution has the virtue of being a particular case of a very general model of revolution against an artistic bureaucracy: the Academy is less interesting as an instrument of domination used by the dominant class than as a bureaucratic form of domination of the artistic field. I think that State commissioning of public art has some invariable properties, and one of my projects is to get a team to undertake a comparative sociology of artistic bureaucracies and State commissions, to enable us to understand Zhdanovism, say, or certain characteristics of Confucian painting. I think that the requirements of the State have some invariable properties. For instance, in Zhdanovist commissions there is of course the petit bourgeois habitus, but also the bureaucratic habitus requiring an uncontroversial painting, an anonymous painting expressing officially validated sentiments (on the family, work and the worker, that is, things that everyone agrees on). I shall not develop this.

In this respect the Third Republic is very significant. The revolutionary painters, and particularly those who started the revolution, were often of very high social origins. It is a kind of law: cultural revolutions are often led by those privileged in the very aspects that they are trying to subvert – heretics often emerge from the clergy – whereas the less favoured people are more submissive to bureaucratic demands. This is understandable: being oblates, who owe everything to the institution, they cannot challenge the institution without destroying the very foundation of their own authority. The Third Republic is very interesting in this respect: it is the people of the lowest social and most provincial origins who benefited from the great State commissions (paintings for the Sorbonne, for municipal buildings, and so on), who were the

Lecture of 23 May 1985 217

object of a democratic distribution. Whereas during this period (I am simplifying, and I apologise to those who know the details, but I have to be schematic if I am to communicate clearly), artistic subversion ([*Bourdieu hesitates to continue*:] I ask myself so many questions that I feel paralysed [*laughter*]) was more likely to occur in people less bereft of specific capital and social capital (relations, language skills, vocabulary) and with the emergence of a free market in art which is obviously the province of the privileged categories, the aristocracy or certain fractions of the upper bourgeoisie.

So the antinomy between the market and art, which leads us to see the market as automatically alienating, is simplistic. There are circumstances in which the conquest of autonomy and liberty may benefit from the help of the market. When liberation from a State bureaucracy is needed, the market can provide freedom, which does not mean that you won't need later to liberate yourself from the alienating kind of liberty that the market provides, with a return to bureaucracy then providing protection from the alienation of the market. I may seem to be using the language of abstract strategy; in concrete terms the question is whether in order to paint in freedom we might not do better to be employed part-time by the State, and whether to practise sociology in freedom we might not do better to be paid by the State rather than leave ourselves open to the requirements of clients funding us. These are eminently practical questions, that each person resolves in their own way . . . In short, it seems to me that there are invariables in the bureaucratic demand, and that we should resist a certain classical temptation that sees the market necessarily as a factor of alienation, for it may provide some freedom.

The collective judgement of the critics

To recapitulate: I have dealt with the social and demographic conditions of the possibility of the Impressionist cultural revolution and I have just referred to the institutional conditions of the institutionalisation of success. Now I would like to briefly mention the resistance of the critics, which will provide some evidence to verify what I was saying at the outset of this series of seminars on the Impressionist revolution, when I 'deduced', so to speak, the properties of *pompier* painting from the academic institution. I shall now undertake a different exercise, trying to deduce the categories of perception that were in force at the moment when the Impressionists started to invent new categories of perception and new institutions to impose those categories, and which

218   *Lecture of 23 May 1985*

are expressed in the judgements of the critics of the revolutionaries. I shall read some very fine studies of the Impressionists viewed by the critics, starting out from the idea that the critics wore spectacles and that those spectacles are revealed when they confront the sort of monstrosity that is Manet. When they speak of Manet what they are expressing is their categories of perception, and their horror is a horror of the monstrous . . . (We could read in the same way the books on May 1968, which are very revealing, not of what happened in May '68 – they hardly mention it – but of the spectacles of those discussing May '68. It seems to me that a historian of mental structures must proceed in this manner – afterwards, he can of course wonder what the books are nonetheless saying about reality.)

First, I shall reveal my sources. The most important is the book by George Heard Hamilton, *Manet and His Critics* (New Haven: Yale University Press, 1954). Then Albert Boime, *Thomas Couture and the Eclectic Vision* (New Haven: Yale University Press, 1980); Joseph C. Sloane, *French Painting between the Past and the Present: Artists, Critics and Traditions from 1848 to 1870* (Princeton: Princeton University Press, 1951). Hamilton is the essential reference. This is one of the laws of academic tradition [. . .]: in a scholarly universe, there is a handful of key studies that the others rework, adding more or less surplus value. It usually takes quite a long time to find the book that all the others have reworked. This book by Hamilton is one of the last that I found [. . .], because it was one of the earliest. We expect to see progress, but in a universe of the humanities, where knowledge is not primarily a cumulative science, the oldest work is often the best. That said, the books by Boime and Sloane are important too. Another extremely important book is Cassagne's *Théorie de l'art pour l'art en France*,[44] because it contains all the elements of a description in terms of field: instead of focusing on Lamartine, Cassagne is interested in the whole 'art for art's sake' movement, and he situates it in the context of other contemporary movements.

For an analysis of the critics, Hamilton is most important, because he gives the reactions provoked by Manet's painting year by year. What I am doing is very superficial and could be much better done. For instance, one thing that I have not considered is the transformation of collective judgement as it is expressed through the critics. This is a major undertaking: you need to make a sociological composition of the field of criticism (which is something that the authors I have mentioned do not enable us to do), that is, possess full details of all the media outlets that publish these critics, and know the relative positions of these organs (which would already give us information about the

Lecture of 23 May 1985 219

social properties of the people who write in these papers . . .). We could then situate the criticism of Manet's work in that space. Ultimately, the kind of collective judgement whose progress I want to describe may perhaps not exist. There is no sense in saying 'the critics' (as in the case of a book entitled *Les Impressionistes devant la presse*[45]). The idea that a space of universal judgement could exist has no sense; the judgements are necessarily differentiated. There is a space of criticism, and the motor of change will to a considerable extent be the struggles within this space, as the critics become a field. This is, moreover, part of the object of our study, since one dimension of the process of institutionalisation of anomie is the institutionalisation of free criticism, whereby the critic no longer sees his only mission as providing the reader with a kind of notice (to explain the history of a work, for instance), but gives as guarantee his personal relations with the author, engaging in a quasi-political way with the struggle within the field.

This is one of the major sources of change. As the years go by, it becomes increasingly clear, and we find an increasing number of charismatic critics, until we reach our own times, with the critic-impresario, who is no longer someone discussing the painting but someone who 'creates' the painting by creating a theory for it. To fully understand this process we would have to simultaneously recreate the social history of the field of painting, the internal struggles between the academic and the avant-garde painters, the internal struggles within the subfield of avant-garde painters, and so on. It is within these latter struggles that the critics will choose, depending on their position (some, for instance, will say: 'After all, Manet is better than the others, because we get used to him in the end'). So we would need to have the whole history of all this. What I have to offer is a much simplified history, that is rather difficult to justify, even in terms of my own categories: I shall be arguing as if the critics formed a collective viewpoint, whereas this is not at all the case.

The three reproaches

What is it in Manet's works that stupefied the critics? What upset them so much? What overthrew their world view? This is one of the properties of cultural revolutions. Some books on May '68 – which was a cultural revolution – say nothing different: 'The world is falling apart, everything is falling apart, my mental coherence is crumbling.' A cultural revolution blows people's mental structures to smithereens. There is nothing more terrible. It is a kind of brainwashing. People

220   *Lecture of 23 May 1985*

suffer a lot. In *Homo Academicus* I referred to this in a couple of sentences by comparing the reactions to May '68 of some high-ranking academics with the reactions of Kabyle elders speaking of the Kabyle youth and their method of ploughing;[46] it was really the same type of reaction: 'Everything is falling apart', 'The world is dead', 'The world is being turned upside down', 'It's like the fourteenth century, the rivers are flowing upstream, the women are going to market', and so on. In other words, the unthinkable becomes thinkable, the monstrous becomes the everyday, the extraordinary, banal . . . and since my mind can't cope with the world, I might as well die. Cultural revolutions provoke enormous symbolic suffering and that is how people react.

Speaking of Manet, they say: 'Manet tortures us' – which means 'Manet tortures our mental structures.' They complain: 'He doesn't know how to paint', 'His painting is flat', and one of the great questions is whether he does it on purpose or not, which raises the question of certification. They say that he can't paint, and that in any case he left Couture's studio too soon: he didn't take any exams, he didn't get the prix de Rome. Since he didn't get any certificates, he is not guaranteed by the institution, 'he doesn't know how'. A famous painting, where we see a *torero* and a bull, I forget the title, was much discussed; the bull is very large and the *torero* very small, there is a flaw in the perspective.[47] Did he do it on purpose or not? They note that having spent five years with Couture he had reached a stage where you know how to achieve perspective: so he must have done it on purpose. This is a great debate among the critics. 'Does he do it on purpose or not?' means 'Does he believe in it or not?' If he believes in it, he is credible. If he doesn't believe, he is a cynic, and is therefore deceiving us.

The problem of the person offering themselves as their own guarantor of their painting activity then becomes very important, and there is a whole debate over the personality of Monsieur Manet. Is Monsieur Manet credible? Is he properly dressed? Someone has shown me an extraordinary text saying: 'but I have met Monsieur Manet, he dresses like you and me [*laughter*], he has a fine presence, he expresses himself very well, so his painting is not a mystification. He is not an imposter or a charlatan.' So we come to the problem of the imposter and the certificate and, in this logic, our only guarantee is the person. One important thing is that by putting these questions the most aggressive critics contribute to the revolution themselves: by demanding guarantees, they contribute to the invention of a universe of painting in which the artist offers himself, and nothing else, as guarantee. Reading the critics of the other persuasion leads us to see the effects of the field.

Lecture of 23 May 1985 221

I must have often told you here that 'My problematic is the "field"'. . . .' This is something I took quite a long time to realise: there is a space of positions and the problematic is relating the positions to one another. In the present case, when someone bursts out asking 'But is he sincere?', all the others feel obliged to reply. In other words, changing a field sometimes simply comes down to entering with a problem that previously did not exist. If you manage to enter the field of journalism with a new newspaper, you present the others with problems, and you have changed the problematic. There the simple fact of raising the question of sincerity elicits replies of the type: 'But yes he is sincere, he suffers for his painting, he can't feed his children' – a partly justified mythology springs up in answer to the most academic question. In this way the academicians, based on their representation of the neatly dressed and decorated master, a member of countless juries, engender a kind of negative creation of the hirsute artist. The others respond in one of two ways: they say 'But no, he is a bourgeois like you', or else 'He suffers', thus inventing the theme of the *artiste maudit*, with starving children, midnight doubts, the absolute masterpiece, etc.

A first point then is: 'They don't know how to paint', 'What they do is flat', 'There's no perspective.' The second is the critics' stupefaction faced with a painting depicting nothing, which is perhaps the most extraordinary scandal: what does it mean to paint things that have no reason to be painted? What is the point of painting things that are absurd? It is the basic idea of the 'representable' that is called into question. A few years ago we made a study of photography in which we showed that we all have an implicit definition of the photographable; at any moment in time there exist things 'worthy of being photographed' and things 'not worthy of being photographed' and a sort of unwritten consensus on the hierarchy of things photographable.[48] It is the same for painting in the nineteenth century: there was an implicit definition of the 'representable', or what was 'worthy of being represented', a hierarchy of paintable objects. People like Manet place themselves right outside this space, they are outside the system of categories, which is dreadful for logicians: what is this thing that won't fit any category . . .? It is something that they can't find words for . . . they don't even know how to question it.

I believe that this is where the attack on intellectual integrity reaches its culmination. Not only do they not paint what is designated [as worthy of being painted], but they take it upon themselves to paint things that are not designated, or even forbidden . . . It is a provocation: as if they were claiming a kind of ontological status for the vacuum, for the social void, for the forbidden. Under these conditions,

222   *Lecture of 23 May 1985*

critics either cry scandal and question their sincerity ('These people are mad', 'It's a provocation'), or else indulge in an unconscious act of recuperation: to escape the tragic experience of finding the insignificant revalued, to suppress the scandal of the insignificant being reclaimed as ontologically meaningful, they grant significance to the insignificant, they seek a meaning for it. Sloane quotes a splendid text by a critic whom he situates among the 'humanitarians' (which means more or less 'mildly left-leaning'). (Sloane is useful alongside Hamilton because he tries to provide some information about the critics; unfortunately his taxonomies are subjective.) This critic finds one painting, *La Dame blanche*, intolerable, with its interplay of whites and colours, and he says: 'Basically, this is the bride's awakening, it is the disturbing moment when the young woman questions herself and is surprised not to recognise in herself the virginity of the night before' [*laughter*], and he compares it to Greuze. In other words he is looking for a lesson. There is then a kind of permanent debate, and field effects will come into play between those who, faced with the scandal of the importance bestowed upon the meaningless, will project meaning, and those who will say: 'But there is no meaning.'

In a sense, those who seek meaning at all costs, with reference to a certain moment in painting (Greuze, for instance) when meaning was compulsory, provoke the riposte 'But it has no meaning', and encourage the transformation of the rejecting of meaning into a project. That did not necessarily have to happen, because the project was not to give no meaning, but to create a play of colour. But in its critical struggles the field of criticism somehow anticipates the actual consciousness of the painter: the critics not only accompany the painters, but they may even precede them, depending on their specific interests. To shout down the critics of a hostile newspaper, they may go as far as to say: 'There mustn't be any meaning', 'It's stupid to look for meaning.' And the papers are rather like those sportsmen who in interviews on radio or television sometimes talk like the pundits [*laughter*]: critics come to tell painters that they must avoid meaning, when they hadn't thought about this at all . . . In truth, Renoir or Monet were not intellectuals . . . but once people say that is what they are doing, they start to say it themselves, and also to work differently by starting to really do what they think they had already been doing.

This is one of the main sources of their development, and we could analyse contemporary phenomena in the same light. For instance, we cannot understand the development of the 'nouveau roman' if we ignore the fact that it is entirely entangled with its relations with the critics (as in the dialogue between Robbe-Grillet and Barthes),[49] where this sort

Lecture of 23 May 1985 223

of explanation of the impact of the artistic intention as perceived by the critic is reflected back to the author of this intention, adapts and transforms the intention, and thereby helps to transform the work. In my opinion there are two major processes at work in the maturation of a cultural producer. The first is this: he believes he is discovering what he is through what people say he is (as much negatively, in fact, as positively, because one of the ways that a producer is dominated by what people say about him is when he rejects or opposes it). The second is the consecration effect, which (unlike biological ageing) provides maturation in specific areas, along with the effect exerted on the producer by the social recognition of his importance. This procedure is important in helping us to understand the careers of the painters, and even more of the writers, to whom we easily grant a prophetic role. We see it clearly in the case of failure, causing effects of resentment, but it is much more subtle in the case of success. The social trap for the artist, then, is the temptation to identify with the consecrating image (the life of Victor Hugo could be seen to follow this pattern). It happens especially to those who are dominant in the field at a certain moment. It is no paradox to say that the most dominated in the field are those who dominate the field (it could be said of Sartre) and owe more and more of their properties to what they must do and be in order to dominate the field. But this critical objectification, and the impact on artistic production of being conscious of this objectification, are I think one of the most important processes we should examine in studying the 'evolution' (as we tend to say using a meaningless, everyday term) of an 'author'.

A third reproach, closely connected with the scandal of meaninglessness that I have just mentioned, is made by looking at all costs for a function and saying: 'It has nothing to say, so it is pointless.' In other words, pure painting is constituted by the scandal that it causes, provoking people to say: 'It is impossible to paint things like that, for no reason.' In fact the scandalised critics create formalist painting by contrasting it with a functionalist definition of painting. Looking at painting with functionalist expectations (it must say something, tell a story, have a moral, activate some cultural history, and so on), and deploring the absence of what they expected, they necessarily formulate its opposite. Ultimately, the greatest contribution to the theory of art for art's sake was produced by the functionalist critics who found it intolerable. We continue to speak of the ruses of history, we wonder who it is who makes history, consciously or unconsciously . . . Here I think we find a kind of 'ruse': those who create the sense of history are those who do not understand its meaning; there is a manner of not understanding that helps to create the sense of the thing to be understood.

I shall stop here. Next time, I shall try to conclude by describing the later phase, when the painters, liberated thanks to the writers, will fight to liberate themselves from the writers.

Lecture of 30 May 1985

Providing a theoretical perspective – The Kantian tradition: symbolic forms – The primitive forms of classification – Historical and performative structures – Symbolic systems as structured structures – The Marxist logic – Integrating the cognitive and the political – The division of the labour of symbolic domination – The State and God

Providing a theoretical perspective

I cannot start this last lecture without saying something about what happened yesterday,[1] because it has a connection with what I want to say today, and it is very important. We are sure to be inundated with indignant moral commentaries on this violence. I think that what is important is to look for the meaning of pure violence, bearing in mind that looking for meaning is perhaps already going too far. There are people who, in a certain state of anomie of the *nomos*, have no other way of gaining attention than violence and there is perhaps a connection between the attitude of the Iron Lady, who has recently broken one of the longest strikes in history,[2] and young people armed with iron bars. Since very few people will make this connection, I wanted to state it: there are people who are condemned by all the social systems and their verdicts, by the education system and the labour market, and who await only the last verdict, that of prison, and I think that violence, even this pure violence, as an aimless ambition, is also a way of forcing recognition of their identity. I do not justify this violence, I describe it, I try to explain the inexplicable. Perhaps others will do this, but I rather doubt it.

That said, I want to try today to do what I said I would, that is, to sum up by providing a theoretical perspective for the analyses

226   *Lecture of 30 May 1985*

that I have been offering. You may well have the impression of some
theoretical sleight of hand, and you might think you are at the Collège
de philosophie.[3] In fact I shall not make a theoretical study, and if I am
saying at the end of my course what others would say at the beginning,
it is precisely because this theoretical discourse comes after the event,
that is, after I have already offered what I see as my small number of
novel insights. If this theoretical discourse is not a 'theoretical work'
(as some were in the habit of calling it at one point in time),[4] we may
wonder what its function is. Its function is one of theoretical verification and control. In fact a philosophical culture, like a political culture
or a theoretical culture in general, seems to me to have as its principal
function to define what you are doing, to enable the person producing a
theoretical discourse – who in any case is situated in a theoretical space
where a certain number of positions are already taken – to discover
what their line is. The autodidact, uneducated in theory, allows the
objective truth of what he is doing to be imposed on him as he wanders
through the space: he cannot even correct the way people receive his
discourse. The principal function of theoretical culture is to define a
theoretical line, to give the person producing an objectively theoretical
discourse the means of mastering the objective sense of his discourse.

I shall therefore turn the theoretical space within which my discourse
has been situated into an object of study. The problem that I have discussed throughout this year is that of the relation between knowledge
and power.[5] It is the problem of the way power is exercised through
its action on knowledge. This presupposes overcoming the traditional
antinomy between power and knowledge (and it is no accident that
others were doing this at more or less the same time), the old Platonic
opposition between politics and theory, between the political preoccupations of the man of the *agora* and the pure, disinterested preoccupations of the philosopher who has the *skholè*,[6] the time, who is in school.
I needed to overcome this classic antinomy between theory and power
in order to suggest that there is a power of theory and to establish
a theory of theoretical power, 'theory' here being understood in the
widest sense of the principles of vision, the explicit principles behind
the establishment of a vision. (Let me explain in passing why I say
'explicit principles'; there are, in the wider sense of the word 'theory'   ,
that I have adopted, implicit theories, and one of the intentions of
this analysis is to discover the principles of these theories of the social
world that social agents have taken on board and which to some extent
constitute this social world.) Obviously, it is as a sociologist that I am
practising this theoretical exercise: I have not undertaken a 'theoretical
study', but I have tried to define the laws of functioning of theoretical

Lecture of 30 May 1985 227

power, the specific conditions of its exercise and its distribution among social agents, which is what philosophers regularly forget to do as they think in terms of pure essence.

Having defined my objective, I shall proceed through a series of syntheses. My discourse will assume a Hegelian air, and I shall appear to be the final thinker who has totalised a series of approaches. Philosophers often proceed in this way, but I warn you in advance that this is not one of my goals at all, I haven't worked that way at all, my history of philosophy is not a philosophy of history. I repeat: what I have to offer, after covering a certain amount of ground (while obviously being aware of the different theoretical positions), is simply a retrospective summary which is bound to take the form of the sum of a certain number of positions. These successive syntheses enable me to show that what I am suggesting combines contributions from philosophers, historians, sociologists or theoreticians normally conceived of as incompatible: essentially Marx, Durkheim and Weber. For this reason I can be reproached (for in some cases it is a reproach) with being Marxist, Durkheimian and Weberian. But I maintain that I am proud of this: a theoretical capital has been accumulated by researchers in the past, and it seems to me that when you situate yourself in a cumulative perspective, scientific study does not imply distinguishing yourself from your predecessors, but accumulating all the knowledge that they have brought, not eclectically, however, but overcoming the contradictions arising from the viewpoints they adopted towards the social world, and at the same time trying to use the viewpoints they adopted towards one another. To understand the thinkers of the past, then, I adopt the same attitude that I constantly apply to the present day: visions of the social world are taken from a particular viewpoint, and in order to accommodate both the view and its blind spots, you need to see the point of view, the point from which the views are pictured, and thereby the blind spots that this implies.

For instance, Marx's blind spots are splendidly seen by Weber. If Weber is something like the end of history in my schema, although I go further than he does (by combining him with others), it is no doubt because he is the one who has least played silly games of 'self-distinction'; he declared 'Essentially, I am a Marxist',[7] although all the commentators are determined to oppose him to Marx, following the ideological fashions of the moment. I think we could say, without exaggeration, that Weber quite consciously brought historical materialism to bear on areas where historical materialism was particularly weak, that is, on the symbolic terrain: where we had a phrase that, however fundamental, was rather simplistic ('Religion is the opium of

228 *Lecture of 30 May 1985*

the people'),[8] and some analyses of the superstructure, Weber took on the construction of a whole theory of religion, the priesthood and the religious vocation, which I believe allowed him to pursue the ultimate consequences of a materialist theory of symbolic forms.

The Kantian tradition: symbolic forms

Having prepared the ground, I shall try for once to say what I want to say, in an hour. The first point ('first' or 'second' is of no importance [other than facilitating the exposition], they are not in some historical or logical order) concerns symbolic systems or forms, depending on the language of the people that I refer to. Cassirer, for instance, wrote *The Philosophy of Symbolic Forms*[9] (another book, more difficult but I think more important, and presenting a viewpoint different from the one that I am adopting today, is *Substance and Function;*[10] an easier read is *An Essay on Man*[11] [. . .]). For Cassirer, who situates himself explicitly in the Kantian tradition, language, religion, myth, science and art are 'symbolic forms', that is, the principles of the 'construction of a world of objects', as he says in a famous article published in the *Journal de psychologie* in 1933.[12] These symbolic forms are structuring structures, that is, categories in the Kantian sense, organising the world we perceive. Cassirer tries to interpret the logic of these structuring structures: as we shall see, in a second phase, he tries, for instance, to show the function and logic of myth, and how that specific logic – which is not that of science, since he attributes a particular form to the principles of causality and identity – goes to construct a particular world. That said, he deals with myth in general (and this will turn out to be a problem); he makes no distinction between specific myths, whether Basque or Bororo, Breton or Zuni.

We seek to understand these structuring structures and we might say a would-be cognitive sociology should aim to analyse these systems of the construction of reality. Thus the ethnomethodological tradition which grew up around Garfinkel's *Studies in Ethnomethodology* [. . .] sets itself the task of explaining the methods that agents ordinarily use to construct the social world: it is an anthropology of the cognitive structures that ordinary agents use to find their way in the world, to implant their own principles of structuring. This cognitive sociology, as we see from its Kantian origins, leads to an idealist vision of the social world. As Bachelard would say, the epistemological vector goes from the rational to the real;[13] the drive to know the social world is projected from the subject onto reality, and the social world is in a way a con-

Lecture of 30 May 1985 229

struct produced by the social subject. We might characterise this form of sociology by paraphrasing the famous title of Schopenhauer's work, *The World as Will and Representation*: ultimately, the social world would be a product of human construction. Thinking for instance of the social classes, there would be no need to look for these classes in the real world, it would be sufficient to study the transcendental genesis, so to speak, of the realities of 'classes'. In fact, it would be through knowing the cognitive structures that we would get to know the social world.

I am caricaturing slightly, but this exercise is important as a theoretical appraisal, because often those who make science progress know not what they do (which is fine, but only up to a point). Not knowing what they are doing, they may possess a philosophy of knowledge without being aware of it. They might be quite astonished to hear themselves characterised as idealists or Kantians, but it might do them good to learn it; they might say: 'Oh yes, and with good reason', or 'Yes, but that is not what I meant to suggest . . .' This is what I was saying at the start about [how providing the perspective that I propose has] a function of theoretical appraisal. Apart from these cognitive sociologies, there are also cognitive linguistics, cognitive psychologies and perhaps cognitive history (history always picks up every passing fancy, usually when it is past . . .). Everyone now is into the 'cognitive', it is all the rage. In fact this too is a consequence of ignorance. Fashions often correspond to the recurrence of very old things returning suddenly at the end of a cycle. So we would do well to have a historical culture.

These cognitive undertakings, which investigate our knowledge of the means of knowledge, tend very naturally towards an idealist vision. Their aim is to analyse systems of classification, taxonomies and theories, in the general sense that I am using, or what I was calling the *nomos*, in the sense of principles of vision and division. Their point of view, which I am summarising rather crudely, can be situated in the neo-Kantian tradition that evolved along two lines [*Bourdieu goes to write on the board*]: one a European tradition, called the Humboldt–Cassirer tradition,[14] and another, the Anglo-American Sapir–Whorf tradition.[15] These two traditions, which developed independently, argue that language is not simply a means of expression, but also a means of constructing the world. It was Whorf who took the hypothesis to the extreme: he tried to find correlations between the structure of the languages of a certain number of indigenous American societies and the structure of representations of the world. There have even been attempts to make experimental verification of the correspondence between linguistic structures and the structures of the world.

230   *Lecture of 30 May 1985*

Ethnology has produced some considerable developments, of which ethnomethodology is one outcome: it is what is called 'componential analysis', a very interesting technique that I have myself used in connection with politics, and have mentioned here previously.[16] It consists in asking respondents to classify things or signs in such a way as to see the principles that they use to classify, but cannot be using consciously. We all possess principles of classification that we are not in full control of. If we want to know your principles of classification in politics, one simple technique consists in writing the names of politicians on slips of paper, asking you to classify them, and then naming the classes that you have used. Thus we try in a way to create an explicit theory of your implicit theory of the political universe. You can master in practice the items to classify, but you do not master these classifications; they are only partly coherent . . . exactly like the oppositions of a mythical system or a ritual system as I have described them for you.[17]

This Humboldt–Cassirer/Sapir–Whorf tradition could be viewed in the light of Saussure's famous phrase: 'It is the viewpoint that creates the object.'[18] Saussure used this formula in connection with the viewpoint of the scholar; he wanted to ground the act of constitution of language as an object in a constitutive viewpoint, which is not constative at all but constructive, where the viewpoint creates the object. According to this logic, myth and religion and the like construct or even produce the world. The problem of the noumena is not pronounced in this kind of argument, but it is there implicitly. In any case, theories of myth bring the world of objects to life; symbolic forms are what give us a cosmos in the sense of an ordered world, rather than chaos. We can say that this philosophy is culturalist and I think that this is the implicit philosophy of the early Foucault [. . .]. Culturalism considers that symbolic forms are historical and linked to tradition. It is distinguished in that respect from the philosophy of symbolic forms, which in its most coherent expression, in Cassirer, considers symbolic forms to be universal, and like Kant posits a transcendental subject, but with one difference. Kant gave himself one single *datum* (physics and mathematics) as matter for reflection in order to extract the forms manifest in the *opus operatum*, whereas Cassirer generalises the Kantian interrogation and says that we need to apply the Kantian mode of reflection to other *opera operata* like myths, religion and art, which are also structured objects in which we may discover structures. That said, Cassirer's symbolic forms are universal structures of the human mind, but there is a problem that Cassirer raises (partially) towards the end of his life, which is to explain why the universal structures of the human mind, like those of myth, find a greater development in primitive societies, whereas symbolic forms like science find a greater development in our societies. I raise these problems very rapidly; they have given rise to whole volumes.

This neo-Kantian tradition, then, may be rigorously Kantian or take on a culturalist form. One important thing to note in passing: this Kantian vision implies a break with Marxist reflection theory. In fact as soon as you follow this way of thinking, you can no longer imagine that our visions of the world are a reflection of the world, and the knowing subject recovers his active powers (I have put this at [the start of this lecture] to underline the break). We could put this in Marxian terms. (Since Marx has said everything, you can always be a Marxist . . . or you may not be, of course . . .) Marx, in one of his theses on Feuerbach, says that the basic drama of materialism is abandoning to idealism the active aspect of knowledge, and that we should restore this active aspect to materialism (as I was in the process of doing); we should reclaim for the knowing subject this capacity to construct the world of objects. That said, it is not a pure, theoretical capacity, and Marx admits this straight away, because he has a perfectly conscious theoretical line: he says that although idealism has rehabilitated the active aspect of knowledge in a way, this was as a cognitive act, whereas it is a practical construction; it is in practice that the instruments of construction are constructed – the subject constructing is a subject in action.[19] I shall not develop this point today, but it links up with my (often rather tangential) reflections on the nature of logical practices.

Neo-Kantianism, then, postulates universal structures. Culturalism is a soft form. It is a soft neo-Kantianism, but historicised: the *a priori* forms become *a posteriori*. They are historical, arbitrary forms, as Mauss[20] and Saussure[21] would say, linked to historical conditions, that is, to the material conditions of existence (geographical, climatic and so on) and basically to cultural chance, because in general, especially in societies with no history (in the sense of written history), ethnologists can only take facts as they are, they cannot return to the founding historical act that might be at the source of some opposition or other. So the culturalist tradition preserves the constructive capacity of the cognitive subject, but it operates a considerable change: these systems of classification are themselves products of history.

This is where Durkheim enters my 'mythical' genealogy. Durkheim has the merit of introducing himself explicitly as a Kantian: in the introduction to *The Elementary Forms of Religious Life* he avoids deceit; he says that he wants to study, but in a way at once empirical, positive and verifiable, the genesis of these categories of thought that we are obliged to presuppose in order to understand what happens in the social world.[22] Thus he wants to make an *a posteriori* science of

232 *Lecture of 30 May 1985*

these *a posteriori* categories in order to escape the alternative of apriorism and aposteriorism, which was the subject of many a thesis at the time.[23] In short, he wants to make a sociology of symbolic forms.

I can illustrate this with a personal anecdote: a collection of some of my earliest studies was translated into German as a 'Sociology of Symbolic Forms',[24] which went down very well in Cassirer's homeland . . . But the combination is shocking: a 'sociology of symbolic forms' is a kind of barbarism, and given the nobility of 'symbolic forms', many German critics saw this as a kind of monstrous, almost bestial coupling of the lower with the higher orders. This is important: the obstacles to the theoretical marriages that I arrange in order to produce what seems to me to be the right theory are often purely social. I am led into what appear to be misalliances according to what people have internalised as *diacrisis* in their minds. People feel: 'Cassirer noble, Durkheim ignoble; how can you marry a lady of easy virtue to a man of ancient lineage?' Problems of theory are often of this order. Which allows me to say in passing that the cognitive structures of the researcher are also always evaluative structures: you cannot say 'high/low' without immediately preferring the high to the low; you cannot say 'masculine/feminine' without immediately privileging the former, even if it's only because it is placed first . . .

The primitive forms of classification

These cognitive structures are symbolic forms that in Durkheim become 'primitive forms of classification'. This is the title of a famous article by Durkheim and Mauss.[25] It is a splendid article in which we find in latent form the whole of structuralism . . . (I say 'in latent form' because it still needed to be transformed into structuralism . . . Those who want to destroy people who have achieved something are always tempted to say: 'It was all there already in X or Y', but obviously we – and I include myself – only see what there is to find in 'The Symbolic Forms of Classification' when we have read Lévi-Strauss, who actually didn't find it there himself . . . which is very important. [. . .] A little historical anecdote: I say that the philosophy of symbolic forms becomes a sociology of the forms of classification, which may appear to be a barbarism, and a philosopher could say that I am confusing the genres, that is, creating a mismatch, mixing 'chalk and cheese', that is, the noble and the ignoble. I sometimes lay traps . . . In fact, it happens that there is a note to this effect in a late book by Cassirer, *The Myth of the State*.[26] Cassirer wrote this book in 1946,[27]

Lecture of 30 May 1985   233

just after his arrival in the United States, at a period when everyone was investigating Nazism. It was his contribution as a philosopher: he attempted to apply his culture to the kind of monstrous question that the reality of Nazism posed: how can a totalitarian State come about? It is a book that is both interesting and naive, because Cassirer was not well equipped to reflect on this question. He certainly had great intellectual powers at the time, but there are always limits to anyone's intellectual powers. Be this as it may, he says in passing in a note to page 16: 'Symbolic forms are the exact equivalent of what Durkheim calls "primitive forms of classification."'[28] The orthodox critics of Cassirer obviously missed this note, but it is important, and not only anecdotally: both authors are in fact indebted to Kant. That said, Cassirer is imprudent in saying this, because the primitive forms of classification are historical, socially constituted forms, whereas Cassirer's symbolic forms are transcendental forms, inherent to the structure of the human mind. He therefore makes a rather imprudent concession, but I am very pleased with this . . .)

With 'The Primitive Forms of Classification', then, Durkheim moved from universal, transcendental forms to social forms, that is, historical and arbitrary forms which are relative to a given use in a given social world. He even went one step further in *The Elementary Forms of Religious Life*, saying that mental structures are social structures that have become mental structures: he says not only that these primitive forms of classification are historical forms, but also that they have been historically generated. They are not merely relative, in Saussure's sense when he spoke of the arbitrary nature of the linguistic sign (to point out that here we say 'table', whereas elsewhere people use a different word); Durkheim tries to show the historical roots of these historical differences. The arbitrary is historical, it is a historical convention.

The primitive forms of classification, then, are engendered, and it is in the structure of groups that we find the foundations structuring the mental structures through which we conceive the world, including, among other things, social groups. These last are not mentioned by Durkheim, because what interested him was grounding his logic in sociology. He was preoccupied with his struggle with the philosophers. He wanted to found an autonomous science, essentially in relation to philosophy, and he spent his life, as in a western, on the frontiers of philosophy, trying to encroach on the philosophers' territory and obviously trying to keep them at bay. This led him to make mistakes. I think that if he didn't argue that structures of groups constitute and found the mental structures which enable us to conceive the world, including its groups, although as a sociologist he thought only of

234   *Lecture of 30 May 1985*

groups, it is because he was too concerned with the philosophers and with problems of logic. Consequently, by adding 'including groups', I am re-reading Durkheim, I am translating him a little, but that is what a true and useful reading really is: I make him say what seems to me to be latent in what he was trying to say, what he should have said if he had fully thought through what he was trying to say.

Durkheim says that our cognitive structures (hot/cold and wet/dry in the mythologies that he studied) are structures that structure the natural world, and I would add that that they also structure the social world. They are group structures (for instance the dualist structures studied by Lévi-Strauss) that became mental structures and then become a structuring principle for the group. This circular process is extremely important and I shall return to it. It is what explains the *doxic* experience that phenomenologists refer to (you see: today I am mixing everything up): the experience of the world as obvious and self-evident seems to me to be founded on this kind of absolute coincidence – which is never completely achieved, but which is more or less complete, depending on the society – between the structures of the thing perceived and the structures of the perceiving subject. When the two structures match perfectly, everything seems absolutely obvious, everything is self-evident, there is no need to comment. This is the supreme form of conservatism, since there is no need even to conserve, since it would not occur to anybody that things could be different. You will note in passing that I have shifted position considerably: I started out from an idealist position, and now I have slipped back into materialism. The cognitive structures are no longer those of a universal subject but those of a historical subject and they are the product of the social world. This is exactly the move made by Marx in his *Theses on Feuerbach*. It is as much as to say: there is an economic and social genesis, and then the economic and social divisions will be reproduced in the shape of principles of division – *principium divisionis* as the scholastics used to say – and vision of the social world. Up to a certain point, you will see the social world in the way that your social world asks you to see it.

By the way, another important reference is the work of Panofsky. Of his principal works, the *Studies in Iconology*[29] are the more theoretical essays, while I am referring here to his *Perspective as Symbolic Form*.[30] As the title of the book suggests, Panofsky was a pupil of Cassirer. (In Cassirer's splendid book, *Individual and Cosmos in the Renaissance*, Cassirer says somewhere in a note: 'I thank my pupil Panofsky for kindly informing me . . .'.[31] This was a time when . . . [*laughter in the audience at the rather 'old-fashioned' style of the note*].)

Panofsky knowingly passes his information on to Cassirer, but he does something more, he traces the history of perspective. He keeps Cassirer's neo-Kantian language (perspective is a structuring principle of the world, etc.), but at the same time, being a historian rather than a philosopher, he sets out a historical genealogy of this viewpoint, with its particular vision of the world, by drawing up a sort of social history of perspective where he compares the perspective of the Romans with the perspective of the *Quattrocento*, for instance. That said, he stays within the idealist tradition, he remains a good pupil of his master, and he will not go so far as to write, as his master did unwittingly: 'Symbolic forms are social forms.'

Thus he writes the social history of a form that we may find unquestionable; when we say: 'Photography is realistic', we are saying that a viewpoint which was only one historical viewpoint among others (there are a dozen or so perspectives), and which the camera reproduces, is objective; it gives us reality. Why is it objective? Because it reproduces reality as we see it, and we see it as we have learnt to see it through a process of socialisation grounded in our perception of representations of the social world, themselves constructed in the light of perspective. I am saying these important things too hurriedly, but you can take them further. Francastel has developed this rather feebly,[32] without citing Panofsky, from whom he has borrowed the essential. Photography then is an example of doxic experience. If it gives us the impression of self-evidence, it is because it conforms to our categories of perception. In so doing, it makes us forget that it is a historical construction and that our categories of perception are historical. When we say: 'It's realistic', this means that we feel the doxic impression that it is 'like I see it', meaning 'it's right', 'that's it'; we don't question the conditions of production of the principles of vision, as the Durkheimian tradition exhorts us to do.

Historical and performative structures

What I have established so far is that our structures of perception and appreciation – which point I shall not develop – are historical. For instance, what we call 'taste' is typically a kind of historical, transcendental subject: taste enables us to make distinctions and classify, it is a principle of *diacrisis*, of judgement. This is an example that I have developed at length:[33] there is a correspondence between the right bank/left bank opposition and the principles of evaluation that we apply in the theatre. Likewise, in Kabyle society the right/left

236 *Lecture of 30 May 1985*

opposition corresponds to masculine/feminine: there are things that men do and things that women do, and never will a man do something that a woman does; the principle of division that we find in social reality becomes a fundamental principle of vision. Likewise, the principles of perception of the aesthetic world and aesthetic objects correspond very closely to the objective oppositions of this world, which are the historical oppositions established at a certain moment in the nineteenth century (which is why what I am constructing in my second sessions is so important:[34] the genealogy of categories of perception that have come to appear self-evident to us).

Aiming to establish a genealogy of categories of perception, the sociology of symbolic forms sets itself in opposition to any attempt to analyse essences. Analysis of essences, which is the alpha and omega of phenomenology, claims to reply to questions of the type: 'What is power?', 'What is beauty?', 'What is taste?' The approach that I have to offer immediately rejects these questions. We obviously need to trace the genealogy of the analysis of essences, of the social conditions of the possibility of this kind of investigation, which is a historical enquiry linked to a tradition. But more profoundly, if I use my approach to ask myself what today is a 'genuinely cultivated habitus', my enquiry will show that it consists by and large in seeing a work as an end in itself, with no outside aim, and in not asking about its function ('What is it for?'). The study of the Impressionists that I have presented you with has consisted in tracing the historical genealogy of this perception and the production of objects corresponding to this perception; it is a historical invention that started before the nineteenth century but which finished in the nineteenth century: in a series of historical analyses I have gradually isolated this sort of essence of pure perception, or the pure work, that an analysis of essences captures naively. An analysis of essences captures the result of a theoretical analysis, believing that it has accomplished an ahistorical study. It thinks it has grasped an eternal structure of the human mind. This is what I reproach it with. And yet this work is not negligible. At the beginning of *Studies in Iconology* there is a very fine passage where Panofsky asks: 'What is a beautiful object?', 'What is the specifically aesthetic gaze as opposed to the practical gaze?' This fine analysis is an analysis of essences, but Panofsky cannot forget that he is a historian. He does not always remember strongly enough, but he forgets less than analyses of essences ordinarily do the fact that the essence he grasps has been produced by a process of filtration.

I may return to this in my second session, but the pure aesthetic disposition described by Kant, the perception of art in terms of an art

Lecture of 30 May 1985 237

beyond any consideration of function, is the product of a process of filtration, in reception as well as production. Haskell, for instance, has quite clearly shown that the birth of the museum as institution corresponds to the appearance of pure aesthetic discourses like Kant's:[35] once you remove an altarpiece, an object that served as a liturgical object endowed with a sacred function, it becomes assessable by the pure gaze. [. . .] This kind of objective filtration, symbolised by museification, is not 'determining', but it does enable, favour and encourage the pure gaze to apprehend the work as such, independently of its functions, whether liturgical, pedagogical or didactic. Ultimately, analyses of essences establish dispositions as transhistorical or ahistorical, whereas they do have a genesis. This does not mean that there are not transhistorical things that are products of history, but this is a problem for science, that I shall leave for the moment.[36]

Oppositions, then, have a social genesis. In previous sessions I have taken the examples of the disabled, of certificates of competence and incapacity: considered objectively, these oppositions tend to become constitutive oppositions. I shall not dwell on this, but I shall just remind you of the themes I have touched on. Group names for instance, which are produced by acts of constitution, become constitutive. A collective study, which has just been published by Maspero,[37] offers a critique of the notion of ethnicity: ethnic names (like the Dahomey, for instance), which are historical products whose genealogy we can trace, become structures of perception constitutive of social reality; these taxonomies come to constitute the identity of the people they designate. Similarly, debates over the notion of a region are interesting. I like to recall that the word 'region' belongs to the same family as the word *rex*, the person who establishes our frontiers and possesses the *nomos*.[38] Another example of a social taxonomy constitutive of reality is the terminology of kinship. An ethnologist, I forget who, said that to tell someone 'She's your sister', is to accuse him of breaking the incest taboo (it is no accident that 'Et ta soeur!' [f... your sister!] is an insult). The constative statement 'She's your sister' is not self-evident: you must already have a genealogy in mind in order to say it; which means that it is constitutive.

I return to the Kantian opposition, which seems to me in this case to be very useful, between the *intuitus originarius* of God (when God sees, he creates, he sees what he creates, he does what he sees, he needs only to think of something for it to exist) and the *intuitus derivatus* of men:[39] things exist and men see them. In fact, they too construct them, they construct them (as I have explained), although they already exist. To be able to tell someone 'She's your sister', something like a girl has to

238 *Lecture of 30 May 1985*

exist, of course, but it is an act *originarius* that constitutes her with an identity implying a series of behaviours and non-behaviours, things to do and not to do, to say and not to say, duties and obligations. The terminology of kinship is the very type of the *categorem* (to use Aristotle's language) that confers existence on what it constitutes.

This is the order of speech creating being, that is, the performative order. (Here I am only developing more fully the idealist tradition.) These classificatory oppositions such as 'She's your sister' have a normative power because they are what we might call trans-personal propositions. When I say 'She's your sister', I have the support of the whole group, and with it the consensus of meaning produced by the concordance of our categories of perception. It is what Durkheim splendidly names 'logical conformism':[40] there has to be validation, everyone speaking must be tuned into saying the same thing, in a state of *homologein* ['saying the same thing']. The sister in 'She's your sister' is a validated sister; everyone will say: 'She's your sister', which makes it serious, it's no laughing matter. Whereas if I say: 'You are an imbecile', it commits nobody but me. This is the difference between a validated *categorem* and an individual *categorem* like the insult.[41]

So I am saying that symbolic systems are structuring structures, but these structures are themselves structured, they have a historical genealogy; these structuring structures are products of history insofar as they are the incorporation of social structures.

Symbolic systems as structured structures

The second point (which I would like to sketch out, but as quickly as possible) concerns the contribution of what has historically been called 'structuralism' in France, which is by and large the tradition of Saussure and Lévi-Strauss. In this tradition, symbolic systems are not merely structuring structures, they are structured structures in the sense of systems. Thus myth is not merely a system of categories of perception of the social world; it is a system in itself. Similarly, language is a system of coherent relations. Symbolic systems, then, have a structure, which opens them up to structural analysis. Here again we meet up with Durkheim, who it seems to me creates a synthesis between the idealist current ('structuring structures') and the structuralist current (symbolic systems are 'structured structures'). He was the first to feel (in 'Primitive Forms of Classification') that primitive mythical structures, which appear at first sight to be completely crazy, have a logical coherence, which is not that of ordinary logic, although they might be

Lecture of 30 May 1985 239

perceived as the origin of the logic of our theories of groups. It is a particular logic, but it can only be discovered if we are prepared to constitute the *opus operatum*, in which we grasp symbolic forms as systems. The difference between the structuralist tradition and the neo-Kantian tradition is that the structuralist tradition is what we might call hermeneutic: it is more interested in the *opus operatum* than the *modus operandi*; it is more interested in mythical systems as myths already composed and narrated, than in what Cassirer called the mytho-poetic act, that is, the act of structuration, construction and production of the myth. That said, Cassirer did anticipate structuralism.

I think that we may call Cassirer the philosopher of structuralism, since no thinker is ever entirely consistent (luckily, they transcend themselves). Cassirer, especially in an article that he wrote in *Word* at the very end of his life,[42] took on the role of the philosopher of structuralism and the philosopher of what Foucault called the *épistémè* – I think that we can find Foucault's philosophy in Cassirer. Cassirer says that we need to grasp the specific logic of a symbolic form: we have to make what he calls, after Schelling,[43] a 'tautegorical' analysis, that is, interpret the myth on its own terms, rather than make an allegorical analysis interpreting the myth in relation to something other (the historical events or economic circumstances that it is supposed to be the expression of, for instance). The same thing applies to art: the tautegorical analysis of art is the internal analysis I have often mentioned, which amounts to saying: 'The key to art is in the art, don't look for it elsewhere.' In Cassirer's logic, art, before being the expression of something other, is a system, and only if you take it to be a system will you be able to understand it.

The most typical formulation of structuralism is obviously Saussure's, since language [*la langue*] for Saussure is the structured system that is the condition of the possibility of speech [*la parole*] and can only be discovered in speech, without ever being reducible to the speech in which it is revealed. In this tradition, language becomes a structured *medium* that we must construct if we wish to explain communication relations: if two subjects understand each other, it is because they associate the same meaning with the same sound and the same sound with the same meaning, it is therefore because they are referring to the same *medium*, which transcends their act of communication and is the truth of their act of communication. Language is this constant relation between sound and sense, this principle of constancy – or veracity as Descartes would have said (for Saussure, language acts rather like the God of Descartes who guarantees that when I say: 'two plus two equals four', the evil spirit won't make them

240   *Lecture of 30 May 1985*

equal five).[44] This principle of constancy is the very structure of a symbolic system.

Now I shall reconcile the idealist tradition with the structuralist tradition, in order to say that the action of symbolic systems produces a particular effect because they are structuring, but structuring through being structured, that is, they impose a structure insofar as they are systems, and the effect of knowledge that they create is reinforced by an effect of coherence. Humboldt has a phrase where he says 'We can only escape one religion by stepping into another':[45] the strength of a symbolic system is that when you are caught up in it you cannot leave it, because the very objections that it provokes are structured by the same structures that compose it. The strength of symbolic systems, and their efficacy, even political, as I shall describe it, depend on their coherence. We might think (here I am taking a risk . . .) that this structuralist philosophy can be found underlying studies like those of Benveniste in his *Dictionary of Indo-European Concepts and Society*, which I have used on several occasions and which consists in using linguistic analysis to elaborate a philosophy of the world (and in particular the social world) that is immanent in language and coherent. If, for example, as I often remind you, I can wander through a semantic field, passing almost naturally from word to word – *nomos, nemo*, 'divide', 'division', *diacrisis*, 'diacritical', it is perhaps because there is a philosophy immanent to language, a realist philosophy, since it is the product of an unceasing dialogue between hypothesis and experience, a centuries-old dialogue between principles of vision and objective divisions.

By combining the idealist vision and the structuralist tradition (according to which symbolic systems are structured and coherent; a myth is not a madman's fantasy but a logic), we are led to say that symbolic systems have a structuring effect through their coherent structures. They offer a coherent vision of the world, and since this is shared by all the social agents who are produced under the same conditions, it is reinforced by consensus, a consensus on meaning being one of the major foundations of objectivity. These symbolic systems, then, offer an objective vision of the objective world: I gave you the examples of perspective and photography. Perception is constantly reinforced, both by reality (to which it owes a part of its structures) and by others' judgements, the *homologein*, the consensus on the social world. Here again we find the theory of this kind of cognitive solidarity in Durkheim, and its development in Radcliffe-Brown;[46] social solidarity, according to this structuralist tradition, is based on the fact that all the social agents share the same symbolic system, the same vision of the world, the same theory of the social world. Symbolism and the symbolic do then have a social function (the word 'function' being understood in the structural-functionalist sense, that is, in the sense of 'function for the whole' – there are other possible functionalisms). Durkheim says that moral, or what we may call 'political', integration depends on logical integration: a group holds together because its members have the same logical categories of perception. There is then a social function of symbolism, which is a political function, a function of communication and knowledge. In performing its task, this function of knowledge also achieves a political function, the example being classification: as the systems of classification are adjusted to fit the social classes, they give a perception of the social world as evident.

I have therefore undertaken a new synthesis: symbolic systems are instruments of knowledge and communication which, having a structure and being 'coherent' (they are coherent only up to a certain point, to unequal degrees, and in different modes: myth is not logical in the same way as science), produce a coherent vision, constantly reinforced both by the world and by consensus. The result is that symbolic systems have a fantastic power, against which revolutionaries can do very little. Symbolic revolutions then are extremely interesting (whence the sense of what I have been telling you during my seminar hours, which focused on a symbolic revolution in the domain of art).[47]

The Marxist logic

Now to introduce the Marxist tradition. I shall simplify and caricature it, but what I have to relate is not one of Marxism's strong points. There is perhaps a gap in Marxist thinking that Durkheimians and Weberians come to fill: symbolic systems are instruments of domination. In fact Marx is not very interested in the structures of symbolic systems (except in *The German Ideology*, where he has fun applying his lively polemical wit to the analysis of the discourse of his theoretical adversaries, revealing their rhetorical procedures and effects).[48] He did not linger over the structuralist level, because it is the function that interests him. When he says 'Religion is the opium of the people', he is saying that what interests him in religion is not how it is put together, how it works, but what it does, what it is used for, what functions it fulfils. Of course this is functionalism, but not in the structural-functionalist sense. For Marx, an institution can have a function that is not a global function, even if it does affect the whole: the function of domination, obviously, works above all for the dominant, even if

242   *Lecture of 30 May 1985*

it is suffered by the dominated. There is no doubt that Marx is functionalist. He is even too much so, in the present case, because he is too interested in the function of symbolic systems, and not enough in their structure. That said, it is important to remind those who may have forgotten, which is often the case with ethnologists, what Marx meant by function. When structural-functionalists apply to differentiated societies functionalist theories taken from Durkheim and Radcliffe-Brown, that are valid up to a certain point for weakly differentiated societies (although, as I have said, 'primitive' societies also mark the difference between the sexes – which is surely not negligible) where the functions of integration are obvious, they fulfil a political and conservative function [. . .].

Marx, then, foregrounds the political function, as opposed to the gnoseological function as I have been describing it ('gnoseological' meaning 'concerning knowledge', 'concerning the construction of the world'). It is the opposition – to be found between the lines in Marx – between myth, which like language is a collective product with no attributable author and which functions collectively (in any case in the Saussurean definition – in reality this is not at all the case), and what Marx calls 'ideology'. *Grosso modo*, myth, like language, has a communicative and integrational function, it enables communication between people, whereas ideology has a differential function: it is the instrument of domination serving a part of the whole and detrimental to the other part. The fundamental principle of ideology that Marx developed may be deduced from its function: ideology has a universalising function, it transforms particular interests into universal interests. We see this function clearly in the case of religion, and I refer you to the text on the religious field that I wrote some years ago.[49] In a Marxist logic reworked through the lens of Weber, it appears that the function of religion is to render absolute the particular and the relative; I am this and not something else, and the religious discourse tells me that I should be as I am. This is the Nietzschean analysis of *ressentiment* (resentment)[50] as a particular case of a more general theory where religion is what enables us to transform something particular, contingent and historical into something absolute, transcendent, universal and necessary.

In Marxist logic the function of religion, as ideology par excellence, would then be to reinforce the integration of the dominant class itself: we should not forget – Marx says it quite clearly – that for the dominant class religion fulfils the function that the Durkheim and Radcliffe-Brown structural-functionalists apply to all symbolic forms in all societies. This function is to unify the dominant class, providing

Lecture of 30 May 1985 243

it with an ethics and a morale. At the same time it fulfils a function of integration of society as a whole, but it is very important to note that it is a fictitious integration. Vulgar Marxists forget that ideologies dominate because they have the properties I have already mentioned (they are structuring and structured). If the ideologies stated crudely: 'The last shall be last', the last would in the end understand, and the ideologies would no longer be dominant. To understand how ideologies dominate, the process of universalisation is very important. It consists in transforming a discourse valid for some individuals into a universal discourse, valid for all: 'What is good for me, says the rich man, is good for all; and even better for the non-rich, since they win their place in heaven.' This kind of universalisation strategy (I am simplifying) is made possible by the very structure of the mythical discourse, which is a complex and coherent discourse that means that you can only pass from a social condition, for example, to a discourse on a particular point ('Should we go on a pilgrimage to Saint-Jacques-de-Compostelle?') if you pass through the mediation and the logic of the whole system, and therefore be subject to the effects of coherence and knowledge. This is what is missing in the Marxist analysis: it has taken only the function, without making the move that I have made through the coherence and complexity of the mythical discourse.

Integrating the cognitive and the political

I shall now make a new synthesis. Communicative relations and acts of knowledge are inseparably power relations (and communication relations – although just a detail, this is in fact the central thesis in my writings on language, in particular *Language and Symbolic Power* – are inseparably power relations that depend, in their structure, form and function, on the capital accumulated by the agents engaged in this communication). The important thing is that symbolic systems fulfil their political functions as structured and structuring instruments of knowledge and communication. In other words, we cannot understand that religion is 'the opium of the people' unless we have in our minds what I have said, drawing on Durkheim and Cassirer, etc. I repeat: it is as structured and structuring instruments of knowledge and communication that symbolic systems, such as systems of classification, taxonomies (masculine/feminine and hot/cold, for instance) or social classes, fulfil their political function of instruments imposing domination and the legitimation of domination. I integrate the cognitive aspects with the political aspects.

244 *Lecture of 30 May 1985*

Thus it is only if we think of them as instruments of knowledge that we can understand their political effect. We cannot understand the phenomena of symbolic power unless we see that symbolic power is exercised as a power of knowledge through the logic of knowledge. Which is what I wanted to say with the word *nomos*. If, to take Weber's expression, religions contribute to the 'control of the dominated'[51] (if anyone had asked me for the author of this formula, I would have said Marx . . .), if they provide the dominant with a 'theodicy of their own privileges' (in Weber's splendid phrase),[52] it is precisely because they act on knowledge.

Here I shall very briefly elaborate the links between the three words 'knowledge' ('cognition'), 'recognition' and 'misrecognition'. I did not invoke the word *nomos* for the pleasure of speaking Greek, but because this word encapsulates everything that I have been saying this year. *Nomos* comes from *nomo* which means 'to divide', whilst also meaning 'to think', that is, 'to know' as well as 'to tell the difference', and therefore *censeo* ('to think' but also 'to tell the difference'); *censeo* leads to *census* which leads to 'censuses' conducted by the INSEE. *Nomos* and *census* are two fundamental words: the *nomos* is a principle of vision and division that is dominant, arbitrary and misrecognised as such, therefore recognised as legitimate and universal. It is because the *nomos* is endowed with coherence (we can say that INSEE's taxonomies, for instance, are based on statistics, mathematics and analysis) that its structuring power is fully effective and that its domination effects can function softly (which is extremely important), that is, in symbolic guise. With the word 'symbolic' (someone asked me for a definition one day), I am adding the idea of misrecognition; a symbolic power is exercised with the complicity of those who are its objects.

This does not mean that 'power comes from below'[53] or another of those faintly repulsive slogans ('the thrill of power',[54] for instance), but that symbolic power is a power that takes effect through the specifically symbolic logic of symbolic systems and the effect of coherence that gives access to acts of knowledge of the social world, which are acts of misrecognition, recognising the *nomos* via the match between objective structures and structures of perception. These are acts of perception which, being structures obeying the same principles as the reality perceived, grant this reality acceptance as absolutely self-evident. It is stupid to try and localise this kind of misrecognition. For millennia people have said that 'power is up there on high' and that the dominated collaborate in their domination. This naive and extreme realist philosophy sees power as a sort of reality which is reified in objects somewhere out there, in a throne or a decree, whereas power, in par-

Lecture of 30 May 1985 245

ticular symbolic power, is everywhere and everything. Like Nicholas of Cusa's God,[55] it is a circle whose centre is everywhere and circumference nowhere, which does not mean, far from it, that everyone has the same power, even if (as the notion of 'field' tells us) the power of the all-powerful cannot dispense with the structures that unite them with and separate them from the powerless. Symbolic power is thus a power premised on acts of knowledge, which operates according to the logic of knowledge and thereby avoids being recognised as power.

Here I must move on [. . .]. The different social agents struggle to impose their understanding of the social world. As a society becomes differentiated, the founding *homologein* – which in societies that are weakly differentiated, and strongly integrated both socially and logically, is very nearly accomplished – disintegrates, and we have a kind of *heterologein*, with dialogue, dispute and struggle over the social world, as the different agents engage individually in the struggle to impose the vision of the social world closest to their interests, wanting to render their particular interests absolute and universal (all social subjects are ideologists who universalise their own position). That said, the most elementary form of the division of labour is no doubt the division of the effort of symbolic production: in this struggle, professional purveyors of a world view or the *nomos* (such as jurists, and priests) very soon emerge, armed with a kind of delegated power and authority to say what the world really is, their verdicts on the world having more force than those of ordinary people. This is how the political field in the true sense of the term is composed (the political field is not reducible to the definition we give it in our societies), as a space of agents, groups of agents and institutions that are engaged in a struggle for classification, using their specific professional competence in a struggle to impose the vision of the social world most favourable to their interests.

The division of the labour of symbolic domination

This brings us to Max Weber, and, I believe, to the last stage of my analysis. In relation to Marx, Weber has something very important to contribute. Marx and Engels named it from time to time (you can always find a text somewhere that more or less formulates the idea you are looking for) when they speak of superstructures, mentioning 'professional corps'. In a famous letter, Engels [. . .] says that there are corps of professionals who enjoy relative independence and who provide a 'symbolic expression of the struggles'[56] (an extraordinary formula). (This is quite a coup for Engels – it is really something other

246   *Lecture of 30 May 1985*

than the tradition of mechanist reflection ... One might almost say that he has had an intuition of the field qua field, that is, a space of professionals who debate the social world, who struggle, and whose standpoints in the struggles over the social world owe something to their position in the subfield of struggles constituted by the field of symbolic production, the political field in the wider sense. This means that what they say about the social world is not a reflection, but a 'symbolic expression' [literally an 'ideological conception']; there is an alchemical process, it is not direct ... But when Engels speaks of the Religious Wars,[57] he falls back to the simplest level – all thinkers have lucky breaks, after which they slip back into their old routines; there are good and bad moments, but we should try to build on only the good moments – he says that the Wars of Religion are class conflicts. This makes the field effect disappear, since he fails to see that at a certain moment the class struggles can only take the form of Wars of Religion because the machinery producing representations of the social world provides nothing but that. This was a parenthesis that I should have avoided . . .)

Weber gives substance to the idea of relative autonomy, which remained rather empty in the Marxist tradition (or so it seems to me), by describing the corps of professionals and in particular what is no doubt the most significant corps of professionals, those producing and commercialising the religious discourse ... I have retranslated this into the language of the field, by establishing the notion of a religious field[58] (it was not given as such in Weber, but expressing it in my terms implies once again attributing to Weber what he intended to say). Weber sees the emergence of a division of labour and a corps of religious specialists who gradually come to hold the monopoly of the production of religious discourse, which means that an opposition arises between the professionals and the profane in the first instance. One important implication that Weber did not develop is that speaking of a religious field signifies that the laymen are dispossessed of their religious self-determination; they have to rely on proxies, on delegates (it is the same thing in the political domain). Once a corps of professionals exists, however much they may fight among themselves, the professionals agree with one accord to combat the laity if they take it into their heads to try to become producers themselves in a kind of religious 'self-service'. To give you a rather rapid and wild analogy, think of the reactions of the press when someone profane like Coluche becomes a candidate for the presidential election.[59] It is not at all Coluche himself who is called into question, but the fact that someone profane and not legitimised by the professional body trespasses onto

Lecture of 30 May 1985 247

the domain of the professionals: the professionals most divided on every other subject come together to denounce the profane man who usurps their professional status . . . [. . .]

The very existence of the profane poses a problem. The professionals need them to remain laymen; and to characterise them as laymen, that is, clients, they need to be characterised as profane, that is, 'unable to serve themselves religiously'. What is needed then is one of the founding acts of the priesthood. Weber says it magnificently: 'The difference between the priest and the sorcerer is that when the sorcerer fails, it is his fault; when the priest fails, it is the fault of the layman, the layman has cheated, etc.'[60] [*laughter*] So the profane must be constituted as profane, that is, as incapable, disarmed, helpless, inapt (given a certificate of inaptitude),[61] for instance for administering the sacraments. In religious reformations, everyone, even the women, starts administering the sacraments. This is a frightening prospect for the priesthood, and the debate is still relevant today:[62] if anyone can administer the sacraments, what becomes of the monopoly of the sacred? It is the end of the 'sacerdotal' (*sacer-doce* = 'giver of sacraments'); by liquidating the *diacrisis* between those who are legitimised to consecrate, who are consecrated to consecrate, who consecrate those who consecrate, and those who are consecrated, being unconsecrated and profane, and whose every religious action can only be profanation, black mass, or the like, we liquidate the monopoly. This *diacrisis* or boundary is capital. But although the boundary between the religious field and the world beyond (the primitive, the barbarian, the Antichrist, etc.) is drawn, there is no consensus within the field; in Weber's terms, there is a struggle for the monopoly of the legitimate manipulation of the goods of salvation: the field, as field, is in agreement to declare that there are titles which authorise possession of the monopoly, but afterwards there is open warfare over deciding who should be consecrated with the right to consecrate.

I shall not take this further, but what Weber points to, then, is the existence of a division of the labour of symbolic domination where we see a field of symbolic power established independently of the field of political power. This is the *bellatores/oratores* opposition. I think that Dumézil's triad, which is a historical triad, can be established in a transhistorical fashion ([. . .] I am saying that hastily; I'm taking a big risk, but I don't have time to develop it). The field of symbolic power is composed independently of the field of political power: one of the problems is to wrest [a part of his symbolic power (?)] from the originary *rex*, the primitive *rex* (as described by Benveniste in his *Dictionary of Indo-European Concepts and Society*)[63] who, like the Achaean king

248 *Lecture of 30 May 1985*

for instance, is an all-powerful theocrat. He is head of the army, but he is also a political *rex*, the person who will *regere fines* and *regere sacra* (I keep repeating this, but it is important), who will say where the boundaries lie, in particular between the groups (which is absolutely capital) and between the sacred and the profane, which is the same thing – the boundaries between the groups are boundaries between the sacred and the profane, insofar as the boundaries of the sacred that are set for the groups represent limits that are not to be transgressed (for example, the boundary between the priests and the laity).

The original *rex*, then, wants all the powers, including the power to say where legitimate power lies: he rejects any idea of power which is not conceived within the sphere of his power (it would be very important to develop this point to see the relations between royalty and symbolic power, as wielded for instance by sculptors and painters). Here the work of Kantorowicz on the struggles in twelfth-century Bologna between jurists and princes is most illuminating.[64] [. . .] The jurists had to struggle inch by inch to restrict the prince's rights, to tell him: 'You cannot judge like that. There are texts; the Romans said . . .' Roman law is very important: the jurists established a capital of specific competence and they managed to convince the king that he could not judge if he had not read the canon law, Roman law and one or two other bodies of law. Little by little they carved out a sphere of autonomy. These spheres do in fact have a historical genesis, and just as I did for the artistic field, we can write the historical genealogy of these spaces of play where each game is irreducible to the games that are played in the adjacent space.

The field of symbolic power, then, emerges with the specific function of being the site of a struggle for the power to impose, and to some extent (through education and the education system) inculcate, systems of classification, categories of expression that although arbitrary, are not recognised as such, but as legitimate. The universal and transhistorical Kantian categories that I mentioned at the outset ultimately become programmes; the Kantian categories of our societies are our examination syllabuses. You are going to think: 'What a theoretical comedown!', but I think that this is a fact. This is reality. Syllabuses are programmes of perception, programmes of knowledge. They define the boundaries between the legitimate and the illegitimate, between what must (or may) be read (*legenda*) and what must not (or may not) be read. They define the categories of the important and the unimportant . . . According to some philosophers of language reflecting on the notion of the 'important', what is 'important' is what matters, what is of interest. The holders of the monopoly of the legitimate vision tell

Lecture of 30 May 1985 249

you what matters, what is worthy of your attention. For instance, the education system today is one of the key pieces of this field of production of the legitimate vision of the world: it helps in its modest way to produce legitimate categories, but above all it has the power to inculcate them durably through its lasting, repetitive operation, which leads us to internalise them profoundly. If we had to find a social location for the imposition of categories of perception – our mental structures – it is likely that one of the most important sites, especially for the cultivated, would be the education system.

The State and God

To recapitulate and conclude. Professionals establish their expertise at the expense of the dispossessed laymen; they operate within a field, they struggle among themselves. The space within which they struggle has a structure which (although I can't explore it today) is homologous with the structure of the social space: the opposition between orthodoxy and heresy, which we find in various forms in the different fields of symbolic production, is homologous with the structure of the social space. Because of this, the producers of religious goods or 'ideological' goods, in Marx's sense, will, in expressing their particular interests linked to their particular position in the field of production, express, on the basis of the structural homology between their field of production and the social field, the interests of those who occupy a homologous position in the social field. Consequently (here I shall say very briefly something that ought to be developed at some length) the symbolic production will function according to the logic of 'killing two birds with one stone'. In saying 'what is good for me' in the university field, the political field (in the restricted sense of our societies) or the religious field, a producer of representations of the social world will automatically say 'what is good' for those who occupy homologous positions in the social space, and who will recognise themselves in what he says, with some minor shifts, linked to the [universalisation (?)] effect. In fact, if I am right, the universalisation effect that Marx attributed to a sort of semi-conscious ideological process is automatic; it is produced by the effects of homology, that is, by the homology between the structures of the fields of production and the social field, which sets the mental structures of the producers concerned with the structure of the field of production in harmony with the mental structures of the perceivers, which are themselves structured according to the structures of the social field as a whole . . .

250   *Lecture of 30 May 1985*

This may not be crystal clear, but you could think of the opposition between high and low (as in fine feelings or base feelings): this opposition can be used to judge a painting, a work of art, or more sophisticated things: an opposition of this kind, which, when functioning in the restricted space of the producers of symbolic goods refers to the structure of this subspace, will be able to function in other spaces with different connotations, for instance for people who have in mind the high and the low of the social space, the vulgar and the distinguished. I think that ideological discourses function almost automatically according to the logic of 'killing two birds with one stone', for they have a sort of structural duplicity. This kind of description is opposed to that of Helvetius or d'Holbach who said: 'The priests deceive, they conceal their interests, they lead the faithful to believe that they believe, whereas they do not believe.' [. . .]

When the field thinks, when the mental structures of someone producing a discourse are the structures of the space within which he produces it, so that the homology between this space and the space in which his audience is situated creates a sort of subjectless communication, the misrecognition effect (what I call the 'symbolic effect') is at a maximum. Ultimately, it is this misrecognition that is equivalent to recognition and that forms the very basis of the social order. The most powerful recognition is the misrecognition of the arbitrary, where absolute misrecognition is able to suppress the very question of 'whether this should be recognised'. This happens when things 'go without saying' . . . This kind of absolute misrecognition seems to me to be a structural effect of the mechanism that I have described.

One last point [. . .]: the problem of the State, which I have raised more than once. What lies behind what I have been saying today about power is what you might call the 'myth of the central bank', that is, the myth of a place where all the acts of guarantee would be guaranteed (I was alluding to this when I talked of the power that 'comes from above' and the power that 'comes from below'). I referred to it last time:[65] when a doctor signs a certificate, who certifies the value of the certificate? When a critic says: 'This painter is a genius', who guarantees the legitimacy of this act of attribution of meaning? The logic that I have described amounts to saying that there are structural effects, and that even within the places where verdicts and sanctions are pronounced there are power relations of a particular form, with effects of concentration of capital, effects of domination, and the like. This is the 'hidden God'.[66] For it seems to me that the 'central bank' is in fact God. Who in the last instance can say who may legitimately pronounce the right to speak, or, to use the formula that I suggested in my com-

Lecture of 30 May 1985 251

mentary of Kafka, who may judge the legitimacy of the judges? Who can say whether the judges have the right to judge? Is it another judge? Is it a king? Step by step, we are referred back to God. Durkheim's phrase, 'society is God',[67] made Raymond Aron laugh – I have never understood why[68] . . . Obviously it was said in a mildly lay and positivist *fin-de-siècle* period, in the context of 'little father Combes',[69] and so easy to mock. But what I am saying has to be taken seriously.

What are we asking of God? What is at stake in Kafka? (Kafka is a noble writer, so I can refer to him.) It is the problem of the last instance: who in the last instance can stop this kind of circular circulation, whose paradigms are the scientific or artistic fields? Who can stop this mad circle, which in the artistic field authorises everyone to say anything they like about absolutely anyone (which is what [in my sessions on the artistic field] I called the institution of anomie)? The monopoly of legitimate consecration, the monopoly of the verdict, is God. In fact, saying that the different social agents inserted in the field of symbolic production are fighting for the monopoly of legitimate violence is to say that they are fighting to be God. In passing [. . .]: I think that this might inspire a reading of theologies. I suggested this, for instance, in the case of Sartre (the opposition between Being-in-itself and Being-for-itself has some connection with sociology), and I said that Kafka could be read as much as a theologian as a sociologist.[70] This is because sociologists in fact speak of theology unwittingly when they discuss the problem of knowing who, in the last instance, has the power to say who is worthy to wield power.

The myth of the central bank and the myth of the last instance are the myth of a place where the power of legitimate distribution and redistribution, not only [of material goods but also of symbolic goods] might be found. All the economists and historians have seen that historically the initial accumulation of power in the emergence of States seems associated with the emergence of places where the social agents have the power to redistribute accumulated wealth. For instance, taxes are collected, but how should they be redistributed, and to whom? To the rich, or the poor? But what I have been describing throughout these lectures is not the power of redistribution of material goods, which has been clearly noted by economists and historians, but the power of redistribution of symbolic goods, in particular the symbolic good par excellence, our identity. This is why I was going to say that the phrase 'Society is God' is far from foolish, because the symbolic power par excellence is the power to tell someone what they are. Categorically. I always return to the opposition between the insult and the verdict. 'You're nothing but an imbecile' is an insult; 'Your IQ is less than 100'

252 *Lecture of 30 May 1985*

means the same thing, but it is a verdict, which makes all the difference. Remember what I said at the beginning about violence: this kind of metaphysical violence seems to me to be a response to a sort of anomie of the *nomos*, distributing verdicts in an absolutely arbitrary fashion.

The central bank is this *nomos* ... It is no accident [. . .] if there is a connection between the [Greek] word *nomos*, the law, and the [Latin] word *numisma*, money. The central bank guarantees the currency of our titles, identities and civil status. As the field of symbolic production has at heart the monopoly of the legitimate enunciation of what social agents truly are (in the truth of the 'verdict',[71] 'in the last resort') – whether they deserve to be condemned or consecrated – we can see that this struggle has a theological dimension. It is a struggle for institutional perception (remember what I said about INSEE), for perception legitimised and validated, and the social agents engaged in this field – the statistical technocrats, the judges and the professors who pronounce these verdicts, each fighting their own corner in their separate subfields – participate in a general field (and, moreover, they can share out their clientele among themselves) where what is at issue is at once the truth of the social world and the truth of each individual, which gives the symbolic struggles a character of formidable violence. To a certain extent, the naive thrust of my scientific project was in fact to give a scientific account of the pathos and extremism of certain struggles that an economic or economistic analysis would be unable to understand: Wars of Religion, language wars, all those conflicts that history is full of and whose stakes are never reducible to their material dimensions. These life-and-death battles are fought over something that is perhaps more important than material conditions, that is, our identity, one of those things [. . .] that we are ready to die for, because it concerns both our reasons for existing and our ability to justify our existence.

If I said just now that religion was the paradigm of all the domains of symbolic production, it is because it goes some way towards answering a social question that is also a metaphysical question (Weber has splendidly demonstrated this – what he says about theodicy is most interesting): How is my existence justified? How can I justify the way that I live my existence? We can say whether we are justified to exist, in the absolute (appealing to principles of sufficient reason, or contingency, for instance), but there is also the question of being 'justified in our social existence', as a mere professor, or being a banker living off profits, or having moods, etc. Religion answers these historical questions in absolute terms and claims to provide social agents with absolute justifications for their existence; it offers them the means to render their existence absolute. In fact I think that the struggles I have discussed, which are struggles over categories of perception, the categories through which people perceive the world but also perceive themselves, that is, struggles for the construction of the identity of the self and others, are in a way life-and-death struggles whose arena today is the State, which is not some entity that would be revealed to you through some sort of anagogy, as in a mystical vision, but the space comprising the playing fields where people who are not too sure what they are doing are fighting at one and the same time for their identity and the power to define the identity of others.

Situating the Later Volumes of General Sociology *in the work of Pierre Bourdieu*

Julien Duval

This fourth volume continues the publication of the Course in General Sociology that Pierre Bourdieu delivered during his first five years of teaching at the Collège de France from 1982, at the rate of eight to ten two-session sessions each year. It contains the lectures given during the academic year 1984–85. One further volume will cover the year 1985–86.

In the words that he used during his very first lecture, the Course in General Sociology presents the 'fundamental lineaments' of his work.[1] The first year of lectures following his inaugural lecture of April 1982 was relatively short. It concentrated on the question of the constitution and classification of groups and 'social classes'. It functions as a kind of prologue to the whole course. During the second year, Bourdieu explained how he envisaged the object of sociological study and developed his thinking on knowledge and practice, then he started to present the major concepts of his sociological approach, expounding their underlying theoretical assumptions as well as the function that he assigned them in the general economy of his theory. He devoted a whole series of lectures to the concept of the habitus, taking account of the fact that the subject in sociology, unlike the subject in philosophy, is a socialised subject, that is, one invested by social forces, and he showed how that concept enabled us to think about social action without falling into the alternative of mechanism and purposiveness. He then made a first, 'physicalist' approach to the concept of the field, presenting it as a field of forces, and leaving to a later stage in the lectures the analysis of the dynamics of the field seen as a field of struggles aiming to modify the field of forces.

The third year focused on the concept of capital. Bourdieu reminds us of the link between this concept and the concept of the field, and then goes on to elaborate the different forms of capital (which are linked

Situating the Later Volumes of General Sociology   255

to the variety of the fields), as well as the different states of cultural capital. He pays particular attention to the codification and objectification of capital: this is designated as one of the sources of the coherence of the social world and an important source of the divergence between pre-capitalist societies and our differentiated societies. The fourth year, which forms the present volume, tackles the concept of field in terms of a field of struggles, insofar as it is the object of perceptions by the social agents, these perceptions being generated by the relation between the habitus and capital. In this fourth year, Bourdieu develops the project of a sociology of social perception, conceived as an inseparably cognitive and political act in the struggle between social agents to define the *nomos*, the legitimate vision of the social world. The fifth year (due to be published later) continues to develop these analyses, but as he prepares to conclude the course of lectures, Bourdieu also seeks to link the two aspects of the concept of the field (the field as field of forces and as field of struggles) through the simultaneous mobilisation of three major concepts. The symbolic struggles aim to transform the field of forces. To understand them we need to introduce the notion of symbolic power and symbolic capital, or the symbolic effect of capital, which is constituted in the relation between habitus and field, a relation of *illusio*. The fifth year finishes with questions arising from the position of the social sciences in the symbolic struggles that aim to impose a certain representation of the social world, and with the idea that the social sciences should combine both structuralist and constructivist perspectives in order to study the social world, which is both a field of forces and a field of struggles that aim to transform it but are also conditioned by it.

Coherence over five years

This five-year-long course of lectures enabled Bourdieu to look back over the theoretical system that he had been progressively constructing. Shortly before the start of this course, and before his election to the Collège de France, he had published two sizable volumes of synthesis, *Distinction* (1979), comprising all his research on culture and social class in France, and *The Logic of Practice* (1980), comprising his investigations in Algeria and the theory of action that he derived from them. The Course in General Sociology covers both research enterprises at once, and aims to elaborate a social theory as valid for pre-capitalist as for highly differentiated societies. Rejecting the usual division between anthropology and sociology, it not only displays the coherence of these

256   *Situating the Later Volumes of* General Sociology

various research projects but also promotes the unity of the social sciences. In 1984–85 and 1985–86 in particular, Bourdieu is a sociologist enquiring into the process that leads from pre-capitalist to differentiated societies, while drawing attention to their continuity. More than once, he points out how pre-capitalist societies act as analysts of our societies: they 'zoom in' on relations between the sexes, they show 'close up' the symbolic struggles that are less perceptible but still at work in differentiated societies (25 April 1985); and he emphasises, for example, what his analyses on social class owe to his work on kinship relations in Algeria (2 May 1985).

The work of synthesis is also applied to the concepts. One of the objectives of his teaching, in fact, is to 'show the articulation between the fundamental concepts and the structure of the relations that link those concepts'.[2] In a concern to clarify, part of the course during the second and third years consists in presenting the three key concepts in succession, with some lessons using the first drafts of the generally rather short theoretical summaries that Bourdieu published in his review *Actes de la recherche en sciences sociales* at the end of the 1970s and the beginning of the 1980s, on the species and states of capital, on the properties of fields, on the effects of the corps, etc. But even at this stage of the course, the concepts remained linked to each other. The concept of capital, for instance, is first introduced in relation to the concept of field and the habitus reappears when the notion of 'information capital'[3] is introduced. The question of codification and institutionalisation, tackled during the third and fifth years respectively, as was the question of the field of power, links up with the relations between capital and the field; and the problem of perception, central to the fourth year, involves the relation between the habitus and the field directly. Countering the temptation of selective borrowing from Bourdieu's sociology, this Course in General Sociology reminds us how far the concepts of habitus, capital and field have been thought through as '"systemic" concepts because their use presupposes permanent reference to the complete system of their interrelationships'.[4]

If Bourdieu takes pains to recapitulate his arguments (more and more often as his teaching progresses), it is because he fears that his concern to 'produce a discourse whose coherence would emerge over a period of years' might escape his audience (1 March 1984). In addition to the spacing out of the lectures over a period of years, there is the fact that Bourdieu is addressing an 'intermittent public' (ibid.) that changes over the years. His style of teaching, moreover, leaves room, within a pre-established canvas, for potential and sometimes quite substantial improvisations and 'digressions'. Finally, the exposition cannot follow

Situating the Later Volumes of General Sociology 257

a perfectly linear course: its nature is to circulate in a sort of theoretical space that authorises different pathways. When he starts the fourth year of his teaching, for instance, Bourdieu says that he hesitated between several possible 'pathways' (7 March 1985).

The lectures were not intended to be published, at least not in their given form,[5] but their 'overall coherence' will perhaps be more apparent to the readers of the transcriptions than it would have been to the audience at the time. The time spent in reading the published lectures is not the same as that devoted to their preparation or that of their oral delivery. Reading acts as a kind of accelerator of the process of thinking that informs the lectures. The juxtaposition of the five volumes, for instance, will show up the loop operated very discreetly in one of the last lectures of the Course in General Sociology as Bourdieu returns to the 'notorious problem of the social classes, which is absolutely central for the social sciences' (5 June 1986), that was at the heart of the first year of his teaching (1981–82). This return to the point of departure, as it might seem on first analysis, demonstrates the coherence of the whole of the course. It allows the reader to measure the distance travelled and become aware of the questions that have been investigated or that have taken on another dimension through the developments proposed in the meantime.

It may also suggest an approach to reading the lectures. The first year, in the spring of 1982, was presented as a reflection on classification and the social classes. The arguments that Bourdieu deployed there drew on insights gained from *Distinction*, but were also based just as much on the research that he was finishing at the time: in particular his book on language, and his analyses of the process of naming or the performative power invested in words under certain social conditions; Bourdieu thus added considerable depth to his theory of the social classes.[6] The movement of the Course in General Sociology could then be understood as a manner of expanding, exploring and generalising the thoughts on the subject of the social classes that he expounded during the first year. For the second and third years, Bourdieu explored his theoretical system, to return in the last two years to the question of the symbolic struggle over the principles of perception of the social world, whose division into classes is a sort of special case. Competition within the 'field of expertise', and the very particular power of the State in matters of nomination, are generally two major aspects of the symbolic struggle in our differentiated societies, which the problem of social classes forces us to face.

Read in this way, the lectures do not come full circle. Far from returning to the point of departure in an attempt at closure, the final

258   *Situating the Later Volumes of* General Sociology

return to the social classes represents an opening out and a progression that are linked to a form of generalisation. It is less of a loop and more of a 'spiralling'[7] movement that he achieved over five years. The image of the 'spiral', like that of the 'constant reworking' of research[8] that Bourdieu also used to describe his manner of working, is relevant not only to the structure of the course; it also applies to the numerous echoes that reverberate from one lecture to another. Because he is afraid of seeming to repeat himself, Bourdieu sometimes specifically emphasises the fact that these are not identical 'repetitions': 'I sometimes pass through the same point on a different trajectory' (17 April 1986); 'I have said this in an earlier lecture, but I shall now rework the theme in a different context' (18 April 1985); 'I have already developed the objective aspect of this argument in a lecture two years ago: I am pointing this out in case you want to make the connection' (15 May 1986). There are themes that recur (for instance the discussion of purposiveness and mechanism and the critique of decision theory, both broached in 1982, recur in 1986), and the same examples may be used to illustrate different analyses: thus the careers of nineteenth-century regionalist authors are referred to within the literary field in which they fall (25 January 1983), but are related later to the space where they originate and terminate in order to show the contribution of these writers to a certain educational mythology (12 June 1986).

The 'improvisations' of the second sessions

The year that the third volume comprises corresponds to the moment when Bourdieu's teaching at the Collège de France settled into a stable form. From the start of his appointment in 1982, Bourdieu had been obliged to abandon the standard format of this institution, which was to deliver a one-session lecture and, at a different time and in a smaller hall, deliver a seminar of the same duration. Researchers who worked alongside him remember how the first seminar session broke down in an atmosphere of great disorder, since the room could not hold the numbers of the public who flooded in.[9] After this experience, Bourdieu decided in 1982–83 to deliver his teaching in the form of two successive session-long sessions with no distinction between a 'lecture' part and a 'seminar' part.

He proceeds somewhat differently in the years published in volumes 3, 4 and 5. As he notes regularly in the course of the lectures, the formula of the open lecture to an anonymous and heterogeneous audience reduced to the role of listener is an ongoing problem for him:

Situating the Later Volumes of General Sociology   259

he finds this framework ill-suited to what he is trying to transmit (a 'method' rather than a body of knowledge in the literal sense),[10] and he refuses to conform to it entirely. He cannot resist the temptation to launch into partly improvised digressions, which lead him very often at the end of a lecture to regret[11] not having said everything that he had intended, and having to postpone certain developments until the following session. At regular intervals he also continues, as he did already during the first two years, to reply to written questions submitted to him during the interval or at the end of the lecture, and which enable him to have at least some contact with his listeners.[12] But at the start of the year 1983–84 he reintroduced a distinction between the two sessions of his teaching on Thursday mornings:[13] while the first session, from 10.00 a.m. to 11.00 a.m., was spent on 'theoretical analysis' (1 March 1984), the second, from 11.00 a.m. to 12 noon, showed a change of subject and tone.[14]

Since he did not feel able at the Collège de France to organise a real seminar, he tries in the second session to give an idea of what a seminar would be, showing how an object of study might be constructed and how a problem might be elaborated, and above all how his theoretical formulae and formulations could be deployed in concrete operations, which is the essence of the craft of the scientist – the art of detecting the theoretical issues to be found in the most singular or banal details of everyday life (1 March 1984). With only a few exceptions, the second sessions of the lectures published in the later volumes are devoted to 'work in progress' (19 May 1984), 'tentative essays, reflections on risky topics' (26 April 1984), or 'improvisations' (17 April 1986). Bourdieu 'allows himself more freedom' than in the first sessions (15 May 1986), in particular to depart from a 'linear itinerary' (12 June 1986) and a 'sustained discourse, with long-term coherence', which would run the risk of being 'slightly enclosed and totalising (some would say slightly totalitarian)' (17 April 1986). As far as possible, he looks for some degree of correspondence between 'the applied studies of the second session and the theoretical analyses of the first session' (1 March 1984). Thus in the fourth year the 'theoretical analyses' concern the perception of the social world and the second sessions focus on a social category, the painters who, with Manet, accomplish a revolution in vision and perception (23 May 1985): the lectures develop in particular the notion of the *nomos*, while the second sessions draw attention to the 'institutionalisation of anomie' operated by modern art.

The second sessions are generally devoted to research that Bourdieu is presenting for the first time. In 1984–85 it is his research into the

260   *Situating the Later Volumes of* General Sociology

field of painting carried out with Marie-Claire Bourdieu. In the years immediately after these lectures, he published the first articles arising from this.[15] At the end of the 1990s he devoted two whole years of his teaching to it.[16] The lectures given in 1985 enable us to judge that this research, probably started at the beginning of the 1980s,[17] was already well under way, even if it still lacked, for instance, the analysis of Manet's works that he was to offer in the 1990s. In 1985 Bourdieu was working in parallel on *The Rules of Art*, which appeared in 1992, and the object of this research seems to lie above all in 'a series of analyses of the relations between the literary field and the artistic field' (7 March 1985): the study of the relations between the painters and the writers takes a central place in the exposition, and some developments refer quite directly to the analyses of the 'invention of the life of the artist' undertaken in the framework of the research on Flaubert and the literary field.[18] At this time Bourdieu was very concerned to show that the process of autonomisation affects the whole range of the artistic field and cannot therefore be entirely grasped in research focusing on a single sector (such as painting, literature or music).

In 1983–84 and in 1985–86, the second sessions concentrate on more limited research projects, which usually last for no more than two or three successive sessions. The first piece of research presented, which Bourdieu says he has 'found while rummaging through [his] notes' (1 March 1984), is his analysis of a 'hit parade' published by the magazine *Lire* in April 1981. He may well have used the lecture to draft the text that appeared as an article a few months later as an appendix to *Homo Academicus* in November 1984.[19] Four years later, he would link it up with the analysis of a sort of 'Chinese game' that he had given a few years earlier.[20] He speaks of a sort of '"masterpiece", such as those made by a medieval craftsman', and presents his approach in these terms:[21]

> I'd say: There's the material, in front of you; it's available to everyone. Why is it badly constructed? What does this questionnaire mean? What would you do with it? . . . You have to question the sample: who are the judges whose judgements led to this list of best authors? How were they chosen? Isn't the set of authors implied in the list of judges chosen and in their categories of perception? . . . And so an idiotic survey of no scientific object if, instead of reading the results at face value, one reads the categories of thought projected in the results they produced . . . you're dealing with already published results that needed to be re-constructed.[22]

Situating the Later Volumes of General Sociology   261

At all events, this research into the ranking list is more than just an exercise in method or style. Bourdieu also uses it as an opportunity to reflect on the properties of the intellectual field, its weak institutionalisation and its vulnerability in the face of a journalistically procured 'social action'. The choice of a limited and easily accessible but also very well chosen and intensively exploited object of study may have something to do with the fact that Bourdieu must certainly have reflected during these years on how he could best continue to engage in empirical research. For his election to the Collège de France brought with it new obligations and necessarily reduced his presence in his research centre,[23] as well as at the École des hautes études en sciences sociales – an institution which, unlike the Collège de France, allows its teachers to direct doctoral theses.[24] His availability for the kind of research that he had been practising since the 1960s was no doubt restricted, even if the enquiry into private housing that he had started during the first half of the 1980s (2 May 1985), like *The Weight of the World*, shows that he managed to launch important new collective research projects based on first-hand material.

Among other research projects presented in the second sessions, several are distinguished by the fact that they are based on literary texts, an approach that Bourdieu had previously practised only in his analysis of *Sentimental Education*.[25] He studies Franz Kafka's *The Trial* (22 and 29 March 1984), Virginia Woolf's *To the Lighthouse* (15 and 22 May 1986), and, rather more briefly, Samuel Beckett's *Waiting for Godot* (19 April 1984) and Kafka's *Metamorphosis* (22 May 1986).[26] He appears to show more interest in literary material and analysis than previously. The analysis of *The Trial* led to a paper read after the end of the academic year 1983–84 in a multidisciplinary colloquium organised at the Centre Pompidou on the occasion of the sixtieth anniversary of Kafka's death.[27] It is possible that this interest in literature is linked to the writing of *The Rules of Art*. Bourdieu does more than find a kind of allegory in *The Trial*, he also in a way practises the 'science of works' whose principles are developed in this book in 1992, in the way that he links the 'Kafkaesque' vision of the world to the insecurity that characterises the literary field that produced it (and Kafka's position in that field). A few years later he notes a slight change in his attitude to literature: he gradually frees himself from the temptation, felt strongly at the beginning, in a context where the scientific nature of sociology was insecure, to distance himself from his own literary education and tastes.[28] In the lectures he retains his concern to circumscribe the place allocated to literary analysis ('I shall not develop this further – since I have already done my little literary turn, you would find that I was

262 *Situating the Later Volumes of* General Sociology

going too far' [15 May 1986]), but his sociologist audience are invited to reflect on their relation to literature.

Explaining his reflections on the 'biographical illusion' exploited by William Faulkner and Alain Robbe-Grillet in particular, Bourdieu draws attention to the 'intellectual double life' led by sociologists, who can make a personal reading of the 'nouveau roman' without drawing conclusions for their professional practice (24 April 1986), and he emphasises how much the repression of the 'literary' by sociologists owes to their position in the space of disciplines; the particular form taken by the opposition between the arts and the sciences in the nineteenth century masks the advantage that writers have over researchers on questions such as the theory of temporality.

Announcing later research

As it intersperses Bourdieu's presentation of projects in progress with reminders of his previous research, the Course is driven by a dynamic in which the contemporary reader can see the bones of some of the studies that Bourdieu was to undertake in the second half of the 1980s, and even during the 1990s.

Above all, the present volumes announce the whole range of the lectures that Bourdieu was to give at the Collège de France from 1987 to 1992. It is no accident if the lecture that opens the third volume remarks in passing on the failings of the French edition of Max Weber: this author will often be referred to during the year 1983–84.[29] A little earlier, moreover, Bourdieu had published in the daily newspaper *Libération* a text entitled 'N'ayez pas peur de Max Weber!' (Who's afraid of Max Weber?!'),[30] which seems to have been triggered by his preoccupations at the time. In his lectures Bourdieu comments on extracts from *Economy and Society*,[31] discussing codification, the notion of the 'discipline' or the sociology of law, which he knows only from the German or English editions. Weber's observations on *Kadi*-justice and the justice of Sancho Panza or Solomon are frequently referred to in the lectures. It is probably during the years that he was giving these lectures that Bourdieu's interest in Weber and the sociology of law developed so strongly. The theme of the *vis formae*, which was never mentioned during the two previous years, is referred to on several occasions during the year 1983–84. His article on the 'force of law' would be published in 1986,[32] that is, during the year of teaching that closes the present set of volumes and which contains references to research in the sociology of law (15 May 1986, 5 June 1986), as well

Situating the Later Volumes of General Sociology 263

as reflections on the juridical field, which would be at the heart of his teaching for 1987–88.

It is not only the law but also more generally the State that becomes the central object of his reflection. The formula that Bourdieu uses to widen Weber's definition of the State ('an enterprise [. . .] that claims the monopoly of legitimate physical coercion') recurs frequently in his lectures in the early 1980s. His critique in 1983–84 of linear interpretations of the process of rationalisation (29 March 1984) prefigures the reflections to be developed a few years later in his lectures on the genesis of the State. The references to the State are very numerous in the last sessions of the fourth year. Indeed, the main theme of social perception leads into a study of the State's monopoly of authorised perception. The analysis of certification also implicates the State, defined in this case as a 'field of expertise, or the field of agents in competition for the power of social certification' (9 May 1985), and the last lecture of the year finishes by acknowledging that a sociology of symbolic struggles should question this 'last analysis' that the State represents. Bourdieu notes that the State has become a major concern for his arguments even before starting his lectures on the State in 1989–90:[33] already in 1987–88 he entitled his course 'Concerning the State'.

The article (1990) and then the book (1998) that he devoted to 'Masculine Domination'[34] may also be seen being sketched out in the lectures. During the year 1985–86 several developments relate to the political dimension of masculine domination or the 'androcentric unconscious' of Mediterranean societies. It is in 1985–86 too that he comments on *To the Lighthouse* (which became an important reference in his later writings on the relations between the sexes); he is particularly attracted to its feminine vision of masculine investment in social games.

While it is more difficult to detect in the lectures the signs prefiguring the work that Bourdieu would publish in the 1990s, today's reader, seeing Bourdieu's methodological reflections on the difficulty of retrieving and explaining the experience of social agents (12 June 1986), cannot help thinking of the organisation of the collective enquiry that culminated in 1993 in *The Weight of the World*. Likewise, it is tempting to connect the study of the 'hit parade' with the analyses that Bourdieu would apply ten years later to the 'grip of journalism';[35] although he does not use this expression in 1984, he sees in the ranking list the sign of a transformation of the balance of power between the intellectual field and the journalistic field in favour of the latter. However, the media and Bourdieu's relations with them were significantly transformed in the ten years or so that separate the analysis of the 'hit parade' (that

264   *Situating the Later Volumes of* General Sociology

Bourdieu published only in his review, and in an appendix to an academic work) from the brief polemical work that he was to publish at the end of 1996 for a wider readership, *On Television*, which is partly a book about 'media-friendly intellectuals'.[36] Essentially, we could say that the lectures published here do slightly pre-date the turning point represented by the privatisation in 1986 of the most popular channel, TF1. At the beginning of the 1980s, the spirit of public service inherited from the beginnings of television remained fairly strong.[37] Bourdieu was still liable to participate in television broadcasts from time to time or to take part in a debate with leading journalists. In 1985, for instance, he intervened in a forum organised by the Comité d'information pour la presse dans l'enseignement,[38] and, encouraged by his Collège de France colleague Georges Duby, he started to participate in the 'educational television' project that would lead to the creation of 'la Sept' (Channel 7), which gave birth to Arte.[39]

The framework of the Collège de France

To understand the space where Pierre Bourdieu was situated in the years from 1983 to 1986 we have to think of the Collège de France. Georges Duby was one of his closest colleagues. Their relationship went back a long way: Duby was one of the founders of the review *Études rurales* in which Bourdieu had published a substantial article (more than a hundred pages long) at the beginning of the 1960s, when he was almost unknown.[40] In the lectures for 1986 where he elaborates the notion of the 'field of power', Bourdieu often quotes his medievalist colleague's book, *Les Trois Ordres, ou l'imaginaire du féodalisme* (1978). He also refers to the analyses of Indo-European triads developed by Georges Dumézil, who had retired in 1968 after nearly twenty years teaching at the Collège de France (he died in 1986). Bourdieu discusses Claude Lévi-Strauss's arguments even more often (although Bourdieu referred to his anthropological studies continuously throughout his career, even when he no longer attended his seminar). Lévi-Strauss retired from the Collège de France in 1982, but a lecture that he gave in 1983 marks a moment of tension between the two men, as reflected in one of Bourdieu's lectures in 1986 (5 June 1986). Bourdieu's lectures also contain glancing allusions to or passing discussions of research by younger professors at the Collège de France: Emanuel Le Roy Ladurie (18 April 1985), Jacques Thuillier (2 May 1985), whom Bourdieu had known from the École normale supérieure, and Gérard Fussman (28 March 1985).

Situating the Later Volumes of General Sociology 265

Bourdieu played his part in the life of the institution. He refers twice to seminars or colloquia which united participants from the different historical and literary disciplines represented at the Collège de France (22 May and 19 June 1986). He participated until his retirement in various events of this nature. In 1984–85 he urged his audience to go to the lectures that Francis Haskell had come to deliver at the Collège de France (18 April 1985, 2 May 1985). Bourdieu's lectures do not refer to any of the works of the 'Collège scientists', but when the right returned to power in 1986,[41] Bourdieu joined several of them (the biologist Jean-Pierre Changeux, the physicist Claude Cohen-Tannoudji, the pharmacologist Jacques Glowinski and the chemist Jean-Marie Lehn) in signing a 'solemn appeal' to the government, which intended to reduce the public funds allocated to research. In addition, the lectures are contemporary with the preparation of the 'Propositions for the education of the future' that the President of the Republic (François Mitterrand) had asked the professors of the Collège de France to prepare in 1984 and which was remitted in March 1985.[42] Bourdieu was the editor in chief, and even, to some considerable extent, the initiator of the project.[43]

During these years, one of the members of the Collège de France whose lectures were most popular was Michel Foucault. Bourdieu was to explain much later what attracted him to and what distanced him from Michel Foucault,[44] whose seminar at the École normale supérieure he had attended. In the 1980s, Foucault and Bourdieu joined forces in appealing to the French government to support Polish trade unionists, but the lectures published here bear witness to a mixture of esteem and distance. Although Bourdieu makes explicit reference to Foucault's work, such as his notion of *épistémè*, the fourth and fifth years' lectures are marked by an ongoing critique of the analyses of power elaborated by the philosopher: in particular the formula 'power springs from below' is seen as showing naive thinking, inspired above all by a spirit of contradiction (17 April 1986). Bourdieu's lectures had already finished just over a month before Foucault's death at the end of June 1984. Bourdieu joined André Miquel and other professors from the Collège de France to attend the ceremony in Paris that preceded his funeral.[45] He published two notices in homage to 'a friend and colleague', one in *Le Monde* and the second in *L'Indice*.[46]

266   *Situating the Later Volumes of* General Sociology

The intellectual field in the first half of the 1980s

The lectures also show the influence of the contemporary intellectual field outside the Collège de France.[47] They contain allusions to major figures from previous decades, such as Jean-Paul Sartre and Jacques Lacan, who had died in 1980 and 1981 respectively, and Louis Althusser, who was interned in November 1980 after murdering his wife. In one of his lectures Bourdieu alludes to the contemporary journalistic debate over finding a 'successor' to Sartre.[48] The dominant figures of the moment who combine intellectual recognition with public notoriety are a group of fifty-year-olds that include Bourdieu, with, principally, Michel Foucault, Jacques Derrida, Gilles Deleuze (and Félix Guattari).[49] They became known during the years preceding May 1968 and shared what Bourdieu calls an 'anti-institutional mood' (2 May 1985). These 'consecrated heretics', according to another of Bourdieu's formulae,[50] took their distance from traditional philosophy and the traditional university. In the first half of the 1980s, they often found themselves signing the same appeals or petitions. However, a younger generation emerged and started to relegate them to the past: in autumn 1985 an essay much hyped by the media took as its target the 'anti-humanist '68 thinking' that they allegedly represented.[51] Bourdieu alludes to this book in one of his lectures (5 June 1986), and on several occasions mentions the thematics of the 'return to Kant' and the 'return to the subject' that its authors stand for.

If he mentions only in passing the development of the 'postmodernism' that dates from the second half of the 1970s (in discussing research into the sociology of science, whose relativism he criticises), he does make several references to the appearance, at roughly the same time, of the 'nouveaux philosophes': 'From the moment that someone intrudes into the space, even a "new philosopher", their existence creates a problem and provokes thought, although that thought may make people think askew, not to mention the fact that it may cause people to burn energy that could be more usefully employed elsewhere' (18 April 1985). The attitude to adopt in the face of this new type of rival, and more generally in the face of the threats that seem to confront 'philosophy' at this time, then provoke debate; several allusions in the lectures reveal Bourdieu's reservations, as he takes his distance from Deleuze's declarations on the 'nouveaux philosophes' (which he finds counterproductive) or from the Estates General of philosophy organised by Jacques Derrida.[52] His analysis of the 'hit parade', however, shows his awareness of the accelerating structural transformations at work at

Situating the Later Volumes of General Sociology   267

this time,[53] and of the danger that they represent for the perpetuation of the intellectual model that he incarnates.

At the beginning of the 1980s, his own status in the intellectual field changed, but according to a logic that is not easy to characterise unequivocally. His election to the Collège de France, for example, or the success of *Distinction*, which made its mark as an important book with an impact well beyond the circle of specialists, increased the recognition of his work, but at the same time make him the incarnation of a discipline and a body of thought that many intellectual schools of thought attacked for being a 'determinist' or even 'totalitarian' 'sociologism'. Among these various criticisms and attacks (which on occasion find an echo in the lectures published here) we could mention, even if they are only a few examples among others, those emanating from collaborators or intellectuals connected with the review *Esprit* or the book that appeared in 1984, *L'Empire du sociologue*.[54]

The subspace of sociology

We find this ambiguity in the subspace of sociology. Since his work was already at a stage that authorised a retrospective viewpoint, Bourdieu sometimes ventures in his lectures to grasp and formulate the general sense of his enterprise; he can insist on the efforts that he has made, in opposition to 'economic and economistic analysis', to highlight 'the decisive role of the symbolic in social exchanges', 'all those conflicts that history is full of and whose stakes are never reducible to their material dimensions' (22 March 1984 and 30 May 1985); he may also point out that his 'historical contribution' will have been to 'take his work as a sociologist to its conclusion, that is the objectification of the professionals of objectification' (19 June 1986),[55] or to 'show due respect to anything that could help us think more deeply about the social world' (14 March 1985). Moreover, he starts working on a synthesis (which includes these lectures) and popularisation. In parallel with his research, Bourdieu started to publish books designed to give accessible insight into his work: in 1980 for the first time he collected in one volume oral presentations given in diverse circumstances.[56] In 1983, one of his first students, Alain Accardo, published the first book that undertook to lay the major concepts of his sociology before a readership of students and militants.[57] His international reputation also grew. Thus just before starting the fifth year of his lectures, he spent a month travelling round the United States, where he gave fifteen seminars and lectures in American universities (San Diego, Berkeley,

268 *Situating the Later Volumes of* General Sociology

Chicago, Princeton, Philadelphia, Baltimore, New York University). In the years that followed, he made similar tours in other countries.

This growing consecration does not mean that he started to exercise a 'mastership'. In sociology, as in the whole of the intellectual field, the growing recognition that Bourdieu attracted seemed to generate even fiercer forms of rejection. In the first half of the 1980s, there were several attempts to describe his sociology as 'out of date', with some talk of an 'actor's last farewell'. The attacks were mounted, in particular, in the name of a 'methodological individualism' that claims to explain social phenomena on the basis of a desocialised *homo sociologicus*. Their leader was Raymond Boudon, who, having been in the 1960s one of the principal importers into France of the 'methodology' of Paul Lazarsfeld (which Bourdieu attacked on epistemological grounds),[58] developed in the 1970s an analysis of educational inequalities challenging the views imposed by *The Inheritors* and *Reproduction*. If Bourdieu in these lectures repeats his criticism of 'methodological individualism' on several occasions, or points out his divergence from the view of his work that it propagates, it is because this current of thought, which was making inroads in the United States at the same time, had entered a particularly aggressive phase. In 1982 Presses Universitaires de France published a *Dictionnaire critique de la sociologie*, edited by Raymond Boudon and François Bourricaud, whose project 'to scrutinise the imperfections, uncertainties and flaws of sociological theories, but also the reasons for their success', is an attack on Marxist- or structuralist-inspired sociology.

Bourdieu's remarks on the 'ultra-subjectivism' and 'facile radicalism' that are emerging in the sociology of science are a response to the appearance in 1979 of the book *Laboratory Life*.[59] Based on the ethnographical study of a laboratory of neuroendocrinology, this book claims to found an approach explicitly different from the analyses that Bourdieu had been offering since the mid-1970s on 'the scientific field and the social conditions of the progress of reason'. Bourdieu rejects this approach, which radicalises to the point of relativism the thesis according to which scientific facts are socially constructed. The authors' insistence on the scientists' search for credibility and their reliance on rhetorical apparatus leads them to ignore the fact that not all strategies are possible in the scientific field (28 March 1985 and 19 June 1986). Some fifteen years later, by which time this 'new sociology of science' had developed considerably, Bourdieu would return to this criticism.[60]

In these lectures Bourdieu also discusses the imports into sociology that took place in the 1980s. These years saw a wave of translations in France of a German contemporary of Durkheim, Georg Simmel, and the 'discovery' of interactionism and ethnomethodology, 'heterodox' currents of American sociology dating from the 1950s and 1960s. At the intersection of sociology and philosophy, the work of the Frankfurt School, largely unknown in France before the 1970s, was also published copiously at the start of the 1980s, particularly by Payot at the instigation of Miguel Abensour. In one lecture Bourdieu offers in passing an analysis of these imports of the 1980s (5 June 1986). Although he mocks the provincialism that leads the French to translate research when it has gone out of fashion in its native land, he cannot help being irritated by these imports when they are introduced by more or less declared rivals in the sociological space and presented as innovations that require immediate attention. In fact they are sometimes explicitly opposed to his own sociology, despite being authors that he had read long before and whom he had helped to make known in France (most of Goffman's work had been translated in the 1970s and 1980s by Éditions de Minuit), and above all whom he had already integrated into his approach.

The political context

The concern to offer teaching that was theoretical but not divorced from the most concrete reality inspires frequent allusions to the political context of the times, to the questions and problems constituted as such in the media and in the political world. Bourdieu finds an almost perfect example of his reflections on the 'science of the State' in the unemployment figures published by INSEE. This statistical indicator in fact became a central stake in contemporary political debate: the unemployment rate was very low until 1973 but then rose continually until the mid-1980s. Among other things, the arrival in France of mass unemployment helped to foreground the question of immigration – the electoral scores of the Front National after 1982 are only the most spectacular manifestation of this. In this way 'current affairs' are a direct illustration of one of the ideas developed by Bourdieu: it is the principles underlying the vision of the social world (and in the event the question of whether the division between immigrants and non-immigrants can replace the division between rich and poor) that are at stake in the struggle. In the first half of the 1980s the growing stigmatisation of immigrants inspired a mobilisation of opposition opinion that Bourdieu associated himself with. Thus he signed a text of support for the march for equality and against racism that took place in autumn

270   *Situating the Later Volumes of* General Sociology

1983,[61] and he played a part in the activities of SOS Racisme, close to the Socialist Party, launched in 1984. In November 1985, for example, he took part in a meeting with the association during which he warned them of the danger of an 'ethico-magical movement' and denounced those who analyse immigration in terms of cultural difference, because this provides a smokescreen hiding the economic and social inequality between Frenchmen and immigrants.

The lectures also include echoes of the rise of neoliberalism, whose acceleration at the start of the 1980s was symbolised by the accession to power of Margaret Thatcher in Great Britain and Ronald Reagan in the United States. The economists of the 'Chicago School', mentioned on several occasions by Bourdieu, are said to have encouraged economic policies which, contrary to the interventionist policies employed in the post-war decades, consider, in a now-famous formula, that the State (or at least its 'left hand') is 'the problem, not the solution'. When at one moment he discusses the difference between private charity and public welfare (9 and 23 May 1985), Bourdieu mentions the attacks that the Welfare State was subjected to at the time. In the last lecture published in this volume, the connection that he establishes between the tragedy that had just occurred at the Heysel stadium and the politics of the 'Iron Lady' announces the theme of the 'law of conservation of violence' that he will use to confront the neoliberal politicians in the 1990s.[62] Moreover, the lectures often echo events and situations that are being discussed in the 'foreign affairs' columns of the French media at the time. Thus Bourdieu alludes to the Iranian revolution or the Irish troubles and offers elements of reflection on them based on his theoretical analyses.

At a national level, the period corresponds to François Mitterrand's first seven-year mandate. The lectures make few allusions to internal political events, apart from some critical comments on the restoration of the school of the Third Republic sought and proposed by the socialist minister of education, Jean-Pierre Chevènement (12 June 1986).[63] The last lecture of the Course makes a few (anecdotal) references to the return of a right-wing government as a result of the legislative elections of March 1986. We can, however, note that, without alluding to this in his lectures, Bourdieu did take public stands on some aspects of the policies implemented by successive governments: he signed several petitions condemning the position of the socialist government towards events in Poland,[64] but also an appeal relating to conditions in prisons and, after the return of the right to power in 1986, appeals against cuts in the budget for research and against the proposal to halt the construction of the new opera house at the Bastille.

Situating the Later Volumes of General Sociology   271

The Lecture of 19 June 1986 that concludes the final volume brings Bourdieu's five-year Course in General Sociology to a close. It was the first general introduction to sociology ever given at the Collège de France. The following year, Bourdieu took advantage of the opportunity that members of the Collège have to suspend their teaching temporarily. He started his lectures again in 1988 with a new title, 'À propos de l'État' ('On the State'). This marks the start of a five-year cycle devoted to the analysis and deconstruction of this institution and, more generally, the start of a period when Bourdieu's lectures at the Collège focus on specific themes: after the sociology of the State[65] came the sociology of the economic field, the sociology of domination, the sociology of a symbolic revolution in painting;[66] then, in a sort of conclusion to his teaching, he analysed research into the sociology of science in general and the sociology of sociology in particular,[67] as if to remind his audience, in opposition to a certain kind of radical relativism, that it is possible, given the right social circumstances – precisely those that constitute the scientific field – to produce truths that are not reducible to the social world that produces them.

Summary of Lectures of 1984–85

Having elaborated the concepts of habitus and field over the last few years, we may now undertake an analysis of the relations between the two notions, and thus move beyond a purely physicalist description of the field as a field of potential forces: social fields are objects of knowledge for the agents engaged in them, and the determining effects associated with holding a position in a space are never purely mechanically exerted. What is needed, then, is a sociology of the knowledge (or perception) of the social world. The knowledge of the social world possessed by agents is part of the present and future being of this world. We argue this against the objectivist vision that tends to reduce agents' representations to more or less well-founded illusions (ideology, or spontaneous sociology) that science has merely to brush aside in establishing its objective viewpoint. But also against the radical perspectivism (or marginalism) that reduces the social world to the universe of viewpoints that can be adopted towards it. It is in the field as a field of forces that the source of the different visions that go to make up a field of forces is to be found: these visions are directly linked to the agent's position by the intermediary of the specific interests that motivate them, and the habitus that is, at least partly, the product of the determining factors associated with their position. This relation between the world perceived and our cognitive structures enables us to understand how the social world commonly presents itself as something that 'goes without saying'.

Insofar as viewpoints are rooted in the same space that enfolds them as they perceive it, visions of the social world are necessarily different or even antagonistic, and the field of forces is at once the source and the goal of struggles over its present and future being: the struggle for legitimate vision and for knowledge as power, in which the scholar, whether he likes it or not, is himself caught up, helps to transform or

Summary of Lectures of 1984–85 273

conserve the field of forces that underlies the agents' standpoints. In this struggle, the holders of cultural capital, which confers in particular the ability to articulate visions of the practical world and translate them into an objectified, public and official, in fact quasi-juridical, state (cf. the link between speaking and laying down the law, observed by Benveniste), possess a considerable advantage. The theory effect, as a power to make things manifest (and make people believe), helps to bring into full existence, even to create, social realities (especially groups) through the power of *nomination* and validation. Because the social world is an object of cognition and recognition, existing socially also means being perceived, being seen and seen-to-be-seen, 'known' (as we say of a writer or an artist) and recognised, *nobilis*, that is, different (from the common or the obscure), but with a recognised and pertinent difference, liable to be recognised by agents possessing the ability to discern the differences recognised as pertinent in a given social universe (the right difference might be based on discretion – one kind of chosen discretion, for instance, might be the unobtrusive (colourless) bourgeois discretion of rejecting socially reprehensible differences, such as the ostentatious vulgarity of the show-off). The passage from a practical, silent vision, unaware of itself, to a vision represented, whether in language or in some objectified form (a work of art or a monument, for instance), is accompanied by a transmutation of the thing represented (whence the importance of the language, including euphemisms, used in political struggles). The theory effect is never more visible than in the political usage of prediction, attempting to make the thing predicted exist by showing it in advance.

We may use this logic to understand all the forms of struggles for classification, struggles aiming to conserve or transform the current classifications (in matters of gender, nation, region, age and of course social status), especially by transforming or retaining the words – which are often euphemisms – used to designate individuals, groups or institutions. Political sociology is thus a sociology of the symbolic forms of perception of the social world and thereby of the construction of this world, or, in a way, a contribution to the empirical analysis of our 'ways of worldmaking': which entail, for instance, all our everyday political efforts to impose our viewpoint particularly of our selves (including the labour of presentation and – objectified – representation of the self) or our own group, or to impose our vision of divisions, connections and distances (with processions, marches and demonstrations where groups display themselves as groups, with their divisions and hierarchies), or to create real connections or separations (such as marriage and divorce). Among all these processes at work in the

274   *Summary of Lectures of 1984–85*

constitution of groups, we should pay particular attention to those that lead to the production of *corporate bodies* (exercising an effect of the corps distinct from the effect of position). The social world is a site of struggle between agents who bring to these struggles on the one hand the power, acquired in previous struggles, that they hold in this world, and, on the other hand, the cognitive structures that are the product of their incorporation of the structures of this very same world.

The political struggle has as its goal the monopoly of legitimate symbolic violence, that is, the *nomos*, as legitimate principle of vision and division (*nemo*). This symbolic power is incarnated in the law and in all forms of official *nomination*, guaranteed by the State (deeds of property, academic qualifications, professional titles, etc.), that assign to individuals their known and recognised social identity. We see in passing that the sociologist is not the nomothete who decides who is right in conflicts over the legitimate vision (of region, nation or class, for instance), but someone who makes a scientific study of the struggle for the monopoly of the nomothetic effect (whence the antinomy between the viewpoint of the jurist and the viewpoint of the sociologist, who presents the jurist not only with a rival viewpoint, but with a sociology of the jurist's viewpoint).

The juridical discourse is essentially performative, that is, magical: it is an act of constitution or consecration (of people or things) which settles conflicts and social negotiations over words and social matters (as exemplified in our civil status, which fixes the names and titles constitutive of an identity): the most typical effect of the reason of State is the effect of validation (*homologation*, from the Greek *homologein*) or *codification* (as the objectification of a consensus) that is exercised through social operations as apparently simple as the awarding of a certificate. The *expert* (doctor or jurist, for instance) is someone who is socially mandated to produce a viewpoint recognised as transcending individual viewpoints (the medical certificate for illness, disability, incapacity – or competence), and who thereby assigns universally recognised rights to the certified individual. The education system, through the award of academic qualifications and certificates of competence guaranteed by the State, exercises an effect that is analogous, but in specific terms that we should analyse. The State economists and sociologists (INSEE), following the model of the Roman *censor*, produce a *census*, that is, a validated, authorised vision, that finally gains recognition as transcending the conflicts between rival visions and divisions. The State thus appears as a sort of central bank, which guarantees all the acts of guarantee (certificates) in the last instance, and whose verdicts on a certain number of key issues put an end to the

Summary of Lectures of 1984–85   275

struggle of all against all to impose their truth on the social world.

In the second sessions [the 'seminars'] we analysed one example of a symbolic revolution: the exercise in subversion of social and mental structures that Manet – and the Impressionists – mounted against the art of the Academy (the study of which will be the subject of a forthcoming publication).[1]

Notes

Editorial Note

1 Pierre Bourdieu, *Science of Science and Reflexivity*, trans. Richard Nice (Cambridge: Polity, 2004).
2 Pierre Bourdieu, *On the State*, trans. David Fernbach (Cambridge: Polity, 2015).
3 Pierre Bourdieu, *General Sociology*, vol. 1, *Classification Struggles*, trans. Peter Collier (Cambridge: Polity, 2018), vol. 2, *Habitus and Field*, trans. Peter Collier (Cambridge: Polity, 2019).
4 See the editors' note in Bourdieu, *On the State*, pp. xi–xii.

Lecture of 7 March 1985

1 In fact Bourdieu starts focusing on this topic in the second session of the next lecture, on 14 March.
2 Robert Alan Dahl, *Who Governs?* (New Haven: Yale University Press, 1961).
3 See the Lecture of 2 May 1985. On the notion of social capital, see Pierre Bourdieu, 'Le capital social. Notes provisoires', *Actes de la recherche en sciences sociales*, no. 31, 1980, pp. 2–3; 'The Forms of Capital', in John G. Richardson (ed.), *Handbook of Theory and Research for the Sociology of Education* (New York: Greenwood Press, 1986), pp. 241–58.
4 Pierre Bourdieu, *Homo Academicus*, trans. Peter Collier (Cambridge: Polity, 1988).
5 When he returns to his analysis of Durkheim the following year, Bourdieu refers to *Pragmatism and Sociology*, trans. J. C. Whitehouse (Cambridge: Cambridge University Press, 1983).
6 Pascal, *Pensées*, ed. L. Lafuma, trans. John Warrington (London: Dent, Everyman's Library, 1960), 217 [399–448], p. 58.
7 The rest of this lecture was not recorded because of a technical problem. The text that follows here has been reconstructed from notes taken by Bernard Convert, which he has kindly transmitted to us, for which we are most grateful.
8 Pierre Bourdieu, 'The Paradox of the Sociologist', in *Sociology in Question*, trans. Richard Nice (London: Sage, 1993), pp. 54–9.

Notes to pp. 7–9 277

9 See Émile Durkheim, *The Rules of Sociological Method*, trans. W. D. Halls (New York: The Free Press, 1982), p. 32, where Durkheim sets as the rule for his method the fact of treating social facts 'as things' (and not that social facts 'are things', as he has been alleged to say, turning a simple methodological precept into an ontological affirmation).

10 Maurice Merleau-Ponty uses this expression in a commentary on Leibniz: *Phenomenology of Perception*, trans. Donald A. Landes (Abingdon: Routledge, 2012 [1945]), p. 69.

11 Karl Marx and Friedrich Engels, *The German Ideology*, Part I (1845), www. marxists.org.

12 Durkheim, *The Rules of Sociological Method*, pp. 32ff.

13 See Pierre Bourdieu, *Forms of Capital*, trans. Peter Collier (Cambridge: Polity, 2021), Lecture of 19 April 1984, pp. 338–9. '"When a man who is happy compares his position with that of one who is unhappy, he is not content with the fact of his happiness, but desires something more, namely the right to this happiness, the consciousness that he has earned this good fortune, in contrast to the unfortunate one who must equally have earned his misfortune. Our everyday experience proves that there exists just such a need for reassurance as to the legitimacy or deservedness of one's happiness, whether this involves political success, superior economic status, bodily health, success in the game of love, or anything else. What the privileged classes require of religion, if anything at all, is this psychologic reassurance of legitimacy." This theodicy of "good fortune" is opposed to a "theodicy of disprivilege".' See Max Weber, *The Sociology of Religion*, trans. Ephraim Fischoff (Boston: Beacon Press, 1964 [1920]), pp. 107, 113; and 'Theodicy, Salvation and Rebirth' in ibid., pp. 138–50.

14 On perspectivism in Nietzsche, see Bourdieu, *Classification Struggles*, Lecture of 16 June 1982, pp. 126–9.

15 Arthur Schopenhauer, *The World as Will and Representation*, trans. Jill Berman (London: J. M. Dent, 1995 [1818]).

16 Probably a reference to the theme of the vulnerability of the social order in Erving Goffman, *The Presentation of Self in Everyday Life* (Harmondsworth: Penguin, 1969).

17 See ibid., where the analogy with the theatre is explicit, in 'Performances', p. 78: 'ordinary social intercourse is itself put together, by the exchange of dramatically inflated actions, counteractions, and terminating replies [. . .]. All the world is not, of course, a stage, but the crucial ways in which it isn't are not easy to specify.'

18 Alfred Schütz, 'Common-sense and Scientific Interpretation of Human Action', in *Collected Papers*, vol. 2 (The Hague: Martinus Nijhoff, 1964). According to a formula of Schütz often quoted by ethnomethodologists (which Bourdieu has in mind during the rest of the paragraph), 'we are all sociologists in a practical sense'.

19 An allusion to Harold Garfinkel, *Studies in Ethnomethodology* (Englewood Cliffs: Prentice Hall, 1967).

20 A reference to the dispute within the First International between Marx's 'authoritarianism' and Bakunin's 'libertarian' socialism. This dispute would have been familiar to the audience of the lectures, since it had been much referred to and commented on in the 1970s.

21 On the figure of the sociologist as sociological midwife, see Pierre Bourdieu et

278 *Notes to pp. 10–17*

al., *The Weight of the World*, trans. Priscilla Parkhurst Ferguson (Cambridge: Polity, 1999), especially the last chapter, entitled 'Understanding', p. 621.

22 A reference to the image of the camera obscura that Marx and Engels use in *The German Ideology*, Part I (1845): 'If in all ideology men and their circumstances appear upside-down as in a *camera obscura*, this phenomenon arises just as much from their historical life-process as the inversion of objects on the retina does from their physical life-process.'

Lecture of 14 March 1985

1 In the three first lectures of the previous year (1, 8 and 15 March 1984), when discussing the 'hit parade of the intellectuals', Bourdieu had mentioned in particular the weak degree of institutionalisation of the intellectual field.

2 Bourdieu may be thinking of the *Kunstkompass*, the annual classification of the most noted living artists, established for the first time in 1970 by the German economic journalist Willie Bongard.

3 This is an echo of the 'provisional morality' adopted by Descartes ('In order that I might not remain irresolute in my actions while reason obliged me to suspend my judgement', René Descartes, *Discourse on Method*, trans. Arthur Wollaston [Harmondsworth: Penguin, 1960], p. 53).

4 In Greek the word *theoria* signifies 'contemplation', 'view of a spectacle', 'intellectual view'.

5 See Émile Durkheim, *The Elementary Forms of Religious Life*, trans. Carol Cosman (Oxford: Oxford University Press, 2001 [1912]), esp. pp. 327–35; Émile Durkheim and Marcel Mauss, 'De quelques formes primitives de classification. Contribution à l'étude des représentations collectives' (1903), in Marcel Mauss, *Oeuvres*, t. II (Paris: Minuit, 1974), pp. 13–89.

6 The French neo-Marxists grouped around Louis Althusser in the 1960s (Althusser et al., *Reading Capital. The Complete Edition* [London: Verso, 2016 [1968]]) took the term 'Träger', used occasionally by Marx, as one of the key words of their 'anti-humanist' approach, within which the social agents were only the supports or the bearers of the role that is assigned to them in the process of production.

7 Barney G. Glazer and Anselm L. Strauss, *Awareness of Dying* (Chicago: Aldine, 1965).

8 This formula, which Bourdieu quotes in different circumstances (see, for example, *Distinction*, trans. Richard Nice [London: Routledge, 1984], p. 444), is in fact due to Maxime Chastaing in *La Philosophie de Virginia Woolf* (Paris: PUF, 1951), p. 48: '[They are] briefly, general ideas. But these ideas are in fact generals' ideas.' The text by Virginia Woolf that Chastaing refers to has not been definitely identified, but it is most probably a passage from the short story *The Mark on the Wall* (1917): 'these generalizations are very worthless. The military sound of the word is enough. It recalls leading articles, cabinet ministers – a whole class of things indeed which as a child one thought the thing itself, the standard thing, the real thing, from which one could not depart save at the risk of nameless damnation ... Generalizations bring back somehow Sunday in London, Sunday afternoon walks, Sunday luncheons, and also ways of speaking of the dead, clothes, and habits – like the habit of sitting all together in one room until a certain hour, although nobody liked it'. Virginia

Notes to pp. 17–25 279

Woolf, 'The Mark on the Wall', in *The Mark on the Wall and Other Short Fiction* (Oxford: Oxford University Press, 2008), p. 6.

9 In this formula Bourdieu may be remembering some remarks by Marx such as 'Only as a personification of capital is the capitalist respectable. As such, he shares with the miser an absolute drive towards self-enrichment. But what appears in the miser as the mania of an individual is in the capitalist the effect of a social mechanism in which he is merely a cog.' *Capital*, vol. 1, trans. Ben Fowles (London: Penguin, 1990), p. 739. Or perhaps: 'The capitalist is just as enslaved by the relationships of capitalism as is his opposite pole, the worker, albeit in a quite different manner' (p. 990).

10 Pierre Bourdieu, 'La production de la croyance. Contribution à une économie des biens symboliques', *Actes de la recherche en sciences sociales*, no. 13, 1977, pp. 3–43. 'The Production of Belief: Contribution to an Economy of Symbolic Goods', trans. Richard Nice, *Media Culture Society*, no. 2, 1980, pp. 261–93.

11 Like physicists or economists, Bourdieu uses the term *hysteresis* (based on a Greek verb meaning 'to be late') to designate a phenomenon that persists when its cause has disappeared. He applies it, in particular in *Distinction*, to the habitus and its categories of perception, in order to express an idea very close to the idea illustrated by the 'Don Quixote' effect: the gap between the conditions of acquisition of the dispositions and their activation.

12 This is no doubt Georg Simmel, 'Female Culture', in *On Women, Sexuality and Love*, trans. Guy Oakes (New Haven: Yale University Press, 1984 [1902]): 'The culture of humanity, even in its pure objective contents, has so to speak nothing asexual and it is not at all placed by its objectivity somewhere beyond man and woman. Even more, our objective culture is everywhere masculine, except in some rare sectors.'

13 Bourdieu had developed this point the previous year, especially in the Lecture of 10 May 1984 in *Forms of Capital*.

14 This is a reference to Erving Goffman, 'Symbols of Class Status', *British Journal of Sociology*, vol. 2, no. 4, 1951, p. 297.

15 S.A.S. was a popular series of spy novels written by Gérard de Villiers. S.A.S. was a kind of aristocratic James Bond. (Translator)

16 Minuit was and is a serious left-wing publisher, whose authors include . . . Pierre Bourdieu. (Translator)

17 Alfred Schütz, 'Making Music Together: A Study in Social Relationship', *Social Research*, vol. 18, no. 1/4, 1951, pp. 76–97.

18 Alfred Schütz, *The Phenomenology of the Social World*, trans. G. Walsh and J. Lehnert (Evanston: Northwestern University Press, 1967 [1932]).

19 'The idea that a prediction may have influence upon the predicted event is a very old one. Oedipus, in the legend, killed his father whom he had never seen before; and this was the direct result of the prophecy which had caused his father to abandon him. This is why I suggest the name "Oedipus effect" for the influence of the prediction upon the predicted event.' Karl Popper, *The Poverty of Historicism* (London: Routledge and Kegan Paul, 1961), p. 13.

20 An allusion to the fact that, approaching questions of justice, Aristotle treats the problems of distribution both in arithmetical terms and in terms of justice: 'Now the points for our enquiry in respect of Justice and Injustice are, what kind of actions are their object-matter, and what kind of a mean state Justice is, and between what points the abstract principle of it, i.e. the Just, is a mean.' Aristotle, *Nicomachean Ethics*, Book V, trans. D. P. Chase (Oxford 1847),

280   *Notes to pp. 26–29*

p. 151.
21 See Émile Durkheim, *Textes, II: Religion, morale, anomie* (Paris: Minuit, 1975), chapter 'Morale et science des moeurs', pp. 255–86.
22 Bourdieu is perhaps thinking of the book by John Rawls, *A Theory of Justice* (Cambridge MA: Harvard University Press, 1971.)
23 During the year 1982–83, in Bourdieu, *Classification Struggles*.
24 The Musée d'Orsay was due to open in 1986. At the precise moment of this lecture there was an exhibition at the Grand Palais of 'Impressionism and the French Landscape', which, following an exhibition devoted to the centenary of Impressionism held in 1974, inspired great enthusiasm.
25 On the lines and elaboration of Bourdieu's research into the artistic field, see Christophe Charles, '*Opus Infinitum:* Genesis and Structure of a Work without End', in Pierre Bourdieu, *Manet: A Symbolic Revolution*, trans. Peter Collier and Margaret Rigaud-Drayton (Cambridge: Polity Press, 2017), pp. 351–61.
26 Bourdieu does not seem to have taken this study of music further. It is an artistic field where he published little, apart from 'Bref impromptu sur Beethoven, artiste entrepreneur' (1981), *Sociétés & Représentations*, no. 11, 2001, pp. 13–18, and 'Les mésaventures de l'amateur', in Claude Samuel (ed.), *Éclats/Boulez* (Paris: Éditions du Centre Georges Pompidou, 1986), pp. 74–5. His journal *Actes de la recherche en sciences sociales* did, however, publish an issue on 'Musique et musiciens' (no. 110, 1995) and a few individual articles, in particular one by Alfred Willener on Haydn (no. 75, 1988) and one by Carl E. Schorske on Mahler (no. 100, 1993).
27 This question will be at the centre of the lectures given by Bourdieu at the Collège de France in 1998–99.
28 Bourdieu had already approached this question in 'L'invention de la vie d'artiste', *Actes de la recherche en sciences sociales*, nos. 1–2, 1975, pp. 67–93 (the article provides one of the starting points for Pierre Bourdieu, *The Rules of Art*, trans. Susan Emanuel [Cambridge: Polity Press, 1996]), and in Pierre Bourdieu and Yvette Delsaut, 'Pour une sociologie de la perception', *Actes de la recherche en sciences sociales*, no. 40, 1981, pp. 3–9.
29 Perhaps 1883.
30 The Villa Medicis, which is the home of the French Academy in Rome, no longer depends on the Institut de France but is still subject to State management, as was shown a few weeks before the lecture, in December 1984, by the nomination of a new director by the President of the Republic.
31 Jules Laforgue, *Oeuvres complètes*, t. III: *Mélanges posthumes* (Paris: Mercure de France, 1903; re-ed. Geneva: Slatkine, 1979), pp. 144–5; trans. William Jay Smith, *Art News*, LV, May 1956, pp. 43–5.
32 For instance: 'Do you know why I have so patiently translated Edgar Poe? Because he resembled me. The first time that I opened one of his books, I was thrilled and horrified to see not only subjects that I had dreamed of but SENTENCES that I had thought up which had been written by him twenty years before'. Letter to Théophile Thoré, 20 June 1864, in Charles Baudelaire, *Correspondance*, t. II (Paris: Gallimard, 'Bibliothèque de la Pléiade', 1973), p. 386.
33 Gustave Courbet, 'Lettre a Maurice Richard', *Le Siècle*, 23 June 1870.
34 Jacques Thuillier, *Peut-on parler d'une peinture 'pompier'?* (Paris: PUF, 1984). (Bourdieu mentions the Éditions du Collège de France no doubt because the book was published in the collection 'Essais et conférences du Collège de

Notes to pp. 29–39   281

35 James A. Harding, *Artistes Pompiers: French Academic Art in the Nineteenth Century* (Hoboken NJ: Academy Editions [John Wiley], 1979).

36 An allusion to two frequently quoted sentences: 'The owl of Minerva begins its flight only with the onset of dusk'. G. W. F. Hegel, *Elements of the Philosophy of Right*, trans. H. B. Nisbet (Cambridge: Cambridge University Press, 1991 [1820]), p. 23. And 'Men make their own history, but not of their own free will; not under circumstances they themselves have chosen but under the given and inherited circumstances with which they are directly confronted'. Karl Marx, 'The Eighteenth Brumaire of Louis Bonaparte', in *Surveys from Exile* (Harmondsworth: Penguin, 1973), p. 146 – often presented in the form of this aphorism: 'Men make history but they do not know what history they are making.'

37 Émile Zola, *My Hatreds*, trans. Palomba Paves-Yashinsky and Jack Yashinsky (Lewiston NY: Edwin Mellen Press, 1991), p. 17.

38 It sounds like Rewald, but John Rewald was a specialist of a later period. Perhaps Bourdieu could have read Albert Boime, 'The Second Republic's Contest for the Figure of the Republic', *Art Bulletin*, vol. 53, no. 1, 1971, pp. 68–83.

39 This term, used during the Vatican II Council (1962–65) to designate the 'modernisation' of the Roman Catholic Church, means 'bringing up to date' in Italian.

40 This is the start of a line from a poem by Horace, whose original sense has been distorted and turned into an academic principle: 'Poetry's like painting: there are pictures that attract you more nearer to, and others from further away. This needs the shadows, that to be seen in the light, not fearing the critic's sharp eye: this pleased once, that, though examined ten thousand times, still pleases.' Horace, *Ars Poetica*, ll. 333–65, trans. A. S. Kline, at https://www.poetryintranslation.com.

41 This is no doubt: 'A work of art is a corner of nature seen through a temperament.' Émile Zola, 'Les réalistes du Salon', *L'Événement*, 11 May 1866.

42 On the fashion designers who in the 1960s and 1970s wanted to 'go down into the street', see Pierre Bourdieu and Yvette Delsaut, 'Le couturier et sa griffe: contribution à une théorie de la magie', *Actes de la recherche en sciences sociales*, no. 1, 1975, esp. p. 13.

43 Joseph R. Levenson, *Modern China and Its Confucian Past* (New York: Doubleday, 1958).

44 Jacques Lethève, *La Vie quotidienne des artistes français au XIXe siècle* (Paris: Hachette, 1968).

45 See Bourdieu, 'The Production of Belief', p. 261.

46 Lethève, *La Vie quotidienne des artistes français au XIXe siècle*, p. 146.

47 Ernst Gombrich, *Art and Illusion* (Oxford: Phaidon, 1960), pp. 162–9. [In fact Gombrich is expounding Vasari's comments on Renaissance art. (Translator)]

48 Nikolaus Pevsner, *Pioneers of the Modern Movement from William Morris to Walter Gropius* (London: Faber & Faber, 1936).

49 Jules Combarieu and René Dumesnil, *Histoire de la musique*, vol. 3 (Paris: Armand Colin, 1955), pp. 467–8.

282 *Notes to pp. 42–45*

Lecture of 28 March 1985

1 The text by Durkheim has not been identified. In his lectures on pragmatism in 1913–14 he says something similar: 'Individual minds, however, are finite, and none can work from all points of view at once . . . Consequently, each mind is free to choose the point of view from which it feels itself most competent to view things. These are probably partial truths, but all these partial truths come together in the collective consciousness and find their limits and their necessary complements . . . Thus, on the one hand, scientific truth is not incompatible with the diversity of minds; and on the other, as social groups become increasingly complex, it is impossible that society should have a single sense of itself.' Durkheim, *Pragmatism and Sociology*, p. 92.
2 Paul A. Samuelson, *Economics* (New York: McGraw Hill, 2009 [1948]). 'Because a labor leader has been successful in several rounds of collective bargaining, he may have the false impression that he is an expert in matters of wage economics. The manager of a firm who has "balanced the books" may, wrongly, consider his opinions on price control to be irrefutable. A banker who has managed to consolidate his funds may conclude (wrongly) that he knows everything there is to know about the creation of wealth . . . When he composes a general introductory treatise, the economist is considering the functioning of the economy as a whole rather than from the point of view of any particular group or unit.'
3 Unless Bourdieu is thinking of a more precise watershed, it was in the 1960s, when the first books by Michel Foucault in particular appeared, and *Nietzsche et la Philosophie* by Gilles Deleuze (1962), that Nietzsche became 'fashionable'.
4 On perspectivism, see also Bourdieu, *Classification Struggles*, pp. 126–8; *Habitus and Field*, p. 55.
5 Friedrich Nietzsche, *Beyond Good and Evil*, trans. R. J. Hollingdale (London: Penguin, 2003 [1886]), § 210.
6 Merleau-Ponty, *Phenomenology of Perception*, p. 69.
7 In 1965 Louis Althusser introduced the theme of the 'epistemological break' to designate the passage from ideology to science in Marx's thought in 1845–46. Louis Althusser, *For Marx*, trans. Ben Brewster (London: Verso, 2006).
8 Émile Benveniste, *Dictionary of Indo-European Concepts and Society*, trans. Elizabeth Palmer (Chicago: Hau Books, 2016), Book IV, chapter 1, *Rex*, pp. 307–12.
9 Georges Duby, *The Three Orders: Feudal Society Imagined*, trans. Arthur Goldhammer (Chicago: University of Chicago Press, 1982); for Georges Dumézil, see especially *L'Idéologie des trois fonctions dans les épopées des peuples indo-européens* (Paris: Gallimard, 1968).
10 In 1982 INSEE's nomenclature of socio-professional categories had been revised, under the influence in particular of *Distinction*. Some of the administrators of INSEE who were active in this revision, such as Alain Desrosières, had been detached to Bourdieu's research centre, the Centre for European Sociology, at the end of the 1970s.
11 Bourdieu is referring to the 'Frankfurt School' of thinkers inspired by Marx, including in particular Theodor Adorno (one of whose books, *Mahler. Une physionomie musicale*, appeared in translation in 1976 in the series edited by Bourdieu at Éditions de Minuit), Max Horkheimer, Herbert Marcuse, Walter

Notes to pp. 46–54 283

Benjamin, and among the generation of Bourdieu's contemporaries, Jürgen Habermas, whose theses are discussed in several passages of Bourdieu's *Pascalian Meditations*, trans. Richard Nice (Cambridge: Polity, 2000).

12 Bourdieu returns to this critique of a branch of the sociology of science in his Lecture of 19 June 1986, and, two years later, more systematically, in *Science of Science and Reflexivity*.

13 Bourdieu had already made a comparison of this kind in his article 'Public Opinion Does Not Exist', in *Sociology in Question*, pp. 149–57, which may be consulted for other points made in this lecture.

14 Bourdieu here is developing the themes of the conclusion to *Distinction*, 'Classes and Classifications', pp. 466–4.

15 An allusion to the etymology of the word 'theory' that Bourdieu often recalls: the Greek verb *theorein* means to 'observe' or 'contemplate'.

16 'The image I get of thinking is that the mind is simply carrying on a conversation . . . I call belief a statement . . .' Plato, *Theaetetus*, trans. Robin H. Waterfield (Harmondsworth: Penguin, 1987), § 190a. [Except that Plato continues: 'but one which is not made aloud and to someone else, but in silence to oneself'. (Translator)]

17 See in particular Goffman, 'Symbols of Class Status', p. 297.

18 See Pierre Bourdieu, *The Logic of Practice*, trans. Richard Nice (Cambridge: Polity, 1990).

19 Claude Lévi-Strauss, *The Savage Mind* (Chicago: University of Chicago Press, 1968 [1962]).

20 Bourdieu had on several occasions during his lectures raised the question of the taxonomies deployed by art critics (for instance, *Habitus and Field*, pp. 132–3, 16 November 1982) and suggested some empirical analyses of these taxonomies in *Distinction*.

21 An allusion to the passage in the *Theaetetus* (172e–173a) that Bourdieu often quotes for the notion of *skholè*: the philosopher has all the time in the world, whereas the lawyers in court only dispose of the time allotted them by the *clepsydre*, a water-clock that, like the hourglass, limits their speaking time.

22 Bourdieu is no doubt thinking in what follows of Louis Marin's study, *La Critique de discours sur la* Logique de Port Royal *et les* Pensées *de Pascal* (Paris: Minuit, 1975). Michel Foucault had also published 'La Grammaire générale de Port-Royal', *Langages*, vol. 2, no. 7, 1967, pp. 7–15.

23 Lucien Lévy-Bruhl, *Primitive Mentality* (Boston: Beacon Press, 1966 [1922]).

24 Vilfredo Pareto, *Traité de sociologie générale* (Paris: Payot, 1917), chapter 13, esp. §2544. (*The Mind and Society*, 4 vols., 1935, *Trattato di sociologia generale*).

25 See Bourdieu, '"Youth" Is Just a Word', in *Sociology in Question*, pp. 94–102.

26 Georges Duby, 'Dans la France du Nord-Ouest au XIIe siècle: les "jeunes" dans la société aristocratique', *Annales ESC*, vol. 19, no. 5, 1964, pp. 835–46.

27 Alain, *Sentiments, passions et signes* (Paris: Gallimard, 1958 [1926]), chapter 15, 'Les ages et les passions', pp. 89–90. For instance: 'The virtue of the adolescent is modesty; and the virtue of the mature man is justice; and the virtue of the old is wisdom' (p. 90).

28 See Bourdieu, *Homo Academicus*, pp. 9–10.

29 In the Lecture of 19 May 1982 (*Classification Struggles*, p. 62). The survey that Bourdieu refers to was conducted by Yvette Delsaut at Denain, near Valenciennes, in 1978.

284 *Notes to pp. 56–66*

30 Referring to comments made during his survey, Bourdieu takes as his example a television personality of the time, Yves Mourousi, the 'popular' presenter of the One O'clock News on Channel One.

31 André Glucksmann for instance had published *The Master Thinkers* (London: Harper Collins, 1980 [1977]).

32 The Indianist Gérard Fussman had been appointed to the Collège de France as professor of the 'History of the Indian World'. The work referred to is perhaps 'Pouvoir central et régions dans l'Inde ancienne: le problème de l'Empire maurya', *Annales ESC*, vol. 37, no. 4, 1982, pp. 621–47.

33 The present town of Volgograd had been named 'Stalingrad' (Russian for 'Stalin's town') in 1925, before being rebaptised in 1961 at the time of 'de-Stalinisation'.

34 The study of these Athenian religious festivities, whose processions are represented in a famous Parthenon frieze, was intended to become the subject of an issue of *Actes de la recherche en sciences sociales* planned by Bourdieu. See Olivier Christin, 'Comment se représente-t-on le monde social?', *Actes de la recherche en sciences sociales*, no. 154, 2004, pp. 3–9 (which reproduces Bourdieu's preparatory notes for the issue).

35 See Marcel Duchamp, *Duchamp du signe, Écrits* (Paris: Flammarion, 1994 [1959]), p. 174.

36 André Gide, *The Counterfeiters*, trans. Dorothy Bussy (New York: Random House, 1973 [1925]), pp. 332–3. Bourdieu returns to this text in *The Rules of Art*, p. 138.

37 This expression, the 'New Novel', refers to the works of a group of French writers, published in the 1950s by Jérôme Lindon at Éditions de Minuit.

38 Bourdieu, 'The Production of Belief'.

39 Bourdieu spent three whole years of his lectures at the Collège de France (1989–92) on the sociology of the State. These lectures were published in 2012 as *Sur l'État* (*On the State*).

40 See Pierre Bourdieu and Erec R. Koch, 'The Invention of the Artist's Life', *Yale French Studies*, no. 73, 1987, pp. 75–103, and the analysis of *Sentimental Education* republished in *The Rules of Art*, pp. 17–81.

41 An allusion to the 'Troubles' in Northern Ireland which started at the end of the 1960s.

42 Marx opposes the '*radical* revolution' to the 'partial, merely political revolution, the revolution which leaves the pillars of the building standing'. Karl Marx, 'A Contribution to the Critique of Hegel's *Philosophy of Right*', in *Early Writings*, trans. Rodney Livingston and Gregor Benton (London: Penguin, 1975), p. 253.

43 An allusion to the 'Iranian revolution' which overthrew the monarchy and established the Islamic Republic in 1979.

44 See Bourdieu, *Distinction*, in particular the chapter 'The Sense of Distinction', pp. 260–7.

45 See *Forms of Capital*, the Lecture of 10 May 1984.

46 *The Funeral of Phocion* by Nicolas Poussin (1648) represents a full-scale landscape, but in relation with a historical subject (Phocion was an Athenian general who had been driven to suicide).

47 The name of the author is indistinct, but it could be Rensselaer W. Lee, *Ut Pictura Poesis: The Humanistic Theory of Painting* (New York: Norton, 1967). On this formula, see above, Lecture of 14 March, note 40.

Notes to pp. 67–73 285

48 Albert Boime, *The Academy and French Painting in the 19th Century* (London: Phaidon, 1971), pp. 19–20.
49 Joseph C. Sloane, *French Painting between the Past and the Present: Artists, Critics and Traditions from 1848 to 1870* (Princeton: Princeton University Press, 1951).
50 Pierre Bourdieu, 'Reading, Readers, the Literate, Literature', *In Other Words*, trans. Matthew Adamson (Cambridge: Polity, 1990), pp. 94–105.
51 After these lectures, Gilbert Dahan gave a translation of a passage from Gilbert de la Porrée (extracted from his prologue to *De Trinitate* by Boetius): 'Not wishing to apply our own authority but desiring to transmit the intentions of the author (*sensus auctoris*) that we have perceived through a preliminary study of the sense, we have been attentive not merely to the words but also to the arguments ... But since there are two kinds of viewers, that of the *auctores*, who formulate their own thoughts, and that of the *lectores*, who report those of others; since among the *lectores*, some are *recitatores*, who repeat the very words of the *auctores*, and decide according to their causes, the others are *interpretes*, who clarify in more explicit terms what had been said in an obscure manner by the *auctores*; we place ourselves in the category of the *lectores*, not as *recitatores* but as *interpretes*, we undertake a labour of explicitation (*reducimus*) of the metaphors into plain language, of the schemas into their developments, of the *novitates* into their rules.' Gilbert Dahan, 'Le commentaire medieval de la Bible. Le passage au sens spiritual', in Marie-Odile Gooulot-Cazé (ed.), *Le Commentaire entre tradition et innovation* (Paris: Vrin, 2000), pp. 214–15.
52 Luc Boltanski, 'Pouvoir et impuissance. Projet intellectuel et sexualité dans le *Journal* d'Amiel', *Actes de la recherche en sciences sociales*, nos. 5–6, 1975, pp. 80–111.
53 An allusion to the 'Letter on Monsieur Pascal's *Pensées*' by Voltaire in his *Philosophical Letters*, 1734.
54 An allusion to the painting *The Romans of the Decadence* by Thomas Couturre (1847), already mentioned in the previous lecture.
55 In one of his lectures on teaching in the Jesuit colleges, Durkheim remarks that 'the Greco-Roman world that the pupils were bathed in was emptied of everything Greek and Roman and had become an unreal kind of milieu, inhabited by people who had no doubt existed in history, but who presented as they were, had more or less no historical attributes'. Émile Durkheim, *L'Évolution pédagogique en France* (Paris: PUF, 'Quadrige', 2004 [lectures of 1905, published in 1938]), pp. 287–8.
56 Michael Baxandall, *Painting and Experience in Fifteenth-Century Italy* (Oxford: Oxford University Press, 1972), translated by Yvette Delsaut as *L'Oeil du Quattrocento* (Paris: Gallimard, 1985). The reference is to chapter 2.
57 Michael Baxendall, 'Jacques-Louis David et les romantiques allemands', unpublished paper, Paris, 7 January 1985.

Lecture of 18 April 1985

1 Bourdieu had started his inaugural lecture at the Collège de France with a similar reflection: 'One ought to be able to deliver a lecture, even an inaugural lecture, without wondering what right one has to do so: the institution is

286 *Notes to pp. 76–80*

there to protect one from that question and the anguish inseparable from the arbitrariness of all new beginnings.' 'Lecture on the Lecture', *In Other Words*, p. 177.

2 This aspect was developed in the first lectures given by Bourdieu, *Classification Struggles*, pp. 6ff.

3 This term alludes to a phrase used by George Berkeley (in Latin, *esse est percipi*) extracted from the following passage: 'That neither our thoughts, nor passions, nor ideas formed by the imagination, exist without the mind, is what everybody will allow. And it seems no less evident that the various sensations or ideas imprinted on the sense, however blended or combined together (that is, whatever objects they compose), cannot exist otherwise than in a mind perceiving them. I think an intuitive knowledge may be obtained of this by any one that shall attend to what is meant by the term exist, when applied to sensible things. The table I write on I say exists, that is, I see and feel it; and if I were out of my study I should say it existed – meaning thereby that if I was in my study I might perceive it, or that some other spirit actually does perceive it. There was an odour, that is, it was smelt; there was a sound, that is, it was heard; a colour or figure, and it was perceived by sight or touch. This is all that I can understand by these and the like expressions. For as to what is said of the absolute existence of unthinking things without any relation to their being perceived, that seems perfectly unintelligible. Their *esse* is *percipi*, nor is it possible they should have any existence out of the minds or thinking things which perceive them.' George Berkeley, *A Treatise Concerning the Principles of Human Knowledge* (Mineola: Dover, 2003 [1710]), Part I, § 3.

4 Bourdieu is no doubt thinking of the sense that the word 'distinguished' had in the past, as illustrated in dictionaries that refer to Molière's Misanthropist, who says: 'I want to be distinguished.' Molière, *Le Misanthrope*, I. I.

5 The Greek word *diakritikos* means 'apt to divide', 'apt to distinguish'. The term has been much used following, if not Saussure himself, then Merleau-Ponty, on the subject of the linguistic sign, to express the fact that 'the terms of language are engendered only by the differences between them ... taken singly signs do not signify anything'. Maurice Merleau-Ponty, *Signs*, trans. Richard C. McCleary (Evanston: Northwestern University Press, 1964 [1960]), p. 39.

6 The Greek words *crisis* and *diacrisis* mean 'action or faculty of distinguishing' and consequently 'action of choosing', 'choice', 'election', 'action of separating, deciding'; the prefix '*dia-*' (in *diacrisis*) reinforces the idea of separation. In the analyses that follow, it may be useful to point out that the Latin equivalent of *diacrisis* is *discretio* ('discernment' or 'discrimination').

7 See the exploration in *Distinction*, passim, on the processes of divulging and vulgarising.

8 Bourdieu is referring to the end of the following passage: 'Therefore, on applying my mind to politics, I have resolved to demonstrate by a certain and undoubted course of argument, or to deduce from the very condition of human nature, not what is new and unheard of, but only such things as agree best with practice. And that I might investigate the subject-matter of this science with the same freedom of spirit as we generally use in mathematics, I have laboured carefully, not to mock, lament, or execrate, but to understand human actions.' Benedict de Spinoza, *A Political Treatise*, chapter 1, § 4, in *The Chief Works of Benedict de Spinoza*, trans. R. H. M. Elwes (London: George Bell and Sons, 1891 [1670]).

Notes to pp. 80–91 287

9 In the seventeenth century the word 'discretion' was close to the Latin word *discretio*. In his *Dictionnaire universel* (1690), Furetière defines it as 'prudence, modesty serving to guide our actions and speech' and as 'judgement, discernment [discrimination]', giving for this sense the following example: 'At the age of seven we reach the age of discretion, we know what is good and what is bad.' This sense of the word 'discretion' lives on today in the expression 'at discretion'. Likewise, the word 'discreet' could signify the fact of having discretion, good judgement.

10 The link is clear in Furetière's definition: taste is 'the sense which is given by nature to discern savours' (ibid.).

11 Georges-Théodule Guilbaud, *Éléments de la théorie mathématique des jeux* (Paris: Dunod, 1968), pp. 99–100.

12 See the Lecture of 22 March 1984 in *Forms of Capital*, p. 330, note 13; and *Habitus and Field*, pp. 82–6.

13 Jeremy Bentham was one of the founders of utilitarian philosophy, which is often given as one of the sources of neoclassical economics (which Bourdieu reproaches with having too narrow a concept of the notions of 'interest' and 'economics').

14 *Habitus and Field*, p. 83.

15 The Latin verb *interesse*, whose main meaning is 'to be between', 'to be in the interval', is formed, like the Latin verb *inesse* (literally 'to be in', 'to belong to'), after the verb *esse* (to be).

16 The State doctorate disappeared in 1984. It coexisted with the third-cycle doctorate (created in 1958) but, especially in the literary and historical disciplines, took much longer to complete.

17 See the Lecture of 28 March above, p. 54.

18 Bourdieu has probably taken this observation from Émile Benveniste, who draws attention to the fact that the word *nomos* belongs to a family of words formed from the root *nem-* expressing a notion of division, legality and therefore 'legal division'. Benveniste, *Dictionary of Indo-European Concepts and Society*, p. 58.

19 This metaphor is probably taken from Bergson's re-reading of a phrase from Spinoza ('Mind and body are one and the same thing, conceived first under the attribute of thought, secondly, under the attribute of extension'. Benedict de Spinoza, *The Ethics* (project Gutenberg EBook #3800, 2017, III, note to proposition II). 'With Spinoza, the two terms Thought and Extension are placed, in principle at least, in the same rank. They are, therefore, two translations of one and the same original, or, as Spinoza says, two attributes of one and the same substance, which we must call God.' Henri Bergson, *Creative Evolution* (1907), trans. Arthur Mitchell, project Gutenberg Ebook #26163, 2008, p. 351.

20 One such collection is *Journal de la commune étudiante. Textes et documents: novembre 1967–juin 1968*, textes choisis et présentés par Alain Schnapp et Pierre Vidal-Naquet (Paris: Seuil, 1969; new augmented edition, 1988).

21 'To hear is used figuratively in mental matters to signify to understand, to enter into the sense of the speaker or writer.' Furetière, *Dictionnaire Universel*, 1690.

22 On the importation of the Russian formalists into France in the 1960s and 1970s, see the Lecture of 7 December 1982, in *Habitus and Field*, pp. 210–11.

23 Lectures of 1 and 8 March 1984 in *Forms of Capital* on 'The Hit Parade of the Intellectuals'.

24 All these points were developed in the two years of lectures that Bourdieu

288   *Notes to pp. 91–98*

devoted to Manet and which were published under the title *Manet: A Symbolic Revolution*.
25 Boime, *The Academy and French Painting in the Nineteenth Century*.
26 At the time of these lectures a 'return to Kant' was in the air (Bourdieu alludes to this again in the following year in his Lecture of 5 June 1986). The mention of a 'return to Fichte' refers no doubt to a movement whose two leading representatives are Luc Ferry and above all Alain Renaut, who in the first half of the 1980s were the translators and editors of a collection of texts by Johann Gottlieb Fichte, *Essais philosophiques choisis (1794–1795)* (Paris: Vrin, 1984) and show themselves ready to invoke the 'contemporary relevance of Fichte' in some of their own essays (*Philosophie politique*, 3 vols., Paris: PUF, 1984–85).
27 Francis Haskell, *Rediscoveries in Art: Some Aspects of Taste, Fashion, and Collecting in England and France* (Ithaca: Cornell University Press, 1976). (The French translation of the book was about to be published.)
28 Apart from one collection of texts published by Félix Alcan in 1912, Georg Simmel's research was not published in France until the start of the 1980s, which saw it 'discovered', above all in the PUF 'Sociologies' series launched by Raymond Bourdon and François Bourricaud, in a wave of translations.
29 Although Herbert Marcuse's books had been translated into French before 1968 (*Eros and Civilization* and *One-Dimensional Man*), translations of Jürgen Habermas, Adorno and Horkheimer appeared only towards 1974. Quite a few had been published by Payot by the time of Bourdieu's lectures.
30 Roger Fayolle, *La Critique littéraire* (Paris: Armand Colin, 1964).
31 Lenore O'Boyle, 'The Problem of Excess of Educated Men in Western Europe, 1800–1850', *Journal of Modern History*, vol. 42, no. 4, 1970, pp. 471–95.
32 Pierre Bourdieu and Monique de Saint Martin, 'La Sainte famille', *Actes de la recherche en sciences sociales*, nos. 44–5, 1982, pp. 2–53
33 Arthur Oncken Lovejoy, *The Great Chain of Being: A Study of the History of an Idea* (Cambridge, MA: Harvard University Press, 1936).
34 This alludes to the expression 'the pope of a discipline' to designate a 'universally recognised' specialist, but also no doubt to Stalin's response to Pierre Laval, then French foreign minister, who in 1935 advised him to make concessions to the Pope: 'The Pope? How many divisions?'
35 Bourdieu may be alluding to the successful sales that Pierre Louÿs, a one-time avant-garde poet, had right at the end of the nineteenth century with his novels *Aphrodite* and *La femme et le pantin*.
36 Ian Watt, *The Rise of the Novel* (Berkeley: University of California Press, 1957).
37 Bourdieu is alluding to the considerable number of young teachers who were recruited into higher education during the years following May 1968, which resulted in blocking the recruitment of teachers for a long time afterwards.
38 An article by Pierre Bourdieu and Luc Boltanski had dealt with the relation between qualifications and posts in the context of France in the 1970s: 'Le titre et le poste: rapports entre le système de production et même de reproduction', *Actes de la recherche en sciences sociales*, no. 2, 1975, pp. 95–107.
39 For Durkheimian sociologists, morphology is a 'special part of sociology which . . . studies groups, the number of individuals that compose them and the diverse ways in which they are disposed in space – this is social morphology'. Paul Fauconnet and Marcel Mauss, 'La sociologie: objet et méthode' [1901], in Marcel Mauss, *Essais de sociologie* (Paris: Seuil, 'Points Essais', 1971), p. 41.

Notes to pp. 99–109 289

40 Emmanuel Le Roy Ladurie was a historian of the same generation as Bourdieu, who most probably knew him from the École normale supérieure. In 1973 he was elected to a chair in 'the history of modern civilisation' at the Collège de France, where he stayed until his retirement in 1999. He described himself on occasion as a 'demographer of the past'.
41 Bourdieu, *Homo Academicus.*
42 A reference to the debates over the question of whether the 'great man' is the product of personal qualities, circumstance, or a conjunction of the various factors.

Lecture of 25 April 1985

1 See, for example, Martin Heidegger, *What Is Called Thinking?*, trans. J. Glenn Gray (New York: Harper and Row, 1968 [1951]).
2 On the Lacanian formula ('It speaks, it speaks even to those who are unable to listen'), see *The Seminar of Jacques Lacan XVIII: On a Discourse That Might Not Be a Semblance*, trans. Cormac Gallagher (London: Karnak, 2002). [The 'it' (*ça*) being Lacan's version of Freud's 'id' (Translator).]
3 Bourdieu here makes reference to the pragmatic and analytic traditions which, although originating in the 'Vienna circle', were developed in particular in America.
4 Bourdieu seems to be thinking of Paul Lazarsfeld (and the sociologists who claim allegiance to him). He often criticised his 'positivism', and the break with (European) 'social philosophy' of the nineteenth century was an important aspect of the 'scientific sociology' that Lazarsfeld, who had studied in Austria, set about developing in the United States, where he was teaching in the early 1930s.
5 Bourdieu went on to develop his critique of these philosophical reflections at length in his lectures in the following year, 1985–86.
6 Bourdieu is most probably thinking of Michel Foucault.
7 Formed from the same verb (*dokeo*, 'to seem', 'to think', 'to believe'), the Greek words *dogma* and *doxa* are in fact sometimes translated by the same word ('opinion').
8 Erwin Panofsky, *Gothic Architecture and Scholasticism* (New York: Meridian, 1957), p. 34. Panofsky describes the *Summa Theologica* as a 'veritable orgy both of logic and of Trinitarian symbolism'.
9 These are notably the questions that Bourdieu had invested in his work on *The Political Ontology of Martin Heidegger*, trans. Peter Collier (Cambridge: Polity, 1991).
10 The term 'nomothete' designates etymologically the legislator, laying down the law. In Athens the word designated the members of a committee charged with ratifying or rejecting draft legislation.
11 Pierre Bourdieu, 'Sur le pouvoir symbolique', *Annales*, no. 3, 1977, pp. 405–11.
12 This may be an allusion to figures in the intellectual world, for example in reviews such as *Esprit*, *Le Débat* or *Commentaire*, who are particularly ready to attribute a 'totalitarian' character to anything they associate with the 'Marxist' left, whether this be their opponents in the intellectual field or members of the Soviet regime. We may note, without this text necessarily being linked to what Bourdieu is saying here, that the review *Commentaire* had in autumn

290 *Notes to pp. 109–118*

1984 published an article by Petr Fidelius with the title 'La pensée totalitaire' (no. 27, pp. 471–6), and remember that Bourdieu's lectures were being given at a time when 'Soviet totalitarianism' was crumbling (Mikhail Gorbachev had just come to power).

13 These approaches were developed from the 1960s onwards ('grammatology' by Jacques Derrida, 'archaeology' by Michel Foucault and 'semiology' by Roland Barthes). They were seen by Bourdieu as an 'effort by philosophers to blur the boundaries between science and philosophy. I never had much liking for these half-hearted changes of label which enable one to draw freely on the profits of scientificity and the profits associated with the status of philosopher.' 'Fieldwork in Philosophy', *In Other Words*, p. 6.

14 Goffman, *The Presentation of Self in Everyday Life*.

15 At the time many adverts for matrimonial and other encounters could be found in the press (including for instance in the daily *Libération*).

16 Bourdieu, *The Logic of Practice*, pp. 170–2.

17 See above, Lecture of 14 March 1985, p. 15, p. 278 note 4.

18 Pierre Bourdieu and Monique de Saint Martin, 'Le patronat', *Actes de la recherche en sciences sociales*, nos. 20–1, 1978, pp. 3–82.

19 This point had already been raised in the Lecture of 28 March 1985, p. 113, p. 284 note 34.

20 Nelson Goodman, *Ways of Worldmaking* (Hassocks: Harvester Press, 1978).

21 In Greek the word *poesis* derives from the verb *poiein* (to make, or create).

22 See nos. 52–3 of *Actes de la recherche en sciences sociales*, June 1984, on 'Le travail politique'.

23 Benveniste, *Dictionary of Indo-European Concepts and Society*, pp. 391–4.

24 Durkheim, *The Elementary Forms of Religious Life*.

25 '[A] complete scheme of rites of passage theoretically includes preliminal rites (rites of separation), liminal rites (rites of transition) and postliminal rites (rites of incorporation) . . .'. Arnold van Gennep, *The Rites of Passage*, trans. Monika B. Visedom and Gabrielle M. Caffee (London: Routledge & Kegan Paul, 1960 [1909]), p. 11.

26 Benveniste, *Dictionary*, p. 392.

27 Ibid., pp. 391–4.

28 Bourdieu developed this analysis of *fides* and its relation to charisma in the following year's Lecture of 24 April 1986.

29 Benveniste, *Dictionary*, pp. 324–7.

30 'The Greek *krainò* is used of the divinity who sanctions (by a nod, *krainò* being a derivative of kára, 'head'), and, by imitation of the divine authority, also of the king who gives executive sanction to a project or a proposal.' Ibid., p. 329.

31 Immanuel Kant, *Critique of Pure Reason*, trans. Paul Guyer and Allen W. Wood (Cambridge: Cambridge University Press, 1998), 'General remarks on the transcendental aesthetic', pp. 185–92. [This translation, however, uses the terms 'pure intuition' and 'empirical intuition' (Translator).]

32 Durkheim, *The Elementary Forms of Religious Life*, pp. 41–4; M. Mauss and H. Hubert, 'Esquisse d'une théorie générale de la magie', in Marcel Mauss, *Sociologie et anthropologie* (Paris: PUF, 1997 [1950]), p. 15: 'Whereas religious rites in general seek to appear in public in broad daylight, magical rites flee them. Even when licit, they hide away, as if evil.'

33 See Erving Goffman, *Asylums* (New York: Doubleday Anchor, 1961), for

Notes to pp. 118–123   291

example his observations on conflicting interpretations, and the 'official psychiatric mandate', pp. 162, 150.

34 See the Lectures of 22 and 29 March 1984 in *Forms of Capital.*

35 For instance: 'In the world of experience I know of only one being that possesses a richer and more complex moral reality than our own, and that is the collective being. I am mistaken; there is another being which could play the same part, and that is the Divinity.' Émile Durkheim, 'The Determination of Moral Facts', *Sociology and Philosophy*, trans. D. F. Pocock (London: Cohen and West, 1965), pp. 35–62 (Routledge reprint of same, 2009, p. 52).

36 Bourdieu returns to the question of the ID card the following year, in the context of a reflection on the 'biographical illusion' (Lectures of 17 and 24 April 1986).

37 Lawrence Rosen, *Bargaining and Reality* (Chicago: University of Chicago Press, 1984).

38 An allusion to the Occitan movement referred to in the first year of lectures (*Classification Struggles*, pp. 86–8, 95), and in Pierre Bourdieu, 'L'identité et la représentation. Éléments pour une réflexion critique sur l'idée de région', *Actes de la recherche en sciences sociales*, no. 35, 1980, pp. 63–72; republished as 'Identity and Representation: Elements for a Critical Reflection on the Idea of Region', in *Language and Symbolic Power*, trans. Gino Raymond and Matthew Adamson (Cambridge: Polity, 1991), pp. 220–8.

39 The British anthropologist Edward Tylor had an evolutionist conception: magic, religion and science represent three forms of knowledge which succeed each other in societies and are distinguished by growing degrees of generalisation, technical efficiency and elaboration. Edward B. Tylor, *Primitive Civilisation* (Cambridge: Cambridge University Press, 2010 [1871]).

40 Bronislaw Malinowski, *Argonauts of the Western Pacific* (London: Routledge, 2014 [1922]).

41 'In the meantime, the Marxist world outlook has found representatives far beyond the boundaries of Germany and Europe and in all the literary languages of the world. On the other hand, classical German philosophy is experiencing a kind of rebirth abroad, especially in England and Scandinavia, and even in Germany itself people appear to be getting tired of the pauper's broth of eclecticism which is ladled out in the universities there under the name of philosophy.' Frederick Engels, *Ludwig Feuerbach and the End of Classical German Philosophy* (1888), at www.marxists.org.

42 John Henry Newman, *Apologia Pro Vita Sua* (New York: Dover, 2005 [1864]).

43 An article by Jean-François Billeter ('Contribution à une sociologie historique du mandarinat', *Actes de la recherche en sciences sociales*, no. 15, 1977, pp. 3–29) had described the examination system that selected officials in China, emphasising the 'individual and collective tensions' that it generated. It mentioned in particular cases of candidates committing suicide during the examinations.

44 An allusion to the parable of the door of the Law at the end of Kafka's *The Trial.*

45 Bourdieu and his audience would no doubt still have in mind the often very painful exclusions operated by the French Communist Party.

46 This point was developed in the previous lecture, 28 March 1985.

47 Bourdieu is certainly thinking of the studies carried out in the United States, in particular the recently published book by Arlie Russell Hochschild, *The*

292   *Notes to pp. 123–134*

Managed Heart: The Commercialization of Human Feeling (Berkeley: University of California Press, 1983).
48 These questions interested Bourdieu very early in his career. In the 1950s he had thought of preparing a thesis under the direction of Georges Canguilhem on the 'temporal structures of the affective life'.
49 See for instance 'Les maladies infantiles de l'indépendence', an issue of the review *Esprit*, vol. 25, no. 6, 1957. The image of 'growing pains' refers to Lenin's book, *'Left-Wing' Communism: An Infantile Disorder* (Rockville: Wildside Press, 2008 [1920]).
50 The phrase is elliptical but Bourdieu seems to draw attention to the word 'sect', noting how through its etymology (the word 'sect' could derive from *scare*, 'to cut off', but also from *sequi*, to follow) he returns to the idea of 'cutting up' evoked during the first session.
51 The expression was current in the second half of the nineteenth century in English literary circles (it is often attributed to the [American] philosopher Henry David Thoreau, who uses it in his *Journal* from 1851). Bourdieu used the idea in 1966 in his first article on the intellectual field ('Champ intellectuel et projet créateur', *Les Temps modernes*, no. 246, 1966, pp. 865–906), developing the arguments of Levin Ludwig Schücking, *Die Soziologie der Literarischen Geschmacksbildung* (Munich: Rosl, 1923).
52 The painting *Incident in a Bullfight*, which Bourdieu refers to here, had been accepted by the Salon in 1864. Yet it was not the first work that Manet had submitted: although *The Absinthe Drinker* had been rejected in 1859, *The Spanish Singer* was nonetheless exhibited at the Salon the following year. Moreover, although the critics mocked the volumes and perspective of *Incident in a Bullfight*, it is not absolutely certain that this was the reason why Manet decided to cut up his canvas and keep only two parts of it, from which, after reworking them, he drew *The Dead Man* (initially *The Dead Torero*) and *The Corrida*. See Françoise Cochin and Charles S. Moffitt, *Manet 1832–1883* (Paris: Éditions de la Réunion des musées nationaux, 1983), pp. 195–8.
53 Bourdieu had developed this idea previously in *Habitus and Field*, pp. 297, 309.
54 All these points are developed in detail in *Manet: A Symbolic Revolution*.
55 Bourdieu and de Saint Martin, 'La Sainte famille'.
56 Maria Rogers, 'The Batignolles Group: Creators of Impressionism', *Autonomous Groups*, vol. XIV, nos. 3–4, 1959, reprinted in Milton C. Albrecht, James H. Barnett and Mason Griff (eds.), *The Sociology of Art and Literature* (New York: Praeger, 1970), pp. 194–220.
57 See in particular François Roustang, *Un destin si funeste* (Paris: Minuit, 1976).
58 Jean Moréas, 'Le symbolisme', *Le Figaro*, 18 September 1886, supplément littéraire, pp. 1–2.
59 Bourdieu gives more information about this in his Lecture of 9 May 1985 (see below p. 189).

Lecture of 2 May 1985

1 This interview comes from the enquiry into private housing undertaken in the 1980s by Bourdieu and other members of his research centre. It led to the report in 1987, 'Éléments d'une analyse du march de la maison individuelle' (Paris: CNAF/Centre de Sociologie européenne), then to an issue of *Actes de la*

Notes to pp. 135–144 293

recherche en sciences sociales, later published in volume form as *Les structures sociales de l'économie* (Paris: Seuil, 2000). The interview referred to here is used in Bourdieu's article 'Un signe des temps', *Actes de la recherche en sciences sociales*, nos. 81–2, 1990, pp. 2–5.

2 This project was to construct a 'European' sociology, mobilising the insights of American empirical sociology, but without abandoning, as it did under Paul Lazarsfeld's inspiration, the theoretical questioning that was so important in Bourdieu's enterprise. Raymond Aron at the end of the 1950s and the beginning of the 1960s was very attached to this, and recognised Bourdieu's capacity to succeed in it.

3 Goodman, *Ways of Worldmaking*.

4 The Latin word *fictio* comes from the verb *fingo*, which means 'to fashion'.

5 Goodman, *Ways of Worldmaking*, p. 7.

6 Bourdieu himself often uses footnotes in this way.

7 On the five operations (composition and decomposition, weighting, ordering, deletion and supplementation, deformation) distinguished by Goldman, see *Ways of Worldmaking*, pp. 7–17.

8 Pierre Bourdieu, *Outline of a Theory of Practice* (Cambridge: Cambridge University Press, 1977).

9 Mikhail Bakhtin (V. N. Voloshinov), *Marxism and the Philosophy of Language* (London: Seminar Press, 1973), p. 71. Bourdieu had already pointed out this error of 'philologism' in his Lecture of 12 October 1982, *Habitus and Field*, p. 40.

10 Jack Goody, *The Domestication of the Savage Mind* (Cambridge: Cambridge University Press, 1977).

11 The recording does not enable us to distinguish between the two very similar words pronounced by Bourdieu: they may be *ethos* (the way of being, which gives us 'ethics') and *ethnos* (the people, from which 'ethnic' is derived).

12 Pierre Bourdieu, 'La parenté comme représentation et comme volonté', *Esquisse d'une théorie de la pratique. Précédé de 'Trois études d'ethnologie Kabyle'* (Paris: Seuil, 2000).

13 See, as well as numerous passages in the current lecture, Bourdieu, 'Espace social et genèse des classes', *Actes de la recherche en sciences sociales*, nos. 52–3, 1984, pp. 3–14.

14 Bourdieu, 'The Social Uses of Kinship', *The Logic of Practice*, pp. 162–99.

15 Rosen, *Bargaining and Reality*.

16 Bourdieu, 'Public Opinion Does Not Exist'.

17 Bourdieu returns to this point at length the following year (see the Lectures of 17 and 24 April 1986).

18 Bourdieu makes this point in other lectures, where he refers to analyses by Durkheim in *The Elementary Forms of Religious Life*.

19 This term became current in France after an article by Louis Roussel in 1978: 'It is rare for the sociologist, to name a phenomenon that anyone can easily observe, not to find a ready-made term waiting to be used. This is, however, the case when it comes to describing the new behaviour of young couples who live together without being married.' ('La cohabitation juvénile en France', *Population*, vol. 33, no. 1, 1978, pp. 15–42).

20 Bourdieu, 'La parenté comme représentation et comme volonté', pp. 164, 178.

21 Bourdieu had already mentioned this word in an earlier year (see the Lecture of 7 December 1982, *Habitus and Field*, p. 230).

294 *Notes to pp. 146–150*

22 The Greek word *theoria* designates the 'act of seeing', in particular 'the act of seeing a spectacle or attending a festival', and by extension, 'the festival itself, solemn festival, pomp, procession, spectacle'. Anatole Bailly, *Dictionnaire français-grec* (Paris: Hachette, 1905 [1895]), p. 933.

23 Max Weber distinguishes between classes, which are defined ultimately by the degree to which an individual may (or may not) dispose of goods and services in order to procure rent and revenue (*Economy and Society*, trans. Ephraim Fischoff et al. [Berkeley: University of California Press, 2013], pp. 302–4), and 'status groups' ('orders' in the French translation), which correspond to 'a plurality of persons who, within a larger group, successfully claim (a) a special social esteem, and possibly also (b) status monopolies . . . by virtue of their own style of life' (ibid., p. 306. See also pp. 926–40).

24 Bourdieu undertook from an early date to go beyond this traditional opposition: 'Condition de classe et position de classe', *Archives européennes de sociologie*, vol. 7, no. 2, 1966, pp. 201–23.

25 '"Status" [*standische Lage*] shall mean an effective claim to social esteem in terms of positive or negative privileges; it is typically founded on (a) style of life, hence (b) formal education, which may be (a) empirical training or (b) rational instruction, and the corresponding forms of behaviour, (c) hereditary or occupational prestige. In practice status expresses itself through (a) connubium, (b) commensality, possibly (c) monopolistic appropriation of privileged modes of acquisition or the abhorrence of certain kinds of acquisition, (d) status conventions (traditions) of other kinds.' Weber, *Economy and Society*, pp. 305–6.

26 The notion of 'conspicuous consumption' is used by Thorstein Veblen in *The Theory of the Leisure Class* (Oxford: Oxford Worlds Classics, 2009 [1899]).

27 See Lecture of 29 March 1984, *Forms of Capital*, pp. 146, 336. Groucho Marx, *Groucho and Me* (New York: Da Capo Press, 1995), p. 321: 'I don't want to belong to any club that will accept people like me as a member.'

28 Erving Goffman, *The Presentation of Self in Everyday Life*, and *Stigma: Notes on the Management of Spoiled Identity* (New York: Touchstone, 1963).

29 Shortly after this lecture, Bourdieu published 'Effet de champ et effet de corps', *Actes de la recherche en sciences sociales*, no. 59, 1985, p. 73.

30 Bourdieu had referred to this notion the previous year only in passing (in the Lecture of 19 April 1984, *Forms of Capital*, p. 160). He had, however, devoted an issue of his journal to it (*Actes de la recherche en sciences sociales*, no. 31, 1980), whose introductory text he had written himself: 'Le capital social. Notes provisoires'.

31 This allusion targets the 'premier recensement des petits bourgeois en France' proposed by Christian Baudelot, Roger Establet and Jacques Malemort, *La Petite Bourgeoisie en France* (Paris: Maspero, 1974), esp. pp. 302–3: 'How many of them are there? Fraction I, commercial, numbers about 1,171,000 active members. Fraction II, petit bourgeois public servants, about 1,194,000. Fraction III, managers in the economic sector, about 1,180,000. That is altogether, in very generous terms, less than four million active members. Is that a lot or a little? It's a lot if we compare them to the ranks of the members of the capitalist bourgeoisie (who are difficult to count). It is less if we remember that in 1968 the proletarian class in the wider sense of the term counted thirteen million workers out of an active population of twenty million. This is cause for reflection in terms of the balance of power.'

Notes to pp. 150–158 295

32 Professionalisation, in the context of the United States, designates the process whereby a professional activity becomes, like medicine, a regulated profession endowed with specific rights. The analysis of this process has given rise to a prolific literature in American functionalist sociology dating from the 1930s.

33 A reference to the termly publication by INSEE of the figures of unemployment, which is considered by many national (and international) agencies as the only valid one.

34 Jacques Thuillier held a chair in 'The History of Artistic Creation in France' at the Collège de France between 1977 and 1998. He was a student at the École normale supérieure in the same year as Bourdieu.

35 Thuillier, *Peut-on parler d'une peinture 'pompier'?*

36 Jacques Thuillier, 'Art et institution: l'École des beaux-arts et le prix de Rome', in Philippe Grunchec (ed.), *Le Grand Prix de peinture. Les concours des prix de Rome, de 1797 à 1803* (Paris: École nationale supérieure des beaux-arts, 1983), pp. 9–17.

37 The Kwakiutl are an Amerindian people situated on the west coast of Canada whose non-mercantile exchanges, the *potlatch*, have been studied in depth by American ethnologists, notably Franz Boas.

38 Bourdieu had drawn this analogy in the Lecture of 18 April 1985 (see above p. 101).

39 Bourdieu, *Homo Academicus*, esp. p. 175.

40 Thuillier, 'Art et institution'.

41 Bourdieu returns to this point at some length in the following lecture, of 9 May 1985.

42 The reference is probably to Max Weber's essay 'Der Sinn der "Wertfreiheit" des ökonomishchen und soziologischen Wissenschaften' ('The Meaning of Value-Freedom in the Sociological and Economic Sciences', in *Collected Methodological Writings*, ed. Hans Henrik Bruun and Sam Whimster [Routledge, 2013 (1917)]). ['Wertfrei' is also variously translated as 'ethically neutral' or 'value free' (Translator).]

43 Pierre Bourdieu, 'Le mort saisit le vif. Les relations entre l'histoire réifiée et l'histoire incorporée', *Actes de la recherche en sciences sociales*, no. 32, 1980, pp. 3–14.

44 'Thus, there remain only two kinds of prophets in our sense, one represented most clearly by the Buddha, the other with especial clarity by Zoroaster and Muhammad. The prophet may be primarily, as in the last cases, an instrument for the proclamation of a god and his will, be this a concrete command or an abstract norm. Preaching as one who has received a commission from god, he demands obedience as an ethical duty. This type we shall term the *"ethical prophet"*. On the other hand, the prophet may be an exemplary man who, by his personal example, demonstrates to others the way to religious salvation, as in the case of the Buddha. The preaching of this type of prophet says nothing about a divine mission or an ethical duty of obedience, but rather directs itself to the self-interest of those who crave salvation, recommending to them the same path as he traversed. Our designation for this second type is that of the *"exemplary prophet"*.' Weber, *Economy and Society*, pp. 447–8.

45 Henry Murger's chronicle, *Scenes of Bohemian Life*, dates from 1851. It is perhaps better known today as having inspired Giacomo Puccini's opera *La Bohème* (1895).

46 A possible allusion to Denis de Rougemont's book *Love in the Western World*,

296 *Notes to pp. 158–164*

trans. Montgomery Belgion (Princeton: Princeton University Press, 1983 [1939]).

47 Bourdieu, 'L'invention de la vie d'artiste', esp. pp. 85, 88–9. Throughout the rest of this lecture Bourdieu refers on a number of occasions to the analysis of *Sentimental Education* that he made in this article and that he repeats in *The Rules of Art*.

48 'Reading the paper in the morning is a sort of realist's matins. We direct towards God or towards the state of the world our attitude towards the world. It provides the same reassurance as to what we are doing here.' G. W. F. Hegel, *Notes et fragments. Iéna 1803–1806*, trans. Catherine Colliot-Thélène et al. (Paris: Aubier, 1991), fragment no. 32, p. 53 [P. C.: my translation from the French].

49 *Science et vie* is a popular scientific monthly review. In the 1970s its readership had been the object of an enquiry by two researchers from Bourdieu's centre: Luc Boltanski and Pascale Maldidier, *La vulgarisation scientifique et son public, une enquête sur* Science et vie (Paris: Centre de sociologie de l'éducation et de la culture, 1977). Bourdieu also mentions this review in *Distinction*, pp. 24–5, 83.

50 This is *L'Hémicycle du Palais des Beaux-Arts* (1841), which represents seventy-five artists. See Haskell, *Rediscoveries in Art*.

51 The issue of *Actes de la recherche en sciences sociales* on the 'Inconscients d'école' (no. 135, 2000) raises questions of this kind.

52 A reference to the phrase 'Let no one ignorant of geometry enter here' which was said to have been inscribed over the entrance to the Academy founded by Plato.

53 Bourdieu, *The Political Ontology of Martin Heidegger*, esp. pp. 78–80.

54 Bourdieu had evoked at greater length Robert Escarpit's sociology of literature (*Sociologie de la littérature* [Paris: PUF, 'Que sais-je?', 1958], and, edited by him, *Le Littéraire et le social* [Paris: Flammarion, 1970]) when he dealt with the literary field in 1982–83 (*Habitus and Field*, pp. 243, 339).

55 See Bourdieu, *The Rules of Art*.

56 Ibid., esp. pp. 104, 106.

57 *Au théâtre ce soir* was a very popular television programme which between 1966 and 1986 broadcast televised revivals of boulevard theatre plays.

58 See Bourdieu, *The Rules of Art*, esp. pp. 101ff.

59 Here and in the passage that follows Bourdieu is thinking in particular of Philippe Sollers (whom he cites by name a little later); ten years later he was to publish a short article resuming the themes touched on here: 'Sollers tel quel', *Liber*, nos. 21–2, 1955, p. 40; *Libération*, 27 January 1995.

60 See Bourdieu, *The Rules of Art*, esp. pp. 8–9, 64, 91–2.

61 Plato, through the voice of Socrates, reproached the Sophists (who, unlike him, were not members of the Athenian aristocracy) for taking payment for their teaching. See, for example, *Hippias Major*.

62 The grisette as part of the bohemian subculture was a frequent character in French fiction of the time. She is the protagonist in Alfred de Musset's *Mademoiselle Mimi Pinson: Profil de grisette*. Possibly the most enduring grisette of all is Mimi in Henri Murger's novel (and subsequent play) *Scènes de la vie de Bohème*.

Notes to pp. 167–172   297

Lecture of 9 May 1985

1 The lecture took place at the end of a period where the very existence of the Order of Doctors was being debated (suppressing it had even been one of the 'hundred and ten proposals for France' presented by François Mitterrand during his campaign for the presidential election in 1981). As Bourdieu remarks later, there were in particular doctors who refused to join the Order of Doctors (because of the political and moral stands taken by the Order). There had been court procedures against them.
2 At the time of these lectures military service was still compulsory in France for all men of French nationality. Grounds for exemption or deferral (temporary of definitive) were principally reasons of health (which had to be certified) or family circumstances.
3 At the time of these lectures, Margaret Thatcher was denouncing, for example, a 'culture of dependency' in the United Kingdom, reactivating the debates of the nineteenth-century philosophers over the 'deserving' and the 'undeserving' poor.
4 See Bourdieu, *The Logic of Practice*, pp. 186–7.
5 The idea that welfare costs too much, that it increases the cost of labour and harms employment and competitivity, was in vogue in the ideological and economic climate of the 1980s when the lectures were being given.
6 Bourdieu had developed his arguments on the notion of intelligence in 'The Racism of Intelligence', in *Sociology in Question*, pp. 177–80.
7 Bourdieu, *Homo Academicus*, chapter 2, 'The Conflict of the Faculties', pp. 36–72.
8 As he had often done in his very first lectures at the Collège de France, especially on the subject of the insult, Bourdieu refers here to the Greek word *idios*, which signifies 'particular', 'belonging to a particular person'.
9 In the following passage, Bourdieu raises points that he had developed the previous year: he had dealt with the notion of *Kadijustiz* (and the examples of Sancho Panza and Solomon) used by Max Weber, particularly in the Lectures of 26 April and 10 May 1984; he had mentioned Kant's critique of the ethics of sympathy in the Lecture of 17 May 1984.
10 Here Bourdieu is referring to the passage where Max Weber describes 'legal domination': 'The members of the organization, insofar as they obey a person in authority, do not owe this obedience to him as an individual, but to the impersonal order. Hence, it follows that there is an obligation to obedience only within the sphere of the rationally delimited jurisdiction which, in terms of the order, has been given to him.' Weber, *Economy and Society*, p. 218.
11 A reference to Kant's 'categorical imperative': 'act only according to that maxim through which you can at the same time will that it become a universal law'. Immanuel Kant, *Groundwork of the Metaphysics of Morals*, trans. Mary Gregor and Jens Timmerman (Cambridge: Cambridge University Press, 2012), p. 34.
12 'Postmen' (*facteurs de la Poste*) had been re-baptised 'mail officers' (*préposés*) in a decree of 1957 (which was in force until 1993), without any real consequences.
13 Claude Thélot, *Tel père, tel fils. Position sociale et origine familiale* (Paris: Dunod, 1982). Claude Thélot was an administrator at INSEE. Bourdieu returns

298   *Notes to pp. 174–182*

to what he sees as a regressive book in *The State Nobility*, trans. Lauretta C. Clough (Cambridge: Polity Press, 1996), p. 136.

14 We might quote, for example, this famous passage: 'In a higher phase of communist society, after the enslaving subordination of the individual to the division of labor, and therewith also the antithesis between mental and physical labor, has vanished; after labor has become not only a means of life but life's prime want; after the productive forces have also increased with the all-around development of the individual, and all the springs of co-operative wealth flow more abundantly – only then then can the narrow horizon of bourgeois right be crossed in its entirety and society inscribe on its banners: From each according to his ability, to each according to his needs!' Karl Marx, 'Critique of the Gotha Programme' (1875), in Marx and Engels, *Selected Works*, vol. 3 (Moscow: Progress Publishers, 1970), pp. 13–30, at www.marxists.org.

15 This was doubtless the official syllabuses and instructions that had been published at the end of April 1985 by the minister of education, Jean-Pierre Chevènement. They insisted particularly on the importance of learning to read, while suppressing 'awakening activities' and reintroducing civic education into the school curriculum.

16 Bourdieu is no doubt thinking of the 'theory of agency' which was formulated in economics in the 1970s and which applies to situations where one agent is empowered to take decisions on someone else's behalf (as, in business, the managers who act in the name of the shareholders, or, in health care, the patient or the doctor who act while the payer may be an insurance company or the national health system).

17 Bourdieu is probably using the word 'idiot' here with reference to the Greek word *idios*, which he has used a little earlier.

18 Bourdieu is connecting the word 'discrimination' (modelled on *crimen*, 'the point of separation') with the word *diacrisis*, whose meaning and etymology he had commented on two sessions earlier.

19 Bourdieu, 'Public Opinion Does Not Exist'.

20 A reference to the 'unwritten unalterable laws' that Antigone opposes to the edict of King Creon forbidding the burial of her brother: 'I do not think your edicts strong enough to override the unwritten unalterable laws of God and heaven, you being only a man. They are not of yesterday or to-day, but everlasting, though where they came from, none of us can tell.' Sophocles, *Antigone*, in *The Theban Plays*, trans. E. F. Watling (Harmondsworth: Penguin, 1947), p. 138.

21 Goffman, *The Presentation of Self in Everyday Life*.

22 'A compulsory political organization with continuous operations will be called a "state" insofar as its administrative staff successfully upholds the claim to the *monopoly* of the *legitimate* use of physical force in the enforcement of its order.' Weber, *Economy and Society*, p. 54.

23 See above, note 1 to this chapter.

24 We may recall that this was Bourdieu's title for the article based on his study of the 'Hit Parade of French Intellectuals' that he presented in his lectures the previous year, just before the sessions devoted to Kafka (in *Forms of Capital*).

25 See the Lectures of 22 and 29 March 1984 in *Forms of Capital*.

26 This was no doubt the 'Estates General of Philosophy' organised in 1979 by Jacques Derrida at the Sorbonne: *États généraux de la philosophie (16 et 17 juin 1979)* (Paris: Flammarion, 'Champs', 1979).

Notes to pp. 184–190 299

27 See the Lectures of 8 and 22 March 1984 in *Forms of Capital*.
28 Pierre Bourdieu, 'Genèse et structure du champ religieux', *Revue française de sociologie*, vol. 12, no. 3, 1971, pp. 295–334.
29 The word 'anomie', which existed in Greek, is formed by the simple addition to the word *nomos* of the privative prefix a-. Émile Durkheim used the term in *De la division du travail social*, and in *Suicide*, without really defining it other than as an absence of collective rules or ethics. Bourdieu used the word in one of his first publications on the Impressionist revolution ('L'institutionnalisation de l'anomie', *Les Cahiers du Musée national d'art moderne*, nos. 19–20, 1987, pp. 6–19).
30 See in particular the Lecture of 8 March 1984 in *Forms of Capital*.
31 Kant, *Critique of Pure Reason*, pp. 185–92.
32 The formula 'God is dead' is associated with Nietzsche (he uses it in particular in *The Gay Science*), who in the 1960s became an important reference for the philosophical avant-garde. At the same time the theme of the 'death of man' was a useful link between, for instance, the structuralism of Lévi-Strauss, the Marxism of Louis Althusser and the thought of Michel Foucault, who uses the formula almost explicitly at the end of *Les Mots et les choses*: 'As the archaeology of our thought easily shows, man is an invention of recent date. And one perhaps nearing its end. If those arrangements were to disappear as they appeared, if some event of which we can at the moment do no more than sense the possibility – without knowing either what its form will be or what it promises – were to cause them to crumble, as the ground of Classical thought did, at the end of the eighteenth century, then one can certainly wager that man would be erased, like a face drawn in sand at the edge of the sea.' Michel Foucault, *The Order of Things* (London: Routledge, 2002 [1966]), p. 422.
33 This is not a quotation but a sort of synthesis of what is said by the painter character Tebaldeo (Alfred de Musset, *Lorenzaccio*, act II, scenes 2 and 6).
34 Bourdieu is thinking of Baxandall's work *Painting and Experience in Fifteenth-Century Italy*.
35 This comes from a note in the first edition of *Jocelyn* appended to the poem 'Les laboureurs': 'On reading these verses the reader cannot doubt that the poet has been inspired by the painter here. The inimitable painting of the Reapers by the unfortunate Robert is obviously the model for this piece. Thus it is that the arts inspire one another and sometimes even translate one another. Fine verse, a fine painting and fine music are the same thought in three different languages; Robert, Rossini and Lamartine can understand one another and share their mutual feelings. They are all at once painters, poets and musicians.' Alphonse de Lamartine, *Oeuvres* (Brussels: Adolphe Walden, 1836), p. 887.
36 Bourdieu borrows this example of the theme of *Mazeppa* from Joseph-Marie Bailbé, *Le Roman et la Musique en France sous la monarchie de Juillet* (Paris: Minard, 1969), p. 4.
37 Bourdieu may be thinking of the thesis by Rémy Ponton that he supervised: 'Le champ littéraire en France de 1865 à 1905', EHESS, 1977, or the article 'Programme esthétique et accumulation de capital symbolique. L'exemple du Parnasse', *Revue française de sociologie*, vol. 14, no. 2, 1973, pp. 202–20.
38 Bourdieu is alluding to the fact that Georges Bataille's writings on transgression, violence and sexuality, with his book *La Part maudite* (1949), are references very often mobilised by many French intellectuals of the time: Jacques Lacan, Jacques Derrida, Philippe Sollers or Michel Foucault, who published a

300 *Notes to pp. 190–197*

famous homage on the death of Bataille ('Préface à la transgression', *Critique*, nos. 195–6, 1963, pp. 751–69) and prefaced the first volume of the writer's complete works (Georges Bataille, *Oeuvres complètes*, t. I, Paris: Gallimard, 1970). As he says explicitly in *Sketch for a Self-Analysis*, trans. Richard Nice (Cambridge: Polity, 2008), pp. 2, 12 and 78), Bourdieu always marked his distance from this author.

39 Bourdieu had discussed this book at some length in the previous lecture.

40 Rudolf and Margot Wittkower, *Born under Saturn: The Character and Conduct of Artists* (New York: Random House, 1963).

41 'When he has mastered the art of sauces, patinas, glazes, gratins, gravies and stews (I am speaking of painting), the *spoilt child* adopts a proud attitude, and continues to tell himself with increasing conviction that nothing else matters.' Baudelaire, 'Salon de 1859. Lettres à M. Le Directeur de la *Revue française*: I L'artiste moderne', in Charles Baudelaire, *Oeuvres complètes*, t. II (Paris: Gallimard, 'Bibliothèque de la Pléiade', 1976), p. 613.

42 This study was published after the lecture course: Dario Gamboni, 'Odilon Redo et ses critiques. Une lutte pour la production de la valeur', *Actes de la recherche en sciences sociales*, no. 66, 1987, pp. 25–34; *La Plume et le Pinceau. Odilon Redonet la littérature* (Paris: Minuit, 1989).

43 Umberto Eco, *The Open Work*, trans. Anna Cancogni (Cambridge MA: Harvard University Press, 1989 [1962]).

44 Bourdieu returns to the way that Duchamp 'leaves hanging in doubt, by irony or humour, the meaning of a work which is *deliberately polysemic*' in *The Rules of Art*, p. 247.

45 *The Unknown Masterpiece* is a novella published by Balzac in 1831. An ageing painter, Master Frenhofer, sets out to paint a canvas, *La Belle Noiseuse* [The Beautiful Shrew], which he has thought about for many years, and through which he hopes to attain a form of perfection and the absolute. See Honoré de Balzac, *The Girl with the Golden Eyes and Other Stories*, trans. Peter Collier (Oxford: Oxford World's Classics, 2012).

Lecture of 23 May 1985

1 Paul Valéry, *Cahiers II* (Paris: Gallimard, 'Bibliothèque de la Pléiade', 1974), p. 1565.

2 Bourdieu tells his audience at this point 'Don't forget these are notes.'

3 Valéry, *Cahiers II*, p. 1566.

4 Jean-Louis Fabiani, 'Les programmes, les hommes et les oeuvres. Professeurs de philosophie en classe et en ville au tournant du siècle', *Actes de la recherche en sciences sociales*, nos. 47–8, 1983, pp. 3–30. Jean-Louis Fabiani had written a thesis supervised by Bourdieu ('La Crise du champ philosophique: 1880–1914; contribution à l'histoire sociale du système d'enseignement', EHESS, 1980) and went on to publish, after these lectures, *Les Philosophes de la République* (Paris: Minuit, 1988).

5 In his re-reading of Max Weber's sociology of religion ('Genèse et structure du champ religieux'), Bourdieu emphasises the passages where Weber highlights the fact that a clergy ensures its domination especially by the designation of a limited number of 'dogmas and canonical writings': 'Most, though not all, canonical sacred collections became officially closed against secular or reli-

Notes to pp. 198–204   301

giously undesirable additions as a consequence of a struggle between various competing groups and prophecies for the control of the community.' Weber, *Economy and Society*, pp. 458–9.

6 Valéry, *Cahiers II*, p. 1557.

7 Ibid.

8 Bourdieu develops this opposition at length in *The Rules of Art*.

9 Bourdieu no doubt has in mind the following remarks: 'False philosophers. Those generated by the teaching of philosophy and its syllabus. They learn problems that they could not have invented and that they have not experienced. And they learn *all* of them! The real philosophical problems are those that torment you and interfere with your life.' Valéry, *Cahiers II*, p. 1567.

10 Valéry, *Cahiers II*, p. 1558.

11 Bourdieu will return to this later; he is thinking in particular of Martin Heidegger.

12 An allusion to the analyses formulated by Kant in *Groundwork of the Metaphysics of Morals*. Bourdieu had already alluded to this in the previous lecture, as in the Lecture of 17 May 1984 (see *Forms of Capital*, pp. 274, 357).

13 Valéry, *Cahiers II*, p. 1558.

14 Bourdieu, 'Postscript: Towards a "Vulgar" Critique of "Pure" Critiques', in *Distinction*, pp. 485–500.

15 Carl E. Schorske, *Fin-de-Siècle Vienna: Politics and Culture* (New York: Random House, 1980), chapter 4.

16 'Luther read the Bible through the spectacles of his whole attitude; at the time and in the course of his development from about 1518 to 1530 this not only remained traditionalistic but became ever more so.' Max Weber, *The Protestant Ethic and the Spirit of Capitalism*, trans. Talcott Parsons (London: Routledge, 2001), p. 43.

17 Ernst Troeltsch, *Die Absolutheit des Christentums und die Religionsgeschichte* (1902), translated after these lectures, *Oeuvres*, vol. 3: *Histoire des religions et destin de la théologie*, trans. Jean-Marc Tétaz et al. (Paris and Geneva: Cerf/Labor et Fides, 1996).

18 A reference to the urinal signed 'R. Mutt' and entitled 'Fountain (1917), a 'ready-made' by Duchamp. See Bourdieu, 'The Production of Belief', p. 42; and, published after these lectures, *The Rules of Art*, pp. 171, 246–7, 291, 391.

19 This may be a reference to the following phrase: 'The fetish of the art market is the master's name.' Walter Benjamin, 'Eduard Fuchs, Collector and Historian', in *Selected Writings*, vol. 3: *1935–1938*, trans. Edmund Jephcott and Howard Eiland et al. (Cambridge MA: Harvard University Press, 2002 [1937]), p. 283.

20 A major exhibition showing 124 works by Pierre-Auguste Renoir had just opened at the Grand Palais in Paris on 2 May 1985.

21 See Edmund Husserl, *Ideas: General Introduction to Pure Phenomenology*, trans. W. R. Boyce Gibson (London: Routledge, 2012), § 88.

22 We imagine that this is referring to the debate on the nationalisations that the socialist government was embarking on in 1982, unless it is the debates around public and private education: the creation of a unified and lay public National Education service was one of the commitments of the socialist government. The draft law presented by the minister of education, Alain Savary, was abandoned in July 1984 when confronted in Parliament with opposition during a major demonstration in defence of l'École libre (private Catholic schooling).

23 Bourdieu is thinking of the judgement of Solomon.

302   *Notes to pp. 205–212*

24 Alphonse Allais, 'Un honnête homme dans toute la force du mot', in *Deux et deux font cinq* (Paris: Paul Ollendorf, 1895), pp. 69–72.

25 In French universities, the 'assistants' and 'maître-assistants' were the lower-grade teachers, who gave lectures while still preparing a doctorate ('de troisième cycle' or 'd'État'). During the period when these lectures were being delivered, there was a reform creating a body of 'maîtres de conférences' (which included the 'maître-assistants') and putting an end to the recruitment of 'assistants'.

26 Bourdieu had developed this criticism of the idea that one could 'put oneself in someone else's place' during the second year of his lectures (see *Habitus and Field*, pp. 36, 86–7, 214).

27 Martin Heidegger, *Being and Time*, trans. John Macquarrie and Edward Robinson (Oxford: Blackwell, 1962), pp. 163–8.

28 Luc Boltanski and Jean-Claude Chamboredon, 'La banque et sa clientèle', report by the Centre de sociologie européenne, 1963.

29 See above, Lecture of 28 March 1985, p. 43, p. 282 note 6.

30 In the Lecture of 28 March 1985, Bourdieu had developed these points, which relate to the fact that the change in nomenclature of the socio-professional categories effected in 1982 drew largely on the analyses of *Distinction*.

31 In the first session of this lecture Bourdieu had already mentioned this exhibition, which had just opened at the Grand Palais in Paris (see above, p. 203, p. 301 note 20).

32 Paul Hayes Tucker, *Monet at Argenteuil* (New Haven: Yale University Press, 1982).

33 A reference to the reflection theory developed by Lucien Goldmann in analysing literary works. See in particular *The Hidden God: A Study of Tragic Vision in the* Pensées *of Pascal and the Tragedies of Racine*, trans. Philip Thody (London: Verso, 2016 [1954]). Bourdieu had developed criticism of this kind of approach in his lectures on the literary field (See *Habitus and Field*, in particular the Lecture of 11 January 1983, pp. 271–3).

34 A reference to the idea developed by Karl Marx and continued by many representatives of the Marxist tradition, arguing that the intellectual products of a society (such as law, politics or art) are the expression or the product of the 'infrastructure', that is, the 'economic structure of society', formed in Marx's words by the 'relations of production appropriate to a given stage in the development of their material forces of production . . . It is not the consciousness of men that determines their existence, but their social existence that determines their consciousness.' 'Preface to *A Contribution to the Critique of Political Economy*', in Karl Marx, *Early Writings*, trans. Rodney Livingstone and George Benton (London: Penguin, 1974), p. 425.

35 See the Lecture of 28 March above, p. 65, p. 284 note 42.

36 An allusion to the exploitation by advertisers of themes associated with May 1968, and to the daily newspaper *Libération*, which was born of post-'68 *gauchisme*, but changed into an 'executives' daily' at the beginning of the 1980s (in 1988 Bourdieu commented on the new profile of its readership; the text was published in 1994: 'Libé, vingt ans après', *Actes de la recherche en sciences sociales*, nos. 101–2, 1994, p. 39).

37 An allusion to a famous passage in *The German Ideology*: 'The ideas of the ruling class are in every epoch the ruling ideas, i.e. the class which is the ruling material force of society, is at the same time its ruling intellectual force.' Karl

Notes to pp. 213–222 303

Marx and Friedrich Engels, *The German Ideology* (London: Lawrence and Wishart, 1990), p. 39.

38 From the beginning of his course of lectures, Bourdieu had mentioned this effect on several occasions (for the first occurrence see *Habitus and Field*, Lecture of 2 November 1982, p. 99).

39 The 'working consensus' for Goffman is an agreement, a *modus vivendi* that the participants in an interaction undertake to realise: it 'does not imply so much that they agree on reality as on the question of knowing who has the right to speak about what'. Goffman, *The Presentation of Self in Everyday Life*, p. 21.

40 For developments of these points, see in particular a lecture that Bourdieu gave in Chicago in April 1989: 'Sur la possibilité d'un champ international de la sociologie', in Catherine Leclerc, Wenceslas Lizé and Hélène Stevens (eds.), *Bourdieu et les sciences sociales. Réceptions et usages* (Paris: La Dispute, 2015), pp. 33–49.

41 The triad of gods worshipped on the Capitoline hill in Rome were Jupiter, Juno and Minerva.

42 Bourdieu returns to this work of purification to some extent in the next session, on 30 May 1985.

43 Raymond Williams, *Culture and Society, 1780–1950* (London: Chatto & Windus, 1958). Bourdieu exploits Williams's analyses notably in 'Champ intellectuel et projet créateur', *Les Temps modernes*, no. 246, 1966 (published as 'Intellectual Field and Creative Project', in Michael Young, *Knowledge and Control: New Directions for the Sociology of Education* (London: Collier-Macmillan, 1971).

44 Albert Cassagne, *La théorie de l'art pour l'art en France chez les derniers romantiques et es peintres réalistes* (Geneva: Slatkine, 1979 [1906]). Bourdieu had already underlined the importance of this book in the lectures he had devoted to the literary field (see *Habitus and Field*, esp. pp. 270–1).

45 Perhaps Jacques Lethève, *Impressionistes et symbolistes devant la presse* (Paris: Armand Colin, 1959).

46 Here Bourdieu is referring to a quotation from a book by Jacqueline de Romilly published in 1969 (*Nous autres professeurs* [Paris: Fayard], p. 20): 'Just like old Kabyle peasants speaking of the heretical methods of cultivation practised by the young, they can only express their stupefaction, their incredulity in the face of the incredible, the world upside-down, the denial of their most intimate beliefs, of all that they hold most dear: "On the other hand, but it's difficult to talk about. Is it true? Might it not be lies or slander? I hear that recently some professors were not only driven to refuse to invigilate exams – which could be defensible as such – but to boycott them, to mark them improperly on purpose. That's what I've heard, but I can't believe it."' *Homo Academicus*, pp. 183–4.

47 See above, Lecture of 25 April 1985, note 52.

48 Pierre Bourdieu (ed.), *Photography: A Middle-Brow Art*, trans. Shaun Whiteside (Cambridge: Polity, 1990).

49 An allusion to criticism of several works by Alain Robbe-Grillet that Roland Barthes had published in the review *Critique*, and to the dialogue between the author and the critic that followed the former's intervention at the Cerisy colloquium devoted to the latter: Alain Robbe-Grillet, 'Pourquoi j'aime Barthes', in *Prétexte: Roland Barthes. Colloque de Cerisy* (Paris: UGE, '10/18', 1978), pp. 244–72.

304 *Notes to pp. 225–229*

Lecture of 30 May 1985

1 This was the tragedy of the Heysel stadium, which had been seen the day before on live television, during the broadcast of the European Cup final between the Liverpool and Juventus football clubs. Before the match, some hooligans from Liverpool invaded one of the terraces of the Juventus supporters. The commotion that followed caused the collapse of a terrace wall, with thirty-nine deaths.
2 A reference to the prolonged strike, between March 1984 and March 1985, of the British miners' union against the closure of loss-making pits, decided by the government of the 'Iron Lady' (Margaret Thatcher's nickname). The latter refused to budge, determined to break the power of the unions once and for all time.
3 An allusion either to the Collège de philosophie founded in 1974 by Jean Wahl or to the Collège international de philosophie, a more recent foundation (dating from 1983) by François Châtelet, Jacques Derrida, Jean-Pierre Faye and Dominique Lecourt.
4 This allusion is aimed at the Althusserians. Louis Althusser had published in particular 'Sur le travail théorique', *La Pensée*, no. 132, 1967, pp. 3–22.
5 A first version of the provision of a theoretical perspective proposed by Bourdieu in this lecture had been presented in 'Sur le pouvoir symbolique'.
6 The Greek word *skholè* means leisure but also the place of leisure (as opposed to a practical occupation) that is the school (*schola* in Latin).
7 For instance, the following comment that Max Weber is said to have made to his students shortly before his death in 1920 has been recorded more than once: 'The sincerity of the intellectual today, and especially a philosopher, can be measured by the way he situates himself in relation to Nietzsche and Marx. Anyone who does not recognise that without the works of these two authors, he would not have been able to accomplish a considerable part of his work, is deceiving himself and others. The intellectual world in which we live has been largely formed by Marx and Nietzsche.' Éduard Baumgarten, *Max Weber. Werk und Person* (Tübingen: Mohr, 1964), pp. 554–5.
8 'Religious suffering is at one and the same time the *expression* of real suffering and a protest against real suffering. Religion is the sigh of the oppressed creature, the heart of a heartless world and the soul of soulless conditions. It is the *opium* of the people.' Marx, 'A Contribution to the Critique of Hegel's Philosophy of Right. Introduction', *Early Writings*, p. 244.
9 Ernst Cassirer, *The Philosophy of Symbolic Forms*, 3 vols., trans. Steve G. Lofts (London: Routledge, 2020 [1923–29]).
10 Ernst Cassirer, *Substance and Function* and *Einstein's Theory of Relativity*, trans. William Curtis Swabey and Marie Collins Swabey (New York: Dover, 1923 [1910]).
11 Ernst Cassirer, *An Essay on Man*, trans. Anne Applebaum (New Haven: Yale University Press, 1962 [1940]).
12 Ernst Cassirer, 'Le langage et la construction du monde des objects', *Journal de psychologie normale et pathologique*, nos. 1–4, 1993, pp. 18–45 (also in *The Warburg Years (1919–1933): Essays on Language, Art, Myth and Technology*, trans. S. G. Lofts and A. Calcagno (New Haven: Yale University Press, 2014).
13 Gaston Bachelard, *Le Rationalisme appliqué* (Paris: PUF, 1949).
14 Wilhelm von Humboldt, *Introduction à l'oeuvre sur le kavi et autres essais (1822–1830)*, trans. Pierre Causat (Paris: Seuil, 1974).

Notes to pp. 229–232   305

15 Edward Sapir, *Culture, Language and Personality: Selected Essays* (Berkeley: University of California Press, 1985); Benjamin Lee Whorf, *Language, Thought, and Reality* (Cambridge MA: MIT Press, 1956).

16 See Bourdieu, *Classification Struggles*, p. 62, and above, the Lecture of 28 March 1985.

17 See the Lecture of 28 March 1985.

18 'What is both the integral and concrete object of linguistics? [. . .] Other sciences work with objects that are given in advance and that can then be considered from different viewpoints; but not linguistics. Someone pronounces the French word *nu* 'bare': a superficial observer would be tempted to call the word a concrete linguistic object; but a more careful examination would reveal successively three or four quite different things, depending on whether the word is considered as a sound, as the expression of an idea, as the equivalent of Latin *nudum*, etc. Far from it being the object that antedates the viewpoint, it would seem that it is the viewpoint that creates the object; besides, nothing tells us in advance that one way of considering the fact in question takes precedence over the others or is in any way superior to them.' Ferdinand de Saussure, *Course in General Linguistics*, trans. Wade Baskin (New York: Philosophical Library, 1959), pp. 7–8.

19 It is the first thesis: 'The chief defect of all hitherto existing materialism (that of Feuerbach included) is that the thing, reality, sensuousness, is conceived only in the form of the *object or of contemplation*, but not as *sensuous human activity, practice*, not subjectively. Hence, in contradistinction to materialism, the *active* side was developed abstractly by idealism – which, of course, does not know real, sensuous activity as such. Feuerbach wants sensuous objects, really distinct from the thought objects, but he does not conceive human activity itself as *objective* activity.' Marx, 'Theses on Feuerbach', in *Early Writings*, p. 421.

20 '*Every social phenomenon* has in fact one essential attribute: whether it is a symbol, a word, an instrument or an institution; whether it is even language itself or the best made science; whether it is the instrument adapted to the best and most numerous ends, whether it is the most rational and most human possible, *it is still arbitrary*.' Marcel Mauss, 'Civilizations: Elements and Forms' [1929], in *Classical Readings on Culture and Civilization*, ed. John Rundell and Stephen Mennell (London: Routledge, 1998), pp. 155–9.

21 'The bond between the signifier and the signified is arbitrary. Since I mean by sign the whole that results from the association of the signifier with the signified, I can simply say, *the linguistic sign is arbitrary*.' Saussure, *Course in General Linguistics*, p. 67.

22 'They embody a large part of human history. This means that to succeed in understanding and judging these categories we must have recourse to new procedures. To know what those conceptions are made of that we have not made ourselves, it is not enough simply to consult our own consciousness; we must look inside ourselves, we must observe history, we must establish a whole science, and a complex one.' Durkheim, *The Elementary Forms of Religious Life*, p. 21.

23 The introduction to *The Elementary Forms of Religious Life* is presented as an attempt to transcend the debate opposing 'empiricism' to 'apriorism'.

24 Pierre Bourdieu, *Zur Soziologie des symbolischen Formen* (Frankfurt-am-Main: Suhrkamp, 1970).

306   *Notes to pp. 232–239*

25 Émile Durkheim and Marcel Mauss, *Primitive Classification* (Chicago: University of Chicago Press, 1963 [1903]).
26 Ernst Cassirer, *The Myth of the State* (New Haven: Yale University Press, 1946).
27 The book was published in 1946. Cassirer died in 1945; he wrote *The Myth of the State* in the last years of his life, after leaving for the United States in 1941.
28 'I have presented a certain number of examples of "primitive" methods of classification in *Die Begriffsform im mythischen Denken*, "Studien der Bibliothek Warburg" (Leipzig, 1922). See also Émile Durkheim and Marcel Mauss, "De quelques formes primitives de classification", *Année Sociologique*, Vi (Paris, 1901–2).' Cassirer, *The Myth of the State*, p. 16, note 15.
29 Erwin Panofsky, *Studies in Iconology: Humanistic Themes in the Art of the Renaissance* (Boulder: Westview Press, 1972 [1939]).
30 Erwin Panofsky, *Perspective as Symbolic Form* (Cambridge MA: MIT Press, 1992). And see also Bourdieu's own translation of *Architecture gothique et pensée scolastique* (Paris: Minuit, 1967).
31 'Erwin Panofsky has very kindly written to inform me that the self-portrait of Roger van der Weyden no longer exists. What has survived is an old Gobelin copy, which is now in the Berne museum.' Ernst Cassirer, *The Individual and the Cosmos in Renaissance Philosophy* (Chicago: University of Chicago Press, 2010 [1927]), p. 31, note 29.
32 Pierre Francastel, *Peinture et société. Naissance et destruction d'un espace plastique de la Renaissance au cubismes* (Lyon: Audin, 1951).
33 See the Lecture of 18 April 1985.
34 A reference to the analyses devoted by Bourdieu to the Impressionist revolution in the 'seminar' part of his course throughout this 1984–85 year.
35 Francis Haskell, 'Les musées et leurs ennemis', *Actes de la recherche en sciences sociales*, no. 49, 1983, pp. 103–6.
36 Bourdieu returns to this problem in *Science of Science and Reflexivity*.
37 Jean-Loup Amselle and Elikia M'Bokolo, *Au coeur de l'ethnie. Ethnies, tribalisme et État en Afrique* (Paris: La Découverte/Maspero, 1985).
38 A reference to the analyses by Émile Benveniste that Bourdieu has mentioned several times in his lectures. On the region, see Bourdieu, 'L'identité et la représentation. Éléments pour une réflexion crtique sur l'idée de région'; republished as 'Identity and Representation: Elements for a Critical Reflection on the Idea of Region', in *Language and Symbolic Power*, pp. 220–8.
39 Kant, *Critique of Pure Reason*, 'Transcendental Aesthetic', § 8, IV, pp. 185–92. Bourdieu had already used this opposition in the previous Lectures of 25 April and 9 May 1985.
40 'So society cannot abandon these categories to the free will of particular individuals without abandoning itself. To live, society needs not only a degree of moral conformity but a minimum of logical conformity as well. Therefore, to prevent dissident views it leans on its members with all the weight of its authority.' Durkheim, *The Elementary Forms of Religious Life*, p. 19.
41 Here Bourdieu rehearses the analyses with which he opened his series of lectures at the Collège de France. See *Classification Struggles*, pp. 12–14.
42 Ernst Cassirer, 'Structuralism in Modern Linguistics', *Word: Journal of the Linguistic Circle of New York*, vol. 1, no. 2, 1945, pp. 99–120. Bourdieu had already mentioned this article in a previous lecture (*Habitus and Field*, pp. 203–4).

Notes to pp. 239–245 307

43 'Mythology is not *allegorical*: it is *tautogorical*. To mythology the gods are actually existing essences, gods that are not something *else*, do not mean something *else*, but rather *mean* only what they are.' Friedrich Schelling, *Historical-Critical Introduction to the Philosophy of Mythology*, trans. Mason Richey and Markus Zisselberger (New York: SUNY Press, 2008), p. 136.

44 A reference to God who, as opposed to a deceiver, is true, and guarantees our knowledge. See René Descartes, *Meditations on First Philosophy*, especially Meditation V.

45 The phrase that Bourdieu borrows relates in fact to language: 'Man lives with his objects chiefly – in fact, since his feeling and acting depend on his perceptions, one may say exclusively – as language presents them to him. By the same process whereby he spins language out of his own being, he ensnares himself in it; and each language draws a magic circle round the people to which it belongs, a circle from which there is no escape save by stepping out of it into another.' Ernst Cassirer, *Language and Myth: On the Names of God*, trans. Susanne K. Langer (New York: Dover, 1953), p. 9, quoting Wilhelm von Humboldt, *Einleitung zum Kawi-Werk*, SW, VI, 60.

46 Alfred R. Radcliffe-Brown, *Structure and Function in Primitive Society* (London: Cohen and West, 1952).

47 Bourdieu devoted two years of lectures (1998–99 and 1999–2000) to analysing the symbolic revolution inaugurated by Manet. See *Manet: A Symbolic Revolution*.

48 In his critique of the Althusserian philosophical critics, Bourdieu shows that they use the same rhetorical procedures as the critical philosophers attacked by Marx. See Pierre Bourdieu, 'Le discours d'importance. Quelques remarques critiques sur "Quelques remarques critiques à propos de Lire Le Capital"', in *Langage et pouvoir symbolique* (Paris: Seuil, 2001), pp. 379–96. [This essay is one of those omitted from the English translated volume *Language and Symbolic Power* (Translator).]

49 Bourdieu, 'Genèse et structure du champ religieux'.

50 Friedrich Nietzsche, *The Genealogy of Morality*, trans. Carol Diethe (Cambridge: Cambridge University Press, 2007 [1887]).

51 For instance: 'As for the European bureaucracy . . . it found itself compelled to pay more official respect to the existing churches in the interest of control over the masses', or again: 'the interest of the privileged classes in maintaining the existing religion as an instrument for controlling the masses, their need for social distance, their abhorrence of educational activities among the masses (as tending to destroy the prestige of elite groups)'. Weber, *The Sociology of Religion*, pp. 90, 136.

52 See the Lecture of 19 April 1984 in *Forms of Capital*, pp. 171, 338–9, and Weber, 'Theodicy, Salvation and Rebirth', in *The Sociology of Religion*, pp. 138–50.

53 An allusion in particular to Michel Foucault, who uses the formula for instance in *The History of Sexuality*, vol. 1, trans. Robert Hurley (New York: Pantheon Books, 1978), p. 94.

54 An allusion to Pierre Legendre, *Jouir du pouvoir. Traité de la bureaucratie patriote* (Paris: Minuit, 1976); *L'Amour du censeur. Essai sur l'ordre dogmatique* (Paris: Seuil, 1974), and perhaps to Jean-François Lyotard. Bourdieu returns to these analyses the following year.

55 This phrase, quoted (among others) by Nicholas of Cusa, is to be found in the

308   *Notes to pp. 245–251*

famous text of medieval philosophy composed of twenty-four definitions of God, including the one positing that 'God is an infinite sphere whose centre is everywhere, and whose circumference nowhere' (*Liber XXIV philosophorum*).

56 Letter from Friedrich Engels to Conrad Schmidt, 27 October 1890, in *Marx and Engels Correspondence* (New York: International Publishers, 1968). [Although Engels does in fact talk of an 'ideological concept' (Translator).]

57 Friedrich Engels, *The Peasant War in Germany*, trans. Moissaye J. Olgin (Abingdon: Routledge, 2015 [1850]).

58 See Bourdieu, 'Genèse et structure du champ religieux'.

59 The comedian Coluche had announced in 1980 that he was thinking of standing as a candidate in the 1981 presidential election, which had triggered extremely virulent reactions from politicians and journalists. Bourdieu joined Félix Guattari and Gilles Deleuze in supporting his candidature. He develops the analysis mentioned here in particular in the article 'La Représentation politique. Éléments pour une théorie du champ politique', *Actes de la recherche en sciences sociales*, nos. 36–7, 1981, pp. 3–24, republished as 'Political Representation: Elements for a Theory of the Political Field', in *Language and Symbolic Power*, pp. 171–202.

60 'In the event of failure, the magician possibly paid with his life. On the other hand, priests have enjoyed the contrasting advantage of being able to deflect the blame for failure away from themselves and onto their god. Yet even the priests' prestige is in danger of falling with that of their gods. However, priests may find ways of interpreting failures in such a manner that the responsibility falls, not upon the god, but upon the behaviour of the god's worshippers . . . The problem of why the god has not hearkened to his devotees might then be explained by stating that they had not honoured their god sufficiently, they had not satisfied his desires for sacrificial blood or soma juice, or finally that they neglected him in favour of other gods.' Weber, *Economy and Society*, pp. 427–8.

61 Bourdieu is referring to the notion of the 'certificate', which he had discussed in the Lecture of 9 May 1985.

62 An allusion perhaps to the emergence in the 1960s and 1970s of a search by the new petite bourgeoisie for a 'personal religion'. Bourdieu and de Saint Martin, 'La Sainte famille', p. 35.

63 Benveniste, *Dictionary of Indo-European Concepts and Society*, pp. 307–12.

64 E. H. Kantorowicz, *The King's Two Bodies* (Princeton: Princeton University Press, 1957).

65 See the Lecture of 9 May 1985.

66 The notion of a 'hidden God' is to be found in the Bible (and again in Blaise Pascal's *Pensées*).

67 See the Lecture of 22 March 1984, in *Forms of Capital*, pp. 121, 332 note 45.

68 As he does to some extent for this year of lectures, Bourdieu concludes his *Pascalian Meditations* by rehabilitating this quotation from Durkheim: 'Durkheim was, it can be seen, not so naive as is claimed when he said, as Kafka might have, that "Society is God".' *Pascalian Meditations*, p. 245.

69 This was the nickname given to Émile Combes (a former seminarist), who, at the end of the nineteenth and beginning of the twentieth century held high political office and was one of the key political figures responsible for introducing the law of the separation of Church and State.

70 See the Lecture of 8 March 1984, in *Forms of Capital*, p. 54.

Notes to pp. 252–259 309

71 As he had done on several occasions during his lectures, Bourdieu is referring to the origin of the word *veredictum*: 'to tell the truth'.

Situating the Later Volumes of *General Sociology* in the Work of Pierre Bourdieu

1 Lecture of 28 April 1982, in Bourdieu, *Classification Struggles*, p. 11.
2 Ibid.
3 'The notion of habitus means that there is a sort of information capital that structures and is structured, that functions as a principle of structured practices without these structures that can be found in the practices having existed before the production of the practices in the form of rules' (10 May 1984).
4 A formula employed in Pierre Bourdieu, Jean-Claude Chamboredon and Jean-Claude Passeron, *The Craft of Sociology: Epistemological Preliminaries*, trans. Richard Nice (Berlin: de Gruyter, 1991 [1968]), p. 35.
5 Bourdieu would certainly have revised the text as was his habit, but an aside ('In fact, what I have to say does exist, or I hope that it will, in book form' [25 April 1985]) and later indications ('This chapter . . . tends to leave aside the specific logic of each of the specialized fields . . . that I have analysed elsewhere and which will be the subject of a forthcoming book.' *The Rules of Art*, p. 380; see also *On the State*, p. 367) indicate that he envisaged publishing one or several volumes. The Course in General Sociology is perhaps one of the lecture courses that were not published for lack of time (on this point see Pierre Bourdieu and Yvette Delsaut, 'L'esprit de la recherche', in Yvette Delsaut and Marie-Christine Rivière, *Bibliographie des travaux de Pierre Bourdieu, suivi d'un entretien sur l'esprit de la recherche* (Pantin: Le temps des cerises, 2002), p. 224. *Pascalian Meditations* (like the volume on the 'theory of fields' that he had nearly finished) was an opportunity to publish some developments from the lectures.
6 The reflections delivered during this first year 1981–82 were to furnish the substance of an important later article: 'The Social Space and the Genesis of Groups', *Theory and Society*, vol. 14, no. 6, 1985, pp. 723–44.
7 'And if I rework the same themes and return several times to the same objects and the same analyses, it is always, I think, in a spiralling movement which makes it possible to attain each time a higher level of explicitness and comprehension, and to discover unnoticed relationships and hidden properties.' Bourdieu, *Pascalian Meditations*, p. 8.
8 See Bourdieu and Delsaut, 'L'esprit de la recherche', p. 193.
9 As noted earlier, this incident explains why the first year of lectures, published in the first volume, *Classification Struggles*, is shorter than the following four (and perhaps also why the second year, *Habitus and Field*, is the longest: Bourdieu had probably envisaged a greater number of sessions in 1982–83 to make up for the sessions that he had not been able to provide in spring 1982).
10 Bourdieu, *Classification Struggles*, p. 4.
11 On the other hand he is sometimes very pleased with this (see, for example, the Lecture of 2 May 1985).
12 'These questions are very useful for me psychologically because they give me the feeling that I have a better idea of your expectations' (23 May 1985).

310   *Notes to pp. 259–263*

13 As a result, the lectures published in this volume all last more or less two sessions, whereas in 1982–83 some lectures lasted considerably longer than the time allotted.

14 Between the two sessions Bourdieu observed a formal break (or an 'interval', as he somewhat ironically calls it, perhaps to remind us of the objectively rather theatrical nature of the occasion).

15 Pierre Bourdieu, 'L'institutionnalisation de l'anomie', *Les cahiers du Musée national d'art moderne*, nos. 19–20, 1987, pp. 6–19; 'La révolution impressionniste', *Noroît*, no. 303, 1987, pp. 3–18.

16 Bourdieu, *Manet: A Symbolic Revolution*.

17 See the indications given on this subject in the Lecture of 14 March 1985.

18 Bourdieu and Koch, 'The Invention of the Artist's Life'.

19 'The Hit Parade of French Intellectuals, or Who Is to Judge the Legitimacy of the Judges?'

20 Pierre Bourdieu, 'Un jeu chinois. Notes pour une critique sociale du jugement', *Actes de la recherche en sciences sociales*, no. 4, 1976, pp. 91–101, and 'Associations: A Parlour Game', in *Distinction*, pp. 546–59.

21 'I'm rather like an old doctor who knows all the diseases of the sociological understanding.' Interview with Pierre Bourdieu by Beate Krais (December 1988), in *The Craft of Sociology*, p. 256.

22 *The Craft of Sociology*, pp. 256–7.

23 We may note that it was in 1985 that Bourdieu ceased to direct the Centre de l'éducation et de la culture.

24 In fact between 1983 and 1997 Bourdieu's graduates completed only half as many theses as between 1970 and 1983 (fourteen as opposed to twenty-nine).

25 Bourdieu and Koch, 'The Invention of the Artist's Life'.

26 Bourdieu refers more briefly to Dostoevsky's *The Gambler* (29 March 1984). During this period he also published an article on Francis Ponge, 'Nécessiter', in 'Francis Ponge', *Cahiers de L'Herne*, 1986, pp. 434–7.

27 Pierre Bourdieu, 'La dernière instance', in *Le siècle de Kafka* (Paris: Centre Georges Pompidou, 1984), pp. 268–70. Reprinted in *Choses dites* (Paris: Les Éditions de Minuit, 1987).

28 Pierre Bourdieu, *Images d'Algérie. Une affinité élective* (Arles: Actes Sud/Sinbad/Camera Austria, 2003), p. 42.

29 The index of the volumes of the *General Sociology* confirms this: Marx, Durkheim and Weber are the authors that Bourdieu refers to most often (they are followed by Sartre, Kant, Hegel, Flaubert, Lévi-Strauss, Plato, Goffman, Kafka, Foucault and Husserl). It is Weber who is cited the most (116 citations against 86 and 81 for Marx and Durkheim), particularly in 1983–84.

30 Pierre Bourdieu, 'N'ayez pas peur de Max Weber!', *Libération*, 6 July 1982, p. 25.

31 In 1962–63, when Bourdieu was teaching at Lille, he had devoted a lecture course to Max Weber and invited his students to read and translate passages from *Economy and Society*. In the 1960s he had made copies of selected passages for his students and researchers. It was only in 1971 that Plon published a partial translation of the book.

32 Pierre Bourdieu, 'The Force of Law: Toward a Sociology of the Juridical Field', *Hastings Law Journal*, vol. 38, no. 5/3, 1987.

33 Bourdieu, *On the State*.

Notes to pp. 263–265 311

34 Pierre Bourdieu, 'La domination masculine', *Actes de la recherche en sciences sociales*, no. 4, 1990, pp. 2–31; *Masculine Domination*, trans. Richard Nice (Cambridge: Polity, 2001).

35 On this reflection (preceded by 'L'évolution des rapports entre le champ universitaire et le champ du journalisme', *Sigma*, no. 23, 1987, pp. 65–70), which includes an analysis of journalism in terms of field, see in particular 'L'emprise du journalisme', *Actes de la recherche en sciences sociales*, nos. 101–2, 1994, pp. 3–9; 'Journalisme et éthique' (Communication à l'ESJ Lille, 3 June 1994), *Les Cahiers du journalisme*, no. 1, 1996, pp. 10–17; 'Champ politique, champ des sciences sociales, champ journalistique (Cours du Collège de France, 14 November 1995)', *Cahiers du Groupe de recherche sur la socialisation* (Lyon: Université Lumière-Lyon 2, 1996), republished in English in Rodney Benson and Erik Neveu (eds.), *Bourdieu and the Journalistic Field* (Cambridge: Polity, 2005), pp. 29–47; *On Television* (Cambridge: Polity Press, 2011), 'Return to Television', in *Acts of Resistance: Against the New Myths of Our Time*, trans. Richard Nice (Cambridge: Polity, 1998), pp. 70–7; 'À propos de Karl Kraus et du journalisme', *Actes de la recherche en sciences sociales*, nos. 131–2, 2000, pp. 123–6.

36 Patrick Champagne, 'Sur la médiatisation du champ intellectuel. À propos de *Sur la télévision*', in Louis Pinto, Gisèle Sapiro and Patrick Champagne (eds.), *Pierre Bourdieu, sociologue* (Paris: Fayard, 2004), pp. 431–58.

37 During the period of these lectures, Bourdieu participated in two sessions of the TV talk show *Apostrophes* (for *Language and Symbolic Power* and *Homo Academicus* and then for the report by the Collège de France on education) and presented two of his books (*Language and Symbolic Power* and *Homo Academicus*) on two television news programmes (one 'regional' and the other 'night-time').

38 Drawing on his analyses of the fields of cultural production, he introduces a sociological reflection on the themes of the disaffection of 'the young' for the press and on the relations between journalism and the educational institution. See Philippe Bernard, 'Exercice illégal de la pédagogie', *Le Monde*, 16 May 1985.

39 See *Pierre Bourdieu et les médias. Rencontres INA/Sorbonne (15 mars 2003)* (Paris: L'Harmattan, 2004). In the years following the seminar (and therefore after the growth of the private channels in France), Bourdieu was one of the instigators of the movement 'Pour que vive la télévision publique' (Long live public television); see Pierre Bourdieu, Ange Casta, Max Gallo, Claude Marti, Jean Martin and Christian Pierret, 'Que vive la télévision publique!', *Le Monde*, 19 October 1988.

40 Remi Lenoir, 'Duby et les sociologues', in Jacques Dalarun and Patrick Boucheron (eds.), *Georges Duby. Portrait de l'historien en ses archives* (Paris: Gallimard, 2015), pp. 193–203.

41 Although the socialist François Mitterrand remained President of the Republic, legislative elections in 1986 compelled him to share power with a right-wing prime minister, Jacques Chirac.

42 *Propositions pour l'enseignement de l'avenir. Rapport du Collège de France* (Paris: Minuit, 1985), a forty-eight-page pamphlet; see also *Le Monde de l'éducation*, no. 116, May 1985, pp. 61–8.

43 On the origins, drafting and reception of the report, see the research in progress by P. Clément (for a first draft: 'Réformer les programmes pour changer l'école?'

312   *Notes to pp. 265–270*

Une sociologie historique du champ de pouvoir scolaire', doctoral thesis in sociology, Université de Picardie Jules-Verne, 2013, chapter 2, pp. 155–240).
44 Bourdieu, *Sketch for a Self-Analysis*, pp. 78–81.
45 Bourdieu mentions this ceremony in *Manet: A Symbolic Revolution*, pp. 318–19.
46 Pierre Bourdieu, 'Le plaisir de savoir', *Le Monde*, 27 June 1984; 'Non chiedetemi chi sono. Un profilo di Michel Foucault', *L'Indice*, October 1984, pp. 4–5.
47 For a detailed analysis of the philosophical field at the time of the lecture course, see Louis Pinto, *Les philosophes entre le lycée et l'avant-garde. Les métamorphoses de la philosophie dans la France d'aujourd'hui* (Paris: L'Harmattan, 1987).
48 See also Pierre Bourdieu, 'Sartre', *London Review of Books*, vol. 2, no. 22, 1980, pp. 11–12.
49 By this time, this intellectual recognition already included American universities. In Foucault's case, for instance, there was a wave of translations in 1977 in the United States. At this time, Bourdieu, who was slightly younger and the only one not to call himself a 'philosopher', lagged behind rather in this respect.
50 See Bourdieu, *Homo Academicus*, pp. 105–12.
51 Luc Ferry and Alain Renaut, *'La Pensée 68'. Essai sur l'anti humanisme contemporain* (Paris: Gallimard, 1985).
52 On this point see Benoît Peeters, *Derrida* (Paris: Flammarion, 2010), pp. 369–80.
53 This model is that of the intellectual combining genuinely intellectual recognition with notoriety for a fairly broad educated public. The beginning of the 1980s (which corresponds, for instance, to the moment when François Maspero sold his publishing house) was a period when publishers started to deplore the scarcity of scholarly authors able to sell in quantity, in a context where academic specialisation seemed to be increasing.
54 Collectif Les Révoltes logiques, *L'Empire du sociologue* (Paris: La Découverte, 1984).
55 We can also refer to his remark on the 'slightly Cubist' character of his sociology (9 May 1985).
56 Bourdieu, *Sociology in Question*.
57 Alain Accardo, *Initiation à la sociologie de l'illusionnisme social. Invitation à la lecture des oeuvres de Pierre Bourdieu* (Bordeaux: Le Mascaret, 1983; republished Marseille: Agone, 2006). This book was followed by a collection of texts edited by Alain Accardo and Philippe Corcuff: *La Sociologie de Bourdieu* (Bordeaux: Le Mascaret, 1986).
58 On the opposition between methodology and epistemology, see *The Craft of Sociology*, pp. 6–7, 11–12. On Bourdieu's relation to Paul Lazarsfeld's enterprise, see Bourdieu, *Sketch for a Self-Analysis*, pp. 72–5. On the 'methodological imperative' that tends to unite the different stages of Raymond Bourdon's sociology, see Johan Heilbron, *French Sociology* (Ithaca: Cornell University Press, 2015), pp. 193–7.
59 Bruno Latour and Steeve Woolgar, *Laboratory Life: The Social Construction of Scientific Facts* (London: Sage, 1979).
60 Bourdieu, *Science of Science and Reflexivity*.
61 On the public positions he adopted during this period, see Pierre Bourdieu, *Interventions 1961–2001: Science sociale et action politique* (Paris: Agone, 2002), pp. 157–87.
62 See for instance Bourdieu, *Acts of Resistance*, p. 40.

Notes to pp. 270–275 313

63 Jean-Pierre Chevènement was minister of education under prime minister Laurent Fabius from 1984 to 1986. He hoped to revive the original mission of the Republican school, which, in addition to promoting civic and lay values, was to level out social inequalities. (Translator)
64 In 1986, activists belonging to Solidarność, the Polish workers' trade union, demonstrated in favour of the release of political prisoners and organised strikes, which defied the regime of General W. Jaruzelski and paralysed the country. Bourdieu and some colleagues signed a petition protesting against the French government's lack of supporting action. (Translator)
65 Bourdieu, *On the State.*
66 Bourdieu, *Manet: A Symbolic Revolution.*
67 Bourdieu, *Science of Science and Reflexivity.*

Summary of Lectures of 1984–85

1 Bourdieu, *Manet: A Symbolic Revolution.* (Translator)

Index

Abensour, Miguel, 269
absolutism, 41–4, 46, 51, 193, 194
abstraction, 136–8
academic art, 29–31, 33–40, 59–72,
  88–95, 125, 151–5, 183–6, 191–2,
  217
academic capital, 4
academic crisis, 4, 33, 92–5, 100–2,
  212
academic eroticism, 70–1
academic field, 3–4, 13, 83, 90, 93–102,
  115, 141, 249, 261
Academy, 28, 30–2, 63, 101, 121–2,
  163, 183, 186–7, 190, 192, 194,
  214, 216, 275
Accardo, Alain, 267
*Actes de la recherche en sciences
  sociales*, 71, 197, 256
action, theory of, 255
administration, 97, 98; *see also*
  bureaucracy
aggiornamento, 32, 127
agrarian rites, 142
Alain, 52, 197, 200
Algeria, 138, 255, 256
Allais, Alphonse, 205
alliances, 112, 119, 143, 145–9, 156–7,
  163
allodoxia, 84
Althusser, Louis, 16, 43, 266
amateurism, 197, 199–200

Amiel, Henri-Frédéric, 70, 71
anachronism, 91, 93, 94, 152, 154, 162,
  191
anarchy, 13, 34, 214
anomie, 184, 186, 194, 212–14, 219,
  225, 252, 259
anthropology, 19, 22, 54, 117, 119,
  228, 255–6; *see also* ethnology
anti-institutionalism, 152–3, 266
anti-utilitarianism, 190–1
Aquinas, Thomas, 105
arbitrariness, 69, 73–4, 86, 208, 233,
  244, 248, 250, 252
architecture, 105
Aristotle, 25, 50, 138, 238
Aron, Raymond, 251
art criticism, 49, 62–3, 65, 69, 93, 126,
  128, 188, 202, 211, 214, 217–24,
  250
art for art's sake, 5–6, 31–3, 60, 62,
  131–2, 161–3, 189, 198, 218, 223,
  236–7
art market, 13–14, 163–4, 188, 215–17
art studios, 100, 125, 154
artisanship, 38, 188–9
artist as character, 187–91, 194
artistic field
  academic art, 29–31, 33–40, 59–72,
    88–95, 125, 151–5, 183–6, 191–2,
    217
  Academy, 28, 30–2, 63, 101, 121–2,

Index

163, 183, 186–7, 190, 192, 194, 214, 216, 275
art for art's sake, 5–6, 31–3, 60, 62, 131–2, 161–3, 189, 198, 218, 223, 236–7
art market, 13–14, 163–4, 188, 215–17
artist as character, 187–91, 194
artist biographies, 60, 63, 65
artists' way of life, 157–9, 161–2, 164, 194, 221
authentication of works, 202
birth of modern artist, 26–40, 59–72, 87–102, 120–32, 151–65, 181–95, 209–24, 259–60
bourgeois art, 31, 161, 191–2
canonisation, 28, 38–9, 63
certification, 184–5, 214, 220
Chinese painting, 36, 216
commissioned works, 37–8, 190, 216–17
competitions, 31, 151–2, 154, 185
consecration, 30, 63, 121, 123–4, 127–8, 130, 194, 214, 223
copying, 36–7, 65
criticism, 49, 62–3, 65, 69, 93, 126, 128, 188, 202, 211, 214, 217–24, 250
Cubism, 187
definitions of art and the artist 30–3, 121, 126, 184, 190, 214
and discourse, 58, 66–8
distinction between artist and artisan, 38, 188–9
École des beaux-arts, 28, 63, 69, 152, 154, 159
finished and unfinished works, 30, 38–9, 66, 89
hierarchy of disciplines, 66–7, 69–70
history painting, 66–7, 69–72
hit parade effect, 13–14, 159
Impressionism, 26, 30, 33–5, 61, 63–70, 87–95, 124–32, 153–5, 163–4, 192, 210–24, 236, 275
landscape painting, 66

and legitimacy, 35, 60, 68, 70, 71, 92, 121, 126, 183–5, 194, 212–14
meaning in works, 62, 67, 193–4, 222–3
nudes, 63, 69–71
open works, 193
painter–writer couples, 191–5
painting as performance, 36–8, 65–6
portraiture, 61
priceless works, 188
prices of works, 64, 188
pure love of art, 157, 158, 187, 190
rapins, 100, 121, 157
readability of works, 31–2, 67–8
relation of artist to object, 37
relation to literary field, 1, 26–8, 32–3, 60–2, 66–7, 131–2, 156–65, 187–95, 260
revolution in, 26–40, 64–70, 87–95, 101–2, 120–32, 153, 156, 163–4, 192, 210–24, 259, 275
Salon, 28, 29, 31, 36, 101, 122, 123–4, 126, 189
Salon des refusés, 101–2, 123–5, 128, 163, 214
sculpture, 189
social art, 31, 161, 198
social conditions of artistic production, 59, 87, 101–2, 213
and the State, 27–9, 63–4, 184, 216–17
studios, 100, 125, 154
structure of, 92–5
technique, 38, 66, 67, 69, 193–4
training of artists, 30, 35–6, 38–9, 69, 89, 92, 220
unique works, 36–7
virtuosity, 36, 38, 65–6, 125, 154
artists' way of life, 157–9, 161–2, 164, 194, 221
Asylums (Goffman), 118
authenticity, 69, 177, 202, 207
authority, 25, 30, 63, 116, 128, 172, 176–7, 197
autocracy, 214

316 *Index*

autonomous fields, 5, 6, 33, 34, 72, 81, 106–7, 188, 211
autonomy, 29, 32, 38, 60, 87, 106–7, 119, 172, 192–4, 212, 214, 217, 246, 248
avant-garde, 34, 124–5, 128, 162–3, 186, 190–2, 219
awareness context, 16–17

Bachelard, Gaston, 9, 228–9
bad faith, 113, 133–4, 141, 142–3
Bakhtin, Mikhail, 138
Bakunin, Mikhail, 9
Balzac, Honoré de, 94, 158, 194
Barbizon painters, 66
Barthes, Roland, 78, 164, 222
Bataille, Georges, 190
Baudelaire, Charles, 28, 191–2
Baxandall, Michael, 71
Beckett, Samuel, 261
being-perceived, 76–7, 79–80, 129, 273
being seen-to-be-seen, 115–16, 120, 273
belonging, 83–4, 98, 139
Benjamin, Walter, 202
Bentham, Jeremy, 81
Benveniste, Émile, 43, 114–15, 116–17, 240, 247, 273
Berlioz, Hector, 132, 189
biographical illusion, 262
biographies, 60, 63, 65, 108, 142
biological reproduction, 99, 204
bluffing *see* simulation
Bohemia, 97, 100, 121, 158
Boime, Albert, 67, 91, 218
Boltanski, Luc, 70
Boudon, Raymond, 268
Boulanger, Louis, 189
boundaries, 25, 42, 44, 114, 142–3, 147, 150, 160, 179–81, 237, 248
Bourdieu, Marie-Claire, 260
bourgeois art, 31, 161, 191–2
Bourricaud, François, 268
bureaucracy, 170, 172–3, 182, 197, 199, 200–8, 216–17

bureaucratic judgements, 204–5
business, 5–6, 81, 98, 112

canon law, 117, 248
canonisation, 28, 38–9, 63, 159–60, 197
capital
    academic capital, 4
    codification of, 3, 255
    concentration of, 250
    cultural capital, 2–3, 4, 6, 21, 23, 138–9, 148, 204, 255, 273
    distribution of, 2, 4, 10, 25–6, 147–8, 204
    economic capital, 2–3, 6, 138–9, 147–8
    forms of, 2–3, 4–6, 254–5, 256
    information capital, 21–2, 256
    objectification of, 255
    power over, 3–4
    and power relations, 243
    relation to the field, 2, 4, 254, 256
    relation to habitus, 256
    social capital, 2–3, 148, 217
    symbolic capital, 111–12, 114–17, 145–7, 150–1, 255
    theoretical capital, 227
    transformation from one form to another, 3
capitalism, 149, 163
Caravaggio, 91
Cassagne, Albert, 218
Cassirer, Ernst, 108, 228, 229–31, 232–3, 234–5, 239
categorial mediation, 203–5
categorisation *see* classification
celebrity, 52
censors, 172, 274
censorship, 105
censuses, 172, 244, 274
central bank myth, 250–2, 274
centralisation, 97
certification, 166–82, 184–5, 201–3, 207–9, 214, 220, 237, 250–1, 263, 274
Cézanne, Paul, 101, 128–9

Index

Champollion, Jean-François, 88
Changeux, Jean-Pierre, 265
charisma, 115, 183, 185, 199, 216
charity, 169, 170–1, 203, 270
Chassériau, Théodore, 189
Chateaubriand, François-René de, 187
Chatterton (Vigny), 157
Chevènement, Jean-Pierre, 270
Chicago School, 270
China, 36, 122, 216
Chinese art, 36, 216
civil status, 118–19, 138, 205, 252, 274
class
    Bourdieu's research on, 254, 255–6, 257–8
    class struggle, 6, 13, 48, 246
    dominant classes, 3, 6, 44, 47, 58, 177, 216, 242–3
    dominated classes, 19, 47, 58
    and the labour market, 97–8
    Marx on, 108, 146, 242–3
classification
    and certification, 170–1, 174–5, 178
    and codification, 51–2, 138, 171, 178
    Kantian perspectives on, 229–30
    medical classifications, 174–5, 178
    official classifications, 45–6, 103–4, 172
    and perception, 77–8, 241
    political classifications, 53–7, 230
    and practical logics, 49–57
    in pre-capitalist societies, 49–51
    primitive forms of, 232–5
    principles of, 20, 54, 64, 229–30
    scientific classifications, 45–6
    structure of systems of, 77–8
    struggle over, 48, 87, 102, 129, 138, 145, 245, 248, 273
    taxonomies, 20, 49–50, 54, 63, 129, 208, 229, 237, 243
    and the theory effect, 55–7
clubs, 146–7, 149–50
codification, 3, 51–2, 117–19, 131, 138, 150–1, 171, 178, 256, 262, 274
Cogniet, Léon, 154

cognitive sociology, 228–9
cognitive solidarity, 240–1
cognitive structures, 17, 18, 22, 29, 228–9, 232–4, 272, 274
Cohen-Tannoudji, Claude, 265
collective bad faith, 113, 133–4, 141, 142–3
collective conversion, 126–8, 130–1, 156
collective decision-making, 148
collective identity, 147, 150
collective judgement, 217–19
collective strategies, 111, 146–7, 148, 150
Collège de France, 73–4, 91, 151, 159, 254, 255, 258–9, 261, 264–5, 267, 271
colonialism, 72
colour, 33, 66, 87, 194, 222
Coluche, 246–7
commissioned works, 37–8, 190, 216–17
common sense, 8, 9, 50, 124
communication, 32, 120, 206, 239, 241, 242, 243
comparative sociology, 44
competence, 179–80, 185–6, 192, 212, 237, 248, 274
competitions, 31, 39, 151–2, 154, 185
componential analysis, 230
Condillac, Étienne Bonnot de, 130
conditioning, 22
Confucian art, 216
consecration, 30, 63, 120–4, 127–8, 130, 148, 160, 167, 191, 194, 214, 223, 247, 251, 274
consensus, 120, 207, 213–14, 238, 240, 247, 274
conservatism, 31, 67, 92–3, 234
conspicuous consumption, 146
constructivism, 255
consumption, 96, 146
continuity, 51–2, 77, 79, 256
conversion, 121–2, 126–8, 130–1, 156
copying, 36–7, 65

318   *Index*

corps effects, 3, 147–51, 256, 274
corps of professionals, 245–7, 249
Counterfeiters, The (Gide), 61–2
Courbet, Gustave, 28–9, 31, 60, 101,
     211
Couture, Thomas, 39, 63, 70, 125, 220
craftsmanship *see* artisanship
credit, 115, 119, 126, 147, 149, 203
crisis, 4, 33, 77, 79, 92–102, 130, 113,
     114, 130, 156, 212
criticism *see* art criticism; literary
     criticism
Critique littéraire, La (Fayolle), 93
Critique of Judgement (Kant), 200
Crystal Palace exhibition, 39
Cubism, 187
cultural capital, 2–3, 4, 6, 21, 23,
     138–9, 148, 204, 255, 273
cultural power, 109
cultural production, field of, 4, 35,
     95–8, 121, 130–2, 153
cultural revolution, 69, 210–13,
     216–220
culturalism, 230–1
Culture and Society (Williams), 215–16
custom, 117

Dahl, Robert Alan, 2
Daumas, Louis-Joseph, 37
David, Jacques-Louis, 71
death, 122, 123, 157, 158, 161, 164,
     187, 191
Début dans la vie, Un (Balzac), 94
decision-making, 134–6, 148
decision theory, 258
decolonisation, 124
definitions, 30–3, 121, 126, 134, 184,
     190, 197, 214
Delacroix, Eugène, 61, 157, 189
Delaroche, Paul, 159
delegation, 65, 148, 176, 185, 199, 245,
     246
Deleuze, Gilles, 22, 266
demography, 98–9, 151, 172, 217
de-realisation effect, 69–72

Derrida, Jacques, 266
Descartes, René, 14–15, 86, 90, 239–40
determinism, 90, 106–7, 176
d'Holbach, Paul-Henri Thiry, Baron,
     250
diacrisis, 77–80, 82, 112, 114, 168, 177,
     185, 232, 235, 240, 247
diagnosis, 168, 169, 171, 174–5, 178,
     180
*Dictionary of Indo-European Concepts
     and Society* (Benveniste), 114–15,
     240, 247
Dictionnaire critique de la sociologie,
     268
differentiated societies, 255–6
differentiation, 5–6, 12, 19, 80–4, 106,
     242, 273
disability, 167–8, 174, 177–8, 181, 237,
     274
discontinuity, 77
discourse
     dominant discourse, 31
     and gender, 117, 118
     hidden discourse, 200
     and institutions, 59, 88, 118
     and the law, 117–18
     monopoly of, 58, 246
     mythical discourse, 243
     official discourse, 117, 140
     and painting, 58, 66–8
     passage from action to discourse,
          84–7
     philosophical discourse, 197, 200
     political discourse, 58, 114
     and position, 84–5, 88–9
     and power, 114–15, 116
     psychiatric discourse, 118
     religious discourse, 242, 246
     scientific discourse, 46–7
     theoretical discourse, 55, 112, 197,
          200, 226–7
discredit, 13, 119, 120, 126, 149, 150
discrimination, 77–84, 85, 87, 114, 177,
     179, 273
dispositions, 17–18

distinction, 76–80, 83–4, 93, 146, 149, 250
Distinction (Bourdieu), 45, 255, 257, 267
distribution
  of capital, 2, 4, 10, 25–6, 147–8, 204
  continuous distributions, 51–2
  of educational success, 172–3
  fair and unfair distributions, 10, 25–6, 168–9, 173–4
  legitimate distribution, 168, 174, 180–1, 251
  of power, 2, 3–4, 25–6, 171, 227
  redistribution, 168–9, 173–4, 180–1, 251
  statistical analysis of, 171–3
  struggle over, 168–9, 173–4, 180–1
  transformation of, 26, 168–9
  of wealth, 172, 251
diversion, 90
division of labour, 18, 19, 20, 53, 99, 245–7
Division of Labour in Society, The (Durkheim), 99
doctors, 167–8, 170–2, 174–6, 177, 179–80, 203, 250, 274
domination
  dominant classes, 3, 6, 44, 47, 58, 177, 216, 242–3
  dominant definitions, 32, 197
  dominant discourse, 31
  dominant positions, 17
  dominant vision, 87, 116, 118, 125, 130, 136–7, 187, 212–13
  dominated classes, 19, 47, 58
  domination effects, 213–14, 244, 250
  domination of the dominant, 17, 223
  ideology as instrument of, 242–3
  Marx on, 17, 241–3
  masculine domination, 263
  and religion, 242, 244
  strategies of the dominated, 19, 101
  symbolic domination, 124, 134, 244, 245–9

symbolic systems as instruments of, 241–2
Don Quixote effect, 19
doxa, 30, 105
doxic experience, 234, 235
dualism, 18, 47, 49–50, 53, 54, 76–80, 83, 86–7, 114, 142–3, 234, 235–6
Duby, Georges, 44, 264
Duchamp, Marcel, 61, 193, 202
Ducrot, Oswald, 135
Dumézil, Georges, 44, 247, 264
Durkheim, Émile
  on anomie, 184
  and demography, 99
  on the division of labour, 99
  Kantianism, 231–2
  on logic, 16, 233–4, 238–9, 241
  on logical conformism, 238
  on magic, 117
  on morphological effects, 98–9
  objectivism, 7–8, 74
  on pedagogy, 70–1
  on primitive classification, 232–4
  on religion, 117, 118, 231–2
  on the sacred, 114
  on the structure of groups, 16, 233–4, 238–9, 241
  on symbolic systems, 238–9, 240–1
  on undifferentiated societies, 5
  on viewpoints, 42, 44
Duseigneur, Jean, 131, 189

Eco, Umberto, 193
École des beaux-arts, 28, 63, 69, 152, 154, 159
École normale supérieure, 59, 101, 153, 154, 264
École polytechnique, 101, 148, 150, 204
economic capital, 2–3, 6, 138–9, 147–8
economic crises, 96, 130
economic field, 5, 81, 98
economic relations, 5
economic revolution, 64, 96
Economy and Society (Weber), 262

320 *Index*

education
  academic crisis, 4, 33, 92–5, 100–2, 212
  and canonisation, 160
  certification, 166–7, 169, 274
  and consecration, 123
  distribution of success, 172–3
  and the family, 203–4
  history of the education system, 95–8
  and inculcation, 160, 248–9
  and the labour market, 96–8
  and legitimate classification, 248–9
  and the literary field, 95–8
  pedagogical principles, 45, 70–1, 91, 107–8
  qualifications, 68–9, 119, 138, 148, 194, 200, 274
  sociology of, 172–3
  specialisation, 95, 196
  State-regulated education, 203–4
  surplus production of graduates, 93–102, 121, 212
  training of artists, 30, 35–6, 38–9, 69, 89, 92, 220
  transformations of the education system, 96
  Valéry on, 196, 198–9, 200
  see also academic field
effect/effects
  corps, 3, 147–51, 256, 274
  de-realisation, 69–72
  domination, 213–14, 244, 250
  Don Quixote, 19
  enquiry, 85–6
  field, 72, 100, 147, 220, 222, 246
  Gerschronken, 213
  hit parade, 13–14, 21, 159, 260–1, 263–4, 266–7
  logical, 109
  Marx, 48, 55, 107–8
  morphological, 98–102, 121, 130
  political, 57, 109
  of power, 176–8
  prophecy, 56, 57

  social, 83, 98, 148
  symbolic, 25, 250
  theory, 15, 24–5, 48, 55–8, 107–8, 273
  Zeigarnik, 181
1848 Revolution, 31, 64, 93, 210
Elementary Forms of Religious Life, The (Durkheim), 231–2, 233
elitism, 9, 97–8
emotion, 123
L'Empire du sociologue, 267
empirical research, 2, 3, 19–20, 48, 85–6, 134–6, 148, 261
Engels, Friedrich, 120, 245–6
England, 96, 104, 108, 117, 134, 149, 215–16, 270
enquiry effect, 85–6
épistémè, 239, 265
epistemological break, 8, 9, 43
epistemocratism, 42–4, 46, 131
epoche, 104
eroticism, 70–1, 158, 162, 190
Escarpit, Robert, 160
Esprit, 267
Essay on Man, An (Cassirer), 228
essences, 227, 236–7
ethnocentrism, 152, 162
ethnology, 18–19, 49–50, 54, 70–1, 86–7, 100, 119, 139–40, 143–6, 230, 237; *see also* anthropology
ethnomethodology, 8, 228, 230, 269
etymology, 15, 79, 80–1, 109, 114–15
Études rurales, 264
Evolution of Pedagogy in France (Durkheim), 70–1
exclusion, 49, 77, 122–5, 164, 186–7
exclusivity, 80, 147
exemplary prophets, 127, 156–7, 158, 189
expertise, 168, 169, 176–8, 179–82, 203, 209, 249, 257, 263, 274

Fabiani, Jean-Louis, 197
faith healers, 179, 184
family, 5, 111–12, 139–46, 148–9, 153,

166, 190, 204, 237–8; *see also* kinship relations
Family Idiot, The (Sartre), 97
fashion, 34
Faulkner, William, 262
Fayolle, Roger, 93
feel for the game, 22, 49, 84–6, 94, 127, 129
Femme Fellah (Landelle), 36
fetishism, 202–3
Fichte, Johann Gottlieb, 91
fields
  academic field, 3–4, 13, 83, 90, 93–102, 115, 141, 249, 261
  artistic field *see* artistic field
  autonomous fields, 5, 6, 33, 34, 72, 81, 106–7, 188, 211
  of criticism, 218–19
  of cultural production, 4, 35, 95–8, 121, 130–2, 153
  and differentiation, 5–6, 19, 106
  distribution of power within, 2, 3–4, 25–6, 171, 211, 227
  economic field, 5, 81, 98
  of expertise, 176–8, 179–81, 257, 263
  field effects, 72, 100, 147, 220, 222, 246
  field of forces, 1–2, 7, 254, 255, 272–3
  field of struggles, 6, 245–6, 254, 255
  fundamental laws of, 5–6, 106, 172
  literary field *see* literary field
  logic of, 90, 93, 97
  political field, 47, 48, 53–5, 93, 214, 245, 246, 249
  positions within, 7, 17–18, 90, 96, 101, 221, 246, 272
  of power, 3–6, 44, 179, 181, 247–8, 256, 264
  relation to capital, 2, 4, 254, 256
  relation to habitus, 7, 255, 256, 272
  religious field, 5, 121, 184, 246–9
  scientific field, 28, 90, 106, 107, 214
  sense of right space within, 21, 49, 56

social field, 5, 12–13, 249, 272
structure of, 2, 3–4, 12–14, 17, 25–6, 92–5, 171–2
transformation of structure, 13–14, 26, 96
Fin-de-Siècle Vienna (Schorske), 200
finished works, 30, 38–9, 66, 89
Flaubert, Gustave, 31, 64, 158, 161, 162, 164–5, 191, 260, 261
forces, field of, 1–2, 7, 254, 255, 272–3
formalism, 36, 51, 71, 89, 143
Foucault, Michel, 230, 239, 265
Francastel, Pierre, 235
Frankfurt School, 45, 92, 190, 269
French Revolution, 97
Freud, Sigmund, 20, 130, 142, 200
Front National, 269
functionalism, 223, 241–3
fundamental laws, 5–6, 106, 172
Funeral of Phocion, The (Poussin), 66
Fussman, Gérard, 58, 264

gambling, 172
Gamboni, Dario, 192–3
games
  feel for the game, 22, 49, 84–6, 94, 127, 129
  game theory, 50, 80–4
  investment in, 81–4, 263
  rules of the game, 140, 151
Garfinkel, Harold, 22, 228
Gautier, Théophile, 127, 157–8, 187, 189, 191
gender
  and discourse, 117, 118
  division of labour between the sexes, 18, 19, 20, 53, 99
  gendered nature of the social world, 20
  masculine domination, 263
  masculine/feminine opposition, 18, 47, 53, 54, 83, 114, 142–3, 236
  and name-transmission, 112
  relations between the sexes, 17, 256, 263

322 *Index*

genealogies, 108, 138, 139, 141, 143–6
'geometral of all perspectives', 7, 43, 207
German Ideology, The (Marx), 241
Germany, 71, 93–4, 232
Gérôme, Jean-Léon, 70
Gerschronken effect, 213
Gide, André, 61–2
Gilbert de la Porrée, 67
Giraudoux, Jean, 59
Gleyre, Charles, 154
Glowinski, Jacques, 265
Glucksmann, André, 155
gnoseological order, 114–17, 242
God, 7–8, 10, 50, 117, 118, 184–7, 194, 207, 237, 245, 250–2
Goffman, Erving, 9, 21, 49, 111, 118, 141, 147, 178, 213, 269
Goldmann, Lucien, 210
Gombrich, Ernst, 38, 89
Goncourt brothers, 191
Goodman, Nelson, 113, 137–8, 143
Goody, Jack, 138
Gothic architecture, 105
Gracq, Julien, 59
Great Chain of Being, The (Lovejoy), 94–5
Greuze, Jean Baptiste, 222
group exhibitions, 214
groups
  and alliances, 112, 119, 143, 145–7, 148–9
  boundaries of, 43, 114, 142–3, 147, 150, 248
  corps effects, 3, 147–51
  Durkheim on, 16, 233–4, 238–9, 241
  exclusion from, 77, 122–5
  formation and reformation of, 110–13, 115, 116–17, 147–50, 273–4
  functions of, 129–30
  power over, 116–17, 248
  self-presentation, 146–7, 148, 151, 273
  status groups, 146, 148

structure of, 16, 139–41, 233–4, 238–9
symbolic capital, 145–7, 150
Grunchec, Philippe, 152
guarantees, 13, 63–4, 103–5, 109, 117–19, 149, 167, 169–76, 192, 201–3, 220, 250–2, 274
Guattari, Félix, 266
Guilbaud, Georges-Théodule, 80–1
Guizot, François, 98, 99

habitus, 7, 15–16, 19, 22, 74, 84, 131, 149, 156, 216, 254–6, 272
Hamilton, George Heard, 218, 220
handicap, 167–8, 170–1, 177–8
Harding, James, 29
Haskell, Francis, 91, 159–60, 237, 265
Hegel, G.W.F., 30, 76, 79, 158–9, 200, 201, 208, 227
Heidegger, Martin, 104, 105, 160, 193, 207
Helvetius, Claude Adrien, 250
heresy, 33, 36, 65, 102, 121, 123–30, 184, 216, 249
heterologein, 245
hidden discourse, 200
hierarchies, 6, 13, 20, 61, 66–7, 69–70, 112–13, 137, 206, 273
hierarchy of disciplines, 61, 66–7, 69–70
historical materialism, 227–8
historical realisation, 70–2
history painting, 66–7, 69–72
hit parade effect, 13–14, 21, 159, 260–1, 263–4, 266–7
Holtzapffel, Jules, 122
Homer, 117, 138
homo academicus, 33–4, 200
Homo Academicus (Bourdieu), 51, 169, 220, 260
homologein, 205, 238, 240, 245, 274
honour, 111–12, 149, 150
housing, 134–6, 148
Hugo, Victor, 131, 189, 203, 223
humanism, 66

Index

Humboldt, Wilhelm von, 229–30, 240
Humboldt–Cassirer tradition, 229–30
Hume, David, 9, 22
Husserl, Edmund, 203, 206
Huysmans, Joris-Karl, 193
hysteresis, 19

idealism, 8–9, 75, 78, 228–9, 231, 234, 235, 238, 240
identity
    civil status, 118–19, 138, 205, 252, 274
    codification of, 118–19
    collective identity, 147, 150
    manipulation of, 147, 150
    monopoly of legitimate giving of identity, 251–2
    and naming, 137
    official identities, 118–19
    social identities, 9, 108, 115, 119, 138, 145, 150, 178, 186, 205, 274
    strategies for establishing, 119
    struggle for, 118–19, 252–3
ideology, 8, 94, 108, 242–3, 245, 249, 272
illusio, 81, 255
immigration, 269–70
implicit definitions, 30, 32
Impressionism, 26, 30, 33–5, 61, 63–70, 87–92, 124–32, 153–5, 163–4, 192, 210–24, 236, 275
imprisonment, 118, 171, 176–7, 225, 270
incorporation, 52–3, 55–6, 83, 122–3, 274
inculcation, 160, 194, 248–9
India, 58
Individual and Cosmos in the Renaissance (Cassirer), 234
individual strategies, 111
information capital, 21–2, 256
infrastructure, 47, 210–11
Ingres, Jean-Auguste-Dominique, 154, 186
inheritance, 204

institutions
    and absolute viewpoints, 44, 45
    and academic art, 33–4, 59–60, 62–3, 69, 88–92, 152–5
    anti-institutionalism, 152–3, 266
    and arbitrariness, 69, 73–4
    and classification, 44, 45
    and collective bad faith, 134
    and consensus, 213–14
    and continuity, 79
    creation of, 212–15, 217–18
    and discourse, 59, 88, 118
    and habitus, 74
    institutionalisation, 13, 151, 186, 205, 212–14, 217, 219, 256, 261
    power of, 121–3
    rehabilitation of, 153–5
    secondary institutions, 100
    sociology of, 59–60
    Valéry on, 198–9
    and validated perception, 205–7
    weak institutionalisation, 13, 261
integration, 8–9, 10, 11, 110, 241, 242–3, 245
intellectual field *see* academic field
interactionism, 8, 16, 111, 141, 147, 269
interest, 80–4, 86–7, 93, 144–5, 176, 182
interviews, 10, 134–6; *see also* questionnaires
Introduction to Psychoanalysis (Freud), 200
intuitus derivatus, 116, 237–8
intuitus originarius, 116–17, 185, 237–8
invalidity, 167–8, 169, 170, 174, 177–8, 203, 237, 274
investment, 81–4, 263
Iranian Revolution, 65, 270
Ireland, 65, 270
Islamic societies, 119

Jaune et La Rouge, La, 150
Jocelyn (Lamartine), 189
Jockey Club, 149

324 *Index*

Journal de psychologie, 228
Journal of Modern History, 93–4
journalism, 90, 221, 261, 263–4, 266
judges, legitimacy of, 182–3, 251
juridical viewpoint, 25, 118, 136–7, 274
justice, 24–6, 114, 168–70, 177, 182, 199, 204–5, 262
justification, 8, 134–6, 169, 194, 252

Kabyle society, 18, 19, 49, 53, 112, 114, 119, 139–41, 144, 146, 149, 220, 235–6
Kadijustiz, 170, 199, 204–5, 262
Kafka, Franz, 118, 122, 182, 184, 185, 251, 261
Kant, Immanuel, 9, 42, 91, 108, 116–17, 120, 135, 159, 170–1, 185, 198–200, 230, 233, 236–8, 248, 266
Kantianism, 108, 197, 228–32, 235, 239
Kantorowicz, E. H., 248
'killing two birds with one stone' logic, 249, 250
kinship relations, 5, 86, 139–46, 148–9, 237–8, 256; *see also* family
knowledge
  absolute knowledge, 42–4
  active aspects of, 231
  acts of knowledge, 12, 14, 24, 76, 243–5
  epistemological break, 8, 9, 43
  epistemocratism, 42–4, 46, 131
  and information capital, 22
  instruments of knowledge, 241, 243–4
  Kantian perspectives on, 228–9, 231
  layperson's knowledge, 8, 9, 43
  and legitimacy, 116
  logic of, 244, 245
  Marx on, 231
  objectivist theories, 7–11, 18–19, 41–4, 46, 74, 272
  perspectivist theories, 7–11, 18–19, 41–4, 46, 186–7, 272
  and power, 116, 226–7, 244–5, 272

  practical knowledge, 49–57, 76, 84, 122
  and recognition/misrecognition, 12, 74, 76, 208, 211, 244, 250
  scholarly knowledge, 8, 9, 43, 45–6, 84
  and symbolic capital, 116
Kristeva, Julia, 78

Laboratory Life (Latour and Woolgar), 268
labour
  and class, 97–8
  division of, 18, 19, 20, 53, 99, 245–7
  and the education system, 96–8
  labour market, 96–8, 225
  strikes, 225
  unemployment, 151, 269
Lacan, Jacques, 104, 199, 266
Laforgue, Jules, 27–8, 60
Lamartine, Alphonse de, 189, 218
Landelle, Charles, 36, 38
landscape painting, 66
language
  arbitrary nature of, 233
  belief language can act on the world, 120
  constructive properties of, 229–30
  and emotion, 123
  etymology, 15, 79, 80–1, 109, 114–15
  invention of words, 214–15
  manipulation of, 114, 117, 143
  painting as language, 30–2, 62
  performative speech, 116, 237–8, 257
  poetic language, 113
  and power, 114–15
  private language, 149
  social philosophy contained within, 79, 103–5
  and sociological method, 103–5, 109–10
  as symbolic system, 238, 239–40

Index

translation, 88, 232
see also discourse; linguistics; naming; philology; sociolinguistics
Language and Symbolic Power (Bourdieu), 243
law
  canon law, 117, 248
  codification of, 117–19
  and discourse, 117–18
  enforcement of, 179
  legal certification, 167
  legal status, 118–19, 205
  and power, 117–18, 179
  rational law, 179, 204
  Roman law, 248
  sociology of, 118, 262
  and the State, 117–19, 179
  vis formae, 262
layperson's knowledge, 8, 9, 43
Lazarsfeld, Paul, 213, 268
Le Roy Ladurie, Emmanuel, 99, 264
Leconte de Lisle, Charles, 191
Lee, Rensselaer W., 66
legal certification, 167
legal discourse, 117–18
Legion of Honour, 63, 65
legitimacy
  and certification, 171, 175–6, 178–82, 184–5, 251
  of definitions, 126, 134, 184, 197
  of distribution, 168, 174, 180–1, 251
  of judges, 182–3, 251
  and knowledge, 116
  and literature, 160, 184, 197
  monopoly of legitimate certification, 171, 176, 178–81, 184–5, 251
  monopoly of legitimate giving of identity, 251–2
  monopoly of legitimate symbolic violence, 64, 178–81, 206–7, 251, 274
  monopoly of scientific legitimacy, 213
  and painting, 35, 60, 68, 70, 71, 92, 121, 126, 183–5, 194, 212–14

struggle over legitimate perceptions, 22–3, 25, 34, 41–4, 46–9, 75–7, 84, 86–7, 109–13, 197, 212, 245, 248–9, 272–4
  and power, 108, 109, 248
  of representation, 35, 70, 71, 221–2
  self-legitimisation, 109
  and the State, 109, 178–81, 184
  and symbolic capital, 115
Lehn, Jean-Marie, 265
Leibniz, Gottfried Wilhelm, 7, 43, 90, 207
Leroux, Pierre, 161
Lethève, Jacques, 37
Levenson, Joseph R., 36
Lévi-Strauss, Claude, 49, 51, 108, 232, 234, 238, 264
Lévy-Bruhl, Lucien, 51
Libération, 128, 262
liberty, 106–7, 190, 191, 217
libidines, 82
limits *see* boundaries
linguistics, 64, 78, 229, 233; *see also* language; sociolinguistics
Liszt, Franz, 189
literary criticism, 62, 93, 157, 192, 222–3
literary field
  Bourdieu's literary research, 261–2
  canonisation, 159–60, 197
  consecration, 120, 160
  criticism, 62, 93, 157, 192, 222–3
  and the education system, 95–8
  history, 91–2, 93, 95–8, 158, 161
  and legitimacy, 160, 184, 197
  nouveau roman, 62, 222–3, 262
  novels, 62, 96, 158, 162, 164–5
  oral transmission, 138
  painter–writer couples, 191–5
  poetry, 32, 62, 113, 131, 138, 157, 189–90, 193
  regionalist authors, 258
  rehabilitation of minor authors, 159, 160–1

326 *Index*

literary field (*cont.*)
  relation to artistic field, 1, 26–8,
    32–3, 60–2, 66–7, 131–2, 156–65,
    187–95, 260
  Romanticism, 26, 157, 187–90, 191,
    194, 215–16
  social conditions of literary
    production, 59
  sociology of literature, 160–1,
    202–3
  a writer's proper place within, 21
literary history, 91–2, 93, 95–8, 158,
  161
literary manifestos, 131
logic
  Durkheim on, 16, 233–4, 238–9, 241
  of the field, 90, 93, 97
  'killing two birds with one stone'
    logic, 249, 250
  of knowledge, 244, 245
  logical conformism, 238
  logical effects, 109
  logical logics, 50–1
  of myth, 228, 238–9, 240
  originating in structure of groups,
    16, 233–4, 238–9, 241
  practical logics, 49–57
  in pre-capitalist societies, 49–51
  rules of logical progression, 21
Logic of Practice, The (Bourdieu),
  111–12, 139, 255
Lorenzaccio (Musset), 187–8
Louÿs, Pierre, 95
love, 157, 158, 163, 190
Lovejoy, Arthur Oncken, 94–5
Luther, Martin, 201

Mademoiselle de Maupin (Gautier),
  189–90
magic, 117, 120, 143, 202, 274
'Making Music Together' (Schütz),
  22–3
Malinowski, Bronislaw, 120
Mallarmé, Stéphane, 33, 34, 127, 199
Manet, Edouard, 30–1, 33, 38, 60–3,

  69–70, 89, 92–3, 101–2, 124–9,
  132, 157, 211, 218–20, 259–60, 275
manifestos, 131
manipulation, 114, 117, 122, 137, 138,
  141–7, 150
marginalist subjectivism, 8–9
markets *see* art market; labour market
marriage, 112, 139–41, 142–4, 146,
  148–9, 150, 273
Marx, Groucho, 147
Marx, Karl
  on class, 108, 146, 242–3
  on distribution, 174
  on domination, 17, 241–3
  functionalism, 241–3
  historical materialism, 227–8
  on ideology, 8, 108, 242–3, 249
  on knowledge, 231
  'Marx effect', 48, 55, 107–8
  objectivism, 7–8, 9
  owl of Minerva reference, 30
  on power, 107–8
  reflection theory, 231
  on religion, 227–8, 241, 242–3
  on revolution, 65, 211
  on symbolic systems, 241–3
  and the theory effect, 48, 55, 107–8
  Weber on, 227–8
Marxism, 34–5, 98–9, 108, 110, 150,
  227–8, 231, 241–3, 268
Masculine Domination (Bourdieu), 263
materialism, 7, 75–7, 130, 188, 231, 234
Mauss, Marcel, 231, 232
mauvaise foi see bad faith
May 1968, 4, 33, 35, 64, 88, 130, 153,
  183, 211, 218, 219–20, 266
Mazeppa, 189
meaning, 62, 67, 193–4, 222–3, 225,
  239, 240
mechanism, 1, 176, 246, 254, 258
media, 164, 178, 218–19, 222, 246–7,
  263–4, 266, 270
medical certification, 167–71, 174–6,
  177–8, 179, 182, 203, 250, 274
medical classifications, 174–5, 178

medieval Church, 117, 121, 184
Mémoires d'outre-tombe
(Chateaubriand), 187
mercenariness, 158, 163–5, 188
Merleau-Ponty, Maurice, 43
Merton, Robert K., 213
Metamorphosis (Kafka), 261
metaphysics, 104, 207, 252
methodological individualism, 268
military service, 167, 171, 175, 182
Miquel, André, 265
Miró, Joan, 202
misrecognition, 12, 74, 76, 208, 211,
    244, 250
Mitterrand, François, 265, 270
modernity, 210
Mondrian, Piet, 69
Monet, Claude, 61, 202, 209–10, 222
Monet at Argenteuil (Tucker), 210, 2
    15
Monet Painting in His Garden
    (Renoir), 209–10
monopolies
    of the Academy over art, 30, 35,
        121, 184–5
    of consecration, 30, 121
    of defining legitimate
        representation, 35
    of discourse, 58, 246
    of legitimate certification, 171, 176,
        178–81, 184–5, 251
    of legitimate giving of identity,
        251–2
    of legitimate symbolic violence, 64,
        178–81, 206–7, 251, 274
    of the sacred, 246, 247
    of scientific legitimacy, 213
    of speech, 55–6
morphological effects, 98–102, 121, 130
motifs, 61–2
Mourousi, Yves, 56
Murger, Henri, 158, 160–1, 190
museums, 68–9, 237
music, 1, 27, 39, 132, 189, 192; *see also*
    artistic field

Musset, Alfred de, 187–8
My Hatreds (Zola), 30–3
myth, 83, 108, 158, 221, 228, 230–1,
    238–9, 240, 242, 243
Myth of the State, The (Cassirer),
    232–3

name-transmission, 111–12, 139
naming, 58, 111–12, 123, 137, 139, 156,
    237, 257, 273
Napoleon, 101, 198–9
National Institute for Statistics and
    Economics (INSEE), 45, 103–4,
    151, 172, 208, 212–13, 244, 252,
    269, 274
'N'ayez pas peur de Max Weber!'
    (Bourdieu), 262
Nazism, 122, 233
neo-Kantianism, 228–32, 235, 239
neoliberalism, 270
neutrality, 67, 83, 86–7, 153, 155, 173,
    207, 208
Newman, John Henry, 122
Nicholas of Cusa, 245
Nietzsche, Friedrich, 8, 42, 47, 242
nobilis, 115, 116, 129, 273
nomic acts, 179, 181, 203
nomos, 87, 106, 109, 116–18, 130,
    136–7, 166–74, 177, 184–6, 205,
    207, 211, 213, 237, 244–5, 252,
    255, 259, 274
Notebooks (Valéry), 196
nouveau roman, 62, 222–3, 262
novels, 62, 96, 158, 162, 164–5
nudes, 63, 69–71
numerus clausus, 98, 100, 150

objectification, 13, 75, 113, 117, 118,
    138–9, 209, 211, 223, 255
objectivity
    elasticity of objective structures,
        12–14, 139
    objective space, 18, 20–2, 46–8
    objectivist theories of knowledge, 1,
        7–11, 18–19, 41–4, 46, 74, 272

328 *Index*

objectivity (*cont.*)
  relation between objective and
    subjective structures, 18–20,
    141–5, 234, 235, 244
obligation, 107, 144, 167
O'Boyle, Lenore, 93
official classifications, 45–6, 103–4, 172
official discourse, 117, 140
official identities, 118–19
Olympia (Manet), 63, 65, 69–70, 163
On Television (Bourdieu), 264
open works, 193
opinion polls, 48, 85, 177
oppositions, 18, 47, 49–50, 53, 54,
    76–80, 83, 86–7, 114, 142–3, 234,
    235–8, 250
oral transmission, 138
Order of Doctors, 167, 180
Orientales, Les (Hugo), 189
Orientalism, 71–2
orthodoxy, 30, 87, 102, 109–10,
    116–17, 121, 126, 212–13, 249
overviews, 8, 17, 42–4, 187, 207
owl of Minerva, 30

painter–writer couples, 191–5
painting *see* artistic field
Panathenaea, 58, 113
Panofsky, Erwin, 234–5, 236
Pareto, Vilfredo, 51, 77
Paris, 18, 94, 97, 162
Parsons, Talcott, 213
partial revolutions, 65, 211
Pascal, Blaise, 7
patrilinearity, 139, 141
pedagogy, 45, 70–1, 91, 107–8; *see also*
    education
perception
  being-perceived, 76–7, 79–80, 129,
    273
  being seen-to-be-seen, 115–16, 120,
    273
  categories of, 16, 18, 20, 33, 64–5,
    76–9, 83, 93, 152, 159, 201,
    217–18, 235–6, 238, 241, 253

and classification, 77–8, 241
dominant vision, 87, 116, 118, 125,
    130, 136–7, 187, 212–13
as investment, 83
politics of, 22–3
practical vision, 84–7, 110–11
relation to objective structures,
    18–20, 141–5, 234, 235, 244
represented vision, 87, 110–11
researchers' perceptions, 19–20,
    208–9, 230
revolutions in, 64–5
self-perception, 122–3
strategies for changing, 111–13,
    128–30
structures of, 15–16, 18–20
struggle over legitimate perceptions,
    22–3, 25, 34, 41–4, 46–9, 75–7,
    84, 86–7, 109–13, 197, 212, 245,
    248–9, 272–4
as system of oppositions, 77–80, 83,
    86–7
transformation of, 110–13, 127–32,
    211
validated perception, 205–7
performance, 36–8, 65–6
performative speech, 116, 237–8, 257,
    274
perspective (in art), 125, 220
Perspective as Symbolic Form
    (Panofsky), 234
perspectivism, 7–11, 18–19, 41–4, 46,
    186–7, 193, 272
Petit Cénacle, 189
Pevsner, Nikolaus, 39
phenomenology, 8–9, 18–19, 22–3, 42,
    86, 177, 206, 234, 236
philanthropy, 168, 170; *see also* charity
philology, 64, 138
philosophical discourse, 197, 200
Philosophy of Symbolic Forms, The
    (Cassirer), 228
photography, 221, 235, 240
Phryné devant l'Aréopage (Gérôme), 70
Piero della Francesca, 159

Pioneers of the Modern Movement
(Pevsner), 39
Plato, 48, 50, 84, 91, 200, 226
Poe, Edgar Allen, 28
poetry, 32, 62, 113, 131, 138, 157,
189–90, 193
points of view *see* viewpoints
political classifications, 53–7, 230
political creation, 53–5
political discourse, 58, 114
political field, 47, 48, 53–5, 93, 214,
245, 246, 249
political effects, 57, 109
political power, 2, 43–4, 114–16,
247–8
political revolution, 64, 102, 131,
210–11
political strategies, 25, 90
political struggle, 10, 24–5, 47, 53,
57, 58, 76, 84, 86–7, 109–13, 115,
273–4
political violence, 57
polycentrism, 214–15
pompier art, 29–30, 33–40, 59–60, 62–3,
66–7, 88–95, 125, 151–5, 217
Ponton, Rémy, 189
Popper, Karl, 25
population size, 98–9
portraiture, 61
positions
creation of new positions, 96
and discourse, 84–5, 88–9
and dispositions, 17–18
dominant positions, 17
effect of position, 17–18
from which viewpoints are taken,
10, 14–18, 41, 84–5, 86, 209, 210,
227, 246, 272
sense of one's right place, 21, 49, 56
space of positions, 7–10, 15, 46, 209,
221
within the field, 7–10, 17–18, 90, 96,
101, 221, 246, 272
positivism, 26, 104, 151, 155, 173–4
postmodernism, 266

Poussin, Nicolas, 66
poverty, 157–8, 168, 177, 221
power
over capital, 3–4
codification of, 3
cultural power, 109
and discourse, 114–15, 116
distribution within the field, 2, 3–4,
25–6, 171, 211, 227
effects of, 176–8
field of power, 3–6, 44, 179, 181,
247–8, 256, 264
Foucault on, 265, 266
over group formation, 116–17, 248
and institutions, 121–3
and knowledge, 116, 226–7, 244–5,
272
and the law, 117–18, 179
and legitimacy, 108, 109, 248
location of, 244–5
Marx on, 107–8
objectification of, 13
philosophy of, 104–5
political power, 2, 43–4, 114–16,
247–8
power relations, 7, 23, 25, 211, 243,
250
psychosomatic power, 121–3
of redistribution, 251
and secrecy, 147
sovereign power, 35, 58, 114,
116–17, 247–8
structure of, 3–4
struggles within field of, 6, 44, 179,
181
symbolic power, 45, 47, 57, 103,
107–9, 117, 122, 126, 169, 177,
180–1, 186, 244–5, 247–8, 251,
255, 274
and theory, 226–7
practical kinship, 143–5, 149
practical knowledge, 49–57, 76, 84–7,
122
practical logics, 49–57
practical vision, 84–7, 110–11

330 *Index*

pre-capitalist societies, 5, 6, 13, 19, 49–51, 64–5, 83, 86–7, 108, 111–14, 120, 122, 138–41, 144, 146, 150, 202, 220, 230–1, 235–6, 242, 255–6
prediction, 24–5, 273
press *see* journalism; media
pricelessness, 188
priests, 65, 94, 197, 245, 247–8, 250
primogeniture, 204
Primitive Classification (Durkheim & Mauss), 232, 238
primitive societies *see* pre-capitalist societies
prix de Rome, 151–2, 154, 220
processions, 112–13, 117, 146, 273
production *see* cultural production; social conditions of production; surplus production; symbolic production
'Production of Belief, The' (Bourdieu), 18, 63
profane, the, 246–8
professional corps, 245–7, 249
professionalisation, 150, 196–8
professions, 45, 54, 103–4, 119, 150, 151, 178, 192, 196–8, 199–201, 207, 212
prophecy effect, 56, 57
prophets, 65, 127–8, 156–7, 189, 197–8
prostitution, 163, 164
protocol, 112–13
Proudhon, Pierre Joseph, 31
Proust, Marcel, 119
pseudonyms, 111, 208
psychiatric discourse, 118
psychoanalysis, 8, 20, 27, 81–2, 89, 142, 164, 200
psychosomatism, 121–3
public opinion, 48, 85, 141, 177
publication, 45–6, 117–18, 120, 142, 143, 149
purchase decisions, 134–6
pure aestheticism, 236–7

pure love, 157, 158, 187, 190
purposiveness, 254, 258

qualifications, 68–9, 119, 138, 148, 194, 200, 274
questionnaires, 48, 85–6; *see also* interviews
quotation, 201

Racan, Honrat de Bueil de, 159
Racine, Jean, 71
racism, 269–70
Radcliffe-Brown, Alfred R., 240, 242
ranking lists, 13–14, 21, 149–50, 159, 260–1, 263–4, 266–7
rapins, 100, 121, 157
rational law, 179, 204
rationalisation, 263
readability, 31–2, 67–8
reading, 137, 201, 234
Reagan, Ronald, 270
realism, 7, 41, 77, 108
reality principle, 84–5
recognition, 12, 74, 76, 115–16, 120, 124, 187, 208, 211, 244, 250, 273
rediscoveries, 91, 159
redistribution, 168–9, 173–4, 180–1, 251
Redon, Odilon, 192–3, 194
regere fines, 43, 114, 248
regere sacra, 43, 114, 248
regionalist authors, 258
rehabilitation, 32, 66, 86, 91–2, 130, 153–5, 159, 160–1, 187
relative autonomy, 246
relativism, 41, 266
religion
  administration of sacraments, 247
  canon law, 117, 248
  changes in the French Church in the 1960s, 127, 156
  conversion, 121–2, 126–8
  and domination, 242, 244
  Durkheim on, 117, 118, 231–2
  and justification of existence, 252–3

Index 331

Marx on, 227–8, 241, 242–3
medieval Church, 117, 121, 184
priests, 65, 94, 197, 245, 247–8, 250
religious discourse, 242, 246
religious field, 5, 121, 184, 246–9
religious revolution, 65
religious rites, 143
and universalisation, 242–3
Weber on, 8, 228, 242, 244, 246–9, 252
Renaissance, 52, 112
Renoir, Pierre-Auguste, 61, 203, 209–10, 222
representation
and legitimacy, 35, 70, 71, 121, 221–2
represented vision, 87, 110–11
self-presentation, 111, 146–7, 148, 151, 154–5, 273
of the social world, 15, 56, 78
re-reading, 201, 234
Restoration, 97
revolution
artistic revolution, 26–40, 64–70, 87–95, 101–2, 120–32, 153, 156, 163–4, 192, 210–24, 259, 275
cultural revolution, 69, 210–13, 216–20
economic revolution, 64, 96
Marx on, 65, 211
partial revolutions, 65, 211
political revolution, 64, 102, 131 , 210–11
religious revolution, 65
specific revolutions, 33–5, 96, 211
in the structure of a field, 13
symbolic revolution, 64–6, 69, 87, 89–95, 101–2, 120–32, 156, 241, 275
theoretical revolution, 211
Richard, Maurice, 28–9
Rise of the Novel (Watt), 96
rites of passage, 114, 142–3
ritual, 49, 68, 114, 120, 142–3, 230
Robbe-Grillet, Alain, 222, 262

Roman law, 248
Romans during the Decadence (Couture), 39, 70
Romanticism, 26, 71, 128, 157, 187–90, 191, 194, 215–16
Rosen, Lawrence, 119, 141
Rotrou, Jean de, 159
rules, 35, 105, 113, 140, 142–3, 145, 151, 190; *see also* law
Rules of Art, The (Bourdieu), 260, 261

sacredness, 114–15, 137, 142, 149, 247
Sade, Marquis de, 162
Saint Martin, Monique de, 94
Salon, 28, 29, 31, 36, 101, 122, 123–4, 126, 189
Salon des refusés, 101–2, 123–5, 128, 163, 214
Samuelson, Paul A., 42
Sancho Panza, 170, 199, 161, 199, 262
Sapir, Edward, 229–30
Sapir–Whorf tradition, 229–30
Sartre, Jean-Paul, 97, 133, 223, 251, 266
Saussure, Ferdinand de, 77, 78, 108, 230, 231, 233, 238, 239–40, 242
Schelling, Friedrich, 239
Schlegel, Friedrich, 71, 93
scholarly knowledge, 8, 9, 43, 45–6, 84
school exercises, 38–9
Schopenhauer, Arthur, 8, 229
Schorske, Karl, 200
Schütz, Alfred, 9, 18–19, 22–3
science
and analysis of distributions, 172–3
and emotion, 123
legitimate definitions of, 134
and logic, 50–1
monopoly of scientific legitimacy, 213
scientific classifications, 45–6
scientific discourse, 46–7
scientific field, 28, 90, 106, 107, 134, 214
sociology of, 46–7, 266

332 *Index*

science (*cont.*)
 and the State, 207–9, 213, 269
secrecy, 19, 117, 143, 147, 149, 150
self-fulfilling prophecies, 25
self-legitimisation, 109
self-perception, 122–3
self-presentation, 111, 146–7, 148, 151,
 154–5, 273
semiology, 32, 67, 89, 109, 201
Sentimental Education (Flaubert), 64,
 158, 162, 164–5, 261
separation, 136–8, 142–3, 145, 149,
 205, 273
sexes *see* gender
sexuality, 54, 158, 190, 191
showing off, 79–80, 112, 146, 147, 273
signatures, 202–3, 208
Simmel, Georg, 20, 91, 269
simulation, 13, 168, 171, 175, 178,
 208
sincerity, 126, 133–4, 221–2
Sloane, Joseph C., 67, 218, 222
social action, 261
social art, 31, 161, 198
social capital, 2–3, 148, 217
social class *see* class
social conditions of production, 59, 87,
 101–2, 213
social crises, 93, 101, 130
social effects, 83, 98, 148
social field, 5, 12–13, 249, 272
social identities, 9, 108, 115, 119, 138,
 145, 150, 178, 186, 205, 274
social mobility, 97–8
social reproduction, 143, 204
Social Security *see* welfare
social topology, 7, 8, 10
social volume, 55–6, 57, 123
social weight, 56
socialism, 32, 270
socio-criticism, 59, 89, 93
sociolinguistics, 56, 59; *see also*
 language; linguistics
sociology
 cognitive sociology, 228–9

comparative sociology, 44
compared with philosophy, 104–5
of education, 172–3
empirical research, 2, 3, 19–20, 48,
 85–6, 134–6, 148, 261
of institutions, 59–60
and language, 103–5, 109–10
of law, 118, 262
of literature, 160–1, 202–3
relation to theories of knowledge,
 7–11, 12
of science, 46–7, 266
sociological relation to the social
 world, 73–5
sociologist-king, 43, 46
specialisation, 95
Sociology in Question (Bourdieu), 7
Socrates, 54, 55, 105–6, 164
solidarity, 129, 149, 163, 240–1
solipsist subjectivism, 8
Sollers, Philippe, 163
Solomon, 170, 262
Sophists, 106, 155, 164
SOS Racisme, 270
sovereign power, 35, 58, 114, 116–17,
 247–8
Spain, 157
specialisation, 95, 196
specific crises, 33, 96
specific revolutions, 33–5, 96, 211
Spinoza, Baruch, 42–3, 44, 46, 52, 80,
 88
sponsorship, 146, 149
Stand, 146, 148
State, the
 and art, 27–9, 63–4, 184, 216–17
 and bureaucracy, 201, 205, 217
 and certification, 63–4, 150–1, 167,
  174–6, 178–82, 203–4, 250–3, 263,
  274
 commissioning of artworks,
  216–17
 and education, 204
 as guarantor, 63–4, 104, 109, 167,
  201, 203–4, 208, 250–3, 274

Index 333

and the law, 117–19, 179
and legitimacy, 109, 178–81, 184
monopoly of legitimate symbolic
  violence, 64, 178–81, 206–7, 251,
  263, 274
and science, 207–9, 213, 269
sociology of, 180–1, 271
State scholars, 151, 172, 207–9, 269,
  274
totalitarian states, 232–3
and validation, 205–8, 274
Weber's definition of, 179, 263
and welfare, 170, 178
status groups, 146, 148
Stigma (Goffman), 147
strategies
  collective strategies, 111, 146–7, 148,
    150
  of the dominated, 19, 101
  for establishing identity, 119
  individual strategies, 111
  for name-transmission, 111–12
  for obtaining certification, 168, 175,
    178, 179
  political strategies, 25, 90
  for self-presentation, 146–7, 148,
    151, 154–5
  symbolic strategies, 13–14, 46–7,
    102, 151, 175
  for transforming perceptions,
    111–13, 128–30
  for transforming the structure of a
    field, 13–14
Strauss, Anselm, 16–17
structuralism, 16, 50, 77, 108, 238–41,
  255, 268
structured structures, 238–41, 243
structuring structures, 16, 228, 238–41,
  243
struggle
  class struggle, 6, 13, 48, 246
  over classification, 48, 87, 102, 129,
    138, 145, 245, 248, 273
  over distribution, 168–9, 173–4,
    180–1

in the field of power, 6, 44, 179,
  181
field of struggles, 6, 245–6, 254,
  255
for identity, 118–19, 252–3
over legitimate perceptions, 22–3,
  25, 34, 41–4, 46–9, 75–7, 84–7,
  109–13, 197, 212, 245, 248–9,
  272–4
over monopoly of consecration,
  121
over monopoly of speech, 55–6
political struggle, 10, 24–5, 47, 53,
  57, 58, 76, 84, 86–7, 109–13, 115,
  273–4
for rehabilitation, 91–2, 130, 153
symbolic struggles, 47–8, 58, 69,
  102, 110, 115, 134, 138–9, 255,
  257, 263
for truth, 212
for validation, 205–6, 207
Studies in Ethnomethodology
  (Garfinkel), 228
Studies in Iconology (Panofsky), 234,
  236
subjectivity, 1, 7–11, 18–20, 41–4, 46,
  141–7, 228–9
Substance and Function (Cassirer),
  228
subversion, 13, 28, 33, 36, 83–4, 91,
  93, 101, 211, 216–17
suicide, 122, 123, 191
Summa Theologiae (Aquinas), 105
superstructure, 47, 210–11, 228, 245
'Sur le pouvoir symbolique'
  (Bourdieu), 107
surplus production, 93–102, 121,
  212
symbolic capital, 111–12, 114–17,
  145–7, 150–1, 255
symbolic domination, 124, 134, 244,
  245–9
symbolic effect, 25, 250
symbolic forms, 75–7, 108, 115–16,
  228–33, 235, 236, 239, 242, 273

334 *Index*

symbolic power, 45, 47, 57, 103, 107–9, 117, 122, 126, 169, 177, 180–1, 186, 244–5, 247–8, 251, 255, 274
symbolic production, 156, 245, 246, 249–52
symbolic profits, 130, 146, 149
symbolic revolution, 64–6, 69, 87, 89–95, 101–2, 120–32, 156, 241, 275
symbolic strategies, 13–14, 46–7, 102, 151, 175
symbolic struggles, 47–8, 58, 64, 69, 102, 110, 115, 134, 138–9, 255, 257, 263
symbolic systems, 47, 228, 238–43
symbolic violence, 57, 64, 178–81, 206–7, 251, 252, 274
Symbolists, 131
synthesis, 41, 108, 227, 243, 256, 267

taste, 80, 82–3, 190, 235
tautegorical analysis, 239
taxation, 136, 172, 251
taxonomies, 20, 49–50, 54, 63, 129, 208, 229, 237, 243; *see also* classification
technique, 38, 66, 67, 69, 193–4
Tel père, tel fils (Thélot), 172–3
television, 264
Thatcher, Margaret, 225, 270
Thélot, Claude, 172–3
theodicy, 8, 244, 252
theoretical capital, 227
theoretical discourse, 55, 112, 197, 200, 226–7
theoretical kinship, 143–5, 149
theoretical revolution, 211
theory effect, 15, 24–5, 48, 55–8, 107–8, 273
Theses on Feuerbach (Marx), 231, 234
Third Republic, 216–17, 270
Thomas, Ambroise, 39
threshold effects, 127
Thuillier, Jacques, 29, 151–5, 264
Time magazine, 215

titles, 119, 138, 151, 178, 205, 206, 252, 274
To The Lighthouse (Woolf), 261, 263
totalitarianism, 109, 233
training, 30, 35–6, 38–9, 69, 89, 92, 220
transcendental philosophy, 229, 230, 233, 235
transformation
   of distribution, 26, 168–9
   of the education system, 96
   of objective space, 47–8
   of perceptions, 110–13, 127–32, 211
   of one form of capital to another, 3
   strategies for, 13–14, 128–30
   of the structure of a field, 13–14, 26, 96
transgression, 113, 125–6, 140, 142–3, 161–3, 190
translation, 88, 232
Trial, The (Kafka), 261
tripartite division, 105
Troeltsch, Ernst, 201
Trois Ordres, Les (Duby), 264
truth, 9, 42, 44, 78, 108, 167–8, 176–7, 183, 185, 207, 212
Tylor, Edward, 120

undifferentiated societies, 5, 6, 19
unemployment, 151, 269
union, 136–8, 142–3, 145, 273
uniqueness, 36–7, 76–7
United States, 26, 38–9, 68, 104, 108, 117, 119, 134, 136, 141, 149, 213, 215, 229, 233, 267–70
universal structures, 29, 230–1
universalisation, 8, 23, 170, 184, 242–3, 245, 249
Unknown Masterpiece, The (Balzac), 194
utilitarianism, 190–1, 198

Valéry, Paul, 80, 196–201, 205, 208, 215

Index

validation, 205–8, 214, 238, 252, 273, 274
Van Gennep, Arnold, 114
verdicts, 118–19, 121, 139, 169–70, 176–9, 181–3, 192, 204, 207, 225, 245, 251–2
Vernet, Horace, 189
Vie de bohème (Murger), 158, 190
viewpoints
    absolute viewpoints, 42–4, 46, 187, 193, 194
    and authority, 25, 116
    conflicting viewpoints, 135–6
    dominant viewpoint, 87, 116, 118, 125, 130, 136–7, 187, 212–13
    of individual social agents, 8, 10, 14–20, 41–2, 47, 186, 255
    juridical viewpoint, 25, 118, 136–7, 274
    overview of viewpoints, 8, 17, 42–4, 187, 207
    of past thinkers, 227
    and position, 10, 14–18, 41, 84–5, 86, 209, 210, 227, 246, 272
    relation to objective structures, 18–20, 141–5, 234, 235, 244
    researchers' viewpoints, 19–20, 208–9, 230
    struggle over legitimate viewpoints, 22–3, 25, 34, 41–4, 46–9, 75–7, 84–7, 109–13, 197, 212, 245, 248–9, 272–4
    and theories of knowledge, 8, 10, 41–4
    transformation of, 110–13, 127–32, 211
    and the transformation of objective space, 47–8
Vigny, Alfred de, 157
Villiers, Gérard de, 21
violence
    law of conservation of violence, 270
    monopoly of legitimate symbolic violence, 64, 178–81, 206–7, 251, 274

motivations for, 225, 270
    political violence, 57
    pure violence, 225
    and revolution, 35, 69, 211
    symbolic violence, 57, 64, 178–81, 206–7, 251, 252, 274
virtuosity, 36, 38, 65–6, 125, 154
vis formae, 262
visibility, 48, 113, 115–16, 117, 120
vision *see* perception; viewpoints
vulgarity, 77–80, 83, 250, 273

Waiting for Godot (Beckett), 261
Watt, Ian, 96
Watteau, Antoine, 130
weak institutionalisation, 13, 261
weak objectification, 13, 138–9
weakly differentiated societies, 242, 245
Weber, Max
    on bureaucracy, 199, 201
    on charisma, 115
    compared with Valéry, 201
    definition of the State, 179, 263
    French translations of works, 262
    and historical materialism, 227–8
    on *Kadijustiz*, 170, 199, 204, 262
    on Marx, 227–8
    on neutrality, 155
    on prophets, 156–7, 197
    on religion, 8, 65, 228, 242, 244, 246–9, 252
    on status groups, 146, 148
    on viewpoints, 44
Weight of the World, The (Bourdieu), 261, 263
welfare, 167–8, 169, 170–1, 174, 176–8, 181, 203, 270
Who Governs? (Dahl), 2
Whorf, Benjamin Lee, 229–30
Williams, Raymond, 215–16
Wittgenstein, Ludwig, 105, 215
Wittkower, Rudolf, 191
Woolf, Virginia, 261, 263
Work of Art, The (Zola), 129

336 *Index*

working consensus, 213
World as Will and Representation, The (Schopenhauer), 229
worldmaking, 113, 273
writing, 137, 138

Zeigarnik effect, 181
Zhdanovism, 34, 216
Zola, Émile, 30–3, 34, 60–2, 68, 127, 129, 132, 194